Milton and the Revolutionary Reader

LITERATURE IN HISTORY

SERIES EDITORS

David Bromwich, James Chandler, and Lionel Gossman

The books in this series study literary works in the
context of the intellectual conditions, social
movements, and patterns of action
in which they took shape.

Other books in the series:

Lawrence Rothfield, *Vital Signs: Medical Realism
in Nineteenth-Century Fiction* (1992)

David Quint, *Epic and Empire: Politics and Generic Form
from Virgil to Milton* (1993)

Alexander Welsh, *The Hero of the Waverly Novels* (1992)

Susan Dunn, *The Deaths of Louis XVI: Regicide and the
French Political Imagination* (1994)

Milton and the Revolutionary Reader

• *SHARON ACHINSTEIN* •

PRINCETON UNIVERSITY PRESS

PRINCETON, NEW JERSEY

Copyright © 1994 by Princeton University Press
Published by Princeton University Press, 41 William Street,
Princeton, New Jersey 08540
In the United Kingdom: Princeton University Press,
Chichester, West Sussex

Library of Congress Cataloging-in-Publication Data

Achinstein, Sharon.
Milton and the revolutionary reader / Sharon Achinstein.
p.   cm. — (Literature in history)
Includes index.
ISBN 0-691-03490-7
1. Milton, John, 1608–1674—Political and social views.
2. Great Britain—History—Puritan Revolution, 1642–1660—Literature and the revolution.
3. Great Britain—History—Puritan Revolution, 1642–1660—Pamphlets.
4. Politics and literature—Great Britain—History—17th century.
5. Literature and history—Great Britain—History—17th century.
6. Revolutionary literature, English—History and criticism.
7. Books and reading—England—History—17th century.   I. Title.
II. Series: Literature in history (Princeton, N.J.)
PR3592.P64A34   1994   821'.4—dc20   94-6647

This book has been composed in Baskerville

Princeton University Press books are printed
on acid-free paper and meet the guidelines
for permanence and durability of the Committee
on Production Guidelines for Book Longevity
of the Council on Library Resources

Printed in the United States of America

1   3   5   7   9   10   8   6   4   2

TO MY GRANDFATHER

Hear'd you not lately of a man
That weekly walkes the streets,
And madly through the City runs,
Wrapt in poor paper-sheets;
It was because, by Parliament,
He did his wits imploy,
Who gave him leave to walke in print,
That he ran mad for joy.

   Mercurius Melancholius, 23–30 October 1647

Millions of spiritual Creatures walk the Earth
Unseen, both when we wake, and when we sleep:
All these with ceaseless praise, his works behold
Both day and night: how often from the steep
Of echoing Hill or Thicket have we heard
Celestial voices to the midnight air,
Sole, or responsive each to other's note

   John Milton, *Paradise Lost* 4.677–83

• C O N T E N T S •

• *A C K N O W L E D G M E N T S* •

AT THE END OF A LONG PROJECT like this one, it gives me joy to recollect all those who have contributed their time, support, and intellectual gifts to help me reach this point. At its inception, Earl Miner, Lawrence Stone, and David Bromwich encouraged me to think beyond the borders of canonical literary study while I was a graduate student at Princeton. All three were generous with me then, and have remained so; at Princeton, I also bene-fited from the advice of Margaret Doody, Victoria Kahn, Richard Kroll, and Kathy Maus, and, while she was visiting there, Lisa Jardine; and from the material support of a Princeton University graduate fellowship, the Whiting Foundation in the Humanities, the Columbia University Council for Euro-pean Studies, and the Donald and Mary Hyde Fellowship for Research Abroad, which first placed me in the British Archives. The Folger Shake-speare Library was a convivial spot to pursue my early research, and there I met and began scholarly conversations with Boyd Berry, Peter Blayney, Jim Holstun, and Gordon Schochet, whom I thank for their encourage-ment, and whose incisive readings of early chapters helped this project grow from a dissertation into a book. In offering a sympathetic yet tough reading of an early chapter, Constance Jordan provided prompt encour-agement of my interdisciplinary interests, and Annabel Patterson read and incisively commented on some of the material in the book, energetically responding to my ideas with her usual toughness of mind. The Milton sem-inar at the Newberry Library offered me a real exchange of ideas, and I am especially indebted to Michael Lieb and David Loewenstein for their model support. At Northwestern University, I have been welcomed by a lively set of colleagues, and thank Jules Law, Lawrence Lipking, Sarah Maza, and Mar-tin Mueller, all who read parts of the manuscript in earlier forms, and Steve Pincus for last minute help. I have been supported in the community of my fellows, especially through the kindness of Helen Deutsch, Karen Pinkus, and Wendy Wall. My research has been aided and funded by the American Council of Learned Societies and Northwestern University; short-term resi-dencies at the Huntington Library in San Marino and the William Andrews Clark Memorial Library in Los Angeles, provided time and the materials to conduct the bulk of the writing and research. I am grateful for permission to reprint material in this book which has been published previously. A first version of chapter 2 appeared in *Prose Studies* 14 (1991), reprinted by per-mission of Frank Cass Publishers. Parts of chapter 4 appeared in *The Witness of Times: Manifestations of Ideology in Seventeenth-Century England*, Katherine Z. Keller and Gerald G. Schifforst, eds. (Duquesne University Press, 1993), reprinted by permission of Duquesne University Press, and in *Milton Studies* 29, Albert C. Labriola, ed. (University of Pittsburgh Press, 1993), published by the University of Pittsburgh Press.

I owe special thanks to David Bromwich, who kept me thinking humanely about Milton and the writing of the past, and who invited me to submit the book to the series. I wish to thank the literature editor at Princeton University Press, Robert Brown, and my copyeditor, Cindy Crumrine. I am especially grateful to Janel Mueller, a reader for the Press, for her equanimity, wisdom, and care in writing a detailed and incisive report. Friends have made all of this possible: Paul Duke, Jessica Hadlow, Lisa Schnell, and especially Martha Hodes. I owe a special debt to Michael Abramowitz for his care and energetic support during the work for this project, and for his willingness to follow its meanderings. My family has been patient and loving with me in sustaining my scholarly choices; and my sister Betty, along with Chad and Emma, gave me a second home.

IN QUOTING from Milton's prose, I have used Don M. Wolfe, gen. ed., *Complete Prose Works of John Milton*, 8 vols. (New Haven: Yale University Press, 1953–82), abbreviated parenthetically as *CPW*; references are to volume and page. All citations of Milton's poetry are from Merritt Y. Hughes, ed., *John Milton: Complete Poetry and Major Prose* (Indianapolis: Bobbs-Merrill, 1957), abbreviated parenthetically as *CP*. References to *Paradise Lost* are to book and line.

In quotations from older texts, I have modernized *i*'s, *j*'s, *u*'s, and *v*'s, but left the spelling and punctuation unchanged. All pamphlet publications originate in London unless otherwise indicated.

Milton and the Revolutionary Reader

THE ENGLISH REVOLUTION was a revolution in reading. Over twenty-two thousand pamphlets were published between 1640 and 1661, surpassing the output of the French revolutionary press over a hundred years later.[1] Readers viewed a drama of political exchange in public, where for the first time in English history, the press was used for open political conflict. Newly freed from the constraints of censorship, the press became the medium for the expression of views not only of the elites in power, but also of serious opposition. During one of the most astonishing moments in British history—where a king was put on trial and was executed by order of Parliament; where partisans fought for a reordering of social structures, of culture, and of political and economic life—the press helped to create a public space in which political argument over such topics could be carried on. While historians have talked of the rise of the political subject in England, they have slighted the impact of this torrent of words, concentrating instead on those works of political theory which emphasize the importance of the public, or of the individual, in political process. Thomas Hobbes, John Locke, the republican theorist James Harrington are all thought to have fathered the liberal political subject. The expansion of the electorate, the increasing number of contested elections, and the existence of political parties have all been interpreted as signs of England's shift toward recognizing both the power of individuals in political process and the power of public opinion as a force in politics.

In *Milton and the Revolutionary Reader*, I explore the concept of the political subject from a different vantage point, looking at its rhetoric, specifically that of the pamphlets. Released from the bonds of censorship, eager pamphlet writers during the English Revolution ushered in a new era of political conduct. They put arguments about the people's rights and duties into actual practice by reaching out to an audience of the people and by presenting matters that had previously been censored. They did this by demanding that their audiences make political choices and that they participate in the political process; in sum, they invoked a revolutionary idea of a reader. In this book, I analyze from a literary perspective the ways pamphlet writers appealed to readers. I examine many kinds of writing during the period, from anonymous hacks, preachers, radicals, and Royalists, to such known figures as John Lilburne, John Cleveland, William Prynne, Thomas Hobbes, and John Milton. In paying attention to these, I seek to picture the political subject from the perspective of the street. Though this perspective may not be as coherent as that reflected in an organized treatise of political theory, it is worth our attention. Indeed, these pamphlets may have had more impact on political practice than did the works of political theory of their day.

John Milton both reflected and contributed to this rhetorical climate by conceiving of his audience as a nation of readers, "fast reading, trying all things, assenting to the force of reason and convincement" (*CPW* 2.537), who were reading, among other things, the political pamphlets of the English Revolution. Milton's vision of an audience exemplifies the way many pamphlet writers made rhetorical constructions of their audiences as reading publics. In their pamphlets, writers like Milton composed their audiences in supreme acts of fantasy, addressing their works to a public, demanding that their audiences read and respond to contemporary issues; they also presented models for public debate by fighting pen-battles in print. Theirs was an imaginative contribution to the English Revolution, and I underscore the literary, and even utopian, dimension of the writers' efforts to instill in their readers these qualities.[2] When writers challenged their readers, offered patterns for them to imitate; when they harassed, prodded, and chastised them; commanded, cajoled, and lied to them, I argue, they did political work. They created the idea of a revolutionary public.

I have three objectives in writing this book, addressing both the historian and the literary critic. The first aim is to enter the debate among historians about whether what happened in England in the midseventeenth century had an ideological component. The second aim is to recommend that Milton scholars pay attention to recent fights among historians, and to revise their picture of Milton accordingly. In my third aim, I speak to the general field of rhetorical study, and press for a consideration of propaganda as well as literary artifact as meaningful objects of analysis.

REVOLUTIONARY FICTIONS

For the historian, I seek to enlarge the study of history to include rhetoric, conceived broadly as the sum of literary customs, the culture of printing and reading, and writers' modes of appeal to audiences. In the book, I describe the rhetorical practices of writers who gave rise to a conception of the public as capable participants in politics, analyzing both their intentions and their habits of reaching readers in the period 1640–60. To delve into this question from a literary perspective requires some understanding of the current historiography of the period, since the historical picture is a disputed one. Historians have tracked the intentions of politicians in the period 1640–60, from Parliament's quest for limits to the king's absolute authority in the Petition of Right in 1628 to the king's trial for treason in 1649. They have examined Parliament's idea that a public should be able to contribute to its own political arrangements and its aim of reconstructing society according to constitutional practice, and they have questioned whether or not Parliament actually did include more of the voices of the populace.[3] What I have to say about the rhetorical conception of the political subject in the pamphlet literature of the English Revolution should add to their political history of the Interregnum period, and specifically to the current debate over the function of ideology in the midseventeenth century. There is presently little agreement among historians about the role of ideology in the English Revolution. So-called revisionist historians are pursuing the idea that there was no profound ideological divide in the mid-seventeenth century, denying that there were long-term preconditions of conflict, in an attempt to topple the Whig interpretive orthodoxy, which had seen the revolution in terms of political progress toward constitutionalism. According to these revisionists, it was not a revolution in the sense that we commonly think about revolutions; in fact, they call it the "rebellion" or the "civil war." According to revisionists like Conrad Russell, there were, rather than fire-breathing revolutionaries, "*ad hoc* gatherings of men reacting to events taking place elsewhere."[4] It was not a revolution. It was, rather, a road accident on the highway of history. These historians have stressed the degree to which civil war politicians agreed, and have demoted the role of constitutional principle while promoting a picture of narrow factionalism among elites. They have also stressed continuities between the Tudor period and that of the Restoration, often in terms of religion, and they have focused on local histories rather than on a national one. By their critique, revisionists have directed attention away from political principles toward practice.[5]

Was there a revolution in England between the years of 1640 and 1660? That all depends upon how one defines *revolution*. Political scientists, sociologists, and historians have fought over that definition and its application to this period for as many years as have passed since the time in question. From Clarendon's *History of the Great Rebellion* to the current revisionist debate in English historiography, there have been different answers to the question of what happened in the middle of England's seventeenth century. If one's definition of revolution includes political ideas, then where do we find the political ideas of the revolution in England between the years 1640 and 1660? In the realm of traditional political theory, when we look for an ideology, Hobbes offers himself as a likely suspect, though Hobbes was no part of the "revolution," if there was one, and remained loyal, it seems, to his monarch while waiting out the civil strife from the safe shores of France. Judith Shklar, a political theorist, has voted down another probable suspect, James Harrington, as the intellectual architect of the Commonwealth regime; he was "not their Marx, and not their Lenin."[6]

When we stop to ask, what kind of political ideas have we been hunting? we recognize that our preconceptions about what counts as a revolution are entering into our analysis.[7] How could they not? As citizens of a century that has seen its share of revolutions, we bring to our historical examinations the memories of the Russian Revolution, the Chinese Revolution, and now, the revolutions in Eastern Europe. Have we been searching for a Lenin, for someone or some group of someones who expressed a coherent program or system? Or have we been looking for the articulation of a timeless set of principles that might be abstracted from their time and made applicable to other times and other places, a political philosophy that transcends the politics of its birth?

If we are looking for these, we shall be looking a good long time yet. The methodological goal of this book is to free English revolutionary thinkers from the bonds imposed by our own search for a consistent revolutionary program. If we are looking for ideology as we know it in the twentieth century we shall not find it in the seventeenth. My method builds upon Quentin Skinner's emphasis on the recovery of the text's position within the framework of its *own* system of communication, with a focus on "the prevailing conventions governing the treatment of the issues or themes with which the text is concerned," and also with attention to "the writer's mental world, the world of his empirical beliefs." From this perspective, the aim of the critic is to decide "what conventionally recognizable meanings, in a society of that kind, it might have been possible for someone to have intended to communicate." As in Stanley Fish's theory, the reader must "construct" meaning. In contrast to Fish, though, Skinner holds that there are meanings there to be understood. For the literary critic, Skinner's method provides a limit to the kinds of interpretations that can be made about texts.[8] Though no history can be written that is not filtered through the ideas and ideological frames we carry around with us, we can attempt to restrict (or at least be conscious of) the ways that our own definitions be allowed to determine our analysis. What makes the search for a coherent political ideology in England in the middle of the seventeenth century so appealing for us is, however, our own sense that what took place then is in some ways *ours* now. It matters to us. It was there, historians of political thought have argued, that the concept of *possessive individualism* was formed. It was there, they have argued, that constitutional ideas were put forward as citizens struggled to limit the powers of their king by means of rule by law. It was there, historians have determined, that we find the "ideological origins of the American Revolution." It was there that the liberal bourgeois state, our hero (and simultaneously our postcolonial villain?), was born.[9]

But what would political ideology have looked like to those early modern English citizens? To them, I think, political theories often appeared as literature. That is to say, the boundaries between the discourses of literature and of political theory were not clear-cut. Here is the likeliest candidate for title of political theorist in the seventeenth century, Hobbes, who begins his introduction to *Leviathan* with these words: "Nature (the Art whereby God hath made and governes the World) is by the *Art* of man, as in many other things, so in this also imitated, that it can make an Artificial Animal." Hobbes begins his profound consideration of the "science of politics" with this fictional gesture, claiming that his own ideas are "Art" or "artificial." Hobbes explains that the state itself is an imagined, an artificial entity: "*Art*

goes yet further, imitating that Rationall and most excellent worke of Nature, *Man*. For by Art is created that great LEVIATHAN called a COMMON-
WEALTH, or STATE, (in latine, CIVITAS) which is but an Artificiall Man;
though of greater stature and strength than the Naturall."[10] James Harrington, the republican political theorist, put his ideas forward in a fictional
utopia, *Oceana*. Literary creation and political theory often converged.

I am not suggesting that their literature holds the "key" to their revolutionary politics, if we can only "read between the lines," properly, as Leo
Strauss has suggested we learn to do. Literature is not strictly politics in
disguise, hidden so as to evade the gaze of the ignorant or the powerful.
Rather, political discussions in the seventeenth century share some characteristics with literature, and in this book, I seek a way to analyze in like
manner these two species of writing that have become now so distinct in our
own day. Now, ideology may always look like literature for its linguistic slip-
periness, for its adherence to conventional genres, or, more broadly speaking, for its organization of signifying practices.[11] My particular interest,
however, is in the intersection between literature and political ideas not at
the level of language or mediation per se, but in the ways political thinkers
resemble creative writers in their fiction-making. When their fictions are
largely apparent, we call them propagandists or utopianists. The political
theorist Sheldon Wolin has suggested that political philosophies always
draw upon the work of the imagination: "Political philosophy," he writes, is
a "means for understanding" what does not exist, both in the way of models
and also in the way of apprehending principles. In his scheme, political
vision involves the imagination:

> Imagination has involved far more than the construction of models. It has
> been the medium for expressing the fundamental values of the theorist; it has
> been the means by which the political theorist has sought to transcend history.
> The imaginative vision to which I am referring here was displayed at its artistic
> best by Plato. In his picture of the political community, guided by the divine art
> of the statesman, reaching out towards the idea of the Good, Plato exhibited a
> form of vision essentially architectonic. An architectonic vision is one wherein
> the political imagination attempts to mould the totality of political phenome-
> non to accord with some vision of the Good that lies outside the political
> order.[12]

Plato had spent a good deal of energy expelling those masters of the imagination, the poets, from his ideal state, for he grasped that poetry was at
odds with philosophy. Plato's ideal state sought a ground in forms rather
than myths. Wolin takes the two in one sweep, however, arguing for the
inseparability of philosophy from the work of the imagination. He asks,
what if forms are myths?

The story I tell in this book depends not upon coherent articulations of
political principle in the writing of the English Revolution, but rather upon
its rhetoric, it myths, which offer us a rich field to study. When we depart

from analyzing the standard texts of political theory of the English Revolution, from the ideas or principles of Harrington and Hobbes and from the "constitutional documents" like the Levellers' "Agreements of the People," we broaden the range of materials we might consider. If we pursue the rhetoric and myths, and not just the principles people fought over, we expand our evidence to include the not-the-very-best political theory, the pamphlets as well as the literary works of the period. John Milton's political tracts, for example, prove relevant to the idea of a political audience. His prose works, which traverse the years of civil war, Commonwealth, Protectorate, and Restoration, give us much to chew on in the way of rhetorical ingenuity, an ingenuity that responded to and helped to transform the character of public discourse in the revolutionary period.

Rather than searching for consistent philosophies, we might become more attentive to the nuances, inconsistencies, and literary qualities of texts. It has been shown that over the course of his writing life, for example, Milton vacillated in his political views, and that this vacillation was a result of Milton's provisional political commitments or of the fact that Milton was just not a very good political thinker.[13] As a full-time member of a revolutionary government, Milton wrote with the needs of that government and the shifting winds of political allegiance always in mind; his political engagement required a rhetorical opportunism at times. Yet from a rhetorical perspective, Milton was surprisingly committed to a single goal, that of making his public fit to achieve self-governance through training in virtue. He persisted in his attempts to formulate an image of the public. Throughout his writing life, Milton had to contend with the actual audiences he hoped to reach in his writing, audiences that were the increasing targets of propaganda. He responded by becoming a powerful myth-maker for the public sphere. I see Milton as a significant case of a revolutionary practice, a writer who shaped his audience not only by his principles and ideas, but by his imaginings.

Historians may never agree whether or not the revolution was at root an ideological conflict, but through my examples, I show how writers made it one; thus I support a modified Whig view. When writers sought to arm readers with equipment with which to fend off enemy opinions; when they invited readers to enter political debate by learning how to read and to understand political rhetoric; when they sought to equip readers to meet the challenge of propaganda, they were making up a new practice of public political conduct. This practice might be called the rhetoric of politics rather than politics itself, but this study seeks to break down the distinctions between the two. In this study, such overt questions of political theory and of historiography are thought of as the arena in which all the revolutionary literary practices must be judged. For instance, it is a powerful testament to the importance of public opinion that the regicides published a record of the king's trial in order to vindicate their acts. By publishing, they exemplified their belief that politics was considered legitimate only when conducted in public.

The English revolutionary pamphleteers participated in some ways in the "structural transformation of the public sphere," as Jürgen Habermas has dubbed it, in which power came to be constructed not out of adherence to the authority of special persons, but by the conditions of rational public discussion. The "public sphere" arose in Europe, Habermas explains, "in which private people, come together to form a public, readied themselves to compel public authority to legitimate itself before public opinion." He has assigned a more recent date—the late-eighteenth century—to the formation of the public sphere in England, in which participatory political processes and the media, along with social and cultural institutions, coalesced to make it possible for the public to become the basis for politics. Habermas stresses the means of political confrontation through which the private people came together as a public—the "public use of their reason"—and the forum for that use, the press. Although the Habermasian scheme has been criticized for its basis in an unreflective notion of "reason," the concept is relevant to analyzing the writing of the English Revolution, to exploring a cultural milieu in which the material conditions were in place for affordable, accessible printing and an intellectual climate of public debate: all these might be said to anticipate Habermas's scheme by a century or so. My argument here is not that what we have in the seventeenth century merely antedates the origins of the "Habermasian public sphere" by a few centuries and thereby proves its existence in the late English Renaissance. Rather, my goal is to show that when people from the past themselves experienced politics taking place in public, their own experiences reveal an incoherence, an ambivalence, at times a brilliant insight, and at others, a marked lack of understanding about the nature of the changes that were happening before their eyes. In his emphasis on the rational basis of the public sphere, Habermas explores the rise of its ideology through the words of political thinkers of the past; for England, for example, he focuses on Hobbes and Locke.[14] Yet my survey of the range of English revolutionary pamphlets suggests that the reactions both to the printing press and to the participation of the public in politics were mixed, and these mixed responses may be charted not through the explicit "ideology" of the key thinkers of the age, but through the rhetoric, the imaginings, and the propaganda of the time. By analyzing contemporary reactions, not all of them "rational," I seek to understand the public sphere as it was imagined by seventeenth-century actors, not through our later sociological concept.[15]

An important outcome of the English Revolution was the development of a notion of a public sphere, in which political negotiations that included the public were to take place. The revolutionaries defined for themselves a public sphere as equivalent to the audience for print. To understand the rhetoric of the pamphlets also means to understand the impact of printing. Printing helped speed the transformation from a closed political arena to an open one, although printing did not cause the revolution. The writers who published their ideas in pamphlet format drew upon existing forms of communication to reach an audience long accustomed to buying sermons, jestbooks, and other forms of popular literature. The most common frame for writers was the quarto pamphlet, of any length from eight pages to over two hundred. Usually pamphlets were eight or sixteen pages long, long enough to argue a single point and to support it with marginalia full of references to other pamphlets and literary works. Such short pamphlets were almost always polemical, and they frequently appeared as responses to other pamphlets, very often referring to those other pamphlets explicitly in their titles. Even news appeared in pamphlet form, and the eight pages of each weekly newsbook were stuffed with up-to-the-minute facts and ideas. The major defense of the commonwealth, Marchamont Nedham's *Case of the Commonwealth Truly Stated* (1650), for instance, was first presented in pamphlet newsbook form. These pamphlets were easy for printers to produce quickly and cheaply. Readers consumed such works with a fury exceeded only by the fury of the press to replace old pamphlets with new ones. As the Stationer commented in his introductory epistle to the reader in the 1645 edition of *The Poems of John Milton*, "the slightest Pamphlet is nowadays more vendible than the works of learnedest men."

To many participants in the civil war debates, not surprisingly, the press *seemed* the cause of all the trouble; Sir Thomas Browne, apologist for Charles, wrote in 1643 against the spate of newsbooks in which "the name of his Majesty [is] defamed, the honour of Parliament depraved, the writings of both depravedly, anticipatively, counterfietly imprinted."[16] To Browne, seeing the king's speech in print without his authorization was a treason. Another Royalist, John Birkenhead, looked forward to the day when there would be no newsbooks, for there would be no news, no change, and no trouble: as he saw it, the newsbooks were a token of that trouble. It is true that publication of parliamentary proceedings proved vital to the parliamentary cause, and that the "diurnals" that appeared weekly in the 1640s presented the conflict between the king and Parliament to the nation at large. The author of the royalist newsbook *Mercurius Aulicus*, for instance, believed that the parliamentary pamphlets had a wide effect: "the London pamphlets are so unexpressibly shameful, that the zealots of New England do both preach and write against them." Noise from the disputes reached across the Atlantic into the settlements in America. John Birkenhead accused the author of *Aulicus* of attracting women readers, who would then entice their husbands "by fair pretences and sugared words." The "lying libels" of *Aulicus* "have tended to naught else, but to animate and encourage their Husbands, and friends to persist in this unnatural war." The pamphlet itself was accused of spreading lies and of inciting readers to war. The wealth of literature in opposition to these pamphlets attests to their high degree of visibility and to their perceived danger. Words might lead to action.[17]

The press had begun to gear up well before the English Civil War, however. Popular writing had existed in England since the sixteenth century, yet the literature of the civil wars was new in that pamphleteers fused the techniques of preexisting low genres with openly political argument and brought political debates from behind the closed doors of parliamentary chambers into the noisy, dusty, crowded street. The pamphleteers of the English Revolution imitated the popular vernacular pamphleteers who had flooded the market in London with their literary novelties since the end of the sixteenth century and who had encouraged a new audience of popular readers to become regular consumers of printed matter. Robert Greene's crime stories, called cony-catching pamphlets, and Thomas Nashe's public quarrel with Gabriel Harvey in the 1590s had established a form of entertainment for the lower stratum of English society that set the stage for the appeal of the civil war pamphleteering to a popular audience. Literacy rates among the lower classes were on the rise, even if the lowest sorts could not write.[18] The civil war pamphleteers' tools of wit, inflated language, and scurrility, as well as the folk genres of the letter, the jestbook, the almanac, the ghost-warning piece, and the ballad, were all forms taken from the vernacular tradition.[19] Sir George Wharton, a royalist astrologer, attacked his rival by accusing him of catering to the vulgar: "you have done very wisely in directing [your pamphlet] to the *People*: none but your seduced Many-headed-Monster *Multitude* will credit you."[20] Popular writings, such as ballads, fiction, plays, and other cheap literature, stood on the cusp of oral and literate cultures and were aimed at an audience that was attractive to writers. Little did these writers mind that their occupation of "popular writer" was deemed disreputable; the money compensated for their failure in social status. Writers used familiar forms—the private letter, "looking-glass" literature, fables, the almanac, newbooks, ballads, and the ghost-story warning-piece—and turned these forms to suit new political uses.

The pamphleteers of the 1640s looked back to the Marprelate Controversy of the 1580s. The Elizabethan Marprelates expressed a radical Puritan opposition to the episcopal form of church government, mounting bold attacks on the status quo through the medium of print. The pseudonymous authors travelled with collapsible presses and stayed at friends' safe houses to escape the recognition of the authorities; they were hounded through the countryside of England in 1588–89. They were finally seized in Lancashire, the associates tried, tortured, and silenced. Some civil war writers liked to think of their own works in that tradition—Richard Overton even went so far as to name his the "Mar-priest" press in 1645 and 1646.[21] To the civil war writers, the Marprelate tracts represented a tradition of political, oppositional prose in print, and their writing imitated the stance and tone of the earlier tracts.[22] The Marprelate tracts contributed to the genre of vernacular scurrility that Luther himself, along with other early Protestant reformers, had established, and they represented an adaptation of the witty jestbook toward a political end.[23] In choosing the pen name "Marprelate," the controversial Elizabethan writers threatened the church order: "Martin" was a name taken from the reformer Luther and "Mar-prelate" denoted violence to come. By joining himself to their cause, Overton reasserted a voice of protest against state authority, and built a dramatic role for himself as an inheritor of their tradition.[24]

Royalists also used the tradition of Marprelate writing, this time to oppose the effects of such popular scurrility. The royalist hack John Taylor played on the Marprelate tradition in his attack on William Prynne. Taylor's *Crop-Eare Curried* (1644), whose title refers in an ugly way to the fact that William Prynne had his ears "cropped" in punishment for politically offensive publications, begins with a dream where the ghost of Tom Nashe offers a vision of Prynne as a viperous "Martinist." Taylor may have been writing with the Elizabethan pamphlets before him at his table, imitating Nashe's accusation in *Saffron Walden* (1596), which accused Harvey of "currying and smudging and pranking himself," *curry* meaning to "beat" or "thrash." The ghost's mission to Taylor is to "stir thee up Nip, and Whip, Strip and Snip, these Matchless, Headless, Heedless Rebels," among whom Prynne is foremost for his "late parricidal pamphlets." The likeness between Prynne and the Martinists is expressed in terms of effects over a mob, and it voices a royalist fear of the public, over which Prynne and his ilk have "persisted in their hellish plots" through "their Pennes and Pulpits."[25]

Who was reading these pamphlets and ephemera? This question is tricky, since evidence of readership is hard to come by. More people could read than could write in seventeenth-century England, so the most humble, but avid, readers left no written record of their reading habits. There were, of course, economic limitations to readership; yet pamphlets and ballads were often consumed in public, shared, or passed around from one person to another. Richard Brathwaite and many others complained about the wide circulation of the ballads from the city into the country, "till at last they grow so common there too, as every poor milk-maid can chant and chirp it under her cow."[26] Evidence from booksellers' stock is slim, since bookshop owners rarely took note of such low literature. But we can estimate who might have been reading them from taking note of literacy and bookselling figures for the period. Historians have estimated that 30 percent of adult males could read; the figures were considerably higher in London, where 60 percent of adult males were literate. Press runs for an individual pamphlet would range from 500 to 1,500 copies, and the number of almanacs produced annually for the Stationers' Company in the 1660s ran between 300,000 to 400,000, or one for every four families.[27] The typical cost of a pamphlet or chapbook was cheap, 2d.–6d.; some of the pamphlets I treat here went into more than one edition. There was a steady market in popular wares such as ballads, and fierce fights broke out among printers throughout the period over copyrights for such golden eggs.[28]

The writers of the civil war period differed from their forbears, however, in their conceptions about their audience and also in their intentions toward politically engaging that audience. Civil war pamphleteers adapted literary conventions and seized upon the popular audience for a new end: to fight a war over opinions, specifically *political* opinions. The Protestant and Catholic literature of the sixteenth century had inaugurated the widespread use of print for polemical purposes, and in the seventeenth century, this medium found political and social avenues to add to the religious ones. As Samuel Hartlib wrote in 1641, "the art of Printing will so spread knowledge that the common people, knowing their own rights and liberties will not be governed by way of oppression." The political pamphleteers of the 1640s conceived of their audience more broadly than had those writing before. With the exception of sermons, prior political writing had achieved limited visibility, since it was written in an oblique style, in secret, or had been smuggled into England from the Continent. The writers had addressed specific elites; the Marprelate tracts, for example, addressed the clergy, and anti-Spanish pamphlets were written in the 1620s for king, court, and clergy (Sir Simonds D'Ewes read them and noted that the king had, too). Yet the nonpolitical writings in the vernacular tradition—the jestbooks, almanacs, and "penny merriments"—could attract a wide audience. In this period, the elite and the popular audiences merged, and political writings were addressed to the public as a whole, and intended to rouse that public into action.[29]

Another key difference was that the earlier pamphleteers wrote under strained conditions, as exceptions to the general rule of political silence. The yearly output of presses prior to the civil war period was small since the printing industry was closely regulated by the governing board of the Stationers' Company, then in the tight reigns of Crown and church. In the 1640s, the output of the press exploded to the thousands. This quantitative difference produced a new degree of audience saturation; forty pamphlets could reach more readers than could four. Few in London at the time of the civil wars could ignore or miss the phenomenon of the pamphlets. The author of a newsbook, *The Exchange Intelligencer*, comments on the changes in his trade in the year 1645: "We had (some years agone) no *Diurnals* [daily newsbooks] of our own affairs in England. We did live then in a so blessed a Time, that we were only curious, and desirous to hear foreign news, and to know the state of other Kingdoms and Nations. And now by a strange alteration and vicissitude of Times we talk of nothing else, but of what is done in *England*." This author fails to acknowledge that censorship of local news by Crown policy had kept information about English affairs suppressed. As this publisher notes (regretfully), most writing in his immediate day concerned topical political matters. One result of this new subject matter was that the readers and writers of these pamphlets began to share a competence in political language.[30]

This was above all writing for action. For example, after the victory of the Parliamentary Army over Prince Rupert's forces at Naseby in June 1644, the king's correspondence was captured. It was published by Parliament as *The King's Cabinet Opened,* and it revealed to the world the king's opposition to peace negotiations with Parliament, his subservience to his Catholic wife's command, and his secret efforts to obtain aid from the Catholic Irish and the pope. The parliamentary preface urged readers to consider the evidence of the letters as sufficiently damaging to the king's cause to change sides: "If thou are well affected to that Cause of Liberty and Religion, which the two Parliaments of England and Scotland now maintain against a combination of all the Papists in Europe almost, especially the bloody Tigers of Ireland . . . thou wilt be abundantly satisfied with these Letters here printed, and take notice therefrom, how the Court has been cajoled . . . by the Papists, and we the more believing sort of Protestants, by the Court." The religious danger, amply expressed in the language of this pamphlet, should provoke a political action. A leading Royalist, Sir Trevor Williams, promptly changed his allegiance. E. Symmons, a preacher, wrote over three hundred pages against this publication and against the conclusions drawn from it in *A Vindication of King Charles . . . from those Aspersions cast upon Him* (1648). This work equates the pen-battle with the battle at swords: "Although you (Dear Sovereign) are not able with your Sword to defend us, yet we must and will with our pens, to the danger of our lives, defend you."[31] Historians will profit from attending to such uses of printing in the early modern political arena.

MILTON'S PUBLICS

My second aim in the book is to offer case studies of Milton's writing both in and out of the English Revolution and, in the final chapter, to offer a reading of Milton's *Paradise Lost* that highlights the debt Milton owed to the political pamphleteering of that period. I present a more nuanced view of Milton's politics than the traditional Whig view—Milton here is presented as an engaged man of considerable literary talent, and his final gestures in his great poem reflected not gloom at the failures of the revolution, but urgency and optimism. In my reading, Milton never gave up on the people of England, and in *Paradise Lost,* the actions of a revolutionary reader become his chief concern. Milton believed that interpretation of events and of words was a chief problem during the English Revolution, as his *Eikonoklastes* fought to prove, and that interpretation of literary and political texts remained a problem in the Restoration. Under the conditions of Restoration political censorship, the only power left to the blind writer was that of writing literature: his aim became not simply to pass on his revolutionary messages in code, but to mold a readership that was increasingly required to know how to decipher conflicting interpretations.

I wish to treat Milton's statement about his "fit audience . . . though few" (*Paradise Lost* 7.31) as a first clue in a detective story: Who is this audience? At times, Milton names his audience directly in his prose, as in *Of Reformation*, where he speaks to "the elegant & learned reader, to whom principally for a while I shal beg leav I may addresse my selfe" (*CPW* 1.807); and in *Colasterion*, he again notes that he speaks to "men of quality" (*CPW* 2.742). Other works were directed at Parliament specifically, as were *Areopagitica* or *Likeliest Means to Remove Hirelings*. In his search for his fit audience in *Paradise Lost*, Milton speaks through a poem written largely after his personal and his political defeat. Individual readers are invited to become part of that "fit audience" by reading the poem.[32] Yet in his poem, Milton offers readers the possibility of assembling into a larger, wider audience. His task is that of "justifying the ways of God to men" (1.26). In this remark, presented early in *Paradise Lost*, Milton's audience is "men," and I emphasize the "to men" aspect of that phrase. Are the "to men" Milton will later seek in his "fit audience" a select group, or are all eligible? In the course of this book, I give an extended commentary on this thorny question of Milton's "fit audience."

When we ask the question, Who was John Milton's audience? scholars studying his poetry give us an innocuous answer: it was a "fit audience, though few," and we wonder if Milton was one of those people who loved humanity in general but hated particular instances of it. Milton's remark about his desired audience in *Paradise Lost* squares with his image as one of the Puritan elect, one who cared only for conversations with rare fellows like himself who were counting down the days—in Latin probably—until the Second Coming. One of Milton's first readers, Andrew Marvell, saw *Paradise Lost* this way, as a poem "deterring the Profane" while it "draws the Devout."[33] Rather than his politics or theology, however, Milton's poetic style has marked him as an "elitist" writer. As C. S. Lewis put it, "it will . . . be unintelligible to those who lack the right qualifications, and hateful to the baser spirits among them."[34] Marvell concurred, recognizing this stylistic difficulty for the audience: "Well mightst thou scorn thy Readers to allure / With tinkling Rhime, of thy own sense secure." It has even been argued that Milton wrote for a coterie—and royalist—audience at least once.[35]

If Milton is an elitist on account of his style in his poetry, in his prose it is on account of his politics. His conception of the public leads him into trouble. Coleridge chastised his hero for holding anti-public sentiments: "It was the error of Milton, Sidney and others of that age, to think it possible to construct a purely aristocratical government, defecated of all passion, and ignorance, and sordid motive. The truth is, such a government would be weak from its utter want of sympathy with the people to be governed by it."[36] Hardly a top-notch political philosopher (or a populist) himself,

Coleridge nonetheless strikes a chord that echoes in the commentary on Milton's prose writings. Though Christopher Hill has bravely attempted to associate Milton with the dust of the street pamphleteers, evidence of Milton's scorn for the people is plentiful in his prose writings, and even Hill finally finds Milton to be no populist, noting the many "contemptuous references to the common people."[37] Marxists have examined Milton for his class biases, and they call the inconsistency between Milton's advocacy of his public cause and his exclusive outlook an "ideological failure"; Milton has been branded an "elitist radical," and chided for his "respectability."[38] Critics have saved the poet from total condemnation for elitism by arguing that Milton did modify his views over time: after the failure of the revolution, he became increasingly—and legitimately, these critics argue—disgusted with his countrymen.[39] Milton's attitudes toward the people have been deduced from his social position, and from descriptive evidence about the public from Milton's text, which is then glossed by historical information about Milton's political milieu. With respect to the kind of evidence used, these critics have taken Milton at face value, that is, they have taken Milton's explicit remarks to be normative statements about the public. This method ignores an important component of Milton's program: the element of the ideal, the rhetorical, or the imaginary. These critics have often confused what Milton said about the historical public with what he wanted—or feared—that historical public to become, and so have seen Milton in only a half-light.

I shall approach the question of who Milton's audience or public was from another view, that of its myths. I see in Milton's career a series of engagements with the double problem of political audience and with the images of the public, a problem produced by civil war writers. In his ideas, Milton was not alone in conceiving of the public in new ways; waving the banner of "the people" was a tactic familiar to seventeenth-century politicians.[40] Yet in his myth making, Milton did make a powerful contribution to civil war thought. Milton helped to define what I call the "revolutionary public" as a political entity by fashioning his audience as a valuable participant in political discussion. Milton, along with the other pamphlet writers of the English Revolution, constructed a positive image for his public. It is true that in many places in his writing Milton scorns the rabble, but it is equally true that in many instances, including *Of Education*, *Areopagitica*, *The Ready and Easy Way*, and even *Paradise Lost*, Milton explains how any rank of citizen may become virtuous—by proper discipline, trial, and reading. In these rhetorical imaginings, we find Milton postulating his public.

There are ambiguities in his postulate, however. In imagining his public, Milton filters his conceptions through the many languages of the revolutionary writers, whose various appeals to an audience helped to shape the character of public discussion during the English Revolution. I shall consider not just those ideas Milton drew from the recognizable languages of political theory and theology—a degraded republicanism or Calvinism, for example—but also the conventions, tropes, and figures used to express those ideas and to put them into practice. These form the languages and rhetorics against which and in which Milton fashioned his own representations. Rather than blaming Milton for his inconsistent portraits of the public or trying to resolve his inconsistencies, I prefer to see the different meanings of the public as a sign of Milton's search for appropriate audiences, for a "fit" audience, and this is indicative of the period's fascination with, and faltering construction of, political subjects in the public sphere.

Milton's task is that of the humanist, educating the people according to the classical model of exemplary learning.[41] Milton himself subscribed to this model in *Areopagitica* when he praised Spenser, melding the classical humanist practice of reading for examples with a Puritan insistence on experience: "our sage and serious Poet *Spencer*, whom I dare be known to think a better teacher than *Scotus* or *Aquinas*, describing true temperance under the person of *Guion*, brings him in with his palmer through the cave of Mammon, and the bowr of earthly blisse that he might see and know, and yet abstain" (*CPW* 2.516). The method for aquiring the virtue of temperance is by experience and not simply by reading precepts; the imagination is a partner to the ethical sense. Yet Milton's vision—and indeed those of the English revolutionary writers in general—also included a Protestant and millennial component that gave such methods of humanist reading the special edge supplied by biblical typology. Reading the Bible to support political argument depended upon a commonplace analogy between England and the biblical people Israel. With a typological perspective, Israel was not just a model for England, as Rome or Greece might be, but England was a recapitulation of Israel. Though parallels between England and Israel had been common parlance since even before the Reformation, the English Revolution added an extra charge to such comparisons.[42] Barbara Lewalski notes: "these parallels, however, are more than analogies: in the charged polemic of the period they are felt as genuine recapitulations in the domain of God's providence, wherein he deals with his new Israel as he did with the old."[43] When Milton and others read their current history typologically, they read with a different kind of authority than when they read classical authors; they read with God's authority. The aim of reading typologically depended upon the special meanings of sacred history for seventeenth-century polemicists, and when they applied this reading, they believed they were completing God's mission.[44] Typological readings "show the nation and the national leader participating in the sanctity of God's providence," according to Steven Zwicker.[45] The typological perspective implied an eschatology, both of self and of nation; a hermeneutic (divine truth could be found in the Bible, if it were only read properly); and an activist role for participants in history (the radical saint).

The typological method of reading thus differed from the humanist method. Like the humanists who read classical history for examples, those who engaged in typological analysis derived their political argument from acts of reading. But the humanist aims of reading examples in order to confer virtue upon the reader or to train the reader in particular habits of thought that would lead to virtuous or discretionary action were only part of the typological mission.[46] Typological analysis raised the stakes of such hermeneutic tasks, invoking ways of reading that embraced, and indeed took part in, a divine plan. Nothing short of a new mode of political consciousness was produced through such readings. Arguments that depended upon typological structures were doing more than appealing to ancient examples; they were turning English people into political activists.[47]

Not only by models would English citizens find their Reformation, but also by this typological vision. Seventeenth-century British thinkers frequently pressed the special connection betweeen England and Israel to justify a spiritual plane for political history. In this line of thinking, the spiritually pure English were seen as types of the biblical "chosen" few, and these latter-day Israelites had a mission to lead England onward to a Second Reformation.[48] Milton himself made abundant use of this "typological" relation between the English Puritan saints and the ancient Israelites to press for a militant response to world events: "Why else was this Nation chos'n before any other, that out of her as out of *Sion* should be proclaim'd and sounded forth the first tidings and trumpet of Reformation to all *Europ*" (*CPW* 2.552). As Arthur Barker puts it, "in executing the King and establishing a 'reformed commonwealth,' the English were erecting a government according to the model provided by God for his chosen people, and were themselves demonstrating their right to that title."[49] Typology, as Boyd Berry explains, was "figurative literalism" in the hands of the Puritans: Puritans "fused a literal with a wildly figurative reading of the Bible, drew their models of conduct from an ancient, literal Israel while they sought to erect an eschatologically typical Israel. . . . Typology . . . was the vehicle by which revolutionaries raised the events of their time above history; it provided a way to equate their struggle with that of Israel, and thereby served to rationalize their revolution as the work of God wrought through his agents on earth."[50] Milton used the equation between England and Israel not just as an interpretive tool, but as a means to put questions of political theory into practice, as he imagines what the people ought to be, which is not as he finds them currently. Nor is it how they were found in the exemplary stories of the past. Milton writes for a public as it "ought" to be, and that "ought" comes out of his imagination, offering in his poetry and prose hypothetical constructions of the people.

Milton has been faulted for the idealizing tendency in his prose, which is deemed to weaken the logic of his political ideas. Keith Stavely writes that "Milton's idealizing impulses consitute his political limitations," so that Milton produced great art, but less than great political theory. Yet the idealizing is part of Milton's greatness, his ability to dream of what the people might become. I do not fault Milton's political theory for the element of the ideal. Rather, in his idealizations, we find the work of the mythographer and the political visionary. The political philosopher Sheldon S. Wolin has written about the role of the ideal in political theory: "Political philosophy constitutes a form of 'seeing' political phenomena and . . . the way in which political phenomena will be visualized depends in large measure on where the viewer 'stands.' "[51] Wolin is not offering to political analysis a version of relativism; he is, rather, explaining that imagination is an important element in traditional political theory. No doubt Milton would reject the idea that he was writing a fiction. As he proclaimed in *Areopagitica*, "to sequester out of the world into *Atlantick* and *Eutopian* polities, which never can be drawn into use, will not mend our condition" (*CPW* 2.526). Refusing to pursue castles in the air, or, more precisely, the likes of Bacon's *New Atlantis*, or More's *Utopia*, Milton locates his task here and now. Michael Fixler explains Milton's rejection of utopian writing by highlighting Milton's commitment to the present needs of state: "Not through models but men would the visible Kingdom of Christ prevail."[52] Yet Milton is not arguing for a kind of pragmatism in his writing; he merely rejects an imaginative practice that has no basis in reality. His own fictions will be, in contrast, reality-based. However Milton denies the place of the ideal in his works, it is there in his rhetorical means. A poet even in his prose, Milton creates out of his brain the very stuff that can construct his new world, here, now.

The contradictory statements about the public in his prose derive in part from the fact that Milton was making up the public, drawing upon the multiple cultural frameworks he inherited, classical republicanism and biblical prophecy being only two of the most notable.[53] There were more ways than one to approach England's political problems, and the writer drafted his answers from the competing and sometimes incompatible languages of political theory.[54] It is true that the conflicting rhetorical tropes do not add up to a single, coherent political program. Rather, they intersect and weave various political languages, and draw together contradictory symbolic frameworks. So in some important sense, Milton's opponents, who accused him then (as now) of expressing contradictory senses of "the people" were right. The different roles Milton crafts for his public were not merely convenient models that Milton deployed for the moment, however. Rather, they were part and parcel of Milton's imaginative construction of a revolutionary public.

The meaning of *Paradise Lost* is here seen as rooted in the hermeneutic climate of the English Revolution, and Milton's concerns that his own readers comprise a "fit audience" derive from that climate. I see the debt Milton owed to the English Revolution, then, not solely in terms of the ideas Milton shared with the radicals, as Christopher Hill has done for this generation, and in terms of the general intellectual climate, as Arthur Barker and Don Wolfe did for the last, but in the ways that Milton's literary performances were saturated with revolutionary attitudes toward readers; his concern to find a "fit" audience is part of those attitudes. My point is not to put Milton in the context of English revolutionary thought—the fact is that he placed himself there—but of its literary practices.

In reading Milton's *Paradise Lost* in light of English revolutionary rhetoric, I aim not only to provide another interpretation of his great poem, but also to address recent historical scholarship that has redrawn the picture of the seventeenth century. My book pries Milton scholars loose from their view that what happened in the middle of the seventeenth century was a revolution pure and simple. Those Milton scholars who celebrate Milton's defense of the right to publish in *Areopagitica*, his opposition to tyranny in *A Tenure of Kings and Magistrates*; who exalt a "Grand Whig Milton," a symbol of the rising bourgeoisie who stood for a party demanding sweeping consitutional reform and whose poetry represented the best—or as feminist criticism has it, the worst—of Renaissance thought, present an outdated historical framework as a background for their claims.[55] Their historical framework, schematically labeled "Whig" by the revisionist historians, persists on a number of levels. Milton is still seen to be a philosophically coherent protoliberal thinker, whose convictions—essentially secular ones—never fundamentally changed over time.[56] This secularity led political historians to see Milton in light of pre-Enlightenment republican theory, as Zera Fink, for example, has done by placing Milton in the solidly bourgeois center of seventeenth-century English political thought.[57] Critics who hold this Whig view of Milton's ideas generally support their claims on biographical grounds, either assuming a fundamental consistency in Milton's philosophy, or at least a developmental model of the author towards the full flowering of his ideals, *Towards "Samson Agonistes,"* as Mary Ann Radzinowicz sums it up.[58] This portrait of a "liberal" Milton adheres to a conception of authorship now increasingly called into question by poststructuralist approaches, but the portrait also contains a progressive narrative that revisionists would balk at as well.[59]

The prerevisionist view of Milton has also turned up in the movement in literary studies called "new historicism," whose critics have sought to reintegrate Milton into what they believe to be the vast economic and social changes of his day. A recent new historicist essay placed Milton into Max Weber's narrative of the emergence of a Protestant ethic, for example, although Weber's "progressive" account is now called into question by revisionist historians.[60] Very recent Milton scholarship still has a tendency to read Milton backward through history almost as much as did the old style liberals or Whig historians, pointing out, rather than his radicalism, Milton's explicit aristocratic biases, his distance from the radical traditions of the English Revolution, his "bourgeois possessive individualism," and his complicity in the terms of sexual oppression.[61] Many new historicist critics have come from the political Left, paying attention to social, and not just to intellectual, or literary, history, and they owe a large debt to Christopher Hill's influential *Milton and the English Revolution.* Hill has left Milton scholars with a Whig image of the English Revolution that stressed ideological combat, real social change, and class clashes. Though, as a historian, Hill is very much a fighter in the blood-sport of early modern historiography, his image of the period is the one usually evoked by literary scholars within Milton studies who wish to return to history. Blind to current historiographical debates, the current literary critics who have turned to Hill's history are thus relying on a contested historical narrative.

One of the thorny disputes within revisionism has been on the role of class. Yet class is still used by Milton scholars to describe their poet. Milton has been seen as an aristocratic "class-warrior," who repeatedly drew a line between himself and the radical, antinomian sectarians.[62] These left-wing critics subscribe to a version of literary history very much like that of the Whigs; the difference is that they put Milton on the "bad" side, along with capitalism and the bourgeois family, and thus they fail to alter substantially the terms of the debate along the lines of revisionist historiography. Their analysis traps critics in one of two opposite models, each monologic—either a "good" Milton (one who furthered the cause of liberty) or a "bad" Milton (one who was elitist and repressive). The historian Lawrence Stone, whom revisionists have called a "grand Whig" himself, has questioned the class-based analysis of the period, and revisionists have hopped on board this train of thought, with J.C.D. Clark noisily asking, how can you have class struggle without class?[63]

If the "Whig" image of Milton is to remain relevant, however, it must be adapted to current historiography of the period. Thus in this book, I seek to read Milton for the postrevisionist generation of Milton scholarship. By outlining the main points of contrast between current Milton scholarship and that of the historians of the seventeenth century, however, I do not mean to endorse the revisionist picture. Rather, I hope to enliven the Whig portrait of Milton by paying attention to recent historiography, on the theory that when Milton scholars make historical arguments, they had better know what counts as history these days. First of all, we need to revise the terms we use to discuss Milton, some of which have gone out of date. Arthur Barker's description of Milton as a "radical but not democratic because he was at once a Puritan and a Christian Humanist,"[64] for instance, needs to be reconsidered, since Barker's very terms have been discredited by historians of the period.[65] But more important, this revisionist movement in history could give new clarity, accuracy, and purpose to the return to history promoted by the so-called new historicism. From the wealth of revisionist historical material, it is now necessary to provide a more thorough grounding for Milton scholarship.

My interest is in the relation between Milton's search for a "fit audience" and the various conceptions of political audiences appearing during the English Revolution. As part of the revisionist program, each rhetorical instance must be examined by itself, before it can be considered as a point along the line of Milton's career. With respect to his audience, for example, at times, Milton thought of a precise, historical group, like the Parliament of England in *Areopagitica*, or a named individual, like Salmasius; at others, his audience was the people of England, the people who betrayed the cause in the "Character of the Long Parliament"; the dazzled rabble in *Eikonoklastes*; or the "Asses, Apes and Dogs" who cry "License" rather than "Liberty" in Sonnet 12. Yet these precise audiences are also infused with fictional or mythical attributes, like the nation of Englishmen celebrated in *Areopagitica* or the heroic citizens in the specific moment in English history in *The Tenure of Kings and Magistrates*. There is contradiction here, and this contradiction should be seen in light of the rhetorical functions of the works themselves. What is particularly interesting is how Milton manipulated his concept of his readers precisely at a time when readers came to take on so many new roles. These contradictions in Milton's thought are not failures of his intellect, but natural consequences of a struggle to reconcile ideals with historical realities, expressed by a man who was no idle theorist about politics, but an engaged partisan. Why is Milton not more like Hobbes, a political scientist friend once asked me, meaning; Why did he not produce a coherent and lasting political theory? The answer may be found in the following pages, which depict the fervor and the range of English revolutionary pamphleteering, where those who were most engaged in polemical activity often displayed an astonishing incoherence. That incoherence was the starting point for much revolutionary discussion about the nature and function of the public in Milton's own time. If my readers take away from my book a new understanding of Milton's poetry, I hope that they will also recognize that Milton's poetry was but one manifestation, though a brilliant one, of a general problem, that of defining an English public.

My own approach thus generally confirms the Whig view that there was an ideological clash in the midcentury, that there was a revolution. In my examples of the pamphlets of the English Revolution, I show a great deal of ideological work going on. I argue that the construction of the revolutionary reader was not an abstract entity, nor a coherent ideology, but the product and sum of political and rhetorical practices of the revolutionary writers, both low and high. A consequence of my rhetorical approach is to press revisionists to pay attention to the workings of rhetoric and literature as ways of understanding political practice. As I pursue a rhetorical understanding of the period, I find that no idea arises without a context, and I have expanded the kinds of contexts allowed to inform our studies of literary artifacts. The relation of cultural artifact to context needs to be rethought in my perspective, since I have found when I examine the "low" pamphlet materials in their rhetorical relation to a "high" work of literature such as *Paradise Lost* or to a work of "high" political theory such as Hobbes's *Leviathan*, it is not the case that high merely influenced low, or vice versa. Rather, I have begun to see that the high and the low are in dialogue, are both parts of the same world of words. To me, it seems inadequate to the task of historical understanding merely to look at the "high."

Propaganda and Literature

However, Milton's *Paradise Lost* is no pamphlet, but rather a significant literary work, an epic poem. Further, some of its most essential concerns are those of literary genre. The methodology of the new historicism cannot adequately address this fact. Texts in the new historicist paradigm seem fixed in a binary struggle between the powerful and the powerless, where distinctions between "text" and "context" are banished in service of the ringing hegemony of "discourse." I have not found the model appropriate here, and my work is an implicit argument against viewing history and literature either sheerly through the gun barrel of power or as a loomless tapestry of discourse. Discourses here are rooted in the available languages of political and literary thought, bound to traditions through form, genre, language, and intention. Though this book is not a work of literary theory, it should contribute to the shift toward cultural history, to further an interdisciplinary understanding of the ways that meaning is made. One way I have done this is by reconstructing a meaningful boundary between propaganda and those works (like *Paradise Lost*) whose writers self-consciously commented on the rhetorical dangers of propaganda, and who worked to preserve a space apart from it. In the last chapter, I address the revolutionary writers' uses of allegory as a literary kind, and then show Milton refusing to make use of allegory in the same way.

My third aim thus addresses more generally the history of rhetoric and propaganda. Because the press was relatively free from constraint during the English Civil War period, this was a time not only for unprecedented political challenges to authority, but also a context in which propaganda flourished. When Milton sought a "fit audience . . . though few," or perversely chided the "hasty multitude" in *Paradise Lost*, he was expressing ambivalence toward the reading public, a public that in his own writing he hoped to shape, but one he knew was vulnerable to seductive rhetoric. For the pamphleteers of the English Revolution, the public was the object of the greatest millennial hopes, but it was also one easily charmed by words. The proliferation of ideas during the relative freedom of the press during the English Revolution only added to the danger that readers would be taken in by propaganda. Thus my analysis of the audience for political literature is also a study of early modern propaganda—its tactics, its assumptions, and its impact on the practices of public political conflict. Of course, English revolutionary propaganda may be traced back to the English Reformation, where propaganda was used by the state for the direction of the people.[66] The Protestant Reformation had first put the public into focus as an object of zeal, and Elizabeth's schemes for educational progress had made religion the impetus for widespread literacy.[67] Pamphlet reading then was tied to action, all in the name of reform.[68] There are important differences between Reformation propaganda and that of the civil war period, however. Not only were Cromwell, Charles, and other revolutionary actors ordering the dissemination of secular political writing, as political leaders had done before them, but many pamphlet writers other than those authorized by the leaders during the English Revolution were busy creating such literature.[69] The most significant difference between the propaganda of the English Reformation and that of the revolution was the wider scope of opinion permitted in the press. Writers of the English Revolution wrote under conditions very like those of a free press, at least until 1655, and their writing was engaged on many sides of the issues.

Propaganda has had a long history, entering the mental lexicon with the Roman Catholic church's response to the Reformation, its *Congregatio de propaganda fide* (Congregation for the propagation of the faith) in 1622.[70] Propaganda has been examined by Marxists, who have looked at instances of propaganda as class exploitation through mystification, as a stranglehold of the powerful over the powerless.[71] For the most part, however, modern theorists of propaganda, both in the fields of communications studies and rhetoric, have slighted the early modern period, deriving their models from examples of twentieth-century fascism. This has tended to essentialize and dehistoricize the study of propaganda. Today's theorists often invoke modern technologies (the communications systems of radio and television), forms of political organization and administration, and cultural norms (urbanism, secularity, and "mass psychology") in their discussions, yet none of these factors matches the seventeenth-century English experience of propaganda.[72] These modern conditions are quite different from the conditions in which Cromwell and Milton struggled, and thus we must revise our modern, anachronistic, understanding of propaganda to understand its presence in the early modern period.[73]

In this book I present a method by which to understand propaganda as a kind of rhetoric. In looking at propaganda from the perspective of those whom it affected, I have found that writers who recognized its power saw propaganda as disallowing readers their freedom to interpret. Jürgen Habermas has suggested that "the elimination of the institution of censorship marked a new stage in the development of the public sphere" in Europe.[74] But it is clear that the weakening of censorship in the 1640s in England did not lead at once to the creation of a public sphere for free political exchange. Rather, politicans struggled with the distortions of propaganda, and this struggle infused the early English public sphere with its peculiar rhetorical character. Writers who engaged in the pamphlet wars of the English Revolution wished to persuade their readers to fight for their causes, but they also sought readers who were fit to withstand the challenges posed by their enemies' propaganda. Writers had discovered that a free press was also a press free for propaganda. These writers appealed to readers as those who were free to make political choices based on a critical practice of reading and decoding enemy propaganda. Their construction of political subjects as capable readers of propaganda is one significant consequence of their understanding of the dangers of a free press, and it is a chief contribution of the English Revolution to the history of political culture.

•

I hope my work represents, in its entirety, an argument for approaching historical texts in a new way, as agents, unwitting perhaps, of ideological change, but not solely reducible to ideology. Our own postdeconstructive moment in literary criticism might demand that we undermine, by a more-than-rhetorical irony, the genuineness of their rhetorical fight. On the contrary: the rhetorical effects of the civil war period had very real consequences for individuals, parties, and institutions, and these consequences may be read in the blood spilled on the battlefields and in the villages, and in the thousands of pages of writing they penned with ferocity and verve. My work then is neither "history" nor "literature"; rather, it draws from methods appropriate to both in order to understand the writing of the past that possessed such power of life and death.

Chapter 1 examines the trials of the radical John Lilburne, who crafted an image of the public, argued for a revolutionary conception of the public sphere, and, like Milton in *Areopagitica*, adopted the model of a jury for his readers. The second chapter looks at conservative responses to these images. I focus on the metaphor of Babel, with which royalist writers registered their opposition to the new kinds of readers, and examine the way this trope linked fears of political anarchy to those of linguistic and literary disorder. Conflicts in the English Revolution took place in, and about, words; but words reflected the social and political currents that were shaking things loose from their traditional moorings. Chapter 3 investigates the theory and practice of pamphlet debate, from the jubilant hopes of the revolutionary writers who believed that in this climate of free exchange, truth would always be the victor, to the Royalists who preferred politics in private. In Chapter 4, I show how those defending the revolutionary public sphere rallied around a vision of a reader fit to withstand coercion by political rhetoric within this climate of conflicting opinions and of propaganda. Milton's *Eikonoklastes* is an instance of a literal challenge to readers to properly interpret rhetoric that was intended to manipulate, but this pamphlet is also emblematic of writers' intense desires to control the intepretations of their readers. In the final chapter, I present Milton's *Paradise Lost* as a reaction to such controlling impulses. Milton uses contemporary references to Satan, I argue, to call into question the nature of literary representation as it was made to serve politics in his own day. In *Paradise Lost*, written after the failure of the revolution, we find Milton still attending to revolutionary readers as ones who must decipher signs with care. In his quest for a "fit audience . . . though few," Milton's poem reiterates the period's intense conflicts, chief among them the battle over the audience for politics. In *Paradise Lost*, Milton summons a reader to reach a heightened awareness of the rhetorical stakes of political writing, as Milton himself applies political lessons to a readership that is increasingly required to know how to make interpretations. His own attempt to defeat the coercive power of propaganda was to train readers to recognize the possibilities for obscurity and manipulation in any kind of interpretation.

The English civil war period and revolution, as I hope this book will make clearer, not only gave writers new opportunities for public expression and provided a setting where writers sought new relations to readers, but equally significantly, raised literary questions, such as those of audience, political content, genre, and style in response to those new circumstances. Writers in the revolutionary period appealed to a wide audience, and literary relations between writers and readers involved polemic, persuasion, and propaganda in a field open to public debate. Milton's *Paradise Lost*, I argue, needs to be seen in this context, one in which these literary protocols may be taken as a given, and one through which Milton is to be seen making his difficult way.

Revolution in Print

LILBURNE'S JURY, AREOPAGITICA,
AND THE CONSCIENTIOUS PUBLIC

And if the Parliament and Military Councel doe what they
doe without precedent, if it appeare thir duty, it argues the
more wisdom, vertue, and magnanimity, that they know
themselves able to be a precedent to others. Who perhaps in
future ages, if they prove not too degenerat, will look up with
honour, and aspire towards those exemplary, and matchless
deeds of thir Ancestors, as to the highest top of thir
civil glory and emulation.

John Milton, *Tenure of Kings and Magistrates*

IN 1649, THE HOUSE OF COMMONS INSTITUTED a High Court of Justice to try
King Charles I, and named commissioners who were to be both judges and
jurors in this unique case. The men who were left to call themselves Parliament
after the purge in 1648 charged the king with the intent "out of a
wicked design to erect and uphold in himself an unlimited and tyrannical
power to rule according to his will, and to overthrow the rights and liberties
of the people, yea, to take away and make void the foundations thereof . . .
which by the fundamental constitution of this kingdom were reserved on
the people's behalf."[1] For this, and for having "traitrously and maliciously
levied war against the present Parliament, and all the people therein represented,"
Charles Stuart was to be put on trial for treason. In late January,
Charles was found guilty and sentenced to die. These revolutionary acts
were done in the name of the people and by order of law. The trial was
illegal, as the king repeatedly pointed out, and the 59 men who signed the
king's death warrant, out of the 150 or so judges listed on the commission,
could hardly be said to represent the will of the people. On 30 January
1649, however, the death sentence was carried out before an astonished
crowd. Public execution in general performed a symbolic function in English
society to legitimize ruling authority. This time, however, the severed
head was the king's, in a reversal of this symbolic act. The execution of

Charles I stunned the English nation and all of Europe. The power being ratified belonged not to the king, but to Parliament.[2]

Writers justifying the trial and execution of the king placed authority in the law of conscience or reason, which they claimed took precedence over custom and kingly prerogative. This logic was potentially revolutionary, since the English legal system relied upon precedent, custom, and kings for authority: these, however, could supply no prior examples to back up the case of the trial and execution of the king. Defending the regicide, John Fidoe had argued: "But if we had no precedent, either Domestic or Foreign, yet the very Law of Reason and Nature were sufficient to clear them in it: As for the laws of the Land, they are all subordinate unto this of Reason, and must give place to it." Milton pursued a similar path in *Tenure of Kings and Magistrates*, arguing that citizens may take action against tyrants by the guide of reason. He opened his tract, "If men within themselves would be governed by reason, and not generally give up their understanding to a double tyranny, of Custom from without, and blind affections within, they would discern better, what it is to favor and uphold the Tyrant of a Nation" (*CPW* 3.190).[3]

The idea that reason is sufficient to "govern" humans, and that the people possessed reasoning capabilities, was expressed often in the aftermath of the king's execution. God's law, as written in the consciences of humans, and the law of reason were above the king's law, defenders of the regicide argued, and the people could administer both. According to Matthew Simmonds, in *The Execution of the Late King Justified, and the Parliament and the Army therein, Vindicated* (1649), "God's Law enjoins the execution of Justice and Judgment; The Parliament in their Late Transactions, have executed Justice and Judgment: Therefore they have obeyed God's Law." John Goodwin used the tools accessible to ordinary citizens, of "clear texts of Scripture, as principles of Reason, grounds of Law, Authorities, Precedents, as well as Foreign, as Domestic," for his justification of Parliament's actions. Robert Robins asked the public to render its word: "now let all the world judge, whether the people have justly recalled their own interest and adjudged him to death for such abuses, and refusing to account" in his pamphlet *Reasons to Resolve the unresolved PEOPLE of the legality of the King's Trial and Judgment* (1649).[4] Just as the regicides appealed to the law of reason and conscience to ask English citizens to support their actions, John Lilburne appealed to the consciences of his jurymen to overturn the views of his judges in his trial for treason in 1649. In this chapter we see how, during the English Revolution, justifications that centered on the authority of a capable public were expressed to a wide audience by the medium of print. In the case of John Lilburne, we see how the public was appealed to as a potent body, was authorized by people's individual consciences to overturn precedent and institutional tradition; in Milton's *Areopagitica*, we see Milton develop an idea of a public out of the same materials of conscience, reason, and right.

PRINTING AND THE PEOPLE

Though the group that sat in judgment of the king was a stripped-down "rump" of the House of Commons, it has been argued that during the seventeenth century more people had more say in government.[5] As early as 1628, with its Petition of Right, Parliament had dared to place limits upon the king's absolute authority, asserting that Charles needed the consent of the Lords and Commons for certain acts; in the words of the Petition: "No man hereafter shall be compelled to make or yield any gift, loan, benevolence, tax or such like charge without common consent by Act of Parliament."[6] With increasing vigor over the course of the seventeenth century, Parliament insisted that the king was to be subject to the law, and battled with Charles over the scope of royal prerogative. The chief struggle between king and Parliament over royal prerogative and rule by law touched upon a wide range of social, political, and religious matters.[7] Some radicals even went so far as to say that the law was made to express the rights of the people, as in the 1647 "Agreement of the People." Revolutionary writers insisted upon the primacy of "fundamental rights" of English citizens, as embodied in Cicero's dictum, *Salus populi suprema lex* (let the welfare of the people be the supreme law), a concept employed by many radicals to overrule the powers of the king. John Lilburne, for example, in his pamphlet *Englands Birth-Right Justified* (1645), treats *salus populi* as a natural political concept. William Walwyn makes the same argument in *Englands Lamentable Slaverie* (1645); from this doctrine, Henry Parker had also advanced a theory of "public consent," a contract theory of authority from law.[8] A pamphlet directed to Charles in 1642, entitled *Vox Populi*, exhorted: "O, then return unto your Parliament, and so unto your people; Return unto your Parliament, and so unto your lawful power."[9] One Royalist complained that "every man who hath but arrived at one sentence in Latin, is ready to beat me down with the irresistable power of axiom . . . *salus populi lex summa*."[10] In taking up arms against him, Parliament concluded that the king had been overstepping his authority in religious and in civil matters in the years of his personal rule; Charles was acting totally out of bounds of the law, *Parliament*'s law.

It is significant that the regicides felt compelled first to try the king in court, and second, to publish the proceedings of his trial in pamphlet form in order to justify their action of killing him. The previously secret operations of the courts, analogous to the secret and unaccountable nature of kingly prerogative, were in these deeds overturned by political actions conducted *in* public and *for* the public. In his trial, Charles was charged in the name of the people of England: "You have been accused on behalf of the People of England of high Treason and other high Crimes." The lord president explained that the authority of the court was the people of England: "This Court is founded upon that Authority of the Commons of England, in whom rests the supreme Jurisdiction," and added an ironic note: "how great a friend you have been to the Laws and Liberties of the People, let all England and the world judge."[11] All England was to render judgment on this comment by reading the official transcript of the king's trial, published during and after the event itself.

At the same time, the king was also fashioning himself into a champion for the people's cause. Charles requested to tell his side of the story, to "give satisfaction to the people of England of the clearness of my proceeding . . . to satisfy them that I have done nothing against that Trust that hath been committed to me." On the fourth day of the case, when the lord president repeated the litany about the king's abrogation of the people's rights, Lady Fairfax, sitting in the crowd, could hold her peace no longer and interrupted the court, saying, "Not half the people!" According to the transcript, the lady "was soon silenced," and was led out of the courtroom. Still, her question acutely pressed defenders of the new commonwealth like John Milton to confront the rather strange picture of "the people" that was presented by Pride's Purge, for only sixty radical Republicans and Independents were left in the "rump" after Colonel Thomas Pride's purge of ninety-six members of the House of Commons, and it was these few who put the king on trial. Even those attending the trial knew that defense by appeal to the people might be stretching the truth a bit. Charles's speech on the scaffold, the later publication of *Eikon Basilike*, along with the thousands of pamphlets protesting the trial's outcome, all rallied the public to his cause: "this is not my case alone, it is the freedom and the liberty of the People of England, and you [the court] do pretend what you will, I stand more for their Liberties," Charles pleaded.[12] Both sides knew of the usefulness of appealing to the people's interest to sway public support.

Printing may have contributed to turning citizens into political actors, but it cannot be said simply to have caused the great changes of England's revolution.[13] Printing presses had been operating for well over a hundred years in England, and though they had produced more than one best-seller, including Foxe's *Book of Martyrs* and King James's Bible, they had yet to their credit no revolutions. In the many cultures where the printing press began to flourish during the Renaissance, the uses of this instrument varied widely, as did its effects on political and social institutions, and upon the lives of ordinary folk.[14] The printing press did not operate in isolation from literacy rates, bookselling topography, patterns of book distribution, the central regulation by the Stationers' Company, police suppression of piracy, and the corps of readers and writers willing to take part in print culture. In short, the communication system of print touched many aspects of English society. During the revolution all these were in continual flux, and writers took advantage of this fluid situation to carve out a niche for the press in the political life of the nation.

The writing of the civil war differed from its precedents, however, in its conceived audience and also in the range of political opinions that appeared. Though literature of religious or political dissent had found outlets before the 1640–41 breakdown of censorship, with Thomas Scott for one exemplifying the possibilities of dissent in the 1620s, when a spate of pamphlets from the pens of the Puritan clergy attacked King James over the Spanish match, incidents of this kind were nevertheless few and far between.[15] Scott's *Vox populi* (1620) ran to four editions in its year of publication, and it even reached the ears of the king, whose anger forced the author into hiding on the Continent, where he continued to publish anti-Catholic materials.[16] Scott did pose a challenge to James's reign of censorship, but he acted as only a tiny minority voice; his claim to represent the interests of the people was yet to be echoed in a huge chorus of civil war writers.

During the 1640s, however, readers were confronted with a variety of political positions in the press. In this climate, everything seemed "up for grabs," as J. H. Hexter puts it. The printing industry was crucial in this unprecedented political conflict, producing over twenty-two thousand pamphlets, sermons, newsbooks, speeches, broadside ballads, and other ephemera. When censorship lapsed in 1640, the explosion of printed material brought such subjects as religion, culture, law, finance, domestic relations, and, prominently, politics, to the attention of the public, an increasingly literate public, it appears.[17] Historians believe 30 percent of adult males in England in 1642 could read; in London, the figure was closer to 60 percent. These were extremely high numbers compared to the rest of Europe.[18] Unlike their precedents, pamphleteers from the civil war period put political controversies before the eyes of the public. Before 1640, for instance, it was illegal to print the proceedings of Parliament and treasonous to print the king's words unless you were the king's printer. After the breakdown of censorship, a number of "diurnals," or journals, published Parliament's goings-on, along with commentary about the governing body's decisions.[19] The printed matter that appeared in the English revolutionary period was thus utterly new. Readers were given access to the workings of the governing body, and could become witnesses to the process of political decision making. Pamphleteering with a political cast was not literally without precedent, however, but the secular political information that was being disseminated and discussed, along with the quantitative change in volume of output, precipitated a qualitative change in the ways people wrote and thought about political ideas.

Where ideas and information were being disseminated to an increasingly politicized public, there was a new political practice, even though the "ideology of the English Revolution" may not have been articulated by a clear "opposition party." Given that historians are yet questioning whether the political nation did expand over the course of the seventeenth century; whether the process of parliamentary selection more accurately reflected the numbers of people voting; and whether the process of politics was increasingly conflictual, we might well give up understanding precisely what printing had to do with all of these. What this unprecedented burst of pub-lication meant for ordinary citizens is hard to determine. Yet there is evi-dence from the numbers in the press that through print, the populace was given access to discussions in and about government. To politicize the pub-lic was not an explicit aim of either side, though the Levellers' platform did tend in that direction, and the royalist one away from it. Still, all sides in-volved the public in new ways by the medium through which they chose to express their conflicts. The politicians seemed to sense the importance and the power of some notion of public opinion in choosing to make their points in public. Thus I see the printing press as a major political agent during the English Revolution.

At the level of political communication, the press improved the quality of political participation of the people. When a pamphleteer like William Prynne attempted to justify Parliament's precedence over the king, for ex-ample, he made use of the press to make "*full vindication* of such *public Truths,* concerning *Public government.*"[20] Vindication, a legal form of exon-eration, could take place in the press, here seen as the public's judicial forum. People were taking sides in a civil war, and they were increasingly thirsty for information, war news, and opinions. The swell of pamphlets in the press indicates that many ordinary citizens were willing to buy news.[21] Impetus for publication also came from opinion makers, those writers and politicians who were increasingly concerned with persuading the people to side with their political views.

What is remarkable about the writing of this period is its "public" charac-ter; exactly what writers meant by "public" is harder to say. The "public" was a setting for the king's execution, for example, and it was the forum for publishing the account of his trial; but the "public" was also an ideological construct of an audience before which writers justified the execution and to which they appealed for support. It is my argument here that with publica-tion an important part of fighting during the English Revolution, writers conceived of their readers as responsible actors in the public forum created in the press. In this chapter, I examine the habits of political writing in which pamphleteers encouraged the public to view, and to take part in, revolutionary politics. The press was instrumental in this encouragment. Writers used the press to fashion a revolutionary conception of an active and informed public as their addressees, and they began to characterize exactly the kind of forum in which such a public would hear their voices.

The tone of the early modern debate over censorship in the press sounds protoliberal in its emphasis on freedom. The Levellers made a free press a keystone of their political program, virtually equating a free press to a free public: "For what-ever specious pretences of good to the Common-wealth have bin devised to over-aw the Press, yet all times fore-gone will manifest, it hath ever ushered in a tyrannie; mens mouth being to be kept from mak-ing noise, whilst they are robd of their liberties," argued the Leveller mani-festo, *To the Right Honourable, the Supreme Authority of this Nation, THE COM-*

MONS OF ENGLAND, published early in January 1649. The Levellers saw the correlation between silence and oppression of the public, piercing through the logic, "specious pretences," of those who claimed to protect the people by censorship. The pamphlet accused those in Parliament who advocated press restrictions of setting up a tyranny over the very populace that had helped them to defeat the tyrant king: "So was it in the late Prerogative times before this Parliament, whilst upon pretence of care of the publicke, Licensers were set over the Press, Truth was suppressed, the people thereby kept ignorant, and fitted only to serve the unjust ends of Tyrants and Oppressers, whereby the Nation was enslaved."[22] Here I see a sense of the public that is potentially revolutionary in its freedoms: under censorship, the people are "fitted" only for oppression; the pamphlet implies that under a free press, they may be "fitted" for freedom. In the Leveller philosophy, religious liberty, as expressed in the idea of liberty of conscience, needed to be guaranteed by civil authorities.[23] As the Leveller William Walwyn put it, "Who can live where he hath not the freedome of his minde, and exercise of his conscience? looke upon those Governments that deny this liberty, and observe the envyings and repinings that are amongst them, and how can it be otherwise, when as if a man advance in knowledge above what the State alloweth, he can no longer live freely, or without disturbance exercise his conscience? What follows then?"[24] As Walwyn asks his rhetorical questions, he begins to outline a philosophy of civil, in addition to religious, freedom. "Freedome of his minde" may run contrary to, or ahead of, the state, as Walwyn suggests here when he asks what happens if a man has knowledge "above what the State alloweth": above is better. Reforming Protestantism, with its drive for the aquisition of new truth, must plunge ahead, and the state must allow it to run freely. In *A Remonstrance of Many Thousand Citizens* (1646), Richard Overton denounced kingship, also opposing censorship in the name of the people: "let the imprisoned Presses at liberty, that all mens understandings may be more conveniently informed." At the time Overton wrote this, he was protesting John Lilburne's imprisonment, and the language of incarceration and slavery applies just as much in this pamphlet to the press, to the people, and to John Lilburne himself, as against "all kings of *Arbitrary government.*"[25]

The debate over censorship in the early 1640s was the occasion for much discussion of the character of the political sphere, now that Parliament was in charge. When control of the press by royal authorities was abandoned in the early years of the English Civil War, chaos erupted in the printing industry, and the Stationers' Company, formerly reliant upon the Star Chamber for regulation of the printing trade, sought help from Parliament. Widespread piracy, lack of proper entrance and copyright in the Stationers' Registers, printers failing to pay fees, and even journeymen and apprentices setting up their own presses in open rejection of the apprenticeship system—all these were signs of total disarray. In an attempt to cap its losses and to regain a tight control—actually a monopoly—over the lucrative system, the Stationers' Company achieved authorization from Parliament in 1643 for an act to put the printing trade back into its own hands. The outcry ensuing the 1643 Ordinance for the Regulation of Printing has earned a place in the Western anticensorship canon, with Milton's *Areopagitica* leading the charge. Milton's lines—"as good almost kill a man as kill a good book"—are invoked frequently today in the face of current forms of censorship, and they are engraved in stone in the foyer of the tower that houses the newspaper in my city, the *Chicago Tribune*. Though modern liberals might wish it otherwise, the seventeenth-century responses to the censorship acts were not influential in reversing Parliament's dedication to control writing. Parliament had enough to think about without surrendering to the pleas of a few radicals and, in fact, needed the printing guilds' cooperation to keep their enemies quiet. Yet Henry Robinson, John Lilburne, Michael Sparke, and William Walwyn all atttacked Parliament's regulation of the press in the early 1640s, and their moves to do so were part and parcel of a radical program that also included legal reform, jury rights, protection of property, and attacks on monopolies: "Oh *Englishmen!*" Lilburne cried out, "Where is your freedoms? And what is become of your *Liberties* and *Priviledges* that you have been fighting for all this while, to the large expence of your *Bloods* and *Estates*, which was hoped would have procured your *liberties* and *freedomes?*"[26]

The rhetorical impact of these appeals is worth our atttention, since arguments favoring toleration drew upon religious and economic, as well as political, languages: all these color our understanding of the early public sphere in which differences of opinion would be tolerated.[27] Defense of freedom in the press was taken by the radicals as a correlate to liberty of conscience, and often religious languages shaded the liberal philosophies. John Lilburne, the Leveller hero of the urban multitude, argued that those controlling the press had chosen to "suppresse every thing which hath any true Declaration of the just Rights and Liberties of the free-borne people of this Nation." For Lilburne, restriction of the press was a restriction of the people's right to hear all sides of an issue, and in *Englands Birth-Right Justified* (1645), he outlined the fundamental liberties of English citizens and included among them freedom from the monopoly of printing.[28] In opposing Parliament's scrutiny of prepublication matter in *Areopagitica*, for example, Milton evoked antimonopolistic rhetoric, stressing that "truth and understanding are not such wares as to be monopolized and traded in by tickets and statutes, and standards" (*CPW* 2.535), asking, "should ye set an Oligarchy of twenty ingrossers over [this city], to bring a famine upon our minds again?" (558–59). Milton's antimonopolistic rhetoric often merged with his anti-Catholicism, as when he compared the censors to "the Popes of Rome engrossing what they pleased of Political rule into their own hands" (501); his opposition to "a fugitive and cloistered virtue" drew upon the rhetoric of the English Reformation: the cloisters in which virtue was held captive in Milton's speech were, of course, the monasteries despoiled in England by the Henrician Reformation.

As anti-Catholicism also shaded the attacks on censorship, that religious discourse was co-opted for a secular cause.[29] Anti-Catholicism, with its images of heroic Protestant virtue, was a language through which libertarian ideas were expressed in many arguments against the 1643 Printing Ordinance. For Milton, truth was not one "that never sallies out and sees her adversary, but slinks out of the race" (515); rather, truth and virtue were imagined as robust, out-of-doors, "scouting" about (517), in public, where Truth "opens herself faster" (521). Printing was to assist in this heroic combat between truth and falsehood: "so Truth be in the field, we do injuriously by licensing and prohibiting to misdoubt her strength. Let her and Falsehood grapple; who ever knew Truth put to the worse, in a free and open encounter. Her confuting is the best and surest suppressing" (561). This sounds a good deal like the heroic virtues found in classical epic, though the subject here, Truth, is female. Truth is like the Amazonian Camilla from the *Aeneid,* or one of those peculiarly English warrior-ladies. Most importantly here, Milton stresses the "openness" of the search for truth, in contrast to the secrecy of Catholic means. For Milton, the activity of finding truth is figured as winning a battle, a race, or an athletic combat. Though the victor here is female, any citizen's reluctance to take part in this combat is unmanly: "And if the men be erroneous . . . what witholds us but our sloth, our self-will, and distrust in this right cause, that we doe not give them gentle meetings and gentle dismissions, that we debate not and examin the matter thoroughly with liberall and frequent audience . . . ?" (567). Only in the open field of a free press can such "gentle meetings" occur (567–68). Debate and discussion, rather than coersion or torture, was to be the means of persuading others; and repeated debate, in public, might be needed. As Henry Robinson argued in *Liberty of Conscience* (1644), "you may, and ought to endeavor in [heretics'] reclaiming, not by compulsive courses, but with brotherly and Christian admonition and instructions, by evidence of Scripture in demonstration of the Spirit, and such other peacable and quiet wayes as are warrantable by the Word of God," and not by torture.[30]

In opposing presbyterian control over the press, John Lilburne echoed Milton's activist rhetoric of epic combat in his arguments against press restrictions, where he saw the press as a field in which political challenges should be carried on in public. In fact, his own writing bore out his theory. Lilburne confronted William Prynne in a public letter, for instance, explaining, "I was determined some weekes since, to have writ you a few lines in a publique way"; using public means, Lilburne also evokes an image of a street. "I send you these ensuing Propositions," he wrote to Prynne, "upon which I will dispute with you, hand to hand before any Auditory in and about the City of London." In this combat with Prynne, "hand to hand" fighting could be witnessed by London spectators, "any Auditory," that is, any collection of persons. Unlike a private duel, Lilburne's "dispute" with Prynne was to be fought and judged before an audience. The language of his argument referred to a tradition of violence, which the rules of the private duel replaced: "And truly it argues no manhood nor valour in you nor the Blackecoates, by force to throw us downe and ty our hands, and then to fall upon us to beat and buffet us, for if you had not beene men that had been affraid of your cause, you would have been willing to have fought and contended with us upon even ground and equall terms."[31] Like the duel, Lilburne's dispute with Prynne should be fought within the rules of fair, and manly, play, this time without censorship on one side. In comparing the struggle to physical combat, Lilburne applies heroic language, reminding us of the field in which Milton's truth and falsehood also grappled, yet this time it is squarely a fight between men. These metaphors of violent physical combat buttress a political point, and they are exemplary of the violent language of the pamphlets themselves, which bristle with vicious, hearty invective and an almost gleefully malicious satire. The level of slander and ad hominem accusation is high, a parallel to the physical violence of war. But they also indicate classical notions of virtue as combat, of manly heroism displayed on the battlefield, this time, however, before a public. The public sphere was coming to be seen as the only legitimate site for such confrontations.

At the same time that he castigates his enemy, though, Lilburne pleads for fairness in abiding by acceptable rules of exchange, based on an idea of equality. Just as Parliament pressed against the rigid hierarchy of social status by dissolving the House of Lords, John Lilburne symbolically refused to take off his cap in his trial, refusing to defer to his social superiors. By this gesture, Lilburne asserted a "natural birthright" due to every "free-born Englishman."[32] In his anticensorship writing, Lilburne called for an ethical, egalitarian code to the practice of public debate. There is a concept of "fair" play that his enemies are not allowing to happen: fight on level ground and with equal "terms," that is, with the same artillery and defenses. Here, the equal "terms" are equal access to technologies, that is, printing capabilities, yet they are also "words." To limit the ability to print is the same thing as to limit the physical movement in a battle. Lilburne sets his conditions of writing in public: "namely that the Press might be as open for us as for you."[33] The metaphor of "even ground" is also important, considering his "Leveller" platform, which was to eradicate differences in rank. The level ground is to be the public space provided by a free press. William Walwyn, too, echoed this sentiment: "let any man's experience witness whether freedom of discourse be not the readiest way both to give and receive satisfaction in all things."[34] Though the radicals did not reverse parliamentary policy, they did articulate a philosophy of the public sphere.

Whether petitioning for free expression or arguing against toleration, writers during the English Revolution presented their ideas in a forum that they created in the press. The lapse of state-sponsored censorship of the press in 1641 gave the printing press a new role to play in this more open politics. By printing their words, writers sought to attract supporters to causes, and they contributed to a body of aggressive partisan literature, which would, as the preacher Lawrence Palmer put it, lead to "the inciting and awakening of the drowsy and indifferent, the shaming of the Neuter."[35] Printing was thought the appropriate means for soliciting this response. Those defending freedoms of the press, writers like John Milton, John Lilburne, and William Walwyn, repeatedly argued that the press defined a space that was the only legitimate space for the conduct of politics, and their constant pamphlet battles put this idea into practice.

The Protestant Ideology of Print

The Protestant Reformation had supplied an ethical ground for the increasing importance of public expression.[36] John Milton's "free and open encounter" between truth and falsehood in *Areopagitica* depended on the Reformation Protestants' insistence that Scripture be accessible to all. Milton expressed his nationalist, millennial impulses by drawing upon a rhetoric of Protestant reform, and in his charge to Parliament in *Areopagitica*, he defended the uses of publicity according to a Christian mission: "Christ urg'd it as wherewith to justifie himself, that he preacht in publick; yet writing is more publick than preaching" (*CPW* 2.548). Could writing possibly outdo the impact of Christ's preaching? Milton seems to imply as much in his bold statement from *Areopagitica*, suggesting that the scope of a single pamphlet could surpass that of Christ's sermon, that the technology of printing could improve upon Christ's methods. In printing, Milton imitated Christ's aim of preaching salvation and reform to the whole world by using the most up-to-date techniques.

The spread of printing has been commonly tied to the Reformation, and Protestant ideology infuses the rhetoric of those who defended freedoms of the press during the English Revolution.[37] John Lilburne employed Reformation rhetoric against censorship as Milton had, comparing his censors to papists—"Chief members of the Kingdom of Darkness"—by which he meant the Anglican bishops, who "had no other argument to convince me with, than to put a Gag in my mouth, lest I should have shaken the foundations of their Antichristian Kingdom, publicly at the Pillory." Like Milton, Lilburne chose a Christian model for his public action of speech: "In all Paul's sufferings, I never read that ever his mouth was gagged, but you have gagged me, for speaking neither lies, faction, nor sedition, but only the naked Truth."[38] For these writers, Paul and Christ were examples of truth-seeking souls, whom writers were to imitate by way of a freer press.

If the press was to be made a tool of true Reformation, a godly mouthpiece of a national pulpit, then the English already were accustomed to a public forum in which an audience could consider political views: the sermon. Sermons during the revolutionary period were providing a critically important forum for the popular dissemination of political ideas.[39] Puritanism had brought many changes to England, and one of them was a determined corps of preachers. Sermons were best-sellers in the printing industry, and civil war polemics drew upon the tradition of preacher-writers. Since they were both spoken and printed, sermons reached an illiterate and a literate public. Sermonizers modeled themselves after biblical prophets, hoping to rouse their readers to action, and used their sermons to construct an ideology of an active public in which readers would be bound together by their common religious mission.

By the arguments of those who opposed press restrictions in the revolutionary period, we can see that ideas about the public sphere came out of a tradition of Protestant lecturing, specifically via the publication of sermons. During the English Revolution, it appeared, more people were taking on the mantle of the preacher, and were printing their utterances. As Milton wrote, "the immediat cause of all this free writing and free speaking, there cannot be assign'd a truer then your own mild, and free, and human government; it is the liberty, . . . which hath rarify'd and enlightn'd our spirits like the influence of heav'n" (*Areopagitica*, *CPW* 2.559). The English nation was busily performing Christ's work: "not only our sev'nty Elders, but all the Lords people are becoming Prophets" (555–56). Publication had merits in this national prophetic movement; by reading, and perhaps rereading, the publications, readers would remember the messages better. The preacher William Mewe stressed this aspect of the compatibility of print to oral communication in his sermon *The Robbing and Spoiling of Jacob and Israel* (1643): "Beside the hearing ear, there is (you know) to be employed a seeing eye, both which are the gift of the Lord." Mewe explained that the purpose of both sensory organs was to press the Christian soul to judge the truth more effectively: "that having brought the truth as tried gold, the filings are not to be lost; that upon your trial (whatever some say) you are willing the wise should judge whether you are taken with sounding brass, or any thing rather than Crown gold."[40] Mewe's reader would return to his pamphlet again and again, "trying" the pamphlet for its truths, and submitting themselves to its repeated testing.

Elizabeth Eisenstein, in her magnificent synthetic work, *The Printing Press as an Agent of Change*, argues that features of print culture "helped to organize the thinking of readers," and she names the various processes of print— standardization of texts, the preparation of indexes, new methods of data collection, and the possibility of improved and corrected editions—as distinct characteristics of a new culture that made an impact on the ways people thought and ordered their thoughts.[41] Of the many attributes of print that led to a qualitative change in the mental set of readers, Eisenstein emphasizes the property of fixity. Manuscripts, she explains, were vulnerable to change because of scribal error and physical deterioration; further, they were "secret" documents, preserved and guarded by the few. Print, on the other hand, could preserve texts in a way that handwritten culture could not; and preservation of texts through print could lead to democratization, as texts became available to more people.

Eisenstein's main point of contrast is between print and manuscript culture. Yet the sermon writers of the English revolution offer another source of contrast: oral culture. Those who published their English revolutionary sermons exemplify the continuity, rather than the difference, between oral culture and printing. Sermon writers noted that printing could widen the audience for printed sermons by accurately reproducing what was in the sermon. The preacher Charles Herle, for instance, hoped "that none be lost, whereby others might be afterwards fed too." Milton, in publishing *Tetrachordon*, defends divorce with the hope that his work "to the people of *England* may, if God so please, prove a memorable informing" (*CPW* 2.716)—all the more "memorable" because it is in print. The reading audience that would read Mewe's sermon, and would perform the test of whether his work was "Crown gold," would do so in the privacy of their own reading. Mewe aimed at a broad public, seeking "to make this Sermon public to the whole (as well as to the representative) body of our Commonality."[42] The sermon was to be recast in print so that the "commonality," a body wider than an audience of sermongoers, might experience it as well. The audience was "all who are concerned," the public. Mewe explained the special qualities of print in his description of the path for the dissemination of their words, "passing" from one sense to another, from ears to eyes, from one hand to another, and from one reader to the next. All these qualities rendered printing especially useful for political communication: printing was more widely distributed and more lasting in its effects than were oral sermons. Printing could construct a cohesive body of readers who did not know each other personally, but who were linked by a common reforming mission.

Many religious writers echoed these reforming sentiments, which continued an oral, public tradition. Claiming their legacy from the Protestant Reformation, these religious writers emphasized the written word, first in reading the Bible, and then in publishing sermons and other forms of religious instruction. When they explained why they were printing their sermons in the first place, religious writers expressed views that the public sphere was the place for spiritual truths to be disseminated. Since sermons were both spoken and printed, they reached both an illiterate and a literate public.[43] "The appetite for sermons, at least in towns, seems to have been insatiable," Christopher Hill comments, explaining that lectures were an unregulated kind of speech that could challenge the traditional hierarchies within the church as well as bring more people into the fold.[44] Sermons heard in the Long Parliament on designated fast days were printed according to orders of Parliament, and in them, preachers named an audience of the people of England.[45] In explaining his decision to print his sermon, for instance, Lawrence Palmer wrote, "The theme and whole discourse tends wholly to invite and urge all sorts within their spheres to be as serviceable as may be, for the promoting of the public; if the printing may conduce more to this end, than the preaching . . . well, the blessing of God go with it."[46] The sermon writers specifically discussed the medium of print as an important vehicle in their reforming mission.

In their printed sermons, preachers made appeals to a public that contributed to a revolutionary conception of a public sphere. In such sermons, the traditional forum of the pulpit as a font of spiritual enlightenment was adapted in an age of print to polemical and exhortative purposes toward civic enlightenment. Charles Herle, for instance, likened his act of publication to Christ's miracle of the feeding of the thousands with only a few loaves of bread (John 6) in his *Davids Reserve and Rescue,* a sermon preached to Commons on 5 November 1644, a day commemorating the Gunpowder Plot. He opened with this analogy: "An honest sermon, I acknowledge . . . hath much of the miracle in it, though but a few barley loaves, yet it may feed many thousands." The reasoning continued, "that none be lost, whereby others might be afterwards fed too." Though he belittled the value of his sermon, insisting that the parliamentary order was the only reason he published it, still Herle made a gesture toward the public by asserting that it was meant for "public use." In the allusion to Christ's miracle moreover, Herle insisted upon the worth of his own work.[47] Matthew Newcomen also printed his sermon out of public zeal: "We whom God hath made Seers to his people must not shut our eyes, and refuse to see what God reveals, nor lay our hands upon our mouths, and fear to declare what we see."[48] The printed pamphlet was to be his public declaration, a modern prophecy. Francis Woodcock explained how the role he played as prophet before his people was transformed by the medium of print. He outlined his mission as God's "people's Watch-men, and his own Remembrancers," an allusion to Isaiah's watchmen on the walls of Jerusalem. The watchman is the organizing image throughout his sermon, where Woodcock is also a "sentinel" and a "trumpet," just as Lilburne himself would be labeled an incendiary "trumpet" by his enemies. These trumpeting images suited the medium of a printed text and denoted broad transmission of his ideas. Woodcock claimed to act for the benefit of "the public itself," and by publishing, he extended the province of the prophet's work, "this same Report which came . . . so acceptable to your ears (I hope your hearts too) might now find the like favor in your eyes also."[49] Milton, like these sermon writers, saw writing as equivalent to public action, mirroring the zeal of radical Puritanism: "when a man writes to the world, he summons up all his reason and deliberation to assist him . . . in this the most consummate act of his fidelity and ripeness" (*Areopagitica, CPW* 2.532). Writing takes place before "the world."

The success of the Reformation may be seen in the high degree of literacy in England, since the Reformation, like no other religious movement, encouraged its public to read. It is important to remember that the English public learned to read in order to read the Bible. Religion, not poetry or plays, was the impetus for widespread literacy. The high literacy figures in early modern England were the result of a burst of popular education in the 1560s, the religious mission of the Protestant Reformation. Evidence of book ownership tells that of all books, the Bible was the most commonly owned, with other kinds of religious literature rating next highest on the list.[50] Printed sermons were everywhere, as preachers leapt into print with zealous exhortations to their readers. The Reformation had made printed literature relevant to action; Protestant literature exhorted, educated, fostered zeal and repentence: "Zeal to promote the common good," was the aim of King James's authorized translation of the Bible in 1611.[51] In this line of thinking, God had sent his chosen people, the Protestant English, to spread the new word (the Protestant word) to the world, and the press was but one artillery in this arsenal. The English felt themselves to be driven toward the fulfillment of a national destiny. The very name "Reformation" attests to the power of this line of thinking. The new literature caught this charge, and as the nation drew closer to civil war, writing came to be considered a necessary part of the fight.

Sermons were intended not only for spiritual growth of the listeners; they were for many, a prime source of political information.[52] In *Saint Paul's Politics; or, A Sermon against Neutrality* (1644), for instance, Lawrence Palmer sought to agitate his audience "to zealous resolution," preaching at St. Margaret's Westminster to an audience that included many in the House of Commons. Palmer urged his audience to serve the public interest, and though he did not directly oppose Charles, he suggested that his audience do this by scrutinizing their monarch, "by the example of all those Kings and Counsellors that have brought ruin on their States and Kingdoms . . . and shew what wicked men they were." The political implication was that listeners, and readers, should begin to resist the king. Palmer summed up the effect printing might have in drawing men to take sides, as they must: "Diverse [souls] that heard it preached, professed they were much affected with it, and told me, that it awakened and roused up some, that were grown cold, and indifferent, to zealous resolution. . . . therefore they conceived, that if the preaching, much more the printing might be of singular use in these cold, declining times." In the sermon, Palmer promoted activism; to be a "neuter" was evil. He characterized his audience as ripe for action, and his own words were intended to stir that audience. Palmer admitted that to publish was an appropriate format for his message of political and religious activism, because it could serve to "make it effectual for the encouraging of the faithful and the constant, the inciting and awakening of the drowsy and indifferent, the shaming of the Neuter, and the discovery of the hypocrite."[53]

In such appeals, sermon writers made a contribution to the construction of the political public sphere out of a tradition of public sermonizing, adapting new technology as the means to reach a wide audience. They began to fashion a potent audience through their self-creation as prophets.

By stressing their Reformation mission, and by identifying with Old Testament prophets, they created a unified set of tropes with which to arouse that audience. Francis Woodcock intended his sermon to spark the audience into action, that "this Alarum which took so well at the main Guard of this Kingdom (the Parliament I mean) may pass from you, to all who are concerned, and be a seasonable warning to them also." The preacher who adopted the role of prophet made use of print to ask the audience to react as a unified body of believers.[54] By their calls to the public, sermonizers made explicit the relationship of writing to action, construing their audience as an active body. John Gauden hoped that his words might have an effect on his audience: "This I am sure, your wisdom and piety are . . . by the publication of this Sermon, more straightly obliged in conscience, to justify before God and man, your desires and opinion of it; which is the Love of Truth and Peace."[55] It was not merely his writing that had power, however; the audience itself was conceived as powerful: "The splendor of so many clear minds, concentrated in Truth, cannot but kindle to a public love of it. And from the sacred light, and beats of so many wise and warm hearts, the life sweetness and abundance of our Peace cannot but grow and flourish." Publication was to lead to awareness and public action. Gauden's sermon was a call for results, a "kindling" of the cause of peace, which the sermon itself would help to "grow and flourish." The printed sermon was to be a stimulation for the public to respond.

JOHN LILBURNE AND THE CONSCIENTIOUS PUBLIC AS A JURY

Although print culture in the English Revolution reinforced the traditions of Protestant reform, there was a qualitative change in how readers came to be included in the political, and not only the spiritual, life of the nation. Ideas were disseminated in the forum of print that encouraged the public to think of themselves in new ways. We see this clearly in the instance of the trial of the radical John Lilburne, who fashioned an image of the public and made full use of the press to vindicate himself from charges of treason. By his appeals to his jury in his trial, Lilburne evoked, crafted, and sparked the public into becoming readers of law who could understand and take part in political process. Lilburne stressed liberty of conscience in his plea for political freedoms, and by adopting the model of a national jury for his audience, first in the courtroom, and then in the press, he contributed to a revolutionary theory of citizen activism, endowing his audiences with the positive powers of authority for judgment. He imagined the public as a body of capable readers, and he used the press as a means to promote this image.

John Lilburne knew how to attract controversy; one wonders what he would have done with a television camera. His trial for treason in late 1649 was a populist media event, a sensation with propaganda, slogans, and crowds. The royalist newsbook *Mercurius Pragmaticus* reported "that which silenceth all other (the news of this week) is the Trial of Mr. Lilburne."[56] The courtroom was bursting with noisy spectators; one reporter noted that his transcription was "as exactly penned and taken in short hand, as it was possible to be done in such a crowd and noise." The judges were repeatedly forced to silence the crowd in attempts to regain order, and the proceedings "pleased the People as well," according to one report, "as if they had acted before them one of Ben Jonson's plays." This analogy between the courtroom and the theater is apt, since the courtroom provided a kind of entertainment sorely lacking after the closing of the theaters in 1641.[57] Lilburne made full use of the power of the press to win his release from prison and gain an acquittal. For Lilburne, celebrity was a means to bypass the judicial system. Although Lilburne was a first-class demagogue, his pleas during his treason trials do give us a glimpse of what appeals to the public could be believed in his day: his public did indeed favorably respond to him.

By 24 October 1649, when he was charged with high treason under acts of Parliament of 14 May and 17 July for printing and distributing seditious pamphlets, Lilburne had already achieved the status of a folk hero on the model of Foxe's martyrs, seeming to spend as much time in prison as out of it for his political activities.[58] His had been already a long career in political dissent. In 1645, Lilburne had fought against the London monopolies in *Englands Birth-Right Justified*, and found himself in prison; in 1647, he had led the army's revolt against Cromwell for full payment and indemnity for soldiers (to prison again). He had supported negotiations with the king briefly in 1647 (to prison again, where he was linked to Royalists plotting in the Tower to release the king); he was one of the authors of the "Agreement of the People," the plea for constitutional reform and manhood suffrage in the name of *salus populi* in 1647, which was the document that gave birth to the Leveller party; in 1649, Lilburne pushed for toleration of religion in a revised "Agreement of the Free People," submitted to the Rump Parliament; and in 1649, he denied that Parliament had a right to put the king to trial, refusing to sit on the High Court of Justice, which parliamentary leaders had asked him to do. What brought him once again to prison in 1649 was his publication of *England's New Chains*, the protest of soldiers asserting their fundamental right to petition; this pamphlet brought on a controversy over the limits of toleration of political as well as religious dissent under the new Commonwealth regime. Parliament was proving to be as arbitrary as the king had been, Lilburne accused, and for this accusation he was charged with sedition; all copies of the pamphlet were ordered destroyed; and John Milton, newly appointed secretary for foreign tongues, was ordered to reply.[59] In 1649, when he he went to prison a full seven months before his trial, Lilburne was already on his way to becoming the "symbolic figure" writers today recognize, the "martyr, folk-hero and demagogue," as William Haller puts it, whose writings on behalf of the English common people's birthrights to freedom earned him the epithet "free-born John."[60] In prison, Lilburne composed *An Impeachment of High Treason against Oliver Cromwell and . . . Ireton* and probably *An Outcry of the Young Men and Apprentices of London,* which were smuggled out, most likely by his wife, Elizabeth. These were his most mutinous pamphlets to date, and for them, Lilburne was brought to trial for treason. In 1649, a royalist newspaper described Lilburne's hold over the people following his leadership of the dissent in the army: "[The commons] were mindful of John Lilburne . . . taking it for granted that these Disorders and Mutinies were all occasioned by his means."[61]

A spokesman for the radical Leveller movement, John Lilburne was "the Leveller incarnate," who had written and published over eighty pamphlets. Lilburne's mission was expressed chiefly by the printed word, through the stories that others wrote and had published about him.[62] Lilburne had long been accustomed to rattling the authorites by the medium of print; in his first trial appearance before the Star Chamber in 1638 he was to be charged with smuggling books from Holland, and after being found guilty, was whipped through the streets of London and pilloried in Protestant martyr tradition. During the proceedings of this earlier trial his mythologizing as a spokesman for "the people" had begun, and, significantly, it began in the press. His friend William Walwyn had appealed to the people of England that Lilburne should not only be an example to all, but actually should stand for all: "Since this worthy man's case is mine, and every man's, who though we be at liberty today, may be in *Newgate* tomorrow, if the *House of Lords* so please, doth it not equally alike concern all the people of *England* to lay it to heart?" Making use of the common image from Exodus, Walwyn figured Lilburne as Moses, leading his people Israel out of the house of bondage: "This noble and resolute Gentleman *Mr. Lilburne,* than whom his country has not a truer and more faithful servant, hath broke the Ice for us all, who being sensible that the people are in real bondage to the Lords . . . hath singly adventured himself a champion for his abused country men."[63] Lilburne's imprisonment in 1647 had sparked the flame of the Leveller party, during which time the informal alliance between Lilburne, Walwyn, and Overton was converted into a serious political movement.

In the Leveller pamphlets, we see Lilburne made into a hero and a spokesman for the common people, and there is a connection between this use of print and the rise of England's first political party. Richard Overton's *Remonstrance of Many Thousand Citizens* (1646) had compared the bondage of the people of England to Lilburne's own imprisonment, and the prisoner himself caused the people to "identify themselves with Lilburne," as Joan Webber has shown. Webber outlines the rhetorical means by which Lilburne encouraged the public to think of him as its symbol—his detailing matters of his private life, autobiographical touches that encouraged the people to see his self-consciousness as a gift to them: "this one person is to be both an ordinary man and a symbol of all men. The insistence that his peril and his rights are those of all runs through his tracts like a refrain."[64] Webber considers Lilburne a performer, acting his political role as a dramatic production for a popular theater. Lilburne's audience, moreover, were no gullible playgoers, taken in by this fascinating demagogue, but rather were intended to be involved actively; yet Webber's brilliant analysis leaves unanswered the means by which they were to be involved. No less than in his own dramatic self-presentation, I suggest, Lilburne created a role for his audience to play. I find that the trial of Lilburne for treason in 1649, along with the thick pamphlet commentary that accompanied it, shows Lilburne's audience exhorted to act as a revolutionary public. Thomas Corns faults the Levellers in general and Lilburne in particular for lacking ideological coherence, arguing rather that Lilburne could offer up only himself as something worth fighting for: "Lilburne tries to turn the English State towards democracy on the improbable fulcrum of his own self-image."[65] Yet that self-image, and the image of the public he conjured up as his partner, promoted a political vision in which we find the important components of a revolutionary public sphere.

As the Commonwealth regime stumbled to gain legitimacy in its first moments, Lilburne presented a great obstacle as spokesman for the Leveller party, a group loosely committed to entertaining rights for all "free-born Englishmen." As leader of a revolt in the army in 1649, Lilburne caught the Commonwealth leaders in a precarious batttle over the loyalties of English citizens, as his threat to their regime possibly bolstered the royalist cause. It is strange, given his earlier opposition to Charles and to monarchy in general, that Lilburne was seized on as a symbol by the Royalists, who saw his rise as the beginning of the end of this new order. Royalists noted with irony how their former enemy had turned friend, and they remarked on Lilburne's voluminous body of writing:

> That painful Quill, which wont to stuff
> Whole volumes with their Treasons,
> And scarcely left margent enough
> To Flank them with his reasons!
> A joyful day we'll set apart
> Whereon to Crown his Actions.[66]

Even for the Royalists, Lilburne's revolutionary activity is emblematized by his writing, though this passage figures Lilburne as writing by hand, using a quill. Lilburne is mocked here as a hasty scribbler, as betrayed by his style, which is irrational: the number of his accusations of treason overwhelmed the "reasons" behind them.

Of course the Royalists would celebrate any snag in the parliamentary plan. Another Royalist tweaked Parliament thus: "Lilburne, Overton, Prince, [leaders of the army revolt] that were but a while ago the very Foxes that these seditious Absaloms tied together with golden chains, to destroy monarchy, and sow sedition in Church and Kingdom, now when they have ended their great Work, to be tied up together in halters. Heaven is just, we see."[67] The royalist press welcomed such weakening into faction among its enemies, joking that Lilburne himself would save Charles II the time and effort of another military campaign: "truly it cannot be much amiss to the Commonwealth, if [Lilburne and Cromwell] were both destroyed, for they be at best but Foxes, and if they do noose and destroy one another, then it will save our young King a labor, destruction arising from themselves is better than from others, and more exemplifies the Judgments of God upon them."[68]

But Lilburne's trial in 1649 would not have consoled the Royalists in other respects. The proceedings of the trial show Lilburne reshaping criminal process, revolutionizing the practice of justice, and specifically appealing to the powers of the public. By his actions, Lilburne upset the standard rules of criminal proceedings: he defended himself with his own knowledge of the law (which was extraordinary for a nonlawyer), claiming "the laws of England, and the Privileges thereof, are my Inheritance and Birth-right," and he refused to swear the oath.[69] He stressed his "down-right Dick" ignorance of law proceedings, acting as an ordinary man like the rest of them: "I being now come before you to answer for my life, and being no professed Lawyer, may through my own ignorance of the practick part of the law, especially the Formalities, Niceties and Punctilios thereof, run myself with over-much hastiness, in snarls and dangers that I shall not easily get out of."[70] In a powerful and dramatic gesture, he called for the door of the courtroom to be opened so the public could look in, a request he deemed a "first fundamental liberty of an Englishman," that "all Courts of Justice always ought to be free and open for all sorts of peaceable people to see, behold and hear, and have access unto." By giving access to the public, Lilburne was inviting the whole people of England to partake of their birthright in listening to and beholding this trial, very much as he had done in his appeal to the censors to allow "even ground and equal terms" for writing against his opponents.[71] However, Lilburne's accusers also claimed to act in the interests of the people, as Chief Justice Jermyn explained: "these are your accusers; who have found you, upon their oaths, guilty of treason, and cry out to the judges for justice against you: and it is they, not we, that proceed against you."[72] For whatever reason, the doors to the courtroom were opened, and Lilburne continued the proceedings in full view. His own trial was becoming a place where citizens were to exercise their birthright by attendance. In turning the world of the courtroom upside down, Lilburne imitated Parliament, which only months earlier had just overturned the rules of judicial proceedings in its trial of the king.

In the course of his trial, Lilburne played his most thrilling card in his appeal to the jury, naming his jury, rather than his judges, as the only authority legitimate to judge him. He suggested that judges themselves had no right, being "no more but Norman intruders: and in deed and in truth, if the jury please, are no more but cyphers to pronounce their verdict." In evoking the myth of the Norman Yoke, Lilburne drew upon a familiar antiauthoritarian, nationalistic, reforming trope. Chief Judge Jermyn responded: "was there ever such a damnable blasphemous heresy as this, to call the judges of the law, cyphers?"[73] Jermyn uses religious terminology here to denounce Lilburne's defiance, suggesting an identity relation between Lilburne's attacks on the judges and an attack on God. It would be "blasphemous heresy" if judges or bishops were merely symbols without powers of positive representation; they would have no authority at all. They could not speak on their own; they could stand positively for any thing or for no thing; their function was to be spoken through—in Lilburne's eyes, to transmit the voices of the jury.

Henry Parker, an avid defender of parliamentary liberty and an antimonarchical theorist, saw the social implications of Lilburne's calling the judges "cyphers." In an attack directed at Lilburne in 1650, Parker wrote: "For you first pull down the Judges from their Tribunal, as mere ciphers, and as Clerks that have nothing to do, but to cry, Amen: and then in their Seats you promote your 12 men," an action that would lead to dreadful results, with authority transferred to those whom Parker deemed least able to exercise it. "The Judges because they understand the law, are to be degraded," Parker feared, "and made servants to the Jurors: but the Jurors, because they understand no Law, are to be mounted aloft, where they are to administer justice to the whole Kingdom." Parker continued his argument through the logic of reductio ad absurdum: "The Judges because they are commonly Gentlemen by birth, and have had honorable education, are to be exposed to scorn: but the Jurors, because they be commonly Mechanics, bred up illiterately to handy crafts, are to be placed at the helm." The result would be the world turned upside down: "And consequently Learning and gentle extraction, because they have been in esteem with all nations from the beginning of the world till now, must be debased; but ignorance, and sordid birth must ascend the chair, and be lifted up to the eminent offices and places of power. Cobblers must now practice Physic instead of Doctors; Tradesmen must get into Pulpits instead of Divines, and Plowmen must ride to the Sessions instead of Justices of the Peace." An inversion of the hierarchies of wealth, status, and education is at the heart of his accusations against Lilburne and his "Levelling philosophy." Henry Parker was terrified lest Lilburne "make the Head which was the Foot; and that the Foot, which was the Head," reviling the social status of Lilburne's supporters, "the greatest part of them consists of women, boys, Mechanics, and the most sordid sediment of Plebeians."[74]

Judge Keble claimed that Lilburne's supercession of the judge's authority by the jury meant that it was Lilburne alone who decided: "You would make yourself judge in your own cause, which you are not, and so make ciphers of us." Henry Parker agreed:

[It] should seem, the judges come upon the Bench to be judged of by Prisoners at the Bar, as well as Prisoners at the Bar come to be judged by the Bench. For if the party arraigned may freely question, and dispute the Authority before which he is arraigned, there must be some other Court to determine betwixt him, and his Judges, or else he and his Judges being both clothed with equality of jurisdiction, must depart on equal terms, without any judgment passed on either side. And if so, what issue, what effect can Justice have? . . . For if there were a freedom of judging due to Prisoners, as well as of Appealing, all impeachments, and criminal charges would be endless, and utterly incapable of determination.

The question here is, who should have authority to interpret the law? Without proper judges, Parker asserts, the law would be "incapable of determination," and Lilburne's move left interpretation of law open to multiple interpretations. The ignorant and unlearned simply were incapable of interpreting the law properly: "Twere absurd that his judgment should be made equal, or superior to the judgment of his Commisioners. . . . What an unlimited liberty do you take to your self?" Even Lilburne himself, according to Parker, has misinterpreted his jurisprudential master, Coke. "You strain your Authorities," Parker wrote to Lilburne, "to all cases and questions of law. . . . you strain your Authorities to all Jurors whatsoever, whether they have knowledge of the Law, or not," contrary to Coke's stipulation that jurors must have knowledge of the law if they are to decide cases. Parker called Lilburne's interpretation into question, citing Coke and Littleton, and he asserted that Lilburne had violated the original meanings: "these words themselves cry out against such a torture." Lilburne's threat, his "unlimited liberty," to the authorities was precisely that he gave the people new interpretations.[75]

Parker placed authority at the bench of judges for social as well as for philosophic reasons: the judges were those whose birth and training had best suited them to maintain and dispense justice. Lilburne's philosophy of jury-right, on the other hand, invoked the fear of popular riot and anarchy. Parker envisions the inevitable result of Lilburne's theory: "we know as well that scarce any thing in the world could be more mischievous to the State, than to leave differences, and suits in Law to judges utterly ignorant and unlearned"; since trouble for the state comes in the form of bloody rebels: "you are an Incendiary and Innovator; as far short of *Perkin Warbeck*, as you are beyond *Wat Tyler*."[76] Lilburne is a rabble-rouser.

In fact it was Lilburne's power over the people of England that the prosecutors found criminal. Using evidence from books alleged to be Lilburne's, the attorney read passages deemed traitorous, laying these passages alongside the recent Statutes for Treason (14 May and 17 July 1649), making the case to look very bad for Lilburne. The attorney buttressed his quotations with accusations; against "The Agreement of the People," he charged that the judges must judge whether it "strikes not at the very root

1. Frontispiece to Clement Walker, *The Triall of Lieutenant Collonel John Lilburne* (1649).

of all government." With this work, Lilburne had declared war on the present government, and had instigated others to do so as well; he had "blown the trumpet, for all that will come in: he hath set up his Centre; he would have it to be a Standard for all his friends to flock to him, and to make them the more quick in betaking them to their Arms." The book was seen as the call to arms for a rebellion against this government; in the trial another of his works was also compared to a trumpet: "This [*The Outcry of the Young Men and Apprentices*] I think is a Trumpet blown aloud for all the discontented people in the Nation to flock together, to root up and destroy this parliament, and so the present government."[77] Perceiving that writing could incite readers to rebellion, Lilburne's prosecutors recognized the power of public opinion.

In his defense, Lilburne reasserted the authority of the people over that of the judges by imagining his jury as a public endowed with the highest authority in the land. In seventeenth-century legal proceedings, the jury was assigned the duty of evaluating evidence, of deciding the guilt or innocence of the accused based on the facts of the case alone. The judges, on the other hand, were to evaluate the law and the legal implications of those facts.[78] The judge presiding at Lilburne's trial was careful to circumscribe the powers of the jury, insisting that, "the jury are judges of matter of fact altogether, and Judge Coke says so: But I tell you the opinion of the Court, they are not judges of matter of law." Lilburne rejected this opinion. In responding that "the jury by law are not only judges of fact, but of law also," he gave to the jurymen what had traditionally been the province of judges. He saw his own mission as a kind of education for his own jury in their rights. Reading aloud from a copy of Coke's *Commentaries upon Littleton*, Lilburne seemed the authority on precedent (though throughout his trial, he alluded to Coke's theory of jury-right without specific references).[79] Lilburne's claims of legal precedent for jury law-finding had great effect, the theatrical performance capped by his holding a copy of Coke's *Commentaries upon Littleton* in his hand during the entire course of the trial.

Among the several groups agitating for law reform in the seventeenth century, the Levellers pressed for the expansion of the jury's role to decide, in criminal cases, not only points of fact, but also of law. John Lilburne's 1649 trial for treason made the role of the jury a central concern, even though his reform was roundly rejected by the more moderate Parliamentarians, who concentrated instead on the regulation and standardization of the selection of judges, on decreasing the delay between arrest and trial, and on the centralization of judicial administration.[80] Lilburne's program for the expansion of jury powers was surely a tactical expedient—since he was almost guaranteed a guilty verdict from the judges, who themselves were his accusers—yet it was also a constitutional principle, based on a theory about jury rule complementing the general Leveller platform of erasing injustices due to rank and privilege. Others who defended Lilburne followed his attack on the judges. John Jones, apologist for Lilburne, railed against the abuses of office of these "rotten Commissary Judges . . . the only monopolizers of Law, to sell, delay and deny Justice to the Free Men of England their Slaves, at their will and pleasures."[81]

But it is his image of his jury that is most powerful in setting forward a philosophy of the public sphere. Lilburne fashioned his jury into his supreme judges, transforming an abstract argument concerning the people's "fundamental liberties" into an actual practice in which he reached out to his jury as embodying the people. He imagined them as "honest fellow citizens" who would be able to perceive his "just and rational motion and request." By his language—flattering, cajoling, and questioning—Lilburne endowed the members of his jury with those attributes which could help him. By claiming the jury was comprised of reasonable men, he was urging that they act reasonably to acquit him; by expressing their identity as his "peers" and "brothers," he was enjoining them to act in consort with him; by endowing them with the powers of rational judgment, he asked them to become judges.

Lilburne constructed a portrait of the kind of jury that would sympathize with his own plight, and one that would rally to his cause, if not to his theories about the role of juries in criminal trials. Lilburne repeatedly appealed to his jury's "consciences, integrity and honesty," which were to serve in a national mission that Lilburne made their own: "my countrymen, upon whose consciences, integrity and honesty, my life, and the lives and liberties of the honest men of this nation, now lies"; the jury was to be "conscientious and tender." Lilburne urged his jury to live out the rule of the Bible, to "put your care in my case, and do by me as you would be done unto by me, if you were in my case and condition." He appealed to the pride of London citizens, specifically to their powers of "conscience" and "judgment": "Truly, I hope there will be no righteous Jury in the world, that will give a Judgment against me for Treason therefore; no I hope for more righteous justice from a Jury of the citizens of *London*, whom I hope to find men of Consciences and Judgment, yea, of such righteous judgment, as that they will abhor to go about to take away my life."[82]

By appealing to their consciences, Lilburne carried on the Leveller torch of defending freedom of conscience. For the Levellers, and for many Protestants, conscience was considered to be a bedrock of human action, an irrefutable justification for dissent. Seventeenth-century writers developed their conceptions of conscience from John Calvin, seeing it as an "extrapolitical factor" that operated as a direct link between humans and God.[83] In Calvin, conscience was a human faculty of discernment that partook in elements of the divine: "when [men] have a sense of divine judgment, as a witness joined to them, which does not allow them to hide their sins from being accused before the Judge's tribunal, this sense is called 'conscience.' For it is a certain mean between God and man, because it does not allow man to suppress within himself what he knows."[84] The image here is the judge's tribunal, and that very like Lilburne's own courtroom. Lilburne made the courtroom become the court of conscience: "I speak here to you [Judge Keble] and to my fellow-citizens the jury, as in the sight and presence of God, that knows I lye not." After making his defense, Lilburne asks his jury to judge the case as if in God's court: "I leave it to the consciences of my Jury, believing them to be a generation of men that believe in God the Father, and believe shall have a portion in the resurrection of the dead, and stand before the tribunal of the Almighty, to give an account unto him, the Lord of Life and Glory, and the Judge of all the Earth, of all their actions done in the flesh: I leave it to their judgments and consciences, to judge righteously between me and my adversaries."[85] Lilburne calls upon his jury to put themselves in the court of God, the court of conscience, to hold their judgment on him to a religious standard. His language echoes that of Calvin, for whom conscience is not just a human faculty, but a joint action between God and humans, "when men have an awareness of divine judgment adjoined to them as a witness which does not let them hide their sins but arraigns them as guilty before the judgment seat."[86] Calvin called conscience the "guardian," the "keeper"; conscience is also "a thousand witnesses," and associated with the idea of natural, or inward law, "written, even engraved, upon the hearts of all." Most important, conscience is an inward guide, as Calvin puts it, "*Dictat lex illa interior,*" an inward law. "A good conscience," writes Calvin, "is nothing but inward integrity of the heart."[87] Lilburne's sense of his jurymens' consciences relies upon these Protestant notions.

According to Calvin, conscience was a component of Christian liberty, the freedom to decide matters deemed inessential to proper Christian teaching, and this could mean civil matters. In Luther, however, conscience was relegated to the spiritual, as opposed to the civil, sphere. In Luther's famous distinction between the two kingdoms, a strict boundary between secular and religious spheres is upheld.[88] But this distinction between civil and spiritual was not always so sharp in Calvinism. The problem, as Calvin had accurately forecast, was when civil laws seemed to threaten a Christian conscience. To resolve this difficulty, Calvin proposed a reading of Paul's command in Romans 13, that "every soul be subject unto the higher powers" because of "conscience," the biblical text that provided justification for obedience to the civil magistrate. Calvin, like Luther, read in Paul a firm distinction between human and divine laws: Paul "does not teach that the laws framed by [magistrates] apply to the inward governing of the soul," since "human laws . . . do not of themselves bind the conscience." Yet even though there is a separation between the two kingdoms in Calvin, nevertheless he admits that difficulties arise in the application of the principle of conscience because many "do not sharply enough distinguish the outer forum, as it is called, and the forum of conscience."[89]

During the civil war opponents of the king had used conscience as grounds for their political activism.[90] The English Puritans built on Calvin's sense of conscience as inherent to Christian liberty, giving conscience a practical component, first to decide "cases of conscience" in the form of traditional casuistry, and then to register political claims against their king within a constitutional framework.[91] William Ames formulated conscience in an active way in 1643: "it appeareth that conscience is not a *contemplative judgment,* whereby truth is discerned from falsehood: but a *practical* judgment," and that meant conscience could lead to a form of knowledge that "may be a rule to him to direct his will."[92] In their drive to construct a "holy commonwealth," the civil war reformers sought to create a political system based on rules acceptable to free consciences. According to many of the radicals of the English Revolution, conscience was a sovereign faculty, incapable of subordination to higher secular authority, and was to be accommodated in a holy commonwealth in terms of freedom of conscience.[93] The Levellers' "Agreement of the People" from 1647 preserved freedoms for conscience for all people, resolving "that matters of religion and the ways of God's worship are not at all entrusted to us by any human power, because therein we cannot remit or exceed a tittle of what our consciences dictate to the mind of God"[94]—their justification to oppose the human powers.

When applied politically, conscience could be a radical concept because of its unimpeachable source of authority. As an innate faculty of humans, it could without external constraint judge right and wrong. The Puritan notion of conscience, as the theologian William Ames pleaded, was based on the idea that only divine agency could give the gifts of faith or salvation: "The conscience is immediately subject to God, and his will, and therefore it cannot submit it self unto any creature without Idolatry."[95] Liberty of conscience from civil authorities was therefore necessary. If the abolition of episcopacy in 1646 served only to establish what Milton and others saw as a tyrannous—national—church system, then it was an encroachment upon the conscience. Defense of free conscience thus required both political and theological justifications.

Yet the question of liberty of individual conscience and of the civil enforcement of uniformity in religious matters came to a crisis in the days following the king's execution. One of Paliament's first acts to make conscience a serious political issue was the Engagement Oath, introduced in early October 1649, just about the time of Lilburne's trial. Soon after the king's execution and the establishment of the Commonwealth, Parliament passed an order in January 1650 requiring oaths of allegiance to its new regime, after considering such action since the previous March. After months of discussion, Parliament ruled that all men over the age of eighteen years of age were to subscribe to "be true and faithful to the Commonwealth of England as it is now established."[96] Many Royalists and Puritans rejected this oath, and it is the unlikely fact that both groups did so on the grounds of conscience. Both held that it compelled a public expression that could not accord with their inner beliefs. Because it was a public oath, Engagement was deemed to involve not just passive acquiescence, but active loyalty.[97]

The Engagement Oath raised the question of the legitimacy of "forcing" obedience to the new regime, and the controversy that ensued in the press shows that the theories of conscience were headed on a collision course. The question was whether the state could exert coercive powers over the individual to secure such an oath. On the one hand, the leaders of the new Commonwealth held they had the right to demand allegiance from their subjects, and this included loyalty in matters that were religious as well as political. On the other hand, opponents to the oath of allegiance charged that such a demand encroached upon the subjects' freedom to think and believe as they wished. Both sides urged their opposing political positions on the grounds of conscience. John Dury, for example, defended the taking of the Engagement Oath based on rules "agreeable to sense, to reason, and to conscience." Dury defined conscience so that it could enter the public realm of politics: conscience is "God's vicegerent over the society of

those to whom his administration doth extend itself." Likewise, the anonymous author of *A Disengaged Survey of the Engagement. In Relation to Public
Obligations* urged subscription based upon "immediate necessity," which
will "satisfy the conscience."[98]

The difficulties of defending conscience are obvious. Conscience becomes its own authorizing principle. The doctrine of conscience is as potentially subversive as it is nonrational: there is no way to ensure standards
of political action. Opponents of the Engagement also used arguments
from conscience to support their positions. Conscience was claimed as the
bedrock of justification of all human actions, especially for swearing oaths.
Robert Sanderson opposed the Engagement, arguing that neither the principle of self-interest nor the necessity of loyalty to the State were sufficient
grounds to take the oath. These are "two desperate Principles," which lead
ultimately to atheism, where "every man, by making his own Preservation
the Measure of all his Duties and Actions, maketh himself thereby an Idol."
Sanderson saw that justifications on the ground of conscience led to a kind
of dangerous individualism.[99] John Aucher refused to take the oath, which
he saw as "the justification, an abetting, or owning (at least in part) of all
those irregular and horrid acts, which have been committed for the bring-
ing about of this change"; he declined on the grounds of conscience, explaining that one does not swear to oaths lightly: "Yet religious and godly
men will make Conscience of what they engage in, declare for, promise,
subscribe (much more) swear unto, and dare not take Gods name in vain,
abuse his Ordinance, delude God or men by seeming to engage in, or swear
that in which they do not really engage." Aucher admitted that the oath
would not "tie the Conscience of the Taker," but that "it will trouble it,
though it do not bind it, it will burden it." His understanding of the oath
agrees with Calvin's reading of the Pauline injunction that "human laws . . .
do not of themselves bind the conscience," but Aucher maintains that such
a civil order could conflict with conscience in some way.[100]

The logic of conscience could lead to resistance against an unjust regime. Lilburne was asking his jury to reject Parliament's definition of treason, guided by the force of their own consciences, and to recognize that
Lilburne was innocent. His self-defense against the oppression of the tyranny of Parliament was that his own activities were not treason at all: "all the
wit of all the lawyers in England could never bring it within the compass of
High Treason, by the old and just laws of this nation, that abhord to oppress
men contrary to law; and then if they seem but to cry out of their oppressions, to make them traitors for words." Lilburne appealed to the "old and
just laws of this nation," just as so often he appealed to the "fundamental
liberties" of the English. His work had been for the betterment of the English people, "and then if I cry out of my oppressions in any kind, I must
have new treason-snares made to catch me." Lilburne takes the role of Jesus
in his resistance to Parliament's oppression: "You have done no more to
me, than the Scribes and Pharisees did to Jesus Christ; and in my dealing

with you, I have but walked in the steps of my Lord and Master Jesus Christ and his apostles." His is a conscientous act in a good Christian martyr tradition.[101]

Repeatedly appealing to the consciences of the members of his jury, Lilburne sought assistance from a force that in his view transcended civil structures: "Truly I hope the jury hath more conscience in them, than to go about to take away my life for giving away a single sheet and a half of paper, that no man swears I was the author of." Conscience, for Lilburne, became the key term on which the jury could hoist its authority. After presenting his account of the facts—denying that he was the author of the pamphlets; asserting that the sheets were given to him, that they were full of printers' errors and were therefore not his own words; that the state was not executing the law fairly and with due process; that some of the writing for which he was indicted, the "Agreement of the People," for example, was written before the treason statute was made into law—Lilburne ventured to suggest that the jury might not only evaluate the facts, but also revise the law on treason. Lilburne knew that the evidence mounted against him looked very bad for his case—most of the trial transcript is filled with passages read out of his own works, which oppose the government—and since the only way out of the death sentence to obtain an acquittal from the jury, his tactic was to ask these jurymen to look beyond the attorney general's evidence. Rather, they had to peer into their own hearts, into the court of conscience: "You the gentlemen of the jury, I appeal to your consciences, and to your judgments, and the Lord set it home to your understandings, that you may not be guilty of the blood of an innocent man."[102] In this trial, Lilburne expressed the belief that citizens must make choices guided by their own consciences and by reason alone, not by civil authority, or even by the law of treason that was interpreted by the state to apply to his pamphlets. Lilburne accomplished this aim by personal appeals to the consciences of his jurors. By attributing supreme power to the jury, Lilburne underscored the mounting powers of the public, and by rewriting their script, he presented a radical conception of what a jury was to be. He had imputed to the jurymen specific characteristics—conscience, reason—and he had given them specific powers—above all, independent judgment. By imbuing the jurymen with these attributes and by charging them with a patriotic mission, Lilburne fashioned their roles as conscientious actors.

Lilburne's approach achieved the remarkable result of an acquittal. A royalist newsbook gleefully reported, "when he was quitted by the Jury, his Judges bit their thumbs for anger, and John laughed them to scorn," presenting Lilburne as a man with Cavalier sensibility: "like a man of a genrous Spirit," the newspaper continued, "at his departure out of Guild-hall, [he] gave the Sergeants that waited 40s to drink; and at night great joy was expressed all the City by Ringing of Bells and Bonfires; while his new Judges were hissed through the streets." Apparantly his jurymen harkened to his call, and decided they could render judgment. At least one witness of the trial, persuaded by Lilburne's legal interpretations, believed Lilburne was a true "defender of the Ancient and known Laws of England." John Jones wrote that "Lilburne did confute [the judges] with good Law, and honest reason, (telling them, that they had prated like Fools, and knew no more LAW than so many Geese) whereupon the *Lubbers* of the *Keepers* of Englands liberties had not a single syllable to utter in defense of themselves or masters, but left it to the Jury." The verdict given out—not guilty—neither confirmed nor denied Lilburne's theories, but Jones was confident that this was indeed a conscientious jury, "a Jury of Mechanics, whose persons or Estates I know not, but that their carriage and Resolution in that manner declare them knowing and understanding men, confirmed in their Verdict, first by God himself . . . but in their hearts and consciences." The medallion struck to commemorate the actions of the jury named each juror, and thus visibly attested to the hope or belief that the jury's consciences had guided their action. The words of the medallion, inscribed around a portrait of Lilburne's head, read, "JOHN LILBURNE, SAVED BY THE POWER OF THE LORD AND THE INTEGRITY OF HIS JURY WHO ARE JUDGES OF LAW AS WELL AS FACT." The medallion, resembling a coin of the land, offers the justification for the radical judgment as one based on Lilburne's theories about jury rights. Jones also asserted that the jury was to be a pattern for other juries, "a precedent for Jurors, and a memorable example for undantable [*sic*], immovable, conscientious Judges of life and death, for the present, and all future ages to imitate." They had become, in short, just the kind of jury Lilburne wanted them to be: judging by the internal authority of their own consciences.[103]

When the jury rendered the verdict of not guilty, the foreman explained to the shocked Judges, "*we have only found him guilty of writing some part of those books he is charged with in the Indictment, but not of High Treason.*" These words, reported the author of *Mercurius Britannicus*, "so astonied the Judges, that they looked as if they would have eaten the Jury, some of them shaking their heads, others threatening them with bug-bear Language"; the jury, however, stood firm in its decision: "but for all this they minded *Lilburnes Reasons* more than the Judges *threats* and stood to their former *verdict.*"[104] The jurors decided that Lilburne's crime was merely that of writing books, not committing acts of treason, and they were in fact interpreting the law by judging what was or was not treasonable writing. Not only did the jurors overturn the judges' authority to determine treason, they were also able to silence the judges in this account. Medusa-like, the jury "astonied" the judges, rendering them impotent. The newspaper colorfully went on to describe the judges as nearly cannibal—"they looked as if they would have eaten the Jury"—but this threat devolves into verbal abuse. The judges are degraded into savage beasts, in contrast to the jurors who stand fast, preferring reason, "Lilburne's reasons," to coercion and threats, as if they were innocent Protestants submitting to Catholic tortures in Foxe's *Book of Martyrs*. The jury delivered up a verdict opposing the judges, a verdict that set a man free. Lilburne had created a conscientious audience, which in turn acted conscientiously on behalf of its creator.

Not surprisingly, Lilburne came to trial again, in 1653 for returning to England after two years of lifelong banishment imposed by parliamentary statute in 1651. This time, he sought to shape more than his particular jury's judgment; he shot for a much larger audience, and found it by way of the press. Acting as a master of media manipulation, Lilburne took his appeal to the streets by printing pamphlet defenses even before the proceedings began. As in 1649, his treason trial was widely publicized—Lilburne was still a popular figure—and a flurry of tracts preceded the hearing. Even before his trial, Lilburne had published a work in which he designated the role his jury was to play. The pretrial pamphlet, *A Jury-man's Judgment upon the Case of Lieut. Col. John Lilburne*, which anonymously appeared within a week of his arrest, attempted to influence public opinion, and in it, Lilburne's jury was now to comprise a national audience, an audience of readers. He was once again asking the jury to evaluate the laws of the land, but this time, the jury was the jury of public opinion. The case, as he saw it, could be won in the press. Lilburne invested his readers with tremendous powers as he rewrote the script of the criminal trial for this national public: "Dear friends," he wrote, "the greatest weight of Trials of men lieth upon the Consciences of the jury-men of England; they are the real Guardians of the peoples lives, limbs, liberties and estates; and they ought not to find any man guilty on any Statute in any case, which appears to have no good ground upon the standing Laws of England."[105] By again appealing to the power of the consciences of his jurymen, and to the consciences of all English citizens as the "real Guardians of the peoples lives, limbs, liberties and estates," Lilburne sought backing from a source of authority apart from the institutions of the law court, implying that the consciences of English citizens were a better guardian of their fundamental rights (lives, liberties, estates) than the laws themselves.

Lilburne expressed the idea of public opinion as the collective consciences of English citizens in designating his own readership as a national jury in the opening pages of *A Jury-man's Judgment*. He exhorted his readers: "Come, my dear Friends and loving Country-men, we the good men of England are continually called forth by law to judge and determine of men in all causes." His current case merely extended the logic, so that Lilburne's jury was not just the twelve men assembled in his courtroom, but all English citizens, deemed capable of judging the fairness of English law. Lilburne relied upon the extrapolitical factor of conscience in this appeal: "Let us all pray earnestly to God," he asks, "that he will be pleased to give us all eyes to see, and hearts to consider, how much the safety and happiness of us all depends upon our sticking close to the old and good laws of the land, and to lay to heart how much it concerns the good men of England, the jury-men especially, who are to determine all causes, to be able to judge, and to distinguish between true and counterfeit laws."[106] Lilburne's jury was now all England, and they were to be guided by God in determining which English laws were true.

Once again the jury of his trial found Lilburne not guilty. Once again the courtroom was packed with his supporters, who, wrote one observer, were prepared physically to fight for Lilburne's life if required to do so by a negative verdict: "There were six or seven hundred men at his Trial with swords, pistols, bills, daggers, and other instruments, that in case they had not cleared him, they would have employed in his defence." When the acquittal was given, "the joy and acclamation was so great after he was cleared, that the shout was heard an English mile." But the words of Gilbert Gayne, grocer, who sat on Lilburne's jury in 1653, reported that the jury heard what Lilburne had to say: "The Jury did as they did," he recounted to an examiner after the trial, "because they took themselves to be Judges of the Law, as well as of the Fact: and that although the Court did declare they were judges of the fact only, yet the Jury were otherwise persuaded from what they heard."[107] With the trial of John Lilburne, the metaphor of trial and judgment by readers had become a political reality, and conscience was the ground on which citizens were to render judgment.

MILTON AND A FIT PUBLIC IN *AREOPAGITICA*

Areopagitica, as we are frequently reminded, had little effect in its own day toward the express purpose for which Milton wrote the pamphlet, the overturning of Parliament's 1643 ordinance requiring prepublication licensing (the ordinance stood). The tract nonetheless marks a significant moment in the conceptualization of the public sphere. In *Areopagitica*, Milton posited a national audience for political and religious reform in general. Milton contributed to a wholly new sense of the public sphere as one in which political discussions should be carried on before a broad reading public, and he based his argument on an assessment of the public that mirrors Lilburne's. Milton gives his arguments grounding in his conception of virtue, which melds the religious notion of conscience with a classical sense of civic duty. He made a powerful political statement by asking Parliament to consider censorship an insult to English citizens, on the grounds that English citizens possessed consciences and reasoning faculties that made them capable to withstand the evil that might be found in printed matter. Citizens were to be free to read any books because they were capable of making judgments for themselves. In *Areopagitica*, Milton envisions a role for printing by melding the classical ideals of oratory with the reforming Protestant mission, and in imagining his ideal citizen as a capable, conscientious reader, Milton gives a full expression to the revolutionary sense of the public sphere.

Flattering his parliamentary audience by comparing them to the Athenian high court of justice, the Areopagus, Milton charged them to carry on the ancient traditions of democracy, reason, and jurisprudence. Milton's comparison of the houses of Parliament to this Greek court is an act of creative fantasy; Milton hoped that Parliament would act in accordance with classical virtues in making its decision.[108] In his plea for the extension of press freedoms in *Areopagitica*, Milton used his classical antecedent as a means to urge Parliament toward further democracy; yet he also took from the classics his posture as a public spokesman for freedom. By this role, Milton gains a potent source of energy for his theories about the authority of the public. Milton's *Areopagitica* is a classical oration, in which Milton seeks "to advise," a stance his classical examples of virtuous citizens adopted. Since classical times there had been a tradition and language for such writing for action: rhetoric. Defined as *dicere ad persuadendum accommodare*, "speech designed to persuade," by Cicero, in *De Oratore*, rhetoric was the means by which men could exercise their God-given reason, as Milton saw it in *The Reason of Church Government* (1642): "persuasion certainly is a more winning and more manlike way to keep men in obedience than fear." Yet the ideal *rhetor* in Renaissance humanistic terms was a great statesman, an adviser to princes; at the very least, he was tied to the court. During the revolution, there was a transformation of the Renaissance humanist practice: rhetoric was turned to the common street. The public, rather than the prince, could give and receive advice.

Milton and the writers of the English Revolution turned rhetoric away from this courtly setting and toward the true Ciceronian mode of rhetoric, where orators served the state by first serving the public. Milton signaled his link to this classical mission by his title-page epigram from Euripides:

> This is true Liberty when free born men
> Having to advise the public may speak free,
> Which he who can, and will, deserves high praise,
> Who neither can nor will, may hold his peace;
> What can be juster in a State than this?

> (*CPW* 2.485)

Milton suggests he is one of those "free born men" who must "speak freely," the exemplary private citizen who acts for the public good, and he takes an advisory stance throughout the course of the speech, imitating Isocrates and Dion Prusaeus.[109] Like Isocrates, Milton represents himself as a citizen giving "public advice" at a time when his country needs him, and he comes forward "from his private house"; like Dion Prusaeus, he acts as "a private Orator." Milton staged his argument as if he were pleading before the Athenian court, the Areopagus, a public place where ordinary mens' voices would be welcome.

Milton constructs his own persona as representative for a national body, making himself into an exemplar of the ideas he wishes Parliament to adopt. The "common grievance" (*CPW* 2.539) is to be his plea, and like Lilburne, Milton makes his own into the nation's common plight, claiming to argue in the defense of the liberties of all the English, thereby establishing his own authority as a speaker: "That this therefore is not the disburdening of a particular fancy, but the common grievance of all those who had prepared their minds and studies above the vulgar pitch to advance truth in others, and from others to entertain it, thus much may satisfie" (539). Though not an admission of populism, this statement reveals that Milton saw himself as spokesman for those with a "common grievance," for those whose first goal is the betterment of humanity, or at least the betterment of the English people. In his other pamphlets of this period, Milton echoes this public, classical role, especially in the context of printed matter. In *Tetrachordon*, Milton explains that his writing in print is a right: "I shall therefore take license," argues Milton, who knows his pamphlet appears without official state approval and thus must appear by Milton's *own* authority, "by the right of nature and that liberty wherein I was born, to defend myself publicly against a printed Calumny, and do willingly appeal to those Judges to whom I am accused" (*CPW* 2.580). His "license by natural right" permits him to speak outside the constraints of the formal licensing of censorship. There is a distinction between the "license" by which he responds to his enemies, and the "liberty" with which he does so. His desire to speak freely takes its authority from his status as a "free-born" Englishman—much the same as John Lilburne's professed authority. For both, the self-proclaimed "natural right" to write and to speak in public are signs of that liberty.

By merging radical Protestantism with classical precedent, the printing press, and the pulpit, Milton appealed to an idea of a public sphere that matched the political needs of the English Revolution. Speaking freely is a precondition of *Areopagitica*, but Milton's tract is not merely a free speech; it is also a question directed at parliamentary readers to make a decision about the kind of ctitizens they imagine the English to be. The choice Milton offered his audience was whether they thought ordinary English citizens were capable of participating in politics or not. Milton posited that difference most clearly in the following words: "consider what Nation it is whereof ye are, and whereof ye are the governours: a nation not slow and dull, but of a quick, ingenious, and piercing spirit" (551). The contrast between these two conceptions is repeatedly stressed throughout the pamphlet, as Milton suggests that Parliament's decision on the matter would expose its attitude toward English citizens. If English citizens were thought to be "slow and dull," then "the whiff of every new pamphlet should stagger them out of their catechism" (537). Milton jokes here, knowing that his beloved fellow Englishmen were nothing of that sort. As a "quick, ingenious" nation, rather, the English public is "musing, searching, revolving new notions and ideas wherewith to present. . . . Others [are] as fast reading, trying all things, assenting to the force of reason and convincement" (554). These two conceptions about audience capabilities—slow and dull or quick and ingenious—can be seen to operate as competing theories of readers in the public sphere, and in presenting these two contrasting images, Milton exposes the assumptions behind censorship he wished to challenge. In Milton's line of thinking, English citizens were qualified as readers, worthy to exercise their reasoning abilities amid a barrage of conflicting opinions.

Milton sets out his image of the capable public by repeatedly distinguishing it from some other audience, creating a series of caricatures that elevates the English at the expense of their enemies. Of his setting of the Areopagus, for example, he comments, "I find ye esteem it to imitate the old and elegant humility of Greece, [more] than the barbaric pride or a Hunnish and Norwegian stateliness" (489). The model for his citizenry is civilized Greece, not uncivilized "barbaric" countries. Repeatedly throughout the tract, he defines his audience by negative comparision: "And out of those ages, to whose polite wisdom and letters we owe that we are not yet Goths and Jutlanders" (489). Milton twice salutes the fortune of place and time in the world's geography and history that have created him a modern Englishman. Adopting this kind of negative comparison again and again during the course of the essay, Milton builds it into the argument as a logic of dichotomy. After presenting a genealogy of censorship, for example, he reminds the Lords and Commons that they are not like the Radamanthite bishops who founded ecclesiastical censorship; they are "not the mercenary crew of false pretenders to learning." Rather, Parliament is "the free and ingenuous sort of such as evidently were born to study, and love learning for it self, not for lucre, or any other end, but the service of God and of truth" (531). While demonizing censors as "Radamanthite bishops," Milton trumpets the positive attributes of the English by contrast, remarking that he had "been counted happy to be born in such a place of *Philosophic* freedom, as [his European hosts] supposed England was" (537).

Not only contrasting the free English to their Inquisitorially subservient neighbors in a fit of patriotism, Milton analyzes the offers a philosophic grounding to the practice of censorship in its conception of the people. In states restrained by censorship, not only is "the privilege of the people nullified" (541), but the people themselves are considered worthless, the "Laity are most hated and despised" (537). Under censorship, "It is to the common people less than a reproach; for if we be so jealous over them, as that we dare not trust them with an English pamphlet, what do we but censure them for a giddy, vicious, and ungrounded people; in such a sick and weak estate of faith and discretion, as to be able to take nothing down but through the pipe of a licenser" (536–37). By adopting a policy of censorship, the state assumes that the people are not to be trusted; opposing this assumption, Milton urges Parliament to conceive of the English people as fit to manage themselves.

We might gloss this unattractive portrait of the people under censorship in a passage from Milton's *Paradise Lost*, where Eve pleads with Adam to allow her to work in Eden apart from him, but Adam is concerned about the greater opportunity for temptation if they work solo. Eve, headstrong, insists, and her argument uses the same logic of choice as that found in *Areopagitica*:

> And what is Faith, Love, Virtue unassay'd
> Alone, without exterior help sustain'd?
> Let us not then suspect our happy State
> Left so imperfect by the Maker wise,
> As not secure to single or combin'd.
> Frail our happiness, if this be so,
> And *Eden* were no *Eden* thus expos'd.
>
> (*Paradise Lost* 9.322–41)

Milton's negative portrait of a people whose ignorance and lack of faith and discretion ought not to be trusted sounds suspiciously like Eve's fatal speech to Adam before parting in the garden in *Paradise Lost*, the prelude to her temptation by Satan. Eve refuses to believe that humanity is not to be trusted, resisting the "narrow circuit" found in Adam's confinement. Trusting that God did not create her to live in fear, Eve argues that she possesses defenses, "Faith, Love, Virtue," with which to resist sin. Eve argues that virtue in the perfect state of Eden would be meaningless if temptation were not possible: "What is . . . Virtue unassay'd?" The implication is that it is not virtue at all. Likewise, in *Areopagitica*, Milton's theory of human virtue involves knowing both good and evil; without the latter component, humans are stripped of their human essence: "When God gave [Adam] reason, he gave him freedom to choose, for reason is but choosing; he had been else a mere artificial *Adam*, such an *Adam* as he is in the motions" (*CPW* 2.527). Since choices are constitutive of free will, as Milton explains ("God therefore left him free"), reason—and choice—are as necessary to humans as life itself. In states that suppress this fundamental liberty of choice, the humanity is stripped from their people. The audience under censorship is "an unprincipled, unedified, and laick rabble, as that the whiff of every new pamphlet should stagger them out of their catechism, and Christian walking" (537). In *Areopagitica*, Milton suggests that the virtue imputed to the people in a censoring society is only a straw virtue, that humans become children or puppets ("Adam in the motions"), and the rabble. That is an audience that cannot think, not an English audience. Milton rejects the idea of a passive public as he parodies it. "They are not thought fit to be turned loose to three sheets of paper without a licenser" (536).

Milton rejects the idea of an incapable public as he parodies it, asking the readers to conclude that this cannot be an English audience. Milton plainly sets out the rival portraits of the English people for Parliament to choose between; either they are "an untaught and irreligious gadding rout" (547) or an audience exercising its free will, able to discern the good from the evil, endowed by God with "the gift of reason to be his own chooser" (514). The unexercised virtue is the one protected by the dictates of the Inquisiton, whereas the exercised virtue is left to decide good and evil for itself, to become its own judge. Milton repudiates the idea of the passive audience (thus attacking the Laudian church [537 n.177]), and he expounds instead his notion of a "fit" audience, in a state where freedom is guaranteed. This audience is the polar opposite of that in the evil states where censorship and tyranny rule over the hapless populace. Milton elaborates this opposite by reference to the liberty that gives character to both government and governed: "It is the liberty, Lords and Commons, which your own valorous and happy counsels have purchased us, liberty which is the nurse of all great wits; this is that which hath rarified and enlightened our spirits like the influence of heaven; this is that which hath enfranchised, enlarged and lifted up our apprehensions degrees above themselves" (559). Liberty, a goal common to Milton and to Parliament, demands an active public, unlike that "sicken[ed] into a muddy pool of conformity and tradition" (543), where truth is fettered. Liberty is known by its opposite, slavishness: "Ye cannot make us now less capable, less knowing, less eagerly pursuing of the truth, unless ye first make yourselves, that made us so, less the lovers, less the founders of our true liberty. We can grow ignorant again, brutish, formal, and slavish as ye found us; but you then must first become that which ye cannot be, oppressive, arbitrary, and tyrannous, as they were from whom ye have freed us" (559). His beloved English could not choose to regress into such a condition, Milton is sure. As Eve will argue in *Paradise Lost*:

> If this be our condition, thus to dwell,
> In narrow circuit straitn'd by a Foe,
> Subtle or violent, we not endu'd
> Single with like defense, wherever met,
> How are we happy, still in fear of harm?
>
> (9.322–26)

Concience is central to Milton's argument. Under censorship, citizens are prevented from exercising their their liberty of conscience; thus Milton sees censorship as a quintessentially papist practice: "the Popes of Rome engrossing what they pleased of Political rule into their own hands, extended their dominion over men's eyes, as they had before over their judgments, burning and prohibiting to be read, what they fancied not" (501–2). Milton applies the language of monopoly and the bugbear of popery to pit the free English against the enslaved Catholics; "engrossers," men who hoarded crops to drive prices up, were also hated figures familiar to seventeenth-century readers. In Milton's account, "any subject that was not to their palate, they either condemned in a prohibition, or had it straight into the new Purgatory of an Index" (503). The suppression of books is equated to the Catholic suppression of liberty of conscience: "a Book in wors condition than a peccant soul, should be able to stand before a Jury ere it be borne to the World, and undergo yet in darknesse the judgement of *Radamanth* and his Collegues, ere it can passe the ferry backward into light"

(505–6). Milton caricatures censors as hellish, in condemning this papist practice that he represents at its birth, as anti-Reformation. The practice was "never heard before, till that mysterious iniquity provokt and troubl'd at the first entrance of Reformation, sought out new limbo's and new hells wherein they might include our Books also within the number of their damned" (506). In comparing censors to Radamanth and his company, the mythical judges of Hades, Milton graphically elides censorship with Counter-Reformation Catholicism.

The history of popery adds horror to Milton's point that the ethical basis of censorship is an affront to any living Christian. By associating censorship with Catholicism, Milton seems to adopt a propagandistic strategy. The frequent evocation of the Inquistion works to elicit a conventional response on the part of the readers, and this tactic, like other forms of propaganda, exploits the "certain words, signs, or symbols, even certain persons or facts, provoking unfailing reactions."[110] Milton strategically uses the myth of the tyrannous papist to clinch his argument with emotional force. Members of his audience are either to be the tyrannous papists who uphold the practice of censorship or they are to act in accordance with their status and power as free-born Englishmen, that is, to repeal the Licensing Act. By his use of two contrasting portraits of the English people, Milton seeks to win Parliament to his cause by persistently forcing them to distinguish their motives and practices from those of the Inquisition. Parliament's choice will no doubt to recognize the virtue of its free-born English citizens.[111] But the stereotypes of Catholicism he uses to make his point are not mere ornaments. There is a philosophic premise Milton is exploring, liberty of conscience. Quite simply, under censorship, there is no space for the individual soul to judge good and evil, no liberty of conscience. The idea of a judge for books was repellent for the same reason that popery was: it reduced learning to brute compulsion and denied the free exercise of choice that is the touchstone of Milton's ethics. In looking at Catholic cases, Milton viewed censorship as a coersive action, rather than a "right" one.

In Milton's line of thinking, if the state instituted a judge for books, the human spirit would be reduced to slavery through these coersive acts; readers would respond only out of fear. "I hate a pupil teacher, I endure not an instructor that comes to me under the wardship of an overseeing fist" (533), Milton fumes. The problem with censorship is that the censor lacks true authority: "who should warrant me his judgment?" (534) Milton asks, fearing that the ultimate authority merely is that of force. There are practical considerations as well as philosophical ones that bother Milton. Practically speaking, a censor might wrongly prevent publication: "He who is made judge to sit upon the birth, or death of books whether they may be wafted into this world, or not, had need to be a man above the common measure, both studious, learned, and judicious"; he is likely to be, rather, "ignorant, imperious, and remiss, or basely pecuniary" (530). If statesmen are to be the makers of judges, then "they may be mistaken in the choice of a licenser, as easily as this licenser may be mistaken in an author" (534).

Milton worries about "the cursory eyes of a temporizing and extemporizing licenser" (531) wrongly exercising "the hide-bound humor which he calls his judgment" (533). He offers historical examples of judges in his "pedigree" of the practice of book licensing (which, as in a law case, amount to precedent) to produce evidence that censors have not judged well. With history supplying examples of only bad judges, this problem of finding a "fit" judge seems insurmountable—perhaps this worry explains why Milton took the job himself six years later.

The choice Milton sets before Parliament is which kind of people they imagine they govern—"Lords and Commons of England, consider what Nation it is whereof ye are, and whereof ye are governors"—and he offers two competing versions of the national identity: "a Nation not slow and dull, but of quick, ingenious, and piercing spirit, acute to invent, subtle and sinewy to discourse, not beneath the reach of any point that human capacity can soar to" (551). In *Areopagitica*, Milton not only charges Parliament to act like the judges of the Areopagus, he forces them to do so by asking them to subscribe to his vision of a good reader. Put simply, a good reader is a judge. A good reader, like a good judge, can make decisions only after surveying all the evidence, true to the dictates of conscience. In *Areopagitica*, his theory of reading is based on the premise that "reason is but choosing" (526). This premise is explained by the conception of virtue, which is actively constituted by seeing, and by rejecting, vice. By his interest in fashioning such a reader, Milton offers *Areopagitica* as a significant expression of a revolutionary theory of citizenship as conscientious readership; his conception would be echoed in many pamphlets by other authors. Milton designates and constructs an audience that was supposed to be active and *activist*.[112] Milton based his program on the notion that readers possessed a fundamental capacity to be judges, endowing them with importance and dignity. In *Areopagitica*, Milton attempted to shape English readers into a body of individuals actively judging what they read, apart from established authority. Milton asked, "what advantage is it to be a man over it is to be a boy at school, if we have only scapt the ferular [rod], to come under the fescu [pointer] of an imprimatur?" (531). In this question, Milton sums up the ground upon which he bases his notion of the capable reader, the revolutionary reader, aiming to turn such schoolboys into men. In describing fit readers as those who have been trained by "trial" of books, Milton does not specify much else about them except that they are worthy of the name of being English citizens. There is only silence about whether women or the poor could qualify as such readers, and there is little explanation about how one might grow up from being a schoolboy, stuck under the ferular, to a man in this scheme. Milton prefers to leave precise details about his reader as a chooser on the plane of the ideal; in this way, he can encompass as large a readership as might exist.

Milton's fit reader is one who has been trained by "trial" of books—books that try him, and he that tries books. We note that it is the book which is effecting the trial here—"that which purifies us is triall" (515), with human virtue a "blank" without the medium of books to provide the trial. Again, this is the idea behind Eve's statement concerning free will; without free will, "Eden were no Eden"; Milton's Adam would be merely an "artificial Adam." The arena for the judgment of books ought not to be the state; rather, it is the individual conscience: this guarantees the exercise of free will, the judging conscience. Milton prefers that the battle between good and evil be tried in the conscience of each individual: "That which purifies us is trial, and trial by what is contrary" (515, 528).

In *Areopagitica*, books are themselves on trial, and Milton asks his readers whether books ought to be tried by official licensers or by readers themselves. Spenser's knight who obtained knowledge through "the survey of vice" (516) succeeded in "trial by what is contrary" by withstanding the attractions of the Bower of Bliss, thus learning through experience. Books, like visions, can enact trials upon their readers: of bad books, "they to a discreet and judicious Reader serve in many respects to discover, to confute, to forewarn, and to illustrate" (512–13). Dionysius Alexandrinus's vision sanctioned reading of all manner of books, because "to the pure all things are pure." The image Milton uses to reinforce this point likens books to meat: "Wholesome meats to a vitiated stomach differ little or nothing from unwholesome; and best books to a naughty mind are not unappliable to occasions of evil. Bad meats will scarce breed good nourishment in the healthiest concoction" (512). According to this concept, a vision, or a book, can "try" a soul, and a good soul will not suffer by contact with a bad book. Finally, choice is necessary to the human condition of free will. Milton employs two slogans used often by the Revolutionary party—"Prove all things, hold fast that which is good" and "to the pure all things are pure" (512); both New Testament texts emphasize the personal basis of authority for judgment.[113] Not the state, but individuals, through their ability to reason, are to make judgments about the value of books. Under censorship, Milton argues in *Areopagitica*, the state usurps the right of the individual to choose.

In the tract itself, readers are persistently involved in acts of self-judgment as they are forced to decide between the two alternative images of the public Milton presents. Yet Milton greatly infringes on the power of his audience to come to just *any* decision. Parliament must assume the role Milton assigns to it, and the people of England must follow their destiny. Thomas Corns has brilliantly analyzed the rhetorical tactics of pamphlets written by John Lilburne and John Milton in 1641, asking whether readers are offered the rhetorical position to make up their own minds regarding the authors' political positions, or whether the author has constrained the possible positions to limit the reader's freedom. Corns argues that Lilburne's pamphlet *The Christian Mans Triall* offers more freedom to readers because in it, Lilburne permits other voices to speak; Milton's *Of Reformation*, on the other hand, is an "unfree text," in that it "excludes from its potential readership all who are not already broadly in agreement with its puritanical assumptions."[114] In my reading, Milton's *Areopagitica* may be seen as just such an "unfree" text, but it is an unfree text that forces freedom. Milton's strategy of offering two alternatives for his audience to choose between builds the logic of choice into his very rhetoric.

•

By insisting on freedom of conscience as his basis of defending freedoms in the press, Milton was echoing and embellishing ideas about the public that were current during the English Revolution. William Walwyn had written, "The people are a knowing and Judicious People; Affliction hath made them wise."[115] Walwyn perhaps best summed up this idea of a capable public: "I carry with me in all places a Touch-stone that tryeth all things, and labours to hold nothing but what upon plain ground appeareth good and useful."[116] Walwyn echoes the reforming Protestant attitude toward the Scripture, that reading the Bible would be sufficient for a soul to understand all. This was foremost an antipapist position, disqualifying the mediation of authorized readers and priests. Yet it had profound implications for political theory as well, as the radicals of the English Revolution proved. Gerrard Winstanley, the founder of the Digger movement, proclaimed the belief that God was in every man, and his plan to reclaim the land of England for the common people was based on a notion of individual abilities and rights that transcended rank and hierarchy. The Ranters took the philosophical position that "to the pure, all things are pure" to justify adultery, as Laurence Clarkson did; the same logic was used by Milton in his *Areopagitica*.[117] Abinezer Coppe, the fervent millenarian Ranter, spoke "by my own Almightiness (in me)," mimicking biblical language throughout his writings to install himself as a capable interpreter of Scripture.[118]

When writers like Milton and the radicals thought of their readers as capable to judge matters for themselves, they made use of these religious directives. Revolutionary writers drew upon the reforming religious tradition in their use of the press, using the Reformation ideal of the individual as the activist saint, as well as the nation as a type of Israel. But they also inherited from Protestant thought the emphasis on the inner worth of the individual, the power of a conscience or inner reason that had little need for an external authority, especially in the church. Those who espoused antihierarchical ideas sought a "more thorough, godly Reformation," and they rejected the institutional orders of the king's church, as they had rejected the Catholicism over a century earlier. They also threw out outward forms of religious practice: the catechism, the altar, and especially the prayer book. The Ranter Laurence Clarkson, in his critique of the church, explained that "I judged to pray was another man's form, was vain babbling, and not acceptable to God."[119] To Clarkson, inner meaning was more important than outward show.

Milton made his debt to this radical reforming tradition clear in *Areopagitica* when he repeatedly referred to prepublication censorship as a Catholic practice, as one that had no place in a Protestant world. Christopher Hill has argued that the radical thinkers contributed significantly to the ideologies of the English Revolution.[120] Though it has been questioned whether the theories of the radicals had any effect on the great constitutional changes of the moment, or effected any institutional reform, nevertheless their premises did gain widespread currency. The words of the radicals also speak from a position made possible only by the freer press conditions of the revolution. The radical scriptural model that promoted individual judgment became an explosive idea with the increasing volume of writing. William Walwyn, favoring liberty of conscience, explains the power of ordinary citizens as deriving from God: "He that bade us try all things, and hold fast that which is good, did suppose that men have faculties and abilities wherewithall to try all things, or else the counsel had been given in vain." Based on a radical assumption about the capability of human judgment, Walwyn urged his countrymen: "If the people would but take boldness to themselves and not distrust their own understandings, they would soon find that use and experience is the only difference, and that all necessary knowledge is easy to be had, and by themselves acquirable."[121]

The radicals were arguing that the citizens of England had certain abilities and rights: for the Leveller John Lilburne, it was a "birthright" of freedom, and for Milton, it was "Reason sufficient to judge aright." When Milton argued in favor of increased freedom of expression, he was voicing a revolutionary conception of the public sphere, and of capable readers within that arena. He transformed the conditions of reading and writing by giving readers a new role to play, and by supplying a vocabulary with which to refer to these readers, a vocabulary drawn from the languages of political theory, of law, and of religion. In *Areopagitica*, Milton did not merely search for an audience, he defined one. While he fought for liberty of expression—a liberty restricted to Protestants, however—Milton also advocated a concept of readers who could foment their own spiritual improvement.[122] When coupled with the power of print, that image of a capable audience or readership was one major conceptual accomplishment of the English Revolution.

In his appeal to the power of the jury to overrule higher authority, Lilburne expressed a conception of a public that echoed that of other writers during the civil war period—a public thought to be active and independent, not one that merely handed back the required verdict to the authorities. The pamphleteers of the English Revolution, including John Milton, addressed and sought to influence this imagined public. In his arguments for a free press, Milton turned authority from external officials and state monitors to the consciences of judging readers, whom he deemed responsible enough to decide matters themselves. Yet instead of recommending that all judges be eliminated, as Lilburne would do, Milton asked that they stay away from making judgments about reading matter. Milton urged that the state "have a vigilant eye how Books demean themselves, as well as men"

(*CPW* 2:492), setting up the analogy between books and defendants. Often compared to prisoners in this speech, books take on human form in lively figures: "debtors and delinquents may walk abroad without a keeper, but unoffensive books must not stir forth without a visible jailer in their title" (536). Books and criminals suffer in the same way under the same process of justice: a book goes on trial where a censor—or a reader—is to be a judge. Milton directed that his readers, rather than rely upon the judgment of censors, themselves be judges of books because his own readers were capable of making judgments for themselves. The ultimate act of judgment for Milton was to take place in the moment of the individual's confrontation with the book; for Lilburne, it was in the moment of the individual's confrontation with the law. For both, the authority for judgment was to be individual reason and conscience. Rather than placing his trust in government-appointed censors, then, Milton returns the power over judgment on books to the public, because they were capable judges. Equipped with a faculty of human reason that is deemed sufficient to "choose aright" (511), Milton's readers must make a choice about the Licensing order, and by so doing, judge for themselves whether they are fit to judge. "Reason is but choosing," he recites; it is within human power to exercise reason by choosing rightly.[123] In 1644, Milton seemed confident that in those scenes of judgment where good and evil battled over human souls, good would triumph. Capable readers were fit to withstand the evil that books might contain.

When writers imagined their readers to possess reasoning capablities, and when they demanded that scenes of judgment take place in public, they based these arguments on the fundamental faith in their readers' powers of conscience, and they sketched a portrait of a revolutionary reader. In Milton's line of thinking in *Areopagitica*, ideal readers of books would be competent to act on their choices, and Parliament would reward their competence by lifting prepublication censorship. John Lilburne appealed to the public to act, and he appealed to his readers as capable of acting in the public sphere. Milton, however, did not go so far as Lilburne in his overruling the authorities and appealing to the public. Lilburne reached over the heads of his judges to address the public, whom he construed as his true judges. Milton, too, reached out to a public, yet he did not render the Court of Parliament powerless. Rather, he hoped to change the minds of the MPs, and thus to work within the established structures of reform. But his methods for doing so were similar to Lilburne's, despite his patent subservience to Parliament. He, too, constructed a revolutionary role for his readers to play. Both Lilburne and Milton considered humans as capable beings, and demanded that they be treated as such: as independent, active, judging— and with authority. Their writing in public was designed to spur readers to take significant action based on their own judgment and with the authority of their own consciences. As the chief justice in the king's trial in 1649 had urged, "Let all England and the World judge."[124] This defiant imperative invested the public with tremendous powers, under whose careful scrutiny even a king's execution might be justified.

So far, we have been examining a model of the revolutionary public imagined by the civil war pamphleteers from the vantage point of the reformers alone. They were not the only ones making use of the organ of the press in order to take their positions to the public, however. Those loyal to the king, though they often cursed the press, also published in droves. In the next chapter, I explore the meanings of a free press to the Royalists. But it is in the reforming writing where the conception of the "revolutionary" public is to be found. If it is true that the radicals do not represent the main part of the political spectrum, it is also true that radicals were sharing philosophic ground with those closer to the center, with those like John Milton, who relied upon conscience as the basis for political duty, and who crafted new roles for the public to fill.

Royalist Reactions

JOHN CLEVELAND, BABEL, AND THE DIVINE RIGHT OF LANGUAGE

And yet is this doctrine still practised; and men judge the

Goodness, or Wickedness of their own, and other men's

actions, and the actions of the Common-wealth itself by their

own Passions; and no man calleth Good or Evil, but that

which is so in his own eyes, without any regard at all to

the Public Laws. . . . And this private measure of Good,

is a Doctrine, not only Vain, but also

Pernicious to the Public State.

Hobbes, *Leviathan*

IF JOHN LILBURNE appealed over the heads of his formal judges to a public, one he endowed with the authority to judge on grounds of conscience, his vision of a capable public was not always well received. Even those who supported the regicide and defended parliamentary liberty foresaw danger-ous consequences to this assumption. Lilburne replaced the authority of judges with the judgments of ordinary citizens, believing that the judges were "no more but cyphers to pronounce their verdict."[1] This was consid-ered "damnable blasphemous heresy" by Judge Jermyn, who understood that by questioning the judges' authority for judgment, Lilburne hit at the very heart of the English legal system: if the judges were ciphers, then they were without value. Jermyn's calling Lilburne's belief "blasphemy" reflects the parliamentary concern with public utterance of unorthodox ideas. Ever since 1648, a committee in Parliament had been considering a blasphemy bill, and measures as strong as the death penalty were urged for those pro-voking religious division.[2] Blasphemy was one term employed by Parlia-ment to denote religious errors; in 1648, one such error was to deny that the Bible was the word of God. In the case of Lilburne, the authorities were thinking over how much dissent they could tolerate.

It is hardly surprising that in the political discussions of the civil war years a strain of pamphleteering emerged in opposition to the notion that the people were an audience fit to participate in public debate at all. In this chapter, I witness antipopular writers coming to terms with public conflict over ideas. During the English Revolution, conservative writers aimed their pens at a new phenomenon, brought on by the lapse of state-sponsored censorship of the press in 1641: the participation of many different voices in political debate. The conservatives feared social disorder would be the result when print reached a previously unlettered public and unorthodox opinions were disseminated to a wide readership. We see an important response to this opening up of the public sphere in this conservative writing. In their attempts to repress those voices now making themselves public, and to unify audiences against them, the conservatives made the revolutionary press, and language itself, the focuses of worries about the condition of political diversity. The conservatives favored an image of Babel for the press, and used it strategically as part of their effort to master, and then to silence, the oppositional and radical voices that they conceived as illegitimate users of language. Parliament, too, was concerned about the public expression of dissent, and they lumped together as "blasphemous" an assortment of dangerous political and religious opinions.[3] Though the 1650 Blasphemy Act softened the punishments for blasphemy and has been considered a gain for religious toleration, especially since so few were convicted under it, still Parliament was nervous about the linguistic habits of English citizens. Significantly, heretical or dissenting religious and political opinions were punishable because they were experienced as verbal acts.

Put simply, to many, the English Revolution *was* Babel. In part, I am talking about Babel as civil war writers did, where ideological disagreements were represented as a war merely about words: "Hard words, jealousies and fears, / Set folks together by the ears," wrote Samuel Butler as he looked back on the civil war years in *Hudibras*. For the writers and fighters of the English Revolution, the conditions of partisan conflict resembled the diversity of tongues at Babel, with the explosion of material in the press and the appearance of numerous religious and political sects, each which appeared to have its own language.

The conservative preoccupation with linguistic anarchy was also mirrored by current linguistic theory, as in the case of the so-called universal language projectors, who sought to resolve linguistic ambiguity by appeals to a common language. John Wilkins's *Essay Towards a Real Character, and a Philosophical Language*, published in 1668 and dedicated to the Royal Society, of which Wilkins was a founding member, aimed to improve international trade, geographical exploration, and, most importantly, to clarify scientific endeavor by replacing the Latin tongue with a "Real universal Character that should not signify words, but things and notions, and consequently might be legible by any Nation in their own Tongue." A new language was needed to express the truths of a new science, and Wilkins hoped that "such a thing as is here proposed, could be well established, [and] it would be the surest remedy that could be against the Curse of the Confusion, by rendering all other Languages and Characters useless."[4] Wilkins, advocate of the new science, preacher of natural theology, sometime master of Wadham College, Oxford, widower to Cromwell's sister, and now bishop of Chester, contributed to a stream of books comprising what historians of science now call the universal language movement. The prevailing motif of the movement was the hope of resolving Babel's linguistic consequences, remedying that "Curse of Confusion," as Wilkins put it. Language projectors repeatedly referred to the biblical story as a prologue to their enterprises—"Babel revers'd," as one urged.[5]

Why did language became the figure for the disputes in the press? I see that concerns about language at this time indicated a great historical shift, the rise of the public sphere. As we saw in the last chapter, that public sphere was imagined by writers as an audience for print, an amalgam made up by Protestant preachers who wished to enlighten a nation to spiritual reform, expressed in the pleas of the radical politician John Lilburne, who overturned conventional forms of justice by appealing to a public, and imagined by John Milton as the forum in which conscientious citizens could seek truth. The public sphere was becoming a place where differences of opinion could be voiced. Contests over political and social authority were represented by figures for clashes in language because political and social differences were becoming apparant by new uses of public expression. I explore the relation between the worry about the variety of languages in the press and the fact of political difference in the first part of this chapter by drawing upon pamphlet texts from the English revolutionary period that were critical of the press itself.

The metaphor of Babel was used in royalist civil war pamphlets to register horror at the fact of political disagreement, and yet the metaphor also reflected that such disagreements were not only expressible *in* language, "hard words," but that they were fundamentally *about* language, about who was speaking language and to what uses language was being put. At a time when alternate languages permeated public discourse, Babel was a figure used by those who were coming to see that language was no transparent medium, that definitions had serious political and social consequences. This is especially visible in the satiric prose of John Cleveland, who is the sample case for study. Cleveland argued that the press was not only a herald of unacceptable political positions, but a constitutor of them. He expressed his fears through linguistic metaphors that suggested an analogy between anarchy in language and anarchy in politics. Cleveland was not the only one who believed that once linguistic errors were corrected, authority would return to the hands of those who rightly deserved to rule, and political and linguistic authority would be one again. Radical sectarians, like the Ranters, also hoped for a singular linguistic and political system—but the Ranters located the authority for that structure with God; Cleveland and his fellow Royalists, with their king. Theories that expressed political difference as linguistic difference during the English revolution could go only so far without divine aid, however; Cleveland's nostalgia for a single voice of truth and, perhaps, Wilkins's project of a universal language both failed to make the epistemological or theological moves necessary for language and politics to become jointly authorized. Thomas Hobbes goes the full distance in his *Leviathan*, where the sovereign, as lexarch, resolves the epistemological and political difficulties of the multiplicity of languages.

The situation of the press in the mid-seventeenth century was highly anomalous: it was largely in the hands of those who resisted monarchical authority, of those who constituted the opposition. The term *opposition* must be taken loosely here, in light of the very great disagreement among historians of the period about exactly what, if any, concrete opposition there may be said to have existed in Parliament.[6] The state as manifested by kingly prerogative was not imposing discipline on its subjects by means of this organ; rather, the press was the medium through which revolutionary ideas were spread. Christopher Hill has shown that the radical literature of the English Revolution can help to tell the story of popular resistance as a history from below, but it is important to remember that during this strange moment in English history, "resistance" literature was the dominant mode. In *Areopagitica*, John Milton was convinced that din was a sign of general reformation: "the people, or the greater part, more then at other times [are] wholly tak'n up with the study of the highest and most important matters to be reform'd, . . . disputing, reasoning, reading, inventing, discoursing, ev'n to a rarity, and admiration, things not before discourst or writt'n of" (*CPW* 2.557).[7] The relative freedom of the press in the early 1640s produced a charged situation in the history of political discourse: scores of disputes began to take place in public, and those disputes often attacked the king or his court.

It did not help their legitimacy that the pamphleteers used traditions of popular genres and relied on literary forms that appealed to a popular audience.[8] Already by the end of the sixteenth century, the pamphlets that flooded the market in London as a "literary novelty" addressed specifically new readers, and these included such groups as women and the poor.[9] Such pamphlets became staples of the printing industry. For example, Thomas Nashe's *Christs Teares over Jerusalem* (1593) was a work of social criticism that sparked many imitations in the seventeenth century.[10] Likewise, Robert Greene's pamphlets, which first appeared in the 1590s, were republished throughout the civil war period. The pamphlets of the late-sixteenth century were diverse in style, but there were prominent genres—the jestbook or the almanac, for instance—which were imitated endlessly. Perhaps most famous, and most powerful in attracting imitations, was the public quarrel between Gabriel Harvey and Thomas Nashe, which presented a series of gossipy attacks between the writers, seven years of a literary feud which was finally ended forcibly by archbishop of Canterbury Whitgift and bishop of London Bancroft in 1599 with a prohibition against satirical works. Scurrility was one of the many modes established by the Elizabethan writers.[11] As reading such pamphlets was already a common practice in seventeenth-century England, a broad audience could potentially be reached for writing which imitated the style of these genres.

Civil war writers used the genres of Elizabethan popular literature, yet they added a charge of overt political content. The astrology book, for example, was a form used by many writers to "foretell" the victory or demise of the king.[12] Though most Christians at this time subscribed to providential schemes of history, astral determinism was still a common language through which to discuss political matters.[13] The royalist John Taylor, in his *Crop-Eare Curried*, predicted that "the King shall prevail in the End"; his fellow royalist Sir George Wharton had nothing but happy predictions: "It is most apparent to every impartial and ingenious Judgment that . . . the several Positions of the Heavens duly considered amongst themselves . . . do generally render His Majesty and his whole Army unexpectedly victorious and successful in all his designs."[14] The parliamentary "Champion of Astrology" William Lilly countered with his own contrary reading, calling Wharton's a "utopian judgment": "his Majesty shall not keep that town [Evesham] very long." Other astrological analyses offered the king a worse fate. John Booker's almanacs were selling about fifteen thousand copies a year in the mid-1660s—a staggering figure.[15]

Other popular forms of writing abounded. Ballads were ubiquitous; they reported events, sang of the wars, and provided political commentary in accessible form. They too took on a political valence. For instance, a 1647 ballad shows Britain, "awake from some six year's dream," and tells the story of the "rebellion." The ballad laments, "Religion once so purely taught, / And Protestant, now's set at naught. . . . How many Feares, and Jealousies, / And Plots . . . Have filled out Pulpits and our Brains," as it calls for a victory for Charles.[16] Another ballad makes its point through allegory, in a game of cards. The title, "Win at First, Lose at Last," explains the meaning of the allegory: "A New Game of Cards; wherein the King recovered his Crown and Traitors lost their heads." Its author sings against "The knave o'th'Clubs [that] hath won the King."[17] Another proroyalist drinking song, called "The Courtier's Health," urged, "Come Boys, fill us a Bumper," and remarked, "I hate those Dissenters."[18] Ballads made an excellent form of propaganda, since they could reach illiterate and literate audiences and could be remembered long after their disposal. Civil war authors also plundered earlier authors for support. Shakespeare and Jonson were made to serve the two causes; as Ernest Sirluck delightedly reports, these two were quoted twice as often by parliamentary writers as by Royalists.[19] One ballad applied the story of King Lear as an allegory for the life of Charles, and concluded with the moral "The crown was left useless, being without a King. / So sad disobedience is the worst of all sin."[20] Edmund Spenser was revived in a pamphlet called *The Fairie Leveller; or, King Charles his Leveller described in Queen Elizabeth's Days* (1648), a vicious anti-Leveller pamphlet that alluded to the communist giant from the fifth book of the *Faerie Queene*.

The writers of the English Revolution knew it was controversial to present political opinions to a popular audience, and some expressed their disapproval by lamenting that literary taste had declined. The newsbook in particular was singled out for abuse, often made the butt of jokes. In the early years of the civil war, newsbooks proliferated at an astonishing rate in the absence of printing regulation, not because Parliament wanted a free press, but because nobody could effectively control them.[21] The results were news productions that represented all shades of the political spectrum, from the king-sponsored *Mercurius Aulicus* to daily reports of Parliament's affairs: *The Dove, The Parliament Scout, The Kingdom's Weekly Intelligencer*. Among many others, *Mercurius Britanicus* and *Mercurius Civicus*, the latter possibly penned by Prynne, were parliamentary papers.[22]

One chief way royalist writers registered their animosity toward the politics of the authors of these popular forms was to attack them for their literary transgressions. These new genres, put simply, were not literature. Newsbooks, for example, were rejected on aesthetic grounds, rather than for the political allegiance of the author. In the pamphlet play *The Great Assizes Holden in Parnassus by Apollo and his Assessours* (1645), the author attacked the diurnals from a literary point of view, putting twelve of them on trial, where Lord Verulam (Francis Bacon) presides as "Chancellor" of Parnassus, Sir Philip Sidney as "High Constable of Parnassus," and "John Picus, Earl of Mirandula" (Pico della Mirandola) as "High Chamberlaine."[23] The court consists of jurists "Erasmus Rotterdam," Justius Lipsius, "John Bodine," Hugo Grotius, Isaac Causabon, among others, "Approved Critics all," and the nine-man jury is composed of Elizabethan and Jacobean literary lights George Wither, Thomas Carew, William Davenant, Michael Drayton, Francis Beaumont, John Fletcher, Thomas Haywood, Philip Massinger, and even William Shakespeare. Ben Jonson is "Keeper of the Trophonian Den," that is, Apollo's prison keeper, who enters "like the old Host of a *New Inn*"; John Taylor is the "Cryer of the Court," a role suited to his continual public announcements in the press, who "hath a better voice, than wit," and Edmund Spenser is Clerk.

The ruler of the poets, Apollo, is also a figure for King Charles, as is made clear by the rhetoric of the character of Joseph Scaliger, appointed "Censor of Manners" in Parnassus. Scaliger approaches his Sovereign, "who rules by Love, and Law, not by the Sword" urging him to "apply Your Sovereign power, and authority, / To vindicate your subjects, and to curb / These Varlets, that your government disturb." Scaliger complains of "some abuses ill," particularly in the press: "which some pernicious heads have so abus'd:"

> This instrument of Art, is now possessed
> By some, who have in Art no interest;
> For it is now employ'd by Paper-wasters,
> By mercenary souls, and Poetasters,
> who weekly utter slanders, libels, lies,
> Under the name of specious novelties.

The literary crimes however, have grave political implications; as Scaliger puts it, "Your Grace will know (I need not to relate) / How Typographie doth concern your state."

The indictments against the diurnals were varied; some were accused of literary offenses. For instance, the *Post* "in felonious sort did steal / From *Euphues*, and *Arcadia*, language gay / Therein his vain relations to array." Another newsbook was accused of having "emptied / The Fountains of the Muses, to fulfil / That appetite which rose from Livers ill," releasing spleen. Most of the indictments, however, were political and not literary in character. *Mercurius Britanicus* was charged with "matters of scandal, and contempt extreme, / Done 'gainst the Dignity, and Diadem / Of great Apollo" in his weekly inky infusion of Mercury, "thereby to murder, and destroy the fame / Of many, with strange obloquy, and shame . . . His ends, and aims, which were his foe to kill." Likewise *Aulicus* was charged with "slanders false" and "forged fictions," which only fueled controversy: "he had his [ink] of burning oil confected, / of Naphtha, Gunpowder, Pitch, and Salt-peter," the chief constituents of gunpowder, increasingly familiar to civil war writers. Those blasting ingredients were said to give force to Aulicus's writing, which "those combustions raised, and made greater." The other newspapers were similarly charged: *Mercurius Civicus* "did enchant / The fancies of the weak, and ignorant, / And caused them to bestow more time, and coin,/ On such fond Pamphlets, than on books divine"; the writer of *Occurrences* is said "to have injured Fame, / And to have disguised falsehood by the name / Of Truth," and also to have "tortured, with his letters large / Ingenuous ears." The chief crime of the newsbooks was their publicizing dangerous ideas, their rousing readers to insurrection by their words. The newsbook is indicted for its role in political effort.

Writers on both sides also worried about the audiences that the pamphlets were reaching. The royalist hack John Birkenhead, author of *Mercurius Aulicus,* was accused of attracting women readers, who would then entice their husbands "by fair pretences and sugared words."[24] The "lying libels" of *Aulicus*, wrote the anonymous assailant, "have tended to naught else, but to animate and encourage their Husbands, and friends to persist in this unnatural war." Not only were pamphlets spreading lies and inciting readers to war, this writer accused Birkenhead, they were being read and written by previously unlettered audiences, specifically by women. Women were not welcomed onto the political scene, either by Parliamentarians or by Royalists, as shown by the example of the anonymous author of *A Brief Representation and Discovery of the notorious falshood and dissimulation contained in a Book styled, The Gospel Way* (1649). The author attacked the Anabaptist Anne Hall, a female prophet, whom he accused of seducing gullible men, like "The Serpent [who] at first beguiled Eve, wounding the man with his own rib; since (finding that way prevalent) he hath used the same Method in all ages of the Church. . . . The same part doth the Devil act in these times, and in this thing, instigating these imposters, to make use of this

female deceiver, for the propagating of their Errors." The author here remarks on the power of this woman over her audience, and in likening her
to the stereotype of the fallen Eve, hopes to discredit her. Hall is not merely
Eve, however; she is a "seducing imposter," potent and persuasive. Strong
measures are needed to resist her words, as he puts it, in order "to reduce
the wandering sheep that decline their careful and painful Shepheards."[25]
Though the anonymous author here dismisses Hall as a type of evil woman,
in the rest of the pamphlet the author takes this woman's words seriously,
offering a close reading of Hall's writing to refute her words with reasons.

It is true that during the English Civil War period, women were coming
to participate in public activity as never before, as military heroes withstanding seiges, but also as political activists, petitioners to Parliament, leaders of
the sects, and prophets.[26] Patricia Crawford's statistical analysis of women's
published writings during the civil war period concludes that this was a
remarkable period for women's publishing. From fewer than ten books in
every five-year period before 1640, to sixty-nine in 1646–50, a level that was
maintained until 1660, the volume of women's writing indeed rose dramat-
ically during the revolutionary period.[27] Women were participating in the
religious sects, and their move to center stage both as prophets and as political petitioners to Parliament brought much contemporary comment.[28]
Women's were among some of the voices that Royalists heard with horror.
The royalist newsheet *Mercurius Pragmaticus* reported on the demonstration
of Leveller women who protested against Parliament over Lilburne and
Overton's imprisonment in 1649, calling these four or five hundred women
petitioners a "Meek-hearted Congregation of *Oyster-wives*," slander that labeled these women prostitutes; the women were also called "*Troops* of *Ama-
zons*," warrior-women who transgressed against the proper female roles.[29]

LINGUISTIC DEVIANTS AND THEIR ENEMIES

A freer press allowed a wider variety of political opinions, and this variety
was something unprecedented in English history. John Lilburne, who coupled the idea of a free press with a free public, argued that those who would
restrict the press sought to "suppress every thing which hath any true Declaration of the just Rights and Liberties of the free-born people of this Nation, and to brand and traduce all such Writers and Writings with the odious terms of Sedition, Conspiracy and Treason."[30] By his terms, "brand"
and "traduce," Lilburne suggested that his enemies' very language was un-
reliable: either those who defended the rights and liberties of the people
were true defenders of the people's freedom or they were traitors.
Lilburne's sense that there were indeed competing languages for describing the same activities is an example of a mode of civil war pamphleteering
that redefined political relations through new uses of language. In his writing, Lilburne attempted to present the people in heroic terms, and to make

the press the battlefield on which that heroism was achieved. But he was aware there was another way of putting things.

To some civil war writers, the fact of public disagreement seemed evil in the first place. For example, *Mercurius Pacificus* (1648) offered his "lectures of Concord" to eliminate the strife between those who were living in what sounds like Hobbes's state of nature: "Divided as far as Hounds and Hares in antipathizing disaffection: Heads divided in opinions, like those of the Serpent Amphisbena, one fighting with another, hearts divided, like fire and water, tongues divided, as still in Babel's confusion, hands divided." The metaphor of Babel was used to represent discord as global, but at the same time most private: "Cities divided . . . Families divided . . . Bloods divided . . . yea houses divided, father against son, brother against sister, mother against daughter; yea beds divided, like oil and water, which cannot mix; husbands and wives snarling in couples."[31] The list of divisions proceeds from the most metaphorical (hounds and hares) to the most intimate (husbands and wives in bed) to illustrate how completely society was riven by discord. This discord was an irreconcilable, oil and water, which cannot mix.

The author conceived of the conflict as a problem in communication, "tongues divided as in Babel's confusion" because the differences derived from verbal acts: "sinister constructions and mis-interpretations, one not rightly understanding another, (as the Orator once complained) that being heard with a left ear, which was spoke with a right tongue, and that which was clear in the fountain's head, being muddied and troubled through the foul pipes and channels of mis-relating mouths, or misconstraining minds." In this seventeenth-century version of our children's party game "telephone," all the trouble seemed to come from garbled messages. The author of *Mercurius Pacificus* thought it possible to achieve peace between the opposing sides, if only the parties could speak clearly to one another. In this account of strife is the view that language can function as a transparent vehicle for thoughts—if we remove the blockages in the "foul pipes and channels" of language, the prefix "mis," for example, we might have true "interpretations," "relations" and "constructions." The author's recommendations were rather like those of Oliver Cromwell at the Putney debates in 1647: "Certainly God is not the author of contradictions. The contradictions are not so much in the end as in the way. I cannot see but that we all speak to the same end, and the mistakes are only in the way."[32]

The idea that "the mistakes are only in the way" expresses a form of linguistic universalism that current linguistic theorists were bandying about. The contemporary scientist John Wilkins hoped to promote the belief that beneath the diversity of tongues were actually common thoughts that could be expressed in a common language. If this were true, Wilkins proposed, then differences in ideologies might not be true differences, but rather tricks of language, "cheats of words." In the years 1640–70, many works were published that sought to resolve such diversity of earthly languages into a common tongue. Wilkins himself had framed this plan as early as 1641 in terms of the biblical story of Babel: "the confusion at *Babel* might this way have been remedied, if every one could have expressed his own meaning by the same kind of Character."[33] The language projectors of the so-called universal language movement often recalled the biblical story as a pretext for their ventures—"Babel revers'd," as one put it.[34] Along with pursuing topics of creating effective shorthand, constructing mathematical models for organizing language, introducing scientific vocabularies, as well as seeking new methods for teaching languages, correcting orthography, fixing pronunciation, bridging the gaps between words and things, and creating a universal grammar, books such as Comenius's *Light to Grammar and All other Arts and Sciences* (1641), Cave Beck's *Universal Character* (1657), John Wallis's *Grammatica Linguae Anglicanae* (1653), George Dalgarno's *Ars Signorum* (1661), and Francis Lodwick's *Common Writing* (1646), among many others, also considered subjects such as secret communication, the correlation between sound and sense, codes, Egyptian and Chinese hieroglyphics, sign languages for the deaf, and the search for the Adamic language that had been lost at Babel.[35]

The chief aims of this movement were scientific and commercial, but universal language and true grammar would also help to resolve international disagreements about religion. As Wilkins put it: "it would likewise very much conduce to the spreading of the knowledge of Religion" and promote the "diffusion of it, through all nations." Wilkins continues, stressing the religious aspects of his plan for linguistic reform:

> This design will likewise contribute much to the clearing of some of our Modern differences in Religion, by unmasking many wild errors, that shelter themselves under the disguise of affected phrases; which being philosophically unfolded, and rendered according to the genuine and natural importance of Words, will appear to be inconsistencies and contradictions. And several of those pretended, mysterious, profound notions, expressed in great swelling words, whereby some men set up for reputation, being this way examined, will appear to be, either nonsense, or very flat and jejune.
>
> And though it should be of no other use but this, yet were it in these days well worth a man's pains and study, considering the Common mischief that is done, and the many impostures and cheats that are put upon men, under the disguise of affected insignificant Phrases.

Wilkins explains that his search for a universal language was prompted by the fact of religious dispute in his day.[36] The language in need of remedy was not safe for true discussion of such matters; rather than conveying clearly the truths of religion, in its present state, language committed "mischiefs," "impostures and cheats," and "disguises" against sense. Aside from being inaccurate, language could be dangerously deceptive.

Wilkins's project, in short, is a manifestation of contemporary concern about language, about who was using political language, how they were using it, for what purposes, and to whom they were speaking it. As we recall Wilkins's hope in the *Essay*: "by unmasking many wild errors, that shelter themselves under the disguise of affected phrases; which being philosophically unfolded, and rendered according to the genuine and natural importance of Words, will appear to be inconsistencies and contradictions" through a universal language.

The English Revolution offered many instances of linguistic confusion, since the radicals often used language to subvert political authority.[37] Ranting style, it has been argued, was a form of political protest. The so-called Ranters, rejecting sin and repression, rejected the distinctions between the sinful and holy, good and evil, heaven and hell. Historians have questioned whether the Ranters formed a coherent political or religious party, but this question is somewhat peripheral to the analysis here, since what is of interest to me is their astonishing use of language as a means to oppose religious authority and conventional morality, and not their precise political location.[38] Ranters articulated their rejections in antinomian uses of language: they delighted in seeing all kinds of contradiction. Laurence Clarkson, for one, believed there was no sin, "but as man esteemed it sin," expressing a theory of language that severed language from a natural or necessary relation to reality; if language was a human construction, then so was morality. Clarkson went on with his logic, "thus making the Scripture a writing of wax," meaning the Bible could be shaped according to any interpreter's intention.[39] Jacob Bauthumley, a more philosophical Ranter, echoed Clarkson's thinking on sin, opining, "For Sin, I cannot tell how to call it any thing, because it is nothing; I cannot give it a name." According to Bauthumley, to make moral distinctions was not possible in human language; only God had that power: "And therefore, as I dare call no man good because there is none good but God: so I dare call no man wicked or ungodly, because it is God only that makes the difference, and who am I to judge another mans Servant?" Good and evil were not acts but words: "neither the evill act or the good act are evill or good, as they are acts; and men can no more do evill then they can do good, as they call it." By this logic, Bauthumley defended swearing and other verbal profane acts: "if this be so, men may drink, swear, and be profane, and live as they list."[40] While these words appear to justify libertinism, Bauthumley pursues rather a purgative, zealous reforming Christianity. Current Protestant practice he deemed utterly corrupt, and that corruption needed to be exposed and eliminated. This purging could be accomplished by repealing even the authority of language to name what is good.

Laurence Clarkson applied this radical antinomianism in his defense before the authorities, using language in a slippery way throughout his interrogation for blasphemy in 1650. At times he contradicted himself outright to his prosecutors, playfully dodging their questions by creatively employing a Ranter style. His literary style differed from the more philosophical Ranters Coppin and Bauthumley, but in his jesting, witty, and colorful language Clarkson refused to play by the linguistic rules of his society. By lying, Clarkson posed another kind of challenge to the authorities; in his very use of language, he was doing the political work of subversion. Because, as he claimed, "I saw all that men spake or acted, was a lye," his own uses of language were to defy that corruption. When accused of fornication and adultery, he replied, "I never lay with any but my own wife." His accusers parried, "No, for you call every woman your wife?" To which Clarkson answered, "I say I lye with none but my wife, according to Law, though in the unity of the spirit, I lye with all the creation." Clarkson redefined "wife," so that "all the creation" could be meant by the word. He performed such redefinitions throughout his writing, asking in *A Single Eye* if God is not "infinite and omni-present in all places, and in all things: as well Hell as Heaven, Devil as Angel, Sin as Holiness, Darknesse and as Light?"[41] Since God was in all these, Clarkson believed it possible to erase the moral distinctions that language imposed on them.

The more preposterous Abinezer Coppe, in his *Second Fiery Flying Roll* (1649), went even farther. Echoing the ecstatic utterances of the inspired prophet, Coppe admitted he spoke in a "riddle," fervently explaining his own adultery thus: "kisses are numbered amongst transgressors—base things—well! by bare hellish swearing, and cursing, (as I have accounted it in the time of my fleshly holiness) and by base impudent kisses (as I then accounted them) my plaguy holiness hath been confounded." In this line of thinking, his kisses, like the verbal act of swearing, are not transgressions, but rather deeds that "confound" what is already a "plaguy holiness." In committing these acts, Coppe defies a corrupt piety. At the heart of Coppe's belief is his mission to replace what is thought base with what is thought holy; only by overturning convenions will morality be cleansed: "I have chosen such base things," he explains, "to confound things that are." In another pamphlet, Coppe sought to revolutionize speech by beginning language over: "All things are returning to their Original, where all parables, dark sayings, all languages, and all hidden things, are known, unfolded, and interpreted."[42] In the originary state of language, words were clear, "known, unfolded," not "dark" and "hidden." By his colorful use of language, and his astonishing use of metaphor, Coppe hopes to return language to this pure condition, making two negatives into a positive.

Ranters may have been "few in number, though prominent in the nighmares of their many enemies," according to the historian Derek Hirst, and from their utterances we can see how they posed a threat not only to religious authority, property, and sexual relations, but also to language itself.[43] The revolutionary regime sought to regulate the uses of language by its Blasphemy Acts, passed by a bloc of moderate Presbyterians and Independents, and thought by historians to be a response to these Ranters and other sectaries on the extreme Left. In August 1650, Parliament directed its act against dissenting opinions and practices, curtailing not only speech, but other forms of political or religious dissent, suppressing the many forms of what it called atheism, prophaneness, wickedness, and superstition.[44] With language itself as a battleground between radicals, Commonwealth-men, and Royalists, the question remained, whose language was it to be?

BABEL AS A POLITICAL STORY

The illustration below, *The World Is Ruled and Governed by Opinion* (1641), represents the consequences of the clash of new voices, and it belongs to a strain of pamphleteering that blamed the press for all the trouble. In this broadside, a female figure rules; her gender signifies the familiar trope of political inversion, a woman on top.[45]

The woman is blindfolded, a parody of Justice, and she addresses the gentleman who approaches her: "'Tis true I cannot as clear judgments see, / Through self-conceit and haughty pride of mind." This does not cause her dismay, since she is happy to see her fruits are growing everywhere: "The fruit those idle books and libels be / In every street, on every stall you find." Her seat of power is in fact a tree bursting with its fruit, pamphlets. The titles of several of these are visible: "Taylor's Physicke," "Brown's Conventicle," "Taylor's Reply," "Hellish Parliament," "News from Elesium." Many of these are the names of actual pamphlets, and the others are at least believable fictions. These pamphlets drop to the ground like ripe fruit. On her left arm lies a chameleon, then, as today, a symbol for ever-changingness, and on her lap sits a globe of the earth in the place of her womb. The womb-as-earth suggests an alternate, and specifically a *female*, creation story—as if she, rather than God, has given birth to the world, in an almost blasphemous parody of a catechism's first question, "Who made thee?" A fool waters the tree below, performing a kind of artificial insemination: "Folly giveth life to thee." The tree of Opinion is a healthy tree, and saplings flourish in its shade. Opinion explains, "Cause one Opinion many doth devise / And propagate 'til infinite they be." Her imperial designs are explicit; the pointer is like a scepter, and the globe on her lap is a symbol of royal power: "I am Opinion who the world do sway," she boasts.

A final symbol rests upon her head, a "tower-like coronet" that represents the Tower of Babel. Opinion explains that the tower shows her "confused way." This sign of Opinion's power is an allegorical reminder that the consequences of rebellion were the profusion of different languages. "The fruit those idle books and libels be / In every street, on every stall you find": the pamphlets are common street literature, catering to the lower elements of society, the "giddie vulgar," and present everywhere. Like other pamphlets that opposed pamphlet debate, this broadside used a story about language to criticize the presence of public debate: too many opinions signaled chaos, and the participation of the lower and middling sorts in the political life of the nation would lead to anarchy.

2. Henry Peacham, *The World Is Ruled and Governed by Opinion* (1641).

More often than not, the story of Babel was cited in order to restore authority to the king's position, and it explained and condemned the origins of political difference. According to the seventeenth-century political theorist Robert Filmer, power was given naturally to Adam, which "continued monarchical to the Flood, and after the Flood to the confusion of Babel: when Kingdoms were first erected, planted, or scattered over the face of the world."[46] Babel represented a state of different and incompatible languages that was God's punishment for political ambition.

Yet, the radicals interpreted Babel differently, associating Babel with the archetypical tyrant Nimrod. In this reading, which is Milton's, Babel's confusion was the result of tyrannical processes. In *Paradise Lost*, for example, Milton associates Nimrod with the suffocating grip of prelatical power and Babel with the pageantry and luxury of kings. As the angel Michael in book 12 of *Paradise Lost* recounts to the fallen Adam the history of man that is to come, he points out the first tyrant, Nimrod, one "Of proud ambitious heart, who not content / With fair equality, fraternal state," who

> Will arrogate Dominion undeserv'd
> Over his brethren, and quite dispossess
> Concord and law of Nature from the Earth;

(12. 24–29)

A tyrant here disrupts the fraternity, the "brethren" of humans, and constructs a hierarchy. The consequence is a breach in the law of Nature, the dispossessing of concord, as if concord is a kind of property of the earth that is banished or vanquished. Milton sees Nimrod's tyranny as a "rebellion" from God, and in punishment for that rebellious tyranny, God sets men's tongues apart, "to sow a jangling noise of words unknown" (12.55).[47] But the tyranny has already created discord, even before God's punishment. Milton agreed with the Royalists that confusion in speech was a consequence of a political sin, yet he saw confused speech as a consequence of tyranny, not of a pluralistic language situation.

Milton also connected the metaphor of Babel with the images of Babylon and the Catholic Church. Catholicism, he wrote in *Eikonoklastes*, enslaved the people by a "spiritual Babel" (*CPW* 2.598). Babel was often associated with Babylon, and the zealous Protestant readers in seventeenth-century England who abhorred popery found analogies between the Babel of their own day and the evils of Catholicism. Thomas Blount's 1656 dictionary equates the biblical city of Babel with Babylon, explaining in his definition of Babel: "tis we use *Babelish* for confused; and *Babylonical* for magnificent and costly, and to *Bable* [*sic*] or *babble*, to twattle, or speak confusedly."[48] If Royalists emphasized the condition of Babel as God's punishment, then anti-Royalists emphasized the causes of Babel—ambition and tyranny—associating Babel with popery. For them, Babel was the metaphor that expressed these ideas.

The competing interpreters of Babel agreed on one thing: there was a plethora of voices to be heard. Whether one argued that Babel was a sign of unlawful resistance to a king, and that God would "suffer those men long to prosper in their Babel who build it with the bones and cement it with the blood of their kings," as was argued in King Charles's defense, *Eikon Basilike*; or that Babel was a sign of tyranny, as Milton wrote in his response to the *Eikon Basilike*, where Babel was "*Nimrods* work the first King, *and the beginning of his Kingdom was Babel*,"[49] the fact of Babel was acknowledged by all. The search for explanations of the conditions of Babel and the search for its cure shared an assessment of the contemporary political theater.

Babel represented competition among different languages for political legitimacy. William Prynne's pamphlet, *New Babel's Confusion* (1647) compared the biblical story to the political situation in England in 1647, when Parliament was divided over the petition called "An Agreement of the People," which asserted that the supreme power resided in the people. Prynne's title makes an analogy between mob rule and Babel; the actions of Parliament in the 1640s reenacted the blasphemous rebellion against right authority that had taken place at Babel. The frequent attacks on the press may be seen as criticisms of the entry of new voices into the political arena, and the likening of the press's activity to Babel was a way of opposing the notion that the people were an audience fit to participate in public debate at all. The example of Babel was cited to enlist support for a conservative antidote to the anarchy of both language and government.

Writers were recognizing that ideological division was represented by verbal action, and that differences might be impossible to reconcile. The public conflict of ideas would lead not to resolution but only to more strife. In an anti-Puritan satire, *Sampsons Foxes Agreed to Fire a Kingdom* (1644), the author compares Puritans to their opposite, papists, and concludes:

> See, two rude waves, by storms together thrown,
> Roar at each other, fight, and then grow one.
> Religion is a circle, men contend
> And run the round, disputing without end.[50]

Strife is figured in terms of a violent storm, and the clashes take place in language. The noise of disagreement had spurred Milton in 1644 to hope that this might be a sign of reformation. But to others (and even to Milton later), noise was not such a good thing. Babble and Babel (even Babylon) were identical. To Royalist John Doughty (1644), the battle cry of the enemy Religious zealot was, "Bibble, Bubble, Babel."[51]

These were clashes *in* language, verbal disputes, but they were also clashes *about* language—about the proper use of words. Sir Thomas Browne, apologist for Charles I, wrote in 1643 against the spate of newsbooks in which "the name of his Majesty [is] defamed, the honour of Parliament depraved, the writings of both depravedly, anticipatively, counterfeitly imprinted."[52] To Browne, printing the king's speech without authorization constituted treason.

In many cases during the pamphlet wars of the English Revolution, those who were represented as threatening natural order were the unruly populace. Thomas Jordan's poem "The Rebellion" presents a vision of anarchy in the many voices of the people. Anarchy in "The Rebellion" is signified by a linguistic condition where the multiplicity of voices, specifically from the lower ranks, create utter confusion:

> Come Clowns, and come Boys, come Hoberdehoys,
> Come Females of each degree,
> Stretch out your Throats, bring in your Votes,
> And make good the Anarchy;

Each voice contradicts the others:

> Then thus it shall be, says *Alse,*
> Nay, thus it shall be, says *Amie,*
> Nay, thus it shall go, says *Taffie,* I trow,
> Nay, thus it shall go, says *Jenny.*

Disagreement is the only observable feature; we do not even know what the matter is.

> Speak *Abraham*, speak *Hester*,
> Speak *Judith*, speak *Kester*,
> Speak tag and rag, short coat and long:
> Truth is the spell that made us rebel,
> And murder and plunder ding dong;
> Sure I have the truth, says *Numphs*,
> Nay, I have the truth, says *Clem*,
> Nay, I have the truth, says reverend *Ruth*,
> Nay, I have the truth, says *Nem*.

The song mixes "common" materials, "tag and rag," and the ballad refrain, "ding dong," to make light of the serious threat of popular rule, and by the names of Abraham, Judith, and Ruth, we see that at least some of these giddy anarchists are Puritans. The poem points to the language in which such rebellion is expressed: "tag and rag," *not* the acceptable language of politics found among educated men. These voices include female ones— Judith, Jenny, Amie—another instance of the slur of "women on top." And they include outsiders—"Taffie," a Welsh name. The moral of the piece, "Thus from the Rout who can expect / Ought but confusion?" is exemplified by making the popular voices express a variety of political opinions, with no apparent reasons:

> Then let's have King *Charles*, says *George*,
> Nay we'll have his Son, says *Hugh*;
> Nay, then let's have none, says gabbering *Joan*,
> Nay, we'll be all Kings, says *Prue*.[53]

The group cannot agree on anything—on a program, on the truth, or on the matter of who shall be king: Babel has come again. The polemical method of this poem is to caricature and distort the opposite side's disastrous disagreement in order to argue implicitly for a political point of view that is, on the other hand, stable, one-voiced, and not confused. At a more sophisticated level, this is the argument of Hobbes's *Leviathan*, as we shall see later.

This poem represents political chaos as a function of class, and indeed, Babel was often the trope assigned to low literature in the schism between "high" and "low" cultures familiar to scholars of early modern culture. The forces at work beneath the distinctions in taste were explicitly political during the English Revolution, as can be seen from poems by Thomas Jordan and others. Printed pamphlets were opposed not only for their sins against taste, but most importantly, because the content of the printed pamphlets posed definite threats to the social and political order. As Gabriel Plattes wrote in 1641: "the art of Printing will so spread knowledge that the common people, knowing their own rights and liberties will not be governed by way of oppression."[54] That multitude now seemed to rule all. Babel was a sign that the many were gaining access to previously inaccessible political energy.

It is not hard to see that the elite attitude was a reaction to pressures from popular literature itself. Writers at this time were aware of a new audience for politics, and some had nothing but scorn for it. According to those who opposed the press, there were too many pamphlets clamoring for authority, too many disparate assertions of truth. The public's contribution to politics seemed to be the Babel of a multitude of voices, no longer the king's single voice of truth. As the sermonizer in *A Remedie Against Dissention* warned his audience in 1644, "have a special eye to them who cause offenses; abettors, barraters [*sic*], authors of libels, and seditious pamphlets, causers of quarrels, men of unclean tongues." Puritans also feared the unruliness of a popular audience.[55] Fear of the mob was not a new phenomenon; Shakespeare's crowds in *Coriolanus* or *Julius Caesar* could be seen to show the worst effects of a republican system.[56] Likewise, the mobs in Spenser's *Faerie Queene* evoked the political memory of mob rebellion like Jack Cade's or Wat Tyler's, and this served to provoke fear among elites.[57] But the conservatives during the seventeenth century had a specific kind of public to fear, one that could express its wants in a language of its own. This was no gullible mass, but rather an entity that was choosing sides, the object of address of a pamphlet literature in which powerful political ideas were being expressed.

JOHN CLEVELAND AND THE DIVINE RIGHT OF LANGUAGE

The royalist pamphleteer John Cleveland made wide use of the conflicting languages in his day to parody those he considered politically illegitimate, and his pieces attacked the language of his enemies as a way of attacking their politics. Cleveland drew an equation between bankrupt language and bankrupt politics, and his three short prose pieces published in 1644, "Character of a Country Committee-man," "The Character of a Diurnal-Maker," and "The Character of a London Diurnal," were satiric attacks on the parliamentary newspapers. During the English Revolution, Cleveland was paid to write as an official spokesman for the king's garrison at Newark.[58] In "The Character of a London Diurnal," for instance, Cleveland mocks Parliament by presenting their actions in their own language. Not surprisingly, Parliament is made to appear ridiculous by its misappropriation of language. In this case, Parliament has misread signs, with disastrous results:

> Suppose a corn-cutter being to give little Isaac a cast of his office should fall to paring his brows (mistaking one end for the other, because he branches at both), this would be a plot, and the next diurnal would furnish you with this scale of votes:—

Resolved upon the question, That this act of the corn-cutter was an absolute invasion of the city's charter in the representative forehead of Isaac.

Resolved, That the evil counsellors about the corn-cutter are popishly affected and enemies to the State.

Resolved, That there be a public thanksgiving for the great deliverance of Isaac's brow-antlers; and a solemn covenant drawn up to defy the corn-cutter and all his works.[59]

Because he is a cuckold, Isaac sprouts antlers (*corni*) on his head as well as having corns on his feet. Since Isaac looks the same at both ends, the corn-cutter makes an error and trims his forehead rather than his feet. Cleveland is not only shaming Isaac (a Puritan by his name) for cuckoldry, but he is also attacking the Puritan's indecorous reversals of natural order: the world is turned upside down. The accusation of cuckoldry is another instance of the woman-on-top theme; just as there has been an illegitimate usurpation in Isaac's domestic hierarchy, there has been usurpation in language. The woman-on-top image was not merely a literary trope, since women in a very real way were participtating in public discourse as they had not before. There is evidence that women's voices were being heard in the political and public arena, as sectarian preachers and in petitions to Parliament.[60]

In the Puritan reading of this incident, the corn-cutter's mistake is treasonous, and the signs take on a wholly different meaning in the frenzied brains of Puritan divines. Isaac's forehead becomes a site representing the city charter, and surgery on this is judged a treachery. Cleveland's parody takes the political metaphor of the "body politic" literally, and shows the Puritan zeal for interpretation gone haywire. Those responsible for the "invasion," of course, were "popishly affected," with the corn-cutter acting not in isolation, but as the instrument of a party. The resolutions call for a response to the "plot," including a "public thanksgiving for the great deliverance"—ridiculous, considering the inanity of the cause. Parliament responds to this situation by passing resolutions, and the second resolution contains a reference to the attack on evil counselors in "Root and Branch Petition" (1640), put forward to initiate a more "godly, thorough, Reformation," and the third, to the *Solemn League and Covenant* (1643). The language used is Puritan, with the full solemnity of their diction mockingly misapplied in a parody.

Cleveland scatters parodic mimicry of Puritan language throughout his "Character" as a means of political attack. Cleveland asks that "some Conjurer translate, and let me know it," casting the Puritan activity of "translation" into work of the Devil, making it a kind of sorcery. It is true that the Puritans had brought a vocabulary derived from the language of biblical interpretation into public discussion. To many like Cleveland, it seemed an abuse of ordinary language. For example, the audience of a giddy people were the object of ridicule in the satirical poem *Ad Populam; or, A Lecture to the People* (1644), in which the author also turns Puritan writing on its head.

Written under the pen name of John Taylor, this pamphlet by Peter Hausted parodied the Puritan "lecture," yet instead of offering enlightenment to its putative listeners, it belittled them at every turn. The writer appealed rather to an audience that shared his distaste for the people, and his writing reversed the popular literary mode of a lecture in order to satirize the public. A Puritan lecture was supposed to edify, and it was the lecture form that first built the public into an audience fit for rational discussion and primed it for political action. Hausted turned the Puritan lecture upside down by using the biblical metaphors that peppered Puritan lectures, but chose ones that undermined the audience's sense of its own worth. For example, when he evoked the Puritans' abhorrence of idol worship—"Ye dull Idolaters, have ye yet bent / Your knees enough to your Dagon-Parliament"—Hausted used the Puritan rhetoric for a huge insult, the accusation that the people worshiped Parliament as if it were Dagon, the Philistine god.[61]

In choosing biblical idols, Hausted made a sophisticated comment on the uses of language in his own day; the incident in the Bible where the Philistine god Dagon is overturned by the power of the Israelites' Ark (1 Sam. 5–7) occurs immediately before the people call for a king to rule over them. Hausted made use of this metonymic relation between the rejection of Dagon the idol and the summoning of a king to reinforce subtly his royalist stance. Yet even this allusion turned conventional Puritan rhetoric on its head. The account of the summoning of the first king in 1 Samuel was used by anti-Royalists to delegitimize kingship, to prove that the origin of kingship resided in the people. Hausted's use, in contrast, reinforces his authoritarian stance. The conflation of religious rule with structures of government (Dagon-Parliament) argues for obedience to a single ruler, to God, and, by political implication, to a king.

In *Ad Populam*, further, Hausted mocks the public as the lowliest of the twelve tribes of Israel: "grosse Ass of Issachar, poor hackney clown, / Betwixt two burdens wilt thou still crouch down." This echoes Jacob's prophecy concerning his sons (Gen. 49:14), which makes the tribe of Issachar a tribe of servants. The author urges his underlings to "Return, return unto your God and King," that is, to return to their proper subordinate station in life. The pamphlet ends with a caustic insult that serves to reiterate the traditional structures of hierarchy and place: "Take up at last, then learn to understand / The Plow and the Sceptre are not for one Hand." As Hausted saw it, the people were unfit for the task they had undertaken, and he should attempt to put them back in their proper place. Though *Ad Populam* could not really have been intended for the general public—it is clearly to insulting to those potential readers, despite John Taylor's "low" associations—the pamphlet does go on to give a serious defense of the ship money issue, a question that divided gentlemen in 1637 over the validity of the semipermanent status of the king's special levy without the consent of Parliament. Hausted tries to convince readers of the royalist position, granting implicitly that the reader has enough sense and judgment to understand and to be persuaded by his argument. This is not the same audience as the one named "ad populam," which lacks reasoning powers altogether. The pamphlet is aimed rather at those who share the aristocratic prejudice against the lower orders, and it attempts to unify those elites against that unreasoning public in order to back the king's financial schemes.

When Cleveland remarks the unnaturalness of Puritan language, however, he forges bridges between it and his own: "In sum, a diurnal-maker is the anti-mark of an historian," he concludes. "He differs from him as a drill from a man, or (if you had rather have it in the saints' gibberish) as a hinter doth from a holder-forth." (*CWSC*, 306). He provides his own meaning, glossed with the Puritan's. His audience is expected to read both languages in order to understand the joke. In fact, Cleveland is so completely aware of other languages that he makes it possible to engage in parody and burlesque. With a sharp ear, Cleveland mimics his opponents' language in order to prove it is without value.

In his attacks on Parliament for uncovering plots of its own fabrication, Cleveland expresses this misreading in terms of one of the great literary misreaders: "Thus the Quixotes of this age fight with the windmills of their own heads, quell monsters of their own creation, make plots, and then discover them" (*CWSC*, 308–9). By this analogy, the Puritans are transformed into readers of romances who have exchanged reality for fantasy, readers who have gone mad. Parliament has misread the entire event of Isaac and his corns in its passage of the resolution on the corn-cutter discussed above, and the minor accident has acquired national significance as a result. The example shows a need for an authorized interpretation—the king's—to prevent such romantic fictionalizing. The diurnal turns from the language of parliamentary activity to that of chivalric romance, suggesting that both are as fanciful as they are discordant. Cleveland mocks the Puritan exploits in this chivalric language: "In the third place march their adventures; the Roundheads' legends, the rebels' romance; stories of a larger size than the ears of their sect" (309). This is true burlesque, applying a high style to a low subject, aggressively perverting reality. Yet the technique of burlesque makes a specific political point: those from the lower orders have usurped the places (and the languages) of their betters.

In the "Character of a London Diurnal," Cleveland outlines the heroic "adventures": Stamford is seen upon "Banks his horse in a saddle rampant"; Sir William Waller's "knight-errantry," shows him a "prodigy of valour." The diction is heroic: "William [Waller] whose lady is the Conqueror . . . the city's champion and the diurnal's delight." The language here is mock-epic, and it makes a political point about Waller, who was notoriously cowardly, informing on his royalist friends as soon as it was expedient, and who changed coats again at the Restoration. The epic rises to a burlesque cheer, self-consciously mock-panegyric when it comes to Cromwell: "But the diurnal is weary of the arm of the flesh, and now begins an hosanna to

Cromwell; one that hath beat up his drums clean through the Old Testament: you may learn the genealogy of our Saviour by the names in his regiment; the muster-master uses no other list but the first chapter of Matthew" (310). And later: "O brave Oliver! Time's voider, subsidizer to the worms, in whom death, who formerly devoured our ancestors, now chews the cud" (311).[62] The mock-panegyric plays upon the convention of chivalric language, but, as in this last display against Cromwell, Cleveland's parodies are grounded on political beliefs and do not merely play with language for play's sake.

Not merely attacking his enemies in Parliament by a parody of their language, Cleveland was concerned with the disturbing social consequences of the revolutionary press. Though it is probable that he wrote for the mercuries of his day, Cleveland opposes news journals and takes advantage of the opportunities for public discussion—only to shut them down. His opposition to the parliamentary press used the metaphor of linguistic order to stand for political order, and we might speculate that Cleveland would have dreamed of the day when there was no public debate. The "Character of a London Diurnal" directs fire at the newsweeklies that reported on the activities of Parliament, and in it, Cleveland opened with an attack on the language used to describe the genre of the newsbook: "The country-carrier . . . miscalls it the urinal" (*CWSC*, 307). By calling its very name into question, Cleveland makes an issue of its legitimacy. Cleveland connects the newsbook to excrement, since they are both waste products.[63]

Naming is also contested in "The Character of a London Diurnal-Maker," where Cleveland refuses to call the producers of these diurnals "authors" so as not to dishonor the art of true authors: "List him a writer and you smother Geoffrey [Chaucer] in swabber-slops." Even to name the diurnal maker is to pose a problem for language.[64] From the very opening, language is shown to be inadequate to describe the current spate of writing, as the "Character" fumbles in its attempts to define its subject: "A diurnal-maker is the sub-almoner of history, Queen Mab's register, one whom, by the same figure that a north country pedlar is a merchantman, you may style an author. It is like an overreach of language, when every thin tinder-cloaked quack must be called a doctor; when a clumsy cobbler usurps the attribute of our English peers, and is vamped a translator" (303). The diurnal maker taking the name of writer, the peddler taking the title of merchant, or the quack of doctor are unmerited usurpations of language. The diurnal maker is certainly not a historian, since "to call him a historian is to knight a mandrake; 'tis to view him through a perspective, and by that gross hyperbole to give the reputation of engineer to a maker of mousetraps." Again there is the topos of aberrant sexuality, with the "mandrake" a common sign for sexual license. To knight a mandrake is to reward the undeserving. Cleveland's definitions serve to put the upstarts in their places.

Although Cleveland fires on his enemy as if the issue were solely verbal illegitimacy, the real issue is political illegitimacy. His account provides an allegory to the House of Commons, filled with "clumsy cobblers," then ruling over the House of Lords. The cobbler "usurps" the privileges of the noble class through an act of "translation," that is, substitution of one language for another. Translation is the term drawn from the very language of Puritan theology, where the activity of any Bible reader can make a cobbler equal to a peer. The prospect of equal opportunities for "translation" horrifies Cleveland, who would like to keep the lower sorts of people at a distance. According to Cleveland, the translation is fraudulent, moreover, since the two languages involved are *not* equivalent to one another: the high may not be exchanged fairly for the low.

Like Wilkins and the universal language movement theorists, Cleveland is concerned with the right and true uses of language, and the similarities between Cleveland's interests and the concerns of the language reformers are even more striking when we consider Cleveland's obsessions with correct definition and proper grammar. Though his motive is political snobbism more than it is a philosophical critique of his enemies' language, Cleveland uses definition as a specific device to challenge the politics of his opponents, as a way to assign a thing a true meaning and to regain control over it. The opening salvo of "The Character of a Country Committee-Man" is a discussion of the the term "committee-man," shown to pose a grammatical paradox in its application of a mass noun for a singular entity. This verbal paradox presents an ideological issue: can political authority be divided among a number of men, including the multitude, and among a number of branches of the government, as the Parliamentarians would have it? Thomas Hobbes expressed horror at the divided authority of such a "mixed government" in *Leviathan*: "For what is it to divide the Power of a Commonwealth, but to Dissolve it; for Powers divided mutually destroy each other."[65] Cleveland spins his puns in analysis of the problem of number, analyzing his opponents' violation of syntax to illustrate his political point: "A committee-man by his name should be one that is possessed, there is number enough in it to make an epithet for legion. He is *persona in concreto* (to borrow the solecism of a modern statesman). . . . It is a well-trussed title that contains both the number and the beast; for a committee-man is a noun of the multitude, he must be spelled with figures" (*CWSC*, 299). This string of phrases, clustered loosely around the term "committee-man," plays on the theme of grammatical misconstruction. According to Cleveland, such a warping of true grammar counts as a political act: "as monstrous as the man, a complex notion; of the same lineage with accumulative treason" (298–99). It is unnatural, "monstrous," and it also constitutes unacceptable political action, "treason." Both bad grammar and political treachery are betrayals of a natural trust. The idea of correct grammar implies a "natural" order in the world, which has been disrupted.

Cleveland points to the examples of ruptured etymology and syntax in hope of illuminating analogous flaws in the politics of these committee-men. In criticizing their diction, Cleveland plays upon the chiefest of their evils, the fact that they divide authority. Collectively, the committee-men are dangerous: "Look upon them severally, and you cannot but fumble for some threads of clarity. But oh, they are termagents in conjunction!" (*CWSC*, 301). He then goes on to portray a few committee-men, concluding, "these are the simples of this precious compound; a kind of Dutch hotch-potch, the Hogan-Mogan committee-man" (302). The "Dutch" were associated with republicanism, and here Cleveland has only derision for their political arrangment. Repeatedly expressing outrage at instances of violated grammar, Cleveland claims, "there is no syntax between a cap of maintenance and a helmet" (300), between laborers and soldiers, and he disparages a time "when so tame a pigeon may converse with vultures" (299). Cleveland believes there exists a proper hierarchy that determines a proper way of talking about matters. The Parliamentarians have usurped this true language by imposing their own fallacious language, just as they have usurped the true, correct politics.

In his acts of definition, Cleveland expresses a definite politics: Only the king has the authority to validate language. In both "The Character of a Diurnal-Maker" and "The Character of a London Diurnal," Cleveland evaluates the names that the Parliamentarians have assigned to things, and he denies meaning to these new names by an appeal to natural linguistic order, snobbishly using metaphors of birth and pedigree. According to Cleveland's definition, a parliamentary "Ordinance" was "A law still-born, dropped before quickened by the royal assent. 'Tis one of the parliament's bye-blows, acts only being legitimate, and hath no more sire than a Spanish jennet that is begotten by the wind" (*CWSC*, 307). For a law to be "still-born," it comes into the world dead, here lacking the "quickening" of kingly or patriarchal potency. The ordinance was a "bye-blow," a child born out of wedlock, illegitimate by law. In these metaphors taken from patriarchal political theory, true paternal legitimacy here would mean royal approval.[66] The next paragraph in the pamphlet draws out the same metaphor, where Parliament's army is like a fatherless offspring: "Thus their militia, like its Patron Mars, is the issue only of the mother, without the concourse of royal Jupiter" (307). The failure of true royalty to provide authority was described as a failure of proper lineage in the genealogical sense.

Genealogy, and the patriarchal political theory it expresses, finds its way into Cleveland's linguistic critique through the device of definition. As in the description of the parliamentary ordinance, Cleveland uses a metaphor of disturbed sexual generation to deny the authenticity of his opponents' politics. Cleveland's wildly creative definitions are not all linguistic play, though they are a good deal of that. They are analogous to the searches for political legitimacy that activists sought from the past, where genealogy gave natural precedent and justification for present actions, as well as for claims to inheritance.[67]

What began as an exercise in definition—what is a diurnal? Or even, what is an ordinance?—has turned into an exposure of his enemy's politics through a study of that enemy's language. Cleveland's use of catachresis is an appropriation of the many languages coexisting in the contemporary political arena, and the *Characters* exemplify the possibilities of exposing illegitimate languages for political uses. In the *Characters*, Cleveland rewrites enemy figures so they appear not in the enemy's language, but in his own. Framed by this one true language, Cleveland presses for the others to be disqualified, both on natural grounds and political ones.

If exposure by framing is possible, he might continue, then truth is a question of linguistic practices and the kind of seriousness with which they are observed. But Cleveland backs away from the radicalism of this general position. One claim, his own, is better than all others. In order to battle with the enemy ideologies, he wars against their languages, revealing his belief that there exists a true language, a real, royal, syntax. The other languages are ungrammatical. Mikhail Bakhtin argues that *polyglossia* may be a feature inherent in any prose work, defining *polyglossia* as the "simultaneous presence of two or more national languages interacting within a single cultural system." This concept of polyglossia is useful in understanding how civil war writers coped with changing conditions in the language of their time. In some sense, it is precisely polyglossia that the conservative seventeenth-century writers wanted to keep out. Bakhtin argues that the "unitary norms of language" are imposed to defend "an already formed language from the pressure of growing heteroglossia," as the two forces play off against each other in a centripetal/centrifugal battle. This interplay is dramatized in the civil war question of authority over language. Bakhtin himself uses the image of Babel to talk about the function of multiple languages in the world: "the prose writer witnesses . . . the unfolding of social heteroglossia *surrounding* the object, the Tower-of-Babel mixing of languages that goes on around any object."[68] For Bakhtin, the Tower of Babel has the positive, liberating resonances of the "open" form of the novel, and is an inevitable consequence of recording spoken language.

But Cleveland, like many civil war writers, would have been worried about the possibility of such a condition. Cleveland attempted to rein in the waywardness of language by an appeal to order and authority. To Cleveland, the condition of Babel was to be eradicated by using proper grammar. Correct grammar and true definition were overarching natural metaphors for political order, and Cleveland's definitions are attempts to regain control of a language that has gone astray. Naming is an issue of power, since whoever controls the language can order the world as he wants it to be ordered. Cleveland sees a necessary connection between language and power, and in this Cleveland resembles Hobbes. But unlike Hobbes, Cleveland does not accept the artificiality of any language; his metaphors above all assert the idea that there is a proper use of language: his own, the King's English.

Thomas Hobbes's Lexarchy

Thomas Hobbes would have agreed with Cleveland that only one model be used for grammar, and that model be authorized by a single authority, yet Hobbes adds that this is not a natural arrangement but a necessarily artificial one. Cleveland runs the risks of a relativistic position with respect to political (and linguistic) authority in his deconstruction of his enemies' language, since he lacks a coherent explanation of how his language is any truer than that of his enemies. Cleveland would not allow that the rhetorical critique of his enemies' language might also be applied to his own; that his own language might also be, as Hobbes would argue, conventional. Though Cleveland's extravagant and memorable uses of catachresis do call into question the propriety of his own language, he does not draw the conclusion that Hobbes will, that the relation of any language to truth is always vulnerable. Cleveland asks the reader to be wary of every language except Cleveland's own, even though he also takes advantage of the situation of writing released by the competition among languages.

Thomas Hobbes supplies a few steps missing between such a critique of language as offered by the civil war pamphleteers' sense of a transparent or true language and the universal language reformers of the late seventeenth century. With Hobbes, we ground in philosophy the responses to linguistic anarchy we have been examining, and we see that the playful defiance of linguistic norms that worries the royalist writers is no mere trifle. With our analysis of Hobbes, we take a detour from literary analysis into political theory in order to examine how linguistic order became a central way that political order was not only understood, but created. *Leviathan* makes explicit the links between the need for authorized speech practices and the public conflict of opinions, between the condition of the multiplicity of languages and the condition of Babel in the press. The first sections of *Leviathan* build up a science of society, and Hobbes makes an account of language germane to his project.[69] Only after explaining that language is conventional will Hobbes argue in *Leviathan* that a sovereign is needed to police linguistic as well as political practice. Hobbes counts on a uniform linguistic practice to counteract the phenomenon of differing public opinions.

Hobbes's version of the story of Babel is set out in chapter 4 of *Leviathan*, "Of Speech." In this account, God instructed Adam how to name, a power that proved Adam's sovereignty and original dominion over the earthly creatures. But, Hobbes continues, "all this language gotten, and augmented by *Adam* and his posterity, was again lost at the tower of *Babel*, when by the hand of God, every man was stricken for his rebellion, with an oblivion of his former language" (*L*, 101). As it was for Filmer, linguistic difference in Hobbes was thus a political fact, incurred not at the Fall, but a result of the human drive for power. Because language *after* Babel was conventional, however, sovereign authority was needed to control it. According to Hobbes, human creatures learned language again after the multiplication of languages at Babel, and this time not according to God's plan, but by their own need and convention: "in such manner, as need (the mother of all inventions) taught them; and in tract of time grew everywhere more copious" (*L*, 101).[70] The account of the origin of languages is somewhat different in *De Corpore*, where Hobbes argues that we must *assume* language is arbitrary: "it is for brevity's sake that I suppose the original of names to be arbitrary, judging it a thing that may be assumed unquestionable." Hobbes asks, "How can any man imagine that the names of things were imposed from their nature? For though some names of living creatures and other things, which our first parents used, were taught by God himself; yet they were by him arbitrarily imposed, and afterwards, both at the Tower of Babel, and since, in process of time, growing every where out of use, are quite forgotten, and in their room have succeeded others."[71] In this story, even God made an arbitrary "imposition" of words on things to "teach" Adam and Eve their language. The passage of time shows not linguistic chaos, but rather a continuous process of the reinvention and forgetting of language, languages constructed by humans.

Hobbes's story of the loss of Adamic language at Babel warrants the sovereign to be chief lexarch. The condition of linguistic arbitrariness requires that the play of language be reined in by publicly accepted rules of speech. Communication through language forges a kind of social order: "names have their constitution, not from the species of things, but from the will and consent of men" (*DC*, 56), like the originating government made from a covenant. Hobbes's theory of language underscores the importance of public utterances for an orderly state, since it is by utterances alone that right and wrong are decided, given the arbitrariness of language to begin with. Since "True and False are attributes of Speech, not of Things" (*L*, 105), an arbitrator is needed to name right and wrong. That authority must set the limits on interpretation: "though it be naturally reasonable; yet it is by the Sovereign Power that it is Law" (323), since "all Laws, written and unwritten, have their Authority, and force, from the Will of the Common-wealth; that is to say, from the Will of the Representative" (315–16). The sovereign oversees the institution of language through the law, that special class of language that determines "the distinction of right and wrong" (312).

According to Hobbes, without sovereign authority, opinions would inevitably create factions—to which the multitude is especially susceptible, being "distracted in opinions concerning the best use and application of their strength, they do not help, but hinder one another" (*L*, 224–25). Faction arises out of private opinions expressed in public, as was set forth in the *World Is Ruled and Governed by Opinion* broadside. When, "a number of men, part of the Assembly, without authority, consult a part, to contrive the guidance of the rest; This is a Faction, or Conspiracy—unlawful, as being a fraudulent seducing of the Assembly for their particular interest" (286).

Like Jordan's "Rebellion," Hobbes's *Leviathan* considers the dangerous consequence of private opinions becoming public without a sovereign to guide human actions: "For in the condition of men that have no other Law but their own Appetites, there can be no general Rule of Good, and Evil Actions. But in a commonwealth this measure is false: Not the Appetite of Private men, but the Law, which is the Will and Appetite of the State is the measure" (697). In a state of nature, humans are driven by the laws of their own appetites, but in a commonwealth, the sovereign's laws must constrain them. Only in the state of nature does private judgment operate, *as expressed in verbal acts*, "calling things Good or evil": "And yet is this doctrine still practised; and men judge the Goodness, or Wickedness of their own, and other men's actions, and the actions of the Common-wealth itself by their own Passions; and no man calleth Good or Evil, but that which is so in his own eyes, without any regard at all to the Public Laws. . . . And this private measure of Good, is a Doctrine, not only Vain, but also Pernicious to the Public State" (697). Public manifestations of private judgments can operate only in the state of nature, and not in a civil society. Unruly expression of "private measure" leads ultimately to anarchy (185), dividing humans to make wars: "And that such as have a great, and false opinion of their own Wisdom, take it upon them to reprehend the actions, and call in question the Authority of them that govern, and so to unsettle the laws with their public discourse, as that nothing shall be a Crime but that what with their own designs require should be so. . . . These I say are effects of a false presumption of their own Wisdom" (341–42). When private judgments are made *public* through "public discourse" they pose a threat to the peacefulness of the state. This fear of the polyglossia of the public sphere is a response to the growing prominence of public discourse. Hobbes belongs to the strain of thought that sets up law as the only possible public expression.[72]

In chapter 29 of *Leviathan*, one cause "Of those Things that Weaken, or tend to the Dissolution of the Commonwealth" is faction, which, surprisingly, Hobbes attributes to talk. Faction derives from men's tendency to "debate with themselves, and dispute the commands of the Commonwealth; and afterwards to obey, or disobey them, as in their private judgment they shall think fit" (365). The belief in the importance of private judgment is a "false doctrine," a chief "poison" responsible for the dissolution of a commonwealth: "*That every private man is Judge of Good and Evil actions*" (365). Though this is the human condition in a state of nature, it will not do for a commonwealth: direct links between private judgment and the public realm must be severed. It is up to the sovereign to *prevent* private judgment of good and evil from becoming public without supervision and authority. The risks of public opinion are too great for it to appear without such authorization. Ideological difference, signified by verbal difference, cannot be tolerated in an orderly state.

Hobbes's account of the subject's surrender to the sovereign obliterates all signs of verbal difference. In the erection of a commonwealth, "[Men] confer all their power and strength upon one Man, or upon one Assembly of men, that may reduce all their Wills, by plurality of voices, unto one Will . . . and therein to submit their Wills, every one to his Will, and their Judgments, to his Judgment. This is more than Consent, or Concord; it is real Unity of them all, in one and the same Person, made by Covenant of every man with every man"(227). Creating a supreme political fiction, Hobbes writes an allegory through which to express his political ideas. By his fiction making, Hobbes carefully shapes his unified state. Hobbes's refusal to equate "Unity" with "consent" or "concord" is crucial. Unity is not a "con-sentire," an "agreeing-together" or a "con-cord," an agreement in combination of hearts. The many are not joined to make a *concordia discors*, or even allied into a consensus. This is not the Rousseauist *volonté générale*. Instead, the "plurality" is by force "reduced," literally *led back*, to a singleness.[73] This is a different conception from Milton's ideal of the charged coexistence of a variety of voices in *Areopagitica*, or even from the kind of consensus that was the aim of the 1640s parliaments. In this linguistic order, the voices of the many are subordinated to the one (*L*, 165). For Hobbes, difference of opinions correlates to linguistic disorder in a profound way: the sovereign is needed to prohibit both. Unlike Cleveland's insistence that language be natural and unified like patriarchal kingship, Hobbes's response to Babel is to acknowledge the arbitrary basis for both language and politics, and to construct laws and a social order to prevent Babel's dangers. Hobbes offers the most definitive answer to the problem of linguistic or political diversity by the annulment of both. In Hobbes's eyes, only dictatorship solves the problem of dissent.

•

The story of Babel in the English Revolution is a complicated one, as writers used the metaphor to express their fears about the appearance of ideological difference in the press. The Royal Society's plan after after the revolution, with its motto, *nullius in verba*, "of nothing in words," sought to reform language to make a plain English the only fit medium for expression, and thus to reduce the number of possibilities of interpretation to one. As Thomas Sprat put it in his *History of the Royal Society* (1667): "to reject all the amplifications, digressions, and swellings of style: to return back to the primitive purity, and shortnes, when men deliver'd so many *things*, almost in an equal number of *words*."[74] Plain style may not only contain an epistemology, but may also espouse a political agenda.[75] In part this desire for simplicity in language was a response to the linguistic situation of the English Revolution. The representation of the fear of popular anarchy as a fear of linguistic chaos reflects the actual nature of the civil war disagreements, where each party seemed to speak in a particular dialect, with words carrying specific meanings that differed according to their use. For a writer like Cleveland, the story of Babel was a conservative story, written in resistance to the pressures of polyglossia in the political sphere. The story offered a providential explanation of current events, as the many languages in public debate were thought to be evidence of divine punishment for rebellion.

In this reading, the authenticity of language was seen as something fundamentally *outside* politics, and language could serve as a standard by which to measure political worth. For Cleveland, and perhaps for the universal language theorists who held that a reorganization of language would eliminate religious differences, language was a model for true order, political and otherwise. What writers who employed this metaphor did not always acknowledge, however, was that their appeal to this story had profoundly unsettling implications for all political communication. If language always provided a base for authority, then wordplay, jargon, and manipulations of language (like the use of a metaphor such as Babel) would all be political as well as linguistic threats. Thus, in the case of John Cleveland and the many writers who used this metaphor, the attack on Babel appears as linguistically problematic as the words of those they were criticizing, since one possible reading of the story of Babel would conclude that all language is conventional, and that any language is as true as any other. Hobbes answers that, yes, language is conventional, and that we had better get used to it.

Babel was an image used both as a representation of the war of words in the press and as a figure for ideological difference in order to stifle the revolutionary press and all its public voices. Linguistic diversity was taken as a sign of deeper trouble. Language here was invested with power in several senses: self-referentiality in language could be used to deconstruct meaning, as in Cleveland, or language could be revealed as having its origins in structures of power, as in Hobbes. The figure of Babel in the seventeenth century did not merely mark the presence of linguistic difference, but it was one response writers had to a new language situation, one in which the expression of many opinions in the press was feared to lead ultimately to political anarchy. Responses to Babel were responses to a new public sphere, where debate and conflicting interpretations about politics were apparent. Even those who responded with fear to the new language situation also contributed to that verbiage, since they too presented their views in the press, paradoxically assailing public discourse in public.

In analyzing the two axes of the metaphor of Babel—the linguistic and the political—I suggest that the pamphleteers who deployed this trope of linguistic disorder used it not only to represent the objects of social and political strife, the lowly and the female, but also to condemn the very grounds of political strife as illegitimate, as nonsensical languages. Conflicts in the English Revolution took place in, and about, words; but words reflected the social and political moorings that were coming loose. The attack on the public shows that writers recognized, if undervalued, the phenomenon of the public conflict of ideas. While asserting the unworthiness of their enemies, royalist writers nevertheless did battle with them in print, in that very public forum they abhorred. Their participation in the pamphlet wars exemplifies the new conditions of writing during the English Revolution, where it was necessary to persuade a public, and thus even Royalists unwittingly fostered the new mode of public debate. Whether Royalists liked it or not, Babel had become a fact of life.

Debate and the Drama of Politics in the Public Sphere

See, two rude waves, by storms together thrown,

Roar at each other, fight, and then grow one.

Religion is a circle, men contend

And run the round, disputing without end.

Sampsons Foxes Agreed to Fire a Kingdom (1644)

MILTON wrote in 1644, "where there is much desire to learn, there of necessity will be much arguing" (*CPW* 2.554). As defenders of the revolutionary public sphere, many partisans agreed with Milton that debate was necessary for resolving disagreements. Oliver Cromwell urged the General Council of the Army in 1647 "that [those who disagreed] should not meet as two contrary parties, but as some desirous to satisfy or convince each other."[1] Argument was the order of the day, in Parliament, on the streets, and of course, in the press. As John Milton wrote in his *Second Defense*, "truth defended by arms be also defended by reason—the only defence truly appropriate to man" (4.553).

While a writer like John Cleveland fancied in this scenario the specter of Babel, to Milton and others verbal disputes were clearing the path for true reformation. Those who held this latter view believed that disagreements in public did not by necessity lead to disaster; rather, airing differences was perhaps the only way to resolve them. They thought open discussions would also keep the public happy, as the Puritan divine John Saltmarsh explained in 1646: "where debates are free there is a way of vent and evacuation, the stopping of which hath caused more troubles in states than anything" (*PD*, Woodhouse, 181). Saltmarsh also thought that politicians must be accountable to the public, writing in a letter to the General Council at Putney: "Let all that preach or print affix their names that we may know from whom . . . If it be the truth they write, why do they not own it? If untruth why do they write? . . . Let all that teach or print be accountable, yet in a several way. If it be a matter of immediate disturbance and trouble to the state, let them account for it to the magistrate under whom we are to live a peaceable and quiet life (I Tim. 2.2); if matter of doctrine, &c., let them be accountable to the believers and brethren who are offended, by conference, where there may be mutual conviction and satisfaction (Gal. 2.11)" (*PD*, 181).[2] Politicians like Cromwell and thinkers like Saltmarsh were articulating new protocols for public discussion, and these are exactly Milton's proposals for authorial accountability in *Areopagitica*.

In this chapter, we see how pamphlet writers invited readers to act in this climate of intense debate by learning how to read and to understand political rhetoric. The pamphleteers I view in this chapter are those who used the literary form of fictional debates to present conflicts on paper, duelling with one another in print. The format of debate goes way back into the poetry and theology of the medieval period; what distinguishes civil war debate from the prior tradition is the explicitness of the political focus. These writers envisioned their readers as those who witnessed the clash of opposing political ideologies, and who would participate in what was becoming a public discourse. Readers were to act not only as spectators of the debates, but were to become a kind of jury in deciding matters. By using the format of debates, writers made political demands on their readers; they imagined their readers as an audience fit to take part in a political spectacle; and they gave their readers practice in defending themselves against their own and their opponents' resistances, counterclaims, and questions. The forms of responsive writing based on rhetorical models were many, with the list of titles beginning with, "An Answer to . . . ," and "Animadversions on . . . ," running well into the hundreds for this period. All this, I argue, adds up to a textual education in participatory politics. By setting competing arguments before the public view, writers asked their readers to choose among the contrary opinions, and this I see as political action.

Christian Jouhaud has analyzed the *mazarinades*, political pamphlets in seventeenth-century France, illustrating how French pamphleteers talked both to each other and to an audience, using traditional forms of public address. His case offers a useful comparison to what we are examining here. Jouhaud argues that the mazarinades constructed a public, a kind of theater audience, because they offered a spectacle, a "mise en scène." Thus he derives the concept of a "public" from the audience of the theater: the audience watches and reacts as they would to a theatrical performance, with laughter, anger, or indignation. In the case of these French pamphlets, the texts themselves fix readers' positions as spectators of the action, performing implicit political acts: "Le texte est représentation et mise en scène de la politique, mais l'action politique elle-même, dans ses manifestations publiques, se veut spectacle."[3] The political action demands to be viewed. This practice makes a political point, that politics should take place in public.

In many ways, the English pamphlets also transformed the members of their audiences into spectators. But more than simply to watch the paper-battles in the press, readers were invited to participate in the fray. The genre of the debate became a mode by which readers were to become part of the action. Both as a literal means to arrive at a position and as literary form, dramatic debates encouraged readers to take sides. The pamphleteers performed public dramas in responding to one another, and many also incorporated genres of drama and debate into their method of presentation. The debate formula was not new; it had been used by Thomas More in his *Utopia* and in books of instruction for the common people since the Tudors. Moreover, the form of debate was encouraged by university rhetoric, since training at school was in oratory and public discussion. The dialogue form suited civil war writers particularly well since its fictionality allowed the author the security of a neutral position: dangerous positions could be cloaked by dramatis personae. Of all its accomplishments, the most important for the civil war polemic was that dialogue allowed for varying perspectives while containing the conflict within the boundaries of its discussion. In dialogues, both sides were usually argued with care, even though there was clearly a "right" and a "wrong" side. It was not always immediately apparent which side the author took; in itself, this could make the process of argument an important part of the presentation. It was not sufficient for readers simply to know the outcome; they also had to know how the outcome was arrived at. It was necessary to know the arguments on both sides, even though those oppositions were manipulated by the author's own hand. By highlighting the process of discussion, the dialogue form taught readers a process of political activity; readers learned to refute opponents' arguments and learned how to make their own. But some writers also feared that readers would not rise to the occasion and would be taken in by false rhetoric, especially when debates represented unbridgeable divides. Since debates allowed all perspectives to be viewed in public, writers worried that readers would fail to distinguish the right perspective from among the many wrong ones.

THEORY OF DEBATE AT PUTNEY

At first, it seemed as if the freedom in the press could lead to only good things. Open debate and public confrontation would resolve all disputes. This was the wish of Oliver Cromwell, who opened the meeting of the General Council of Officers at Putney, 28 October 1647, by explaining the procedures for what would become a most remarkable debate in English history: "That the meeting was for public business; those that had anything to say concerning the public business, they might have liberty to speak" (*PD*, 1). He cleared the way for speakers with differing perspectives to exchange ideas in what turned out to be a four-day political argument about the fundamentals of government. This was no idle forensic exercise: the participants at Putney were the victors in the first civil war against the king, and at Putney they sought to settle the form of government in England that would prevent the king from doing mischief in the future. While the debaters all agreed that the king must be prohibited from exercising arbitrary rule— they had fought the first civil war for this—they disagreed in the particulars.

In the late fall of 1647, several meetings took place in or near a church at Putney, where the groups who had fought with the king expressed their differences: Independents (Cromwell included) and the more radical parties of the Left, including the Levellers.[4] The Presbyterians (who were not present at the debates, but whose opinions were responded to nonetheless) had opposed toleration, seeking a national church controlled by the state, and they sought sovereignty from Parliament, emphasizing in addition to religious uniformity the need for protection of property. The Independents, in the center, advocated toleration for dissenters, yet agreed with Presbyterians on the protection of property if not on the means to effect that protection. Mistrustful of the Long Parliament, Independents sought a principle of biennial parliaments to limit the possibility of parliamentary tyranny. Then there were the radical groups, the parties of the Left, the sectaries, religious and political, who agreed on little but on religious toleration and freedom of conscience. The soldiers in the army, themselves aligning with the parties of the Left, had elected representatives, called "agitators," to press for their rights of back pay and to argue against negotiating a peace with the king whom they had just captured. They also advocated a much wider franchise than their allies the Independents did, and pressed for the implementation of the Levellers' "Agreement of the People," the attempt at a written constitution for the people of England.

The Putney debates widened the rift between the Independents and those on the Left. Natural law was at the center of this difference; the radicals John Wildman and Colonel Thomas Rainborough argued for a wide franchise, echoing the Levellers' campaign for universal manhood suffrage, and basing their arguments on natural law (*PD*, 38). Henry Ireton the Independent, on the other hand, wanted that right restricted to property holders. The ground of the Levellers' argument was as revolutionary as its proposals: they appealed to reason and natural law, as against custom, in their opposition to absolutism. At Putney, Rainborough, Wildman, and Ireton dominated the conversation, but many other men's voices were heard. The Putney debates themselves have occasioned much commentary, particularly with respect to the history of democracy.[5] They have been hailed as revolutionary: we hear, "almost for the first time in history, the case for a truly representative government being made."[6] Historians have found "implicit in it all—becoming explicit when necessary—the idea of *equal* rights, which is the distinguishing idea of democracy."[7] Putney was one example of the widening of political scope that began to include many opinions in the planning of government, a process that had begun during the Long Parliament's sitting. As one historian put it, during the Long Parliament, "the organic political nature had become pluralistic," and Putney served only to further this process.[8] At least at Putney, if not throughout much of the literature of the late 1640s, political participants hammered out their programs in a give-and-take that depended upon the "liberty to speak." If the Putney debates failed to achieve a political or practical resolution, they did succeed in terms of the process they validated. At Putney, I shall argue, the disputants may not have reconciled the divisions between the army and Parliament, but they did inaugurate a theory and a practice of debate, in word and in deed.

The participants in the debates at Putney were revolutionary not only in their political aims, but also in their methods: they called for freedom for all to speak; they urged protocols of debate, as the radical Captain John Clarke did in suggesting that "there might be a temperature and moderation of spirit within us; that we should speak with moderation, not with such reflection as was boulted from another, but so speak and so hear as that which [is said] may be the droppings of love from one to another's hearts" (*PD*, 75). Though Clarke advocated the law of nature rather than property as the basis for the franchise, his Christian language infused all the debaters' talk about their commitment to the process of debate, as when Cromwell reflected, "if I had not come hither with a free heart to do that that I was persuaded in my duty, I should a thousand times rather have kept myself away" (75–76). The articulate Leveller John Wildman urged that "we might proceed only in that way, if it please this honourable Council, to consider what is justice and what is mercy, and what is good, and I cannot but conclude that that is of God" (108). They debated in the spirit of Christians seeking God's way. Most important for us here, they debated not to display difference and to wage a battle, but to overcome differences and achieve "mutual satisfaction," which meant more than consent. Cromwell, who presided over the discussion, urged "that they should not meet as two contrary parties, but as some desirous to satisfy or convince each other" (22). For Cromwell and for the men who debated at Putney, the purpose of debate was "satisfaction," not specifically the arrival at truth. In this statement, in contrast to some that were to be made later in the debate, Cromwell promoted a practice of sharing differences of opinion in order to come to a political solution that did not represent certainty or political truth.

The first premise of the Putney debates was freedom of speech. Cromwell opened with an invitation to all, "that had anything to say concerning the public business, they might have liberty to speak": this was a call for free participation, without restraint of censorship. The army radical William Allen put it simply in a preface to his remarks: "Men have been declaring their thoughts, and truly I would crave liberty to declare mine" (102). Many times in the course of the discussions, this first principle was reiterated, and even widened in scope, for example, by Leveller Colonel Thomas Rainborough, who added that their debating should not only allow free speech but that it should also take place in public: "I think it an advantage that it should be as public as possible, and as many as may, be present at it. The debating this thus publicly may be an advantage to us" (44). The principle upon which the public debate rested was that all deserved to know the reasons for decisions, including those who were in disagreement: "And if we were satisfied ourselves upon debate, and yet there should be one party, or one sort of men, that are of a judgment at present contrary, or others that should come over to us, it would cost some time hereafter to know the reasons of their contrary judgment or of their coming over" (43–44). Speakers in the debate had to be accountable not only to each other, but also to others who were not present, for whom the outcome of the debates had profound consequences.

Free speech had its costs, however, as the participants at Putney knew. Time was first, as the radical Captain Lewis Audley expressed in weighing the practicalities of such public debate: "While we debate we do nothing. I am confident that whilst you are doing you will all agree together, for it is idleness that hath begot this rust and gangrene amongst us" (44). For Audley, unity could come only from action; debate was detrimental to that end. He likened the discussions to rust and gangrene, metaphors denoting the physical effects of neglect and inaction. Cromwell agreed with Audley only up to a point: "I make some scruple or doubt whether or no it is not better to adjourn the debate. I know that danger is imagined near at hand, and indeed I think it is; but be the danger what it will, our agreement in the business is much more pressing than the pressing of any danger, so by that we do not delay too long" (43). For Cromwell, a course of action was out of reach until some agreement had been made: "Let us be doing, but let us be united in our doing" (44). Cromwell was confident that in the end they would all agree, but he also knew that discussion was a prerequisite for unity.

Cromwell was sure that "satisfaction" was possible because he believed, as others did, that the differences between the debaters were not irreconcilable and that a fundamental agreement underlay all the apparent disagreement. The main task was to find it. Cromwell remarked that in the variety of opinions, "there have been several contradictions in what hath been spoken. But certainly God is not the author of contradictions. The contradictions are not so much in the end as in the way. I cannot see but that we all speak to the same end, and the mistakes are only in the way. The end is to deliver this nation from oppression and slavery, to accomplish that work that God hath carried us on in, to establish our hopes of an end of justice and righteousness in it. We agree thus far" (104). Cromwell's sense that disagreements were minor, "not so much in the end as in the way," meant that the debaters should expel their superficial disagreements once they remembered their mutual unity of purpose. In a sense, there was a unity of purpose; those who convened at Putney had all shared in the victory against the king's forces in the first civil war. Since their disputes were internal to Parliament and the army, the sense that they agreed despite minor differences was warranted. Cromwell attributed their differences to surface distortions that needed to be cleared away in a process of "unmasking" or "undeceiving." Captain John Merriman seconded Cromwell on this: "I think that when this Oedipus riddle is un-opened, and this Gordian knot untied, and the enemies of the same unmasked, it will be found that the dictates of the Spirit of God are the same in both, and the principles of both are the same" (35). Merriman's images make a bold comparison: the apparently irreconcilable disagreements at Putney are like the mythical Oedipal riddle and the Gordian knot, which prompted acts of epic heroism. Oedipus and Alexander the Great, both heroes, responded to these classic mysteries—by answering the riddle and cutting the knot—and their acts were among their first trials of heroism. Merriman's comparison expressed confidence that the conflicts at Putney would be resolved, like those mythical puzzles, and he further implied that their solution was on the same order as the epic heroes' primal feats.

But Cromwell's sense that contradictions were only temporary resting points along the road toward unity depended on an idea that the purpose of debating was to discover God's purpose. Cromwell asserted that "certainly God is not the author of contradictions" (104), and "if in sincerity we are willing to submit to that light that God shall cast in among us, God will unite us, and make us of one heart and one mind" (17). The task was to attain God's full perspective, which was uncontradictory and lay at the end of debate. John Wildman put it this way: "I observe that the work hath been to inquire what hath been the mind of God, and every one speaks what is given to his spirit" (107). The human conversation was prompted by God's spirit, and by conversing, these debaters would reach an understanding of God's designs.

During the English Revolution, politicians were having to get used to increasingly divisive issues, however; the ideal of a God-given single truth seemed increasingly remote. For the debaters at Putney, the idea of truth as agreement, where politics could be settled by mutual consent, could also lead down a more skeptical path of political praxis. As Colonel Ireton said, in dismay that no consensus could be reached on the question of property and the franchise, "when I see the hand of God destroying King, and Lords, and Commons too, [or] any foundation of human constitution, when I see God hath done it, I shall, I hope, comfortably acquiesce in it. But first, I cannot give my consent to it, because it is not good" (68–69); and later, "If God will destroy King or Lords he can do it without our or your wrongdoing" (123). God's message was not unequivocal; therefore, Ireton looked elsewhere for a conclusion. Likewise, the debaters at Putney pressed for consent and unity, and did not base their arguments on divine inspiration. The prominent army agitator Captain Edmund Rolfe put it thus: "I conceive that, as we are met here, there are one or two things mainly to be prosecuted by us; that is epecially unity, [the] preservation of unity in the Army, and so likewise to put ourselves into a capacity thereby to do good to the kingdom" (79–80). Unity was first. The idea that agreement was possible whether or not God's ultimate plan was known led to the striking appeal to the method of dialogue as a means of settling disagreements.

The idea of agreement being the goal of debate resembles the skeptical tradition of arguing *in utramque partem*, arguing on both sides of the question for rhetorical effect. In the pamphlet debates, writers relied upon their traditional education in disputation. While students at university, they were given topics to argue for or against and competed with one another on the floors of the public assembly. The chief rhetorical model for grammar school and for university students was Cicero, whose position as an orator and a statesman provided a goal for training boys into a life concerned with public affairs. This practice of humanist debate, learned at school, served politicians well in their civil war writing years. Like the Ciceronian orator, the debaters at Putney and elsewhere were concerned with matters of state. Such a training in classical oratory might have given educated men a tendency toward failed conviction, aware as they were that both sides of the question could be argued with strength. Humanist dialogue often did more exploring than settling of questions.[9]

Yet few at Putney had received university education; furthermore, their goal was not to explore all sides of a question but to reach a political agreement. Those at Putney could ill afford the luxury of *in utramque partem* disputation; as Audley had admonished, "while we debate we do nothing" (44). Settling on a course of action could be at odds with humanist training: the pamphlets were not like humanist dialogues, where skepticism often prevented a clear-cut conclusion. This skepticism about settling debates had to be left aside during the broiling civil war period, as debaters were arguing for their lives and souls. Though all had learned their schoolboy exercises, the participants in any case did not argue strictly according to the traditional forms of debate. Writers seemed to patch together what they could to persuade each other of their positions, aware that the audience was looking for persuasive reasons to side with one or another cause. But some of the skeptical tradition remained in the assumption that truth could be found in argument, and in moments of political necessity, this skepticism led to justifications for political actions based on public appeal.

FICTIONAL DEBATES AND THE DRAMA OF THE READER IN POLITICS

In *Areopagitica*, Milton claimed disagreement was not an end in itself, but a temporary condition on the way toward achieving truth. Other writers who used the model of debate were far more pragmatic; they sought mutual understanding, satisfaction, and accord rather than truth. By seeking accord in their debates, writers were reflecting a practice of political conduct that required public discussion and that was based on public opinion. By their preference for accord rather than truth, writers were admitting that contrary views were permissible, and even encouraging them. Both the ideology and the practice of public debate in the press give a blueprint for the public sphere, that arena in which open disagreement over issues could take place. The practice of writing in the public sphere was embraced by not only revolutionary writers; even the most committed Royalists, to whom the paper war was a sign of the disorder of the times, joined the debate in the press. By their very participation in the pen-wars, they conceded that argument in print could serve a purpose, and that the public conceived of as readers should be aware of more than one side.

The debates written during the civil war period differed from the traditions of rhetoric in one important respect, however: they were fiction, and they relied upon the literary concept of speaking through indirection. As Thomas More hinted in his *Dialogue of Comfort*, the medium of dialogue could protect the author from charges of treason, since authors could present dangerous positions without committing themselves to any one by writing under the disguises of personae.[10] As a fictional genre, the debate relieved authors of responsibility for all the opinions expressed in their works. Drama had long been a tradition in which political discussions could take place, under the clasp of censorship, as Margot Heinemann has shown; a Renaissance dramatist like Thomas Middleton presented criticism of Crown policy by putting into characters' mouths the dangerous ideas.[11] The pamphlet debates offered performances that continued this oppositional practice even after drama was banned.

The fiction of debate allowed the expression of divergent, and potentially radical, views. Thus through the format of the dialogue writers seized the opportunity to make free speech. For example, the writer of *A Dialogue betwixt a Rattlehead and a Roundhead* (1641) found that the dialogue was formally useful in exploring the many sides of an issue. In this pamphlet, two characters, a "Rattlehead" and a "Roundhead," overcome their differences by realizing that they both share an enemy, the Canterbury bishops. The Roundhead had hoped to lead his interlocutor down "that perfect road, by which, [to] tread the ready way to heaven"—this is surely an echo of Arthur Dent's best-selling *The Plain-man's Pathway to Heaven* (1601)—if he'd only "renounce your Church you follow now, and turn to us." The Rattlehead, too, wanted to convert the other: "hear me speak, and but compare your form of government with ours, I'd soon transport you to a heaven of happiness, by changing your opinion, and confute you by your own words."[12] Their dispute was broken up, however, by a third, "Neutralis," who, by presenting the bishops as an enemy to both, unifies the two sides. This pamphlet dates from 1641, a very early year in the conflict, when hopes for such a mutual resolution were realistic. Later, as we shall see, the differences would become too great for such temporary accord.

The author of *The Soldier's Language; or, A Discourse between two soldiers, showing how the Wars go on* (1644) exploits the freedom of a literary form to speak dangerous words, putting criticism of the king in the mouths of the characters. In the sixteen-page pamphlet, Jeffrey and Nicholas discuss the matters of the wars, considering some of the criticism of the king they have heard. Both have fled Roundhead routs, one at York, and the other at Bristol, and they lament the defeat of Prince Rupert and the king's forces, identifying themselves as supporters of Charles. While at first it seems that this is a royalist tract, the conversation between the two men reveals the true allegiance of the pamphlet as soundly antiroyalist. Through the technique of ventriloquism, the author is able to present a point of view (here a phony Royalist's) while at the same time providing an ironic commentary on it.[13] Jeffrey asserts that Prince Rupert's mistake was in not engaging enough papists to fight on his side, since only papists would remain loyal to him: "I would have him put none into his great office, or place, of trust, but such as were absolute Papists." The implication is that only a papist would support the king. Reason would persuade any but papists to change allegiance: "whereas if he choose any one that stand indifferent, when he is better informed, he will recant, and revolt." Jeffrey reassures Nicholas that the king's forces are strong nevertheless, reinforced by "all the Papists generally from the greatest to the least, the devil cannot turn them; we have the Pope, Cardinals, Jesuits, Monks, Friars, Abbots; we have the Bishops, Deans, Prebends, yea all rank of them, from the Archbishop, that sits with one foot on the throne, even to the journey-man Curate." To boot, the king can rely upon "almost all the ignorant people" because, as Jeffrey reasserts the "Papist's" claim: "Ignorance is the mother of Devotion, for we may see by experience where ignorance bears the most sway, the King has best subjects."[14] The two characters are "dummies," two personae the author has employed to do the work of persuasion.

The characters themselves speak the accusation that the king's court is thoroughly papist, rather than the author speaking it himself, as they discuss Parliament's objections to the judges and bishops and denounce the king's misuse of prerogative. The finally agree however that argument alone shall not decide these matters, but that force will try the strength of the cause: "for all that they shall know that we have martial law, and what we want with the Word, we will make up in the Sword: and what we want in arguments we can make up in stones." In his ironic conclusion that violence is the answer, the author rejects the process of discussion altogether. For these soldiers, actions mattered, not words. The ultimate message of the pamphlet is despair. Neither character is ideologically committed to his cause, as Nicholas reveals when asked what he would do if the Roundheads won. He admits he would submit to either regime: "I will cut off my locks, and be as zealous as any of them all: but if I see the Papist get the better, I will go along with them to Mass for company, as dogs go to church." The jab is at the papist, who is a servile beast. Further, Nicholas sees no real difference between the two sides: "I have been with them many times at Mass, and I see little difference between it and our Common Prayer, only the one is in English, the other is Latin, otherwise for aught I know, the one may be as good as the other." The author indirectly treats the controversy over the prayer book, which the Scots and Puritan ministers made the chief issue in their dispute with the king. Nicholas's statement is a pro-Puritan ironic comment on the book: he asserts, as they did, that it is indistinguishable from a papist document. But this soldier cares little whether it is "Papistical" or not, since it matters little to him which side wins.[15]

Through ventriloquism, the author has managed to lodge several barbs in the side of the Royalists, taking advantage of the form of the literary dialogue to present the real situation to the eavesdropping reader, who hears the soldiers speaking freely. The reader learns the king's forces are stuffed with papists. The author is protected by passing the responsibility for his treasonous words to his fictional characters. *The Soldier's Language* shows how the form of dialogue allows the writer the freedom to explore dangerous topics, and to express views that could not be stated directly. The conversants in *The Soldier's Language* explored many views, and ultimately, the reader would have to choose which one was right. By presenting their opinions through such fictions, writers could invite readers to interpret for themselves.

In *A Dialogue Betwixt a Courtier and a Scholar* (1642), for instance, though two sides never come to an agreement, the reader is left in the position of deciding among the positions. The Courtier and the Scholar meet while traveling and they discuss "several passages of state" along the way, since the Courtier wants to know which of the two sides is favored "by the Vulgar." Though the Scholar informs him that Parliament is their choice, and explains why, nevertheless the Courtier adamantly asserts he will not be swayed from his allegiance to Charles. The pamphlet is filled with the Scholar's thoughts on the king's abuses, yet what holds the Courtier back is his repeated declaration: "I am a Courtier"; nothing will change that. The Scholar complains that such intransigence is precisely the problem: "such hath been the corruption of courtiers . . . that it hath begot a universal diffidence in the people."[16] The Scholar may not have convinced his auditor in this particular case, but he may have made the reader rethink a position or two.

The author admits that his mission on the title page was, like the mission of most debate pamphlets, "for the further satisfaction of the common people." Yet by this fictional form, the author is self-censored, saved from the dangerous consequences of his indictments by this fiction of indirectness. The writer hopes that, unlike the fictional figure of the intractable Courtier, "common people" may be persuaded by what the Scholar says or what a Courtier might recant. And the pamphlet is not all puff; rather, during the course of the debate, the reader is forced to consider a list of the king's offenses: monopolies, his forced loans, ship money, and his "endeavor to advance the Prerogative beyond its due limits," reigning "over us as a conquered people by his will."[17] After reviewing this list, readers of this pamphlet come to understand Parliament's specific grievances against their king in a way that the Courtier, ever loyal to this tyrannical king, cannot. Though the Scholar and Courtier are locked in an irreconcilable situation, the pamphlet may have some real effect on its readers to change their minds.

The press, whose freedom had allowed the expression of a much wider spectrum of political thought than had been published before, was becoming the vehicle of full-scale open debate. The tract *Against Universal Liberty of Conscience* (1644) takes the form of the "Animadversion," a literary mode that presented both sides of an argument for the reader to judge.[18] The two points of view are presented side by side on the pages of the pamphlet, which the reader must compare. Though the "right" choice is announced by the title (*against* liberty of conscience), the enemy argument nevertheless is entertained seriously. In a reversal of the expectations of the reader, the author at first vouches, "I every day grow stronger for an universal liberty of conscience." In the course of the pamphlet, however, the reader is drawn through a process of refuting this opening statement. The typographical layout of the tract forces the reader to confront directly both sides of the question, since arguments of the pamphlet are presented in two columns. The column on the left (pro) is glossed by the right-hand column (con). The right-hand animadversion "reads" the left-hand assertion and provides judgment and commentary: "An universal conscience, is an universal liberty to sin, to maintain heresy, to practice Idolatry, to vent Blasphemy; in a word, an universal liberty to dishonor God, under pretence of serving him." The pamphlet continues in this manner, presenting an assertion as well as an opposing commentary. Caught in the tension between the two, the reader must decide which is right. The animadversions form shows a dialogue in action, a kind of conversation between two opposing sides. In *Against Universal Liberty of Conscience*, and in many other pamphlets like it, the author allowed that there were two possible sides to take on the issue, and did take each one seriously. Readers come away with more than an opinion; they are shown also how to make objections; how to "read" political assertions properly; and how to refute them. The pamphlet gives readers means to defend themselves against their enemies, not by censoring the enemy position, but by including it in the process of persuasion.

Writers used the dialogue form not to allow the reader to come to any conclusion, however, but rather to educate the reader to view both perspectives, and to choose the "right" one. In imitating the religious dialogue form, further, writers drew upon a genre traditionally intended for the religious instruction of the common people in this period, in which questions would be posed by a beginner and answered by a teacher, representing the process of indoctrination into the church. During the civil war period writers used the genre of catechism to urge readers to make political commitments, as they reached for a popular readership. The literary model of catechistic teaching was a tried-and-true publishing success; Arthur Dent's *Plain Man's Pathway to Heaven* (1601) was the best-selling religious tract of the seventeenth century, having gone through twenty-five editions in forty years. Dent, the rector of South Shoebury in Essex, was renowned as a preacher and popular sermonizer, and he represented his Puritan Essex brethren in his clashes with Bishop Aylmer over matters of religious practice. His dialogue, which was intended to educate even the simplest of readers in the rudiments of faith, took place in a meadow between a divine and an "honest man," who engaged in religious discussion, at the honest man's urging. The honest man stood for the reader and represented a commoner. By writing in the dialogue form, Dent embraced readers of all kinds: "I write to all of all sorts: I speak not to some few of one sort."[19] The two debaters were joined by two other villagers, an "ignorant man," who, at the end of the four-hundred page octavo, thanks the divine for his "true conversion unto God"; and "a caviller," also called an atheist, who provided comic relief by acting the part of the gadfly. This work accommodated the honest, the ignorant, and the caviling. The form itself created a drama for the reader, an instruction not in how to refute the interlocutor but, instead, in how to learn to answer questions.[20]

Given the solid tradition of such a popular form, it is no surprise that the genre of religious debate was snapped up by the political writers of the English Revolution who sought to convince a popular readership of their own doctrines. For instance, *A Soldier's Catechism* (1644) was a handbook for men fighting on the parliamentary side, and the author used the question-and-answer form to explain Parliament's cause. The respondent in the pamphlet answered questions about the causes of the war and about the proper conduct of soldiers while his interlocutor probed the particulars of the parliamentary line. The authoritative answer is merely a question for the soldier, however: "Hath not the King published many Protestations that he will maintain our Laws, Liberties and Religion? Why then do we fear the subversion of them?" The soldier is supposed to act in this pamphlet, not merely to receive doctrine. The reader/soldier is peppered with questions that urge him to take an active part in thinking about politics: "How can you that are Soldiers for the Parliament, answer that place of Paul, Rom. 13.1,2,3, etc."[21] Paul's exhortation to the Romans to be subject to higher powers becomes a site of contention, as the reader is questioned about Parliament's legitimacy in rebelling from the king. In directing questions to his readers, the interlocutor raises concerns that every English citizen had to answer in order to choose sides, questions that were vital for the justification and legitimation of Parliament's army. In this pamphlet, the student was not only to use his ears; he was supposed to ask good, hard questions that indicated a high degree of interest and willingness to learn about the matter. The reader, reading this pamphlet, was to become judging and judicious.

Indeed, the didactic debates could make the reader attuned to the nuances of rhetorical argument by the very process of probing. The debates provided readers with a voice, and made it legitimate for them to ask questions. They taught the student ultimately to become the teacher, to be able to interrogate authorities, and to fend off objections on his or her own. The example of Elizabethan religious writing provided a model for civil war writers who adapted this tradition of dialogue with some of the same aims as their predecessors: they directed their writing toward a popular audience, with a didactic intention. Yet the civil war writers took the religious formula into a new arena: political warfare. Indoctrination was necessary for political, not only for religious, commitment, as *The Soldier's Catechism* shows. Most important, the civil war dialogues themselves, though sometimes presenting little in the way of real exchange, nevertheless provided readers with active roles in fending off adversaries.

Fictional debates did not always lead to a clear-cut conclusion, however, with the "student" merely parroting the authority's opinions at the end. It was part of the revolutionary practice of debate not only to impart knowledge, as the evangelical model would, but to engage readers in specific ways: to make them alert, active, critical judges. In a patently unresolved debate, a writer risked turning readers over to possible enemies as a necessary gamble in this process of political education. For example, the reader has to play an active role in the civil war dialogue pamphlet, *A Late Dialogue, betwixt a Civilian and a Divine* (1644), in which the citizen, rather than acting as a passive vessel for the Divine's knowledge, has been busy reading and is full of questions himself. The citizen is in need of instruction and guidance, to be sure, but the character is shown thinking, probing, acutely aware of important issues of the day. The writer of the fictional dialogue forms engaged readers by directing them to identify psychologically with the character—here, the pupil—represented on the page. In *A Late Dialogue*, the pupil engages with his tutor over the issue of independency, questioning the relation of the church to the state. The title page of this pamphlet sports the Puritan slogan "Prove all things: hold fast that which is good" (1 Thess. 5:21). This slogan stands as a motto for allowing readers to choose; it forces the good and the bad to be tested together, as two debaters in argument, where both sides must be presented for view, a version of Milton's trial by contraries in *Areopagitica*, which also deploys this slogan (2.512). Only if both sides are presented can the good be known.

Though the aim of the pamphlet is to convince the civilian to agree with the teacher, in *A Late Dialogue*, the civilian's specific questions are an important part of the process. The pupil begins by asking his teacher about the pamphlets of the Presbyterian William Prynne, with whom he is inclined to agree on the issue of one national (uniform) church. The pupil has read Prynne's *Independency Examined* and *An Answer to a Letter to a worthy Gentleman*, and has found these convincing. The civilian's questions are intelligent, and his sympathy for Prynne is respected: Prynne is quoted directly and fairly. In the pamphlet, however, the "divine" spends a good bit of time repairing the civilian's error. Prynne is criticized respectfully: "Though Mr. Prynne be a man much esteemed by me," the divine insists, "both for his sufferings, and much good service done by him in the Church, yet I must say, he wrongs both the Truth and himself, in taking upon him to go against the whole current of Interpreters" on the question of the shape of the re-formed church.[22] The Divine is sensitive to the citizen's preferences in reading material.

The citizen is represented as a reader of controversial texts; his conversation with his superior is based on his reading. It is significant that his questions derive from reading not only the Bible, but also the pamphlets. This citizen/reader brings an active political sensibility to the teacher, and receives a training in *how* to think about such pamphlets, almost as much as he learns *what* to think. The Divine confesses that he too has "seen and read the book [*The Answer*]," though he was not taken in by it. The Divine worries that "simple people, who never yet saw a Presbytery, may be made afraid of it, as of some hellish monster," because of the writing made powerful "by the special Inspiration of the father of lies." He assures the citizen that "men of understanding will not be taken with such bold and shameless calumnies as come from the pen of that son of Belial."[23] Though readers come to agree with the teacher's position over the course of the pamphlet, and come to reject Prynne's views, they also engage in arguments with the teacher about their reading. The world represented in this text is a world of readers who are arguing about what they read.

The idea of a capable readership found its way into many of the pamphlet exchanges of the period. William Prynne replied to an enemy's attack not by making a sustained self-defense or refutation, but by urging that his readers act on his behalf by comparing his own words with those of his enemies: "I shall desire the ingenious Reader, only seriously to peruse the several quotations this Cobler [his enemy] hath botched together," with the result that "then the Fallacies, Falsities, and Calumnies of this Anonymous Patcher . . . will need no further Refutation." Judging readers must come to Prynne's defense. Though Prynne's exhortation to the jury of readers is preceded by four pages of accusations against his assailant, the author urges readers to make up their own minds. Encouraging readers to check the disputed sources for themselves, Prynne suggests that the source texts are shared by the whole reading community at large and are open to public examination. "*Si judicas, cognosce*, was the ancient rule: I pray therefore get and read my quoted authors . . . hereafter, before you presume to charge me with misquotations," rattles Prynne, citing the Senecan dictum.[24] Final authority for interpretation—and thus his own vindication—derives from the reader's ability to make judgment (*judicas*). Prynne assumes that his reader will make a "right reading," provided that the reader has access to those texts and may personally confront them. Simply to force his audience to read, he believes, is to muster sufficient support.

Prynne's use of the Senecan rule *Si judicas, cognosce* dictates a theory of "right" understanding, which his opponent's "misreciting, dismembering, other men's works, to be a seeming refuter of them" has failed to achieve. The attacker has used Prynne's text falsely, as a "botcher" might. Demanding that his reader compare the enemy text against his own, Prynne points to several evidences of misquotation, where that enemy reader has "taken unnecessary pains, to cull out here and there a word or line, out of his [Prynne's] writings on several subjects, and then patched them up together into inferences and arguments of his own forging." Prynne's assailant has read incorrectly, arriving at an interpretation that was untrue to his text, true only to himself, "fighting only with his own shadow, and mangling, misreporting, perverting all the passages he recites (as the reader may at first view discern) instead of answering."[25] Prynne's conception of a "bad" reader, then, is one who sees only "his own shadow," who reads only pieces of the body he does not perceive as a whole, and who thereby dismembers and "mangles" that body out of recognition. The "bad" reader does these things not only for himself, but also for others to whom he "misreports" his readings. The last accusation makes sense only in a context of printed, disseminated, and shared texts, in a world where texts attract a public.

The assumption is that there is a proper way of reading Prynne's texts, one not employed by the author of *The Fallacies*. Prynne asserts that a good reader "may at first view discern" the failings in his assailant's interpretation, and thus he gives a compliment to the reader of his own pamphlet, who is being educated as a "good" reader. That reader must view both texts at once—his own and his assailant's—in a public space of free judgment, like Milton's "free and open encounter" between Truth and Falsehood presented in *Areopagitica* (2.561). At the end, the author of *The Falsities* throws his own defense to the judgment of his readers. The charges of "other pretended points of Popery, perverting of Scripture, of Laws, Treasons, and betraying of the Cause," are "so abundantly answered, refuted in my Books at large, in the pages quoted by this Author, that I shall wholly appeal to them, and the indifferent perusers of them, both for my Purgation and Justification, in all particulars." His books and his readers will defend him, and the reader for Prynne is the judge.[26]

This world of readers further included unlearned members, who, though they were used to reading religious printed material, were not before this moment the targets of political conflict. For this group, political controversy was imagined to be a new, and a potentially dangerous matter. Simple readers are the focus of the pamphlet, *A Medicine for Malignancy* (1644), in which the author explains the choice of the literary form of the dialogue, "that it may be profitable to all," thus reiterating the motive of religious catechistic writers to reach the common people. In deference to these readers, the author claims to "have observed a very plaine method, and homely style, not desiring to clothe that with elegant expression that is intended for vulgar satisfaction." The point is that "the ignorant be informed, the wilful reformed, the seduced undeceived." In the pamphlet, the author presents his dialogue between a Royalist and a Loyalist: a supporter of the king and a supporter of Parliament. The Royalist poses questions to the Loyalist in a debate. But, as in the pamphlets examined above, the royalist auditor does not passively accept the Loyalist's ideas. Though the Loyalist talks most in the pamphlet, the Royalist asks questions that penetrate right into the heart of the conflict between king and Parliament. Near the end of the ninety-four page pamphlet, the Royalist claims to be converted: "I do heartily thank you for the satisfaction you have given me in all, now I see abundance of people in the Kingdom are wonderfully deceived, I shall by God's grace hereafter adhere to and assist Parliament to my utmost."[27] In *A Medicine for Malignancy,* as in other debate pamphlets, "satisfaction" comes only through answering questions and overcoming objections. The formula of debate gives the reader an enlarged role in the polemical literature of the period.

DEBATE OR DISAGREEMENT: IRRECONCILABLE POLITICAL CONFLICT

While the debates both at Putney and in some of the pamphlets considered in the early part of this chapter present discussions between members of roughly the same side (pro-Parliament), many of the pamphlets that represented confrontations between members of opposite sides, Parliament and Royalist, have a different character. In these cases, there were no illusions that agreement could be reached amicably. Rather, writers clashed as opposites, stuffing their pamphlets full of insults, taking any opportunity to attack one another, certainly not searching for common ground. In representing debates between parliamentary and royalist sides, writers fashioned political arguments as irreconcilable, producing the polarities of propaganda campaigns. During the course of the war period, when allegiances hardened, agreement seemed almost impossible at times. When Calibut Downing republished his 1641 pamphlet, originally called *An Appeal to Every Impartiall. . . Reader: Whether the Presbyterie or Prelacy Be the Better Church Government,* he chose a new title in 1644: *The Clear Antithesis or Diametrical Opposition Between Presbytery and Prelacy,* reflecting the polarization of political discourse. What appeared to be possible for the "impartial reader" to adjudicate in 1641 was no longer capable of being settled in 1644. Rather, readers now had to decide between two contrary positions.

The point of this divisive writing was sometimes not for one side to appear the victor in the debate, but for the conflict to be resolved by the viewer. In their increasing polarization of the options for readers, writers demanded that readers themselves pick sides. In *A Dialogue betwixt a Horse of War and a Mill-Horse* (1644), the author presents a discussion in the form of a beast fable, where enemy horses discuss the wars.[28] The author, using the familiar artistic representations of the Cavalier and Roundhead to satirize both sides—the Cavalier whose bravado is in excess of his ideological commitment and the Roundhead who is morose to a point of humor—implies that those who fight on either side are beasts. The Horse of War is a dandy: saddled, boasting spurs, an ornate saddle, and a long mane—all accoutrements fit for a cavalier. To make the point typographically, the

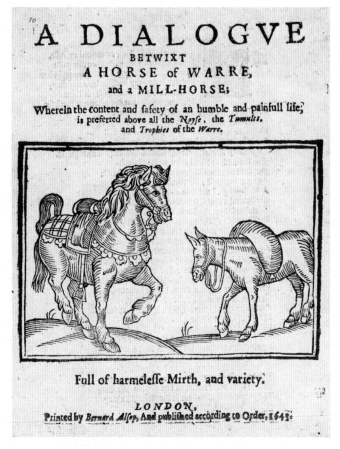

3. Frontispiece to *A Dialogue betwixt a Horse of Warre and a Mill-Horse* (1644).

author chooses "White letter," or the roman font, for the Horse of War's speech. The Mill-Horse, on the other hand, speaks in "Black letter," the typeface used in works meant for the common people, and also to signal radical Protestantism. The Mill-Horse is a beast of burden, and he stands with his head and eyes turned piously downward, without a mane or ornamental bridle.

The (Cavalier) Horse of War urges the Mill-Horse to join in what he sees is the best fun of the day. He admits, "I care not for the liberty nor laws, / Nor privilege of subjects, nor the cause," but fights mostly because "I have no more Religion than a Horse." The Mill-Horse would rather stay at the mill than fight the wars, and is rewarded for this cowardly admission by the Horse of War with "a round answer with some kicks." The action of the pamphlet ends with violence, as if there can be no resolution between these two sides but through force. The dialogue seems to offer yet another occasion for a drama of hate, but the author finally offers his own judgment: "the country is by Cavaliers undone," intoning that, "the content and safety of an humble and painful life is preferred above all the Noise and Trophies of the War." In this debate, where force is seen to shut down discussion, both sides in the political conflict are demolished through satire: both are beasts.

Other writers were pessimistic about the possibilities of resolving such political discussions, representing arguments that seemed to lead nowhere. In *A Dialogue, or Rather a Parley between Prince Rupert's Dog . . . and Toby's Dog* (1643), for instance, violence is imagined as the only conclusion to debate. The title page features a picture of two dogs, Puddle and Pepper, surrounded by their human friends and owners. Again, stereotypes of Cavalier and Puritan are pictorially mimicked in the presentations of these animals: Prince Rupert's dog, Puddle, bears the marks of a Royalist—the long, curly hair, spurs on his fat legs, and a tail that looks suspiciously like the plume in a Cavalier's hat—and Toby's dog, Pepper, fits the stereotype of the Puritan—thin to the point where his ribs stick out, with short hair and a plain tail. Pepper barks at his rival, addressing him as "Cavalier Dog," and his enemy snaps back, "Roundhead Cur." Their masters call out, "to him Puddle," and "Bite him, Pepper," as incitement to the two to fight. Instead of brawling right away, Toby's dog insists, "I'll bark before I bite, and talk before I fight," mimicking the human war of words. Toby's dog admits he is of a "More reformed condition" than Rupert's dog, and calls the other a "popish profane Dog," who is "no more than half a devil." Still, he is persuaded by Rupert's dog, who manages to convince him to swear an oath of allegiance to the Cavaliers, to promise to bark henceforth at Roundheads, on the grounds that Lent is coming up, and Toby's dog dreads losing his meat. "I desire to be better fed than taught," Toby's dog admits before converting. The pair are interrupted however by a third dog, Prince Griffin's, who attacks Prince Rupert's for preying upon such an innocent: "Thou worm of wickedness, fritter of Folly, spawn of doggedness, and piece of mongrel stuff"; Toby's dog, Pepper, is not his match: "no, he is too mild for thee: thou should have given notice of your treaty and discourse to me who am thy equal."[29] This third dog chases Puddle off the scene with threats, furiously defending the honest but seduced Toby from the Cavalier.

The author has made literal the insulting metaphor "Dog" by presenting real dogs at battle: to this writer both sides are dogs. By reducing a political motivation to the issue of feeding time, the author also cynically interprets how people in general were thought to be making decisions. Skeptical of the entire process of public debate, this author implies that innocent folks like Toby's dog have been choosing sides according to the dictates of their bellies or by flowery rhetoric of their betters, and not according to reason. The third dog, who rescues the seduced innocent, only reasserts traditional rank, since in his defense he merely joins in the battle rather than working

4. Frontispiece to *A Dialogue, or Rather a Parley between Prince Rupert's Dog . . .
and Toby's Dog* (1643).

toward some resolution of difference. Even this victor seems reluctant to
take on the issues of political conflict. The differences, it seems, are too
deep to be considered reconcilable, and the only job left is to cancel the
effect of the Cavalier dog by force or by conventional hierarchy. The third
will do this by promising to "proclaim thee [Rupert's dog] a coward in
print, and set thy name upon every whipping post and pissing place, for all
the dogs in the Town to lift up their legs to piss against." Vitriol is the final
and winning mode.[30]

Many pamphleteers thus rejected a model of rational debate and mutual
persuasion, claiming that force rather than logic would win arguments. In
an oppositional libel by Royalists, might has already overpowered right, as
the Rump song "The Power of the Sword" (ca. 1653) chides:

> Lay by your Pleading, Law lies a bleeding
> Burn all your Studies down, and throw away your Reading;
> Small power the Word has, and can afford us
> Not half so many Priviledges as the Sword has.

The pamphlet also asserts, "'Tis not in season, to talk of Reason, / Or call
it Legal, when the Sword will have it Treason." A winning kick, or a sword,
had more power than an acute *refutatio*: "Take books and rent-um, who
would invent'um / When as the Sword replies, *Negatur argumentum*."[31] Such
pamphlets repudiated rhetoric and mistrusted the methods of argument
and debate.

The Leveller John Wildman, one of the representatives for the army at
Putney, had warned the soldiers of the army to "take heed of crafty politicians and subtle Machiavellians, and be sure to trust no man's painted

words; it being high time now to see actions." He continued in his attack on the practice of delay that Ireton and others seemed to be using to wear down their opposition in the Putney debates: "One of the surest marks of deceivers is to make fair, long and eloquent speeches, but a trusty or true-hearted man studieth more to do good actions than utter deceitful orations." Wildman is aware of the protocols at Putney, but he is distrustful of them: "One of the surest tokens of confederates in evil is not only, when one of his fellows is vehement, fiery or hot in any of their pursuits, to be patient, cold or moderate, to pacify his partner, and like deceitful lawyers before their clients to qualify matters, but sometimes seem to discord or fall out, and quarrel in counsels, reasonings, and debates, and yet nevertheless in the end to agree in evil." Wildman suggests that the Putney debate may fail to settle questions at all, and he attacks Cromwell and Ireton specifically, calling them "false sophisters" and "treacherous deceivers," who are "like the former courtiers, [who] can always play the hypocrites without any check of conscience." Wildman urges his readers to end their discussions with these leaders since there seems to be no possible solution to questions of the franchise and parliamentary sovereignty: "But if you will show yourselves wise, stop your ears against them. . . . Hold not parley with them, but proceed with that just work ye have so happily begun, without any more regarding one word they speak."[32]

Wildman's attacks on the proceedings at Putney underscore a central question raised about the literary form of debate, particularly in light of those pamphlets which substituted brute force for rhetorical argument: To what extent were the pamphleteers who represented their ideas in debates interested in real exchange? Was agreement really possible? In many cases, instead of leading to rational argument, persuasion, and agreement, literary debates only hardened polarities by setting up irreconcilable oppositions. Debates did initiate readers into participatory politics, but they also encouraged readers to become fighters, and to be suspicious of the war of words.

PAPER-PELLETS AND PEN-WARS

Were these writers offering a sincere invitation to readers to entertain opposing ideas, or were they closing off debate by appealing to the known prejudices and habits—both literary and political—of their expected readerships? Regardless of the ideological orientation of the writer, evidence comes in on both sides of this question. In their pamphlet duels, these writers sometimes spoke less to convince an undecided audience than to shore up support for their own side. Though the war of words in the press could enact a revolutionary drama of public political exchange, however, in their literary warfare, authors also sharpened their disagreements by drawing stereotypes, often narrowing the range of political discourse to two stark alternatives. As we shall see, the pamphlet culture included both kinds of appeals.

Like the Puritans who adopted the biblical slogan "He who is not for us is against us," the political and religious leaders of the seventeenth century forced citizens to choose sides in terms of polar opposites. In the English civil wars, the lines were often drawn with such absolute certainty. Pamphlets written about the "Anti-Parliament" in Oxford, during the king's residence there in 1644, constructed a binary formula, where two sides of an identical sign system told exactly opposite stories. This Anti-Parliament was the negative version of the "true" Parliament sitting in Westminster. The rivalry between the newspapers *Aulicus* and *Britannicus* was a token of the same split. Many pamphlet titles with the prefix "Anti-" circulated in this period, madly attempting to negate and undo the power of their inverted target: *The anti-confederacie* (1644), *The Anti-Covenant* (1643), *The Anti-Remonstrance* (1641) are examples; to these we might add the many "Antidote" titles, which expressed differences in terms of health and sickness, disease and remedy. Even the term "Malignants," Parliament's name for those loyal to the king, derived its power from the opposition between health and sickness. The labels "Kingdom" or "Commonwealth" told opposite versions of state organization. The ever-familiar Cavalier/Roundhead diad drew upon the sharpness of the opposition.[33] Anti-popery posed the most glaring example of this style of propaganda, preying upon popular fears and armed by the long vernacular tradition of anti-papist sentiment and imagery. The dichotomies are visible in the rhetorical strategies of the works as well as in their titles. Through inversions, exaggerated language, and popular stereotyping, writers called out to their readers to decide between two options in severe terms. Such a starkness forced readers into a tightly constricted space.

Debate could occur even within the imagery of a single pamhlet. We have seen Milton use dichotomizing rhetoric in *Areopagitica* when he asked his readers what kinds of judges they were going to be. Were they going to be like the Inquisitors, with "the privilege of the people nullify'd" (*CPW* 2.541), or were they to fulfill their destiny as a "Nation chos'n before any other" (552) to complete the work of the Reformation? Milton, however, limited his readers' choices to two, and one of these was not really a choice, since Milton used the Inquisition images to strengthen his own position. Nonetheless, Milton's whole argument is cast as a set of decisions the reader must make, even though there was a "right" answer implicit in the options. By construing his world in terms of either/or statements—The English are either "slow, dull" *or* "quick, ingenious" (551); an "untaught and irreligious gadding rout" *or* "judicious, learned, and of a conscience" (547); should they suffer "servitude," whether Philistine or Italian, *or* live under "English liberty"—Milton forced the reader to side with the free English. Milton's ample use of anti-Catholicism makes the choice appear easy to make.[34] In his images and by his name calling—the practice of censorship is "Spanish"

(519), though it derives ultimately from Catholic Italy (530)—Milton urges Parliament to unite against a common foe, by means of a "unification device" that stands as a keystone in his argument.[35] In *Areopagitica*, Milton seems to present a choice between two options that is at times no choice at all.

The kind of caricaturing that gave Milton's pamphlet its peculiar charge was common to the polemical writing of the civil war period, as stereotypes of the opposite sides were represented with striking regularity in pamphlets throughout this period. In *Areopagitica*, Milton set a choice before Parliament in a kind of debate. By repeatedly distinguishing his chosen nation from those degraded ones, Milton hoped to win readers to his cause by forcing them to demarcate their motives and practices from those living under Catholicism. With ferocity and persistence, Milton evoked the Inquisition to elicit a formulaic response on the part of the readers, exploiting the age-old tactics of anti-papist propaganda.[36] Throughout his tract, Milton strategically uses the myth of the tyrannous papist to clinch his argument with emotional force. But he countered these myths of the tyrant or of the papist with a myth of his freedom-loving reader, as we saw in chapter 1. Milton distinguishes between those places like Italy, where tyranny holds sway, and England, home of philosophic freedom. Like those authors of pamphlet debates, Milton represents the English people by these two irreconcilable images in order to challenge his readers. In *Areopagitica*, Milton dares his readers to reject the ugly picture of what they might become, and sets out his theory of capable readers who were to exercise their choice by viewing the two examples, and by choosing to become free. In *Areopagitica*, Milton built the theory of the capable reader into the rhetoric of his piece by facing the reader with two alternatives. In the debate between these two positions, however, there is clearly a "right" answer. What seems as important as coming up with that right answer, however, is following a process of reasoning that involves choice between two alternatives. Milton's dichotomizing strategy reflects the nature of civil war discourse, and reiterates in its theory of choice the contemporary genre of debate.

In the fictional debates, characters were imitating actual civil war writers who battled with one another in the press. When John Taylor shot at John Booker in his *No Mercurius Aulicus*, for example, John Booker and an army of imitation "Bookers" fired right back with *No Mercurius Aquaticus, but a Cable-Rope Double twisted for John Taylor*; John Taylor responded with, *John Taylor, being yet unhanged, sends greeting to John Booker that hanged him*; Booker soon answered this by a request that Taylor kill himself, in *A Rope Treble-twisted for John Taylor*. This entire war of words took place in the space of three months in 1644.[37] Even those to whom the paper war was a sign of the illness and fraudulence of the times joined the written debate. By their very participation in the pen-wars, they conceded that argument in print could serve a purpose, though they railed against the frenzy of "paper-pellets," likening the cacophony of voices to Babel, as we have seen. It was common practice for a single pamphlet to set in motion a volley of pamphlets in response. At times, the arena of pamphlet conflict seemed to be inhabited by very familiar suspects, a small clique of writers who mentioned each other by name. The authors assumed there was a world of shared texts in which the readers were reading. Though more immediately, Booker's first pamphlet responded to the July pamphlet in which Taylor had taken up "the breaking of BOOKER," whom he called "the Asse-tronomical London Figure-flinger," in *No Mercurius Aulicus*; Booker's new response pamphlet, *No Mercurius Aquaticus but a Cable-Rope Double twisted*, answered to Taylor's January pronouncements as well. A "Cable-Rope double twisted for John Taylor," was the means by which Taylor was to hang himself, and this allusion referred to yet another pamphlet in the war of words, his own *Rope for a Parrot*, printed four months earlier. A single text thus referred to a network of texts. Such exchanges would be forgotten the next month, as another pamphlet war would take center stage.

The political culture of the English Revolution thus veered in two directions: toward opening up political exchange by inviting readers to participate in making up their own minds by reading, and also toward shutting down conversation by seeking to engage readers as partisans through propaganda. Closing off real debate between opposing sides, the two principal newsweeklies, for example, became symbols for their respective causes, so that merely the name *Mercurius Aulicus* became a code word for the king's cause (the Latin title literally transplanted the court orientation to the medium of print), and *Mercurius Britanicus* for Parliament, as easy to identify as the Roundhead and Cavalier stereotypes whose pictures adorned the ballads and the pamphlets of the period. Pen-battles between the two figures raged throughout the pamphleteering of this period, as these two newsheets took human form and personalities became characters in the satirical poetry and drama of many pamphlets. The clash between Aulicus and Britannicus shows the degree to which confrontation between two opposing sides could lead to no resolution, evidence of the wide gulf between partisans. Daniel Featley took a shot at *Britanicus*, the parliamentary paper, for example, in *Sacra Nemesis . . . or Mercurius Britanicus Disciplined*, disapproving of "every hackney pamphleteer, every mercenary scribler . . . among these Britanicus is the busiest."[38] Even Milton in *Areopagitica* made an allusion to *Aulicus*, writing of "that continu'd Court-libell against the Parliament and City, Printed as the wet sheets can witness, and dispers't among us" (*CPW* 2.528). The antics of these two newspapers were represented in many pamphlets, and the paper war between the two seemed to epitomize the entire political conflict. *Aulicus his Hue and Cry after Britanicus* was a six-page drama showing Aulicus searching the streets and taverns of London for his adversary, finding Britanicus at last sick in bed at Westminster, unable answer the string of invective Aulicus lets loose at him.[39] *The Recantation of Mercurius Aulicus* for example, was an antiroyalist parody of the royalist newspaper. *The Recantation* presented Aulicus as "the Darling of the Court, that [courtiers] prefer it before the Bible." In this caricature, Aulicus pompously laments that he is no longer believed, that his enemies have won more support because they write in "plain English," admitting that this was a battle not only over ideologies, but over styles.[40] When writers alluded to the split between the two newspapers, they were very often commenting on the starkly opposing content of the two sides in contemporary political argument.

Attacking names and titles was a kind of stereotyping, necessary for the mobilization of an audience around a symbol. In attacking his enemy, the parliamentary apologist John Booker had asserted that [John] "Taylor" was no single person, but a "name," a synecdoche for his whole party. He evoked this name in his long title, *A Rope Treble-twisted for John Taylor, or rather for his Malignant friends in London, which make use of his Name to slander and abuse the Parliament, and well affected party in their pernicious pamphlets*, and insinuated that royalist pamphleteers were using Taylor's name to attract readers. His evidence for this accusation that others had been writing under Taylor's pen name was that the pamphlet *John Taylor, being yet un-hang'd* was printed in London, when it was known that Taylor was in residence with the king at Oxford. Booker concluded that Taylor's associates were printing the material in London, and that Taylor was but one of a group of royalist writers. This is why Booker attacked the Malignants as a group rather than John Taylor alone.

The pamphleteers repeatedly used the names of the pamphlets to stand for their parties, a sign that partisan battle was quite firmly embedded in the thinking of the time. A supporter of Booker, self-styled as "Philo-Bookerus" in his *Mercurius Vapulans*, directed his atack at the same George Wharton whose almanac had evoked Booker's reply. Philo-Bookerus claimed, "your party are very sufficient Railers, even Naturalized into detraction and lying." Choosing to attack a "party" in addition to the stated target of the single writer, Philo-Bookerus continued, "Every one of you is as another *Aulicus*."[41] By this account, "Aulicus" had become the code name that stood for *any* Royalist. The choice of the code name Aulicus is significant, not only for political allegiance it signified, but because the actual *Aulicus* was not a person, but a written and a published document. By evoking the name Aulicus, authors assigned human properties to an ideology or political position, and made the activities of writing and publishing pamphlets the very symbol of royalist enterprise. The titles of many Mercury pamphlets (e.g., *Mercurius Aquaticus, Mercurius Melancholius, Mercurius Pragmaticus*) were also used as if they were names of persons. The names referred of course to the pamphlets' authors, but the practice of identifying pamphlets with authors suggested that pamphlets themselves were human and could exercise human power; or that they represented identifiable political positions. Prynne's *name* was made into an abstract concept by his enemies: "his name only has rendered his subitane Apprehensions, in deed and truth such, to seem good and solid Reasons."[42] The *name*, rather than the man, was able to exert such power. Such abstraction I take as a sign of ideological battle.

If every Royalist was an Aulicus, as the author of *Mercurius Vapulans* claimed, then every anti-Royalist was a Booker. One's enemies would be predetermined by the name under which one chose to write. Both sides participated in these name-cloaking devices, but since both Taylor and Booker were paid party hacks, in making the individual names stand for a cause or party, writers accurately assessed political responsibility as belonging to parties. The battles in print between writers then involved not only the writers, but also their friends, backers, and, ultimately, the English public as a whole. The pen-wars thus show the workings of a patronage system reapplied to current political needs.[43] The profession of letters had only just begun to be freed from the constraints of aristocratic patronage, with the public beginning to take up the role as patron.[44] During the civil war, however, political participants began to see the use, indeed, the necessity, of writers. Both sides depended upon hired writers to present their cases to the public; Parliament voted several times for favorable books to be dispersed; Cromwell had ordered a propaganda campaign to diffuse the mutiny in the army in 1647; and the king had surrounded himself with a loyal band of writers in his hideout at Oxford in 1644.[45]

Though there may not have been clearly defined structures of party patronage during the civil war period, and though there may not have been clearly articulated party positions, from these pamphlets, nevertheless, we can infer the existence of some kind of organization, even if it worked only at the level of rhetoric. Still, this level was highly significant in eliciting public support. The texts themselves refer to the political contours of literary patronage. When John Booker replied to John Taylor's attack, he fired back at Taylor with *No Mercurius Aquaticus*, designating his target, Taylor, in the title. Yet Booker writes that his reason for returning Taylor's accusations is his concern for *Parliament's* reputation, not his own. These are his opening words: "I should be loath to foul my fingers with any base pamphlet that comes from Oxford, if the venom of their malicious spleens were darted only against my particular self; But when through my sides they wound the honour of Parliament, and our Armies abroad, I cannot but set Pen to Paper, and pay them back again in their own kind."[46] Booker writes not only to defend himself, but also to defend publicly his political allies in Parliament (that he was rewarded by Parliament accounts for his loyalty).[47] Likewise, when Booker attacked Taylor, his accusations were not merely directed at Taylor alone, but at those whom Taylor supported by his writing, the king's men. Booker accused Taylor of writing only for money, and worried that his own attack was merely "giving you occasion to raise a fortune with scribbling pamphlets." It is true Taylor was then in the king's service at Oxford. "Thou art a most expert Taylor"—Booker pokes fun at his adversary's name—"and canst easily take measure of the University Intellects, and fit their Phantasies with a paper-work presently."[48] This accusation plays on a rhetoric of deference due to rank; Taylor is a servant to those university intellects, both as a fitter to their clothing—a mouthpiece for their opinions—and also as their hired underling. Through this metaphor, Booker exposes Taylor as a tool of these "University Intellects," lower in social status than they, servile to their interests, willing to "fit" their desires by his productions. Taylor is a clothier, an employee only with an eye to please his patrons; elsewhere, he is figured as a "parrot," an inhuman reproducer of human sounds.

In their paper wars, the authors are self-conscious about the place of patronage and politics in the literary system. In his response, *John Taylor, being yet unhanged, sends greeting to John Booker that hanged him lately in a pamphlet called a Cable-Rope double-twisted* (1644). Taylor goes on to accuse not only Booker, but also Booker's colleagues: "thy Consorts," whom Taylor proceeds to name: "May, Wither, Britanicus, the Scout, the Dove and all the Rabble of lying and reviling rebels," mixing the mens' names with titles of proparliamentary newsweeklies. Taylor's battle, finally, is not with Booker, but with a crowd of writers with whom Booker is allegedly allied, *and* with the ideas he represents. "Booker" has become a composite character *and* a political ideology. While Taylor hastens to identify Booker with his confederates, he is evasive, however, about his relation to his own associates. On the one hand, he reveals his allegiance to his friends at Oxford: "we at Oxford are true Protestant pen-proof, and the King, Queen, Princes, Clergy, University, Army, Magistrates, and Commons, are slander-proof, so that neither your rebellious fighting, or reviling writing, can wound, blemish or sully the majestic lustre of Royalty in the sovereign, or the obedient expression of duty in the subject"; on the other hand, he dissociates himself from the king in order to protect him, arguing that Booker ought to attack the writer and leave the king alone. "It was I that galled and spur-galled thee to the quick," Taylor vouches, "and thou (like a blind Jade) could not see me alone that did it, but thou must fall a snapping and snarling at the King, the Queen, etc. . . . thou shouldst only have meddled with me that mumbled thee." Taylor thus substitutes his own person for the issue at hand, preferring to sacrifice his own reputation rather than to see his king suffer. Thus by ad hominem gestures, Taylor reduces the power of Booker's writing to no more than a personal attack:

> But 'tis the old trick of your Pulpiteers and Pamphleteers, to draw the more attention, and entire Coxcombs and Knaves to buy your damnable roguish riffe raffe, to mix and blend some scandalous lies, and traiterous jeers against our Sovereign, and his most gracious government: for it is a Rule among you, that if there be no Treason in the Sermon, or lying Calumniations in the printed pamphlet, the one will never be liked or rewarded, nor the other be bought and sold.

Leaving only the sting of personal invective in a typical "reducing" display of satire, Taylor refuses to take on the real issues in Booker's writing. By turning the political into the personal, Taylor easily distracts attention from the ideological substance of the pamphlets and concentrates instead on manners; this move closes down political discussion altogether. Taylor transformed debate in the pamphlet into a personal struggle and erased the ideological matter.[49]

In his reply two months later, Booker refused to play this game. In *A Rope Treble-twisted for John Taylor, or rather for his Malignant friends in London,* Booker named the addressees boldly; it was now not just Taylor but also his "friends" who were identified by a code name, "Malignant," which contemporaries would read as those counselors to the king who were leading him astray, according to the parliamentary account of the day. The title made clear that John Taylor was not the enemy, but rather that all the Malignants were—and Malignants not in Oxford but in London. In this pamphlet, Booker sees through Taylor's feint of treating their dispute strictly as a personal one, claiming that Taylor "strives not so much to clip Mr. Booker's credit with his Popish scissors, as to wound the Parliament, and all those that are well-affected to their Cause and just Quarrel." Booker suggests that real object of Taylor's attack is not the man (here himself), but the powerful institution behind him: Parliament. Booker defends Parliament by showing that it is the real target of Taylor's attack; he calls his enemy's book "John Taylor against the State," asking, "was ever such language as this vented against the honour of a Parliament?" Booker then defends Parliament, rather than himself, by taking up the exact language of Taylor's pamphlet: "neither your Peers, Clergy, University, Army, Magistrates, are Pen-proof, because they are neither Parliament-proof, nor Reason-proof."[50] The twist is that Booker has substituted the words "Parliament," and "Reason" for Taylor's phrases "Royalty in the sovereign" and "duty in the subject," as the ultimate authority over allegiance. This substitution, like Milton's calling his pamphlet *A Defense of the People of England* in response to Salmasius's *Defence of the Rights of Kings,* of course, made the crucial point on which his party stood: the location of authority rested in the Parliament, not in the king. Yet the two men also assert different relations to their parties; the parliamentary John Booker defends his cause while the royalist John Taylor defends only himself. The distinction between the two parties' tactics here is politically significant. The royalist Taylor retreats from ideological arguments, and chooses instead personal forms of attack and defense. The proparliamentary author Booker, rather, takes on the ideological weight of the battle. Both sides could look as if they were playing at the same game, but they were really expressing very different philosophies of public appeal in their pamphlets.

PERSONAL POLITICS AND ROYALIST PROPAGANDA

The royalist Taylor figured his political ideas through personal attack and thus avoided the realm of ideological debate, the public sphere. Those defending the monarchy did take their case directly to the people by publishing, as did Taylor, yet they dismissed the notion that the people ought to participate in politics by ridiculing and chastising them. The royalist press, set up at Oxford in 1641, worked along with clandestine presses in London to perpetuate an image of a divinely authorized king in order to discourage those whom they called rebels from persisting in their rebellion. The royalist weekly squib, *Mercurius Aulicus,* which began publication out of Oxford in 1643, was aimed at the upper classes, as designated by its price: three pennies in 1643, rising to eighteen pence by 1645; in to contrast *Mercurius Britannicus,* the parliamentary newspaper, which sold for a penny (the price of a quarter pound of beef).[51] *Aulicus* had a wide readership, to be sure, with its five thousand weekly press run passing from one hand to another, but its buying audience precluded those of the middling or lower sorts.

Royalists often opposed the political participation of the people, and they did so not just through political theory, but through personal attack. Debate was avoided in favor of satiric name-calling. The election to the Commons in 1649 of Philip Herbert, fourth earl of Pembroke, who had once been Charles's lord chamberlain of the royal household, caused quite a stir in the press as the royalist pamphleteers skewered Pembroke in a series of pamphlets that took him severely to task for being a turncoat. Satirized for his prostration before the people, Herbert is reported to have wooed his voters by a speech in which he claims, "The Place I stand for, is, Knight of the Shire. None but Kings can make Knights, make me your Knight, you are all Kings."[52] The author mocks the notion that the people thought they could take the king's place. Another royalist pamphlet reported Herbert's maiden speech before Parliament, in which he explained his change of allegiance: "I am not very good with speeches, but had rather make twenty i'th'Lower house here, than one upon the Scaffold. . . . For a Lord to turn Knight is only to wear his coat the wrong side out. Its a hard world now; Lords may be forced to turn their clothes." As Pembroke cravenly saves himself from the same fate as met King Charles, the antipopular thrust of the pamphlet is painfully clear: "I would I had been a Brewer, or a Cobler, or any thing but a Lord." Pembroke's habits of swearing and his love of the hunt appear in this satire, which finally suggests that his love of beasts attracted him to Parliament: "Mr Speaker, I hope 'tis not unlawful to keep Dogs, Keeping Dogs, Mr Speaker, is no swearing. I love Dogs, and I love the Parliament; I may love Dogs, and yet not love Kings; I must love Dogs now, Mr Speaker, for else why was I chosen Knight of Barkshire?"[53] The pun adds the crowning effect. Another pamphlet—there are at least five that concern Pembroke's political defection in 1649—recounts a speech in which Pembroke works to secure "the people's liberties": "We are the keepers of their Liberties; and if we keep their Liberties, we ought to keep their Money too, their Law and Religion, nay, their very Wives if it please us."[54] Rather than expressing an antipopular theory of politics, these pamphlet authors pressed their messages through personal attack, assuming Pembroke's switch was based upon personal gain rather than upon a political position. Not only did Pembroke's suing for the people's support in his election campaign come under fire, but the message was that by catering to the people's wishes, Pembroke was catering to a pack of dogs. The idea that the people deserve no place in politics is here expressed through personal satire.

These pamphlets reveal a royalist practice of "personal politics," which is fully in line with the rhetoric through which Charles ruled his courtiers: a rhetoric of love and personal loyalty. During his reign, Charles himself had cultivated influential subjects rather than the people in general when it came to important state matters.[55] As Kevin Sharpe explains, "in a society organized around personal connections, in a commonweal founded upon patronage and clientage, personal relationships were often intrinsically and obviously political, as indeed political relationships were personal."[56] Sharpe here does not outline precisely what he means by "political," though in his thorough and close-contextual treatment of Caroline court poetry in his book *Criticism and Compliment*, his sense of politics is narrowly construed as "high politics," and not politics in the broad sense of the power relations that interest American new historicist literary scholars. In his analysis of love poetry and masques, Sharpe emphasizes the Stuart court's neoplatonic, spiritualized themes, proving the court's inundation with political interests via aesthetic forms.[57] Sharpe properly argues that the Stuart masques and country poetry, as kinds of Cavalier poetry in general, were not exercises in escapism; rather through them, men seriously engaged with moral and political topics. And through the conventional forms of love poetry and the neoplatonic masque, Sharpe and others have argued, criticism of Charles's policies reached the king himself. By drawing upon the languages of love and courtliness, political discussion could take place, one-sided and covert though it may have been.[58]

Royalist political practitioners thus avoided open debate. Recent literary scholars have argued that masques do not monolithically deliver unreflective flattery of the king, but rather show how political disagreement was conducted through them at court. Patronage affiliations and court personalities may have been the marks of royalist power relations, but royalist political protocols allowed that political disagreement could take place in the private setting of the king's playing chamber, filtered through literary convention, within the constraints of patronage relationships. Courtly love poetry was not merely about human effections or eros; love, rather, was the bond that held humans together in society and was thus the language through which to negotiate political and social arrangements. "Private languages sustained quite public argument," write Steven N. Zwicker and Kevin Sharpe.[59] Along with the masque, an excellent example of the "private" public sphere in which political confrontation could occur is the royalist preoccupation with romance as a genre during the civil war period. Both king and queen identified with romance as their personal genre, and, with their marriage held up in countless poems of praise, as Annabel Patterson has argued, this choice strengthened his political image. Pastoral and romance were habits of thought inculcated by Royalists; the name of the royalist newsbook *Mercurius Rusticus*, for example, held up the pastoral image of court. During the Interregnum, allegory and romance became vehicles for royalist political expression and discussion. By their allegories, royalist authors' texts, as Patterson sees them, "would have been either inscrutable to Cromwell's censors, or sufficiently oblique to avoid direct confrontation."[60] Royalist romance thus sought a coterie audience, not a general crowd, as its readers.

If the masque's function was to teach and criticize the king, the means for this instruction and criticism were nevertheless not for the public's eye. Royalist political practice was therefore intensely antipublic in the sense that Royalists often resisted direct and open confrontation with political issues. The Interregnum saw a spate of royalist works published, many of them collections of pastoral poetry that engaged in political issues only obliquely. Allegorical romances, too, were a favorite genre of Royalists. The noted plagiarist Robert Baron offered "Fortune's Tennis-ball: A Moral Fable," an account of the life of a prince brought up by bees in a forest:

> In an old hollow Oke, whose top a Swarme
> Of Bees (the Muses Birds) had made their hive
> They left the Child, with Gold, and 'bout his arm
> Bracelets and Jems whose Shine with's eyes did strive.[61]

The oak, where Charles I had purportedly hidden from parliamentary troops, had become a symbol for the Stuart monarchy, and this poem, in slightly veiled language, expresses its hopes for the young Charles II. The prince's natural majesty and riches are safeguarded by bees, long a politically charged insect, standing for a natural political order in an Aristotelian fable often used to support divine right monarchy. Baron's poem continues its allegorical description, using the language of Stuart court patronage to describe the bees' caretaking of the young king: "These their Loves gave, that who so him should find / Might be, if not their Loves, for wealth's sake kind." Romances such as this one, and Cavalier poetry in general, asserted a natural hierarchy that found expression in aesthetic as well as in political principles.

Royalist sensibility flourished through such works, which used the language of pastoral and romance to express antipopular, antiparliamentary sentiments. Lois Potter's excellent study *Secret Rites and Secret Writing: Royalist Literature, 1641–1660* analyzes how genres such as romance and tragicomedy were codes signifying royalist allegiance. According to Potter, for instance, Davenant's *Gondibert*, while not articulating a coherent royalist ideological position, was nonetheless a "coded narrative [whose point is the] creation of a world where, as in royalist propaganda, private motives are privileged over public consequences." Potter demonstrates how in royalist writing the two Charleses "acted out virtually every role available to a ruler in romance or drama: the disguised lover, the husband parted from his wife/kingdom, the loving father of his country, the sacrificial victim, the wandering prince." This dramatic role reflected the royalist perception of reality. "For royalists," Potter explains, "the world after 1642 *was* an appalling confusion of classes, creeds and genres, and the only acceptable model for events was one in which a divine purpose could be seen fulfilling itself slowly but surely." Potter argues that royalist literary practice in the Interregnum cultivated a "philosophy of secrecy," in which Royalists chose the only means available to a suppressed group, "enabling communication and consolidating its sense of itself as an elite," thus agreeing with Patterson's formulation of censorship as a determining condition of such writing.[62] Yet my argument here is that Royalists wrote through a "philosophy of secrecy" not only because of the conditions of censorship and political oppression, but also because something in royalist political thought preferred secrecy to publicity. Royalists chose the private sphere in which to conduct politics because to them, politics *was* a private matter. Coterie art, and "personal rule," as historians call the years during which Charles ruled without parliaments, were the preferred means of kingly political reflection. It is significant that covertness and indirectness were features of Caroline poetics even before and after the conditions of Interregnum censorship, and these literary qualities may be seen as the conditions of the royalist public sphere.

If political conversations between subjects and their ruler were private, this practice was buttressed by the political theory most often used to prop up Stuart kingship, patriarchy. James I had set out the patriarchal theory of kingship in his *Trew Law of Free Monarchies* (1598): "The king towards his people is rightly compared to a father of children, and to a head of a body composed of divers members, for as fathers the good princes and magistrates of the people of God acknowledged themselves to their subjects."[63] Sir Robert Filmer, setting down the classic of partiarchal political thought, sums it up in *Patriarcha*: "I see not how the children of Adam, or of any man else, can be free from the subjection of their parents." Filmer explains that the order of things does not leave "it any place for such imaginary pactions between kings and their people as many dream of."[64] As J. P. Sommerville explains, "patriarchalism was at once an account of the origins of government and a description of the nature of political power."[65]

England under Charles may have been operating under a mixed monarchy,[66] a theory elaborated by Philip Hunton in his *Treatise of Monarchy* (1643), yet the imagery of King Charles, all his cultural force, was patriarchal in style. The words given to Charles in *Eikon Basilike*, a work purportedly his meditations in prison before his execution, are full of patriarchal imagery. Not only are English citizens likened to the king's children—"If they [the people] had been my open and foreign enemies, I could have borne it; but they must by my own subjects, who are, next to my children, dear to me"—but the story of Noah and his transgressing sons is brought out to chastise those who published the king's correspondence: "I am sure they [those who seized the letters] can never expect the divine approbation of such indecent actions, if they do but remember how God blessed the modest respect and filial tenderness, which Noah's sons bore to their father; nor did his open infirmity justify Cham's impudency, or exempt him from that curse of being servant of servants; which curse must needs be on them who seek by dishonourable actions to please the vulgar, and confirm by ignoble acts their dependence upon the people." In this analogy, the disobedient people have acted as Noah's sons, "forgetting that duty of modest concealment which they owed to the father of their country."[67] Here duty to one's country is figured not as an abstract commitment to virtue or contract or rights, for example, but as filial loyalty, and that entailed secrecy.

In consequence, the subscription to a familial understanding of the relations between sovereigns and subjects bore on the royalist practice of political disagreement . If family relations were the basis of politics, then there could be no ideological disagreements between subjects and their king, merely personal or generational grabs for power. As Charles was purported to have lamented, "they hate me with a deadly hatred without a cause." Repeatedly his courtiers and his subjects in *Eikon Basilike* were rebuked for their ingratitude and personal disloyalty to Charles, who bemoaned "the ungrateful insolencies of my people," finding that this ingratitude was a test of God: "we see God is pleased to try both our patience by the most self-punishing sin, the ingratitude of those who, having eaten of our bread and being enriched with our bounty, have scornfully lifted up themselves against us; and those of our own household are become our enemies." Finally, the cause of the entire civil war was only personal: "the production of a surfeit of peace and wantonness of minds, or of private discontents, ambition, and faction, which can easily find or make causes of quarrel, than any real obstructions of public justice, or parliamentary privilege."[68]

The most popular of royal romances, *Eikon Basilike* beautifully illustrates the point that royalist politics preferred to take place in a private sphere. *Eikon Basilike* spoke a private language, a letter between a father and his son, yet through it, Royalists reached out to an audience of the English nation at large. *Eikon Basilike* reflects a practice of presenting history or political ideas in the form of a letter, a fictional genre that suggests immediacy, veracity, and freshness.[69] In Charles's case, this long letter to his son was clearly intended for a readership of English citizens, but *Eikon Basilike* preserved its personal intention by appearing as a private document in every way. From the book's published format—the earliest editions were duodecimos, tiny books that could be slipped into one's pocket—to its chapter-by-chapter prayers, *Eikon Basilike* purports to be the private musings of a man facing death. The "penitential meditations" reflect Cavalier poetry of meditation, and the whole style of the piece is remarkable in its private public sphere. After the king gives an account of his actions—the calling of the Long Parliament or the signing of the execution of warrant for earl of Strafford—he presents a prayer, calling on God to witness that the acts were taken against his conscience, or that God can judge the rightness of his acts. After the public statement comes a private one. The work was a culmination of a personal style of politics, making its political points through private means.

Patriarchalism as a political theory had consequences for the style of politics of the Stuart court. The rhetoric of love and personal loyalty worked within the general theory of patriarchal political thought to which Charles and the rest of his court subscribed. Critics have explored how patriarchalism infused every aspect of the aesthetic and cultural practices of the Stuart courts.[70] The royalist notion of political conduct as a private matter, the *arcana imperii,* was of an altogether different color than the theory of debate at Putney, or than much of the practice of polemical controversy in the press.

•

Debates had opened up the possibilities for real exchanges of ideas, but the fact of English revolutionary debates did not always bear out this ideal. Rather, debates offered occasions for propaganda and coercive rhetoric, especially visible in pamphlets written under the sign of one or another patron. Debates had promised a free exchange of ideas and indeed presented occasions for true conversation and conversion, as had happened with the antiroyalist disputants at Putney. Yet literary debate served another purpose: to sharpen issues, forcing readers to participate by choosing between only two options. The literary form of debate could harden existing oppositions while protecting the writers from the possible implications of those polarities. As many of the civil war fighters and writers insisted, "he who is not for us is against us," and by constricting the parameters of discussion, writers contributed to the symbolic divisions that resulted in propaganda. In the next chapter, we shall examine how writers expressed their growing awareness of both kinds of propaganda as they sought to combat its coercive effects over readers.

Reading in the Revolution

EIKONOKLASTES *AND THE BATTLE OF PERSPECTIVES*

Fighting only with his own shadow, and mangling,
misreporting, perverting all the passages he recites (as the
reader may at first view discern) instead of answering.

William Prynne, *The Falsities*

Nor shall their black veiles be able to hide the shining of My
face, while God gives Me a heart frequently and humbly to
converse with him, from whom alone are al the
Eradications of true glory and Majesty.

Charles I, attr., *Eikon Basilike*

And those *black vailes* of his own misdeeds he might be sure
would ever keep *his face from shining*, til he could refute
evil speaking wilth wel doing.

John Milton, *Eikonoklastes*

BY 1647, Oliver Cromwell's revolutionary army had defeated Charles's
forces on the battlefield and had forced the king to surrender at Oxford.
Rather than celebrating their successes, however, Cromwell's army was dividing into factions. The mutiny in the army began with the soldiers' call for
back pay, but soon London radicals added their own demands for "fundamental liberties of free-born Englishmen," in their "Agreements of the People." Cromwell believed that the parliamentary cause could not survive
such divisions. By May, strong measures had to be taken to quell the rebellion of the army, since any negotiations for peace with the king could be put
at risk by such disunity in the parliamentary cause. Responding to this new
challenge, Cromwell charged his military council not to use force against

the mutineers, but to wage a different kind of battle: "keep a party of able pen-men at Oxford and the Army," he ordered, "where their presses be employed to satisfy and undeceive the people." He further stipulated, "Do all things upon public grounds for the good of the people, and with expedition, to avoid divisions and for the prevention of bloodshed."[1]

These injunctions amount to a propaganda campaign, authorized by a desperate Cromwell, who, like our own leaders, saw the necessity of good press coverage. As a supplement to the force of combat, he believed, war must also be won in the press. In requiring his supporters to pay attention to how their actions were represented, Cromwell tacitly acknowledged that rhetoric was a constitutive element of his own power, to be manipulated according to a desired political end. Cromwell's public contradiction of his enemies belongs to an era where politicians became newly self-conscious of their political conduct and made themselves accountable to the public, where subjects' allegiances were to be decided by airing issues, not by traditional patronage, not by monarchical injunction, not by the pulpit, but by the leadership of those who had to convince others of their legitimacy through public appeals.

By his injunction, Cromwell admitted that readers were having to grapple with conflicting perspectives. Cromwell's missive offers us a firsthand reflection on the political conflict taking place in the press as he ordered his own writers to correct the erroneous or "deceptive" interpretations of his enemies. He acknowledged that in the climate of polemical debate, readers' allegiances might be drawn away by enemy rhetoric. Many of the pamphleteers during the English Revolution were deeply concerned that their readers be taught to resist enemy opinions or "deceptions." Cromwell's program to "undeceive" in his plan to defeat the mutiny among his soldiers involved a battle over a public thought to be held captive by an enemy. In "undeceiving" the people, Cromwell used a word derived from the Latin root *capere*—"capture," taking prisoners, thus evoking the idea of a military rescue—yet this campaign was not to free a soldier, but a reader. As the volume of writings published during the revolutionary period suggests, books were prime ammunition in what was becoming a war of words.

How were these readers going to avoid being taken in by propaganda, "deceived," as Cromwell put it? In this chapter, I explore how writers equipped readers to read properly. Writers, Cromwell's "pen-men" included, sought to retrieve those readers from seductions by more writing. They posed the debate between contrary political positions as a question of interpretation, a subject that is taken up in this chapter's discussion of that most successful piece of royalist propaganda, *Eikon Basilike*. This work's detractors, John Milton included, claimed that the book had "dazzled" men out of a true perspective. In his own writing, Milton aimed to unmask the king's rhetoric so that the truth could shine out, and he presented to his readers an education in reading and resisting propaganda. The function of debate may have been to teach readers how to refute, and thereby to resist their opponents; the pamphleteers I examine in this chapter take these lessons for readers a step further, seeking to educate readers in interpreting political rhetoric.

To understand propaganda as a phenomenon in its full cultural significance is beyond the scope of this book, which is primarily concerned with the fashioning of an audience by rhetorical means. Yet we may make some preliminary observations here based on our understanding so far of the seventeenth-century pamphleteers' rhetorical practices and with the foundation in theory provided by Jacques Ellul's classic study, *Propaganda: The Formation of Men's Attitudes*. Ellul analyzes propaganda as a sociological, rather than as a strictly rhetorical, phenomenon, though his discussion of the mutual relation between the producers and consumers of propaganda holds promise for our understanding of the ways this kind of writing works. Ellul is concerned to show that propaganda is possible (and indeed necessary) in democratic societies; surprisingly, he argues that propaganda is a feature of societies in which people's opinions *count*. Propaganda is not created by an evil few to dupe the many, argues Ellul; rather, there is a mutual relation between the propagandist and the propagandee. Propaganda responds to the fact that a people are hungry for news and information and opinions; the propagandist complies with that need. Propaganda works only in those societies in which the public can be informed and can think of itself as politically meaningful. In thinking about those qualities in the public which make propaganda possible, Ellul suggests that indeed, "the informed opinion is indispensable for propaganda."[2] Traditional studies of propaganda have examined how propagandistic writing evokes a system of signs, how the producers of propaganda manipulate their audiences by orienting those systems of signs and by drawing on their power.[3] In the early modern period, that anti-Catholic masterpiece, Foxe's *Acts and Monuments*, which preyed on English citizens' fears of popery and which itself influenced panics among the populace at repeated intervals in English history, is an excellent example of the kind of propaganda that makes use of a symbolic system.[4] In fact, English revolutionary propaganda does rely heavily on seventeenth-century society's worst fears—that Charles was secretly a papist or that those in Parliament were an anarchic mob.

Our interest, however, is not strictly in the semiotics of propaganda, but in propaganda's demands upon its audience, since those demands parallel the notion of a fit readership that is this book's subject. Ellul's understanding of propaganda as a two-way relation between producer and consumer is therefore more helpful to our understanding of the English revolutionary reader than the semiotic approaches taken by historians and sociologists. In Ellul's scheme, what propaganda does with the public's need is rhetorically significant. To that hungry public, propaganda offers information that is filtered through the intentions and opinions of the producers, and "aims less at modifying personal opinions than at leading people into action. This is clearly its most striking result: when propaganda intervenes in public opinion, it transforms the public into an acting crowd or, more precisely, into a participating crowd."[5] Propaganda mobilizes a group into an active public.

When I look at this English revolutionary propaganda, Ellul's thinking leads me to ask, what are the relations between author and audience? During the English Revolution, writers' conceptions about audiences were precisely the grounds of differences in opinion. In the fictional pamphlets of the English Revolution, we see that some authors were not allowing that the public might be a player in politics at all, and they employed an authoritarian rhetoric whose premise was that the audience was not fit to make decisions for itself. Such English revolutionary writers offered few choices to readers because they worried about the effects of opinions in public over an unlearned public. Hobbes, for example, compared the common people's minds to clean paper, suggesting that they were impressionable to any powerful idea: "the Common-peoples minds, unlesse they be tainted with dependence on the Potent, or scribbled over with the opinions of their Doctors, are like clean paper, fit to receive whatsoever by Publique Authority shall be imprinted in them."[6] In this attitude, we see a rejection of the notion that the people could participate in politics. Yet this kind of statement admits that politics was becoming a two-way affair between leaders and their public. In my historically attuned examination of author's assumptions about audiences, I suggest that such a hostile attitude toward the public was a marker of the rise of the public sphere: writers recognized, even in their hostility, that political writing was involving the people in powerful way. Propaganda was being recognized as a potentially dangerous force because the people were viewed as participating in its success.

GULLIBLE READERS AND THE WAR OF INTERPRETATIONS

With as much bombast as hope, Milton addressed his fellow countrymen in *Areopagitica* as "a Nation not slow and dull, but of quick, ingenious, and piercing spirit, acute to invent, subtle and sinewy to discourse, not beneath the reach of any point that human capacity can soar to" (*CPW* 2.551). In his concern that English citizens side with the quick and ingenious rather than with the dull and simple, Milton was responding to a powerful myth circulating during the English Revolution, the myth of what might be called the "gullible reader." As conservatives looked out on the level plain of the press, they saw political novices—gullible readers—taking part in the national reading revolution. Horrified at this vision, they imagined a second Babel had arrived, as we saw in chapter 2, as they conceived of most English citizens as incapable of making judgments for themselves. To add to their fears of social anarchy and popular insurrection, they believed that the populace would be powerless against the seduction by persuasive writers. They saw their writing as a rescue mission for those naive readers.

For writers using the myth of the gullible reader, this reeducation had a hermeneutic component: writers felt compelled to show readers *how to read* the enemy arguments properly. In his pamphlet *The Contra-Replicant* (1643), for example, Henry Parker feared that readers were being duped by the superior rhetoric of the king's writers. Like the Prince's dog, Puddle, who won Pepper to his side because of his greater rhetorical prowess in *A Dialogue . . . between Prince Rupert's Dog . . . and Toby's Dog* (1643), Parker claims the king's pen-men are able to "catch" the popular sort by rhetoric. "None but the duller sort of people are to be catcht by pure Oratory," Parker writes. "The wiser sort are well enough instructed. . . . [The king] aims not at the satisfying of wise men, but the dazzling of simple men."[7] The task for Parker and for writers like him is to educate that audience of "simple men" to resist being duped.

William Prynne offers us a case of a writer thought to hold enormous sway over his gullible readers. Prynne, it must be remembered, was the most prolific English writer of the seventeenth century. Known for his diatribe against the theatre, *Histriomastix*, and for the loss of his two ears, Prynne was a mythical figure among the pamphleteers because of his unstoppable pen. During the course of his long writing career, he managed to antagonize and to suffer punishment from just about every possible authority, from Charles I and Archbishop Laud in the 1630s, to the Independents and the army during the Interregnum. After the Restoration, he backed the returning King Charles II, and was rewarded for it. With over two hundred pamphlets to his name, it is no wonder that he was embroiled in some of the most fiery pamphlet battles of his day. A graduate of Oriel College, Oxford, and a Lincoln's Inn lawyer, Prynne had been educated as a gentleman, but was accused of catering to the vulgar tastes of the public for reasoning badly, if simply. Both his royalist enemies and his Puritan supporters deplored his popularity. Like John Lilburne, Prynne made himself a spokesman for "the people," as he did in the pamphlet *Vox Populi*, where he urged the king in 1642 to "return unto your Parliament, and so unto your people," yet unlike Lilburne, he trusted Parliament adequately to represent the people.[8] He took his authority from his role as a public representative, recalling the king to his primary duty to the public.

Prynne was unpopular with those who wanted to exclude the public from political discussion, who doubted that the public had any reasoning powers of their own. Royalist writers feared that strong leaders like Prynne could convince the people to support any cause. In fact, these writers were partly right, since pamphleteers and sermon writers were mobilizing the public in new ways. The writers who waged a war against Prynne condemned his enormous effect over gullible readers, and their condemnation reveals a pressure point in the revolutionary writing culture. The theory that

Prynne's readers were credulous simpletons was set out in the pamphlet *The Fallacies of Mr. Prynne* (1644). Prynne's power over his audience was said there to be even greater than that of the preachers: "Mr. Prynne's books are more prevalent than their sermons. Our Preachers indeed have persuaded the people effectually to this pious War, but persuasion itself seemeth to dwell in the lips of Mr. Prynne." This was exactly what elites feared most: that the public, ever passive, would turn to a new authority, and that Prynne could command their unquestioning obedience. The author of *The Fallacies* called Prynne the "Popular Doctor," and asked him, "why hast thou . . . taught the People thus barbarously to kill one another?"[9] Hezekiah Woodward, an Independent, worried that Prynne's reputation had become so powerful that his faulty reasoning would be overlooked because of his fame: "His name only has rendered his subitane Apprehensions, in deed and truth such, to seem good and solid Reasons; and so to pass through the city, as having Truth and Reason in them . . . the weakest and slightest as ever came from so solid a man . . . yet they take with the people."[10] Prynne's "subitane Apprehensions," that is, his hastily produced arguments, were spreading subversive ideas about town. Woodward was troubled that Prynne's name alone would provide the authority to cap an argument, and that more valid courses of reasoning would be ignored.

Woodward envisioned an audience of "the people" that "takes" the shoddy reasoning for the truth. The people are "taken" with Prynne's reasonings in several senses of the word. They "take" to him: are pleased, charmed, and attracted. Yet they are also "taken" *in* by him: misled, duped, or deceived. In seventeenth-century English, one could also be "taken with" the plague. It is unclear in which sense Prynne relates to the people, and this ambiguity leaves open the question of whether Prynne acts upon the people (taking them in) or whether the people act upon Prynne (taking to him). Woodward points to both relations between writer and audience in his criticism of Prynne; he is afraid of the man who incites the audience, and also afraid of the incendiary audience. For the journalist Marchamont Nedham, then a Royalist, there was no ambiguity about Prynne's danger. Prynne takes in readers with his deception: "Feeding the Phantasie with such Fears and Jealousies as the weaker sort of men (fruitful enough in these times) create unto themselves out of what they read."[11] Prynne has been "feeding" the people with his "fears and jealousies," that is to say, with his ideas. The metaphor denotes activity going in one direction, from feeder to eater, from Prynne to a passive public, which is, as we would say, "swallowing" the stuff whole. Nedham's metaphor shows his conception of the public as passive and obedient to their new master, yet his argument also envisions that public active in a new and dangerous way. It was not only persuasion of the public that worried contemporaries, it was Prynne's particular political line that was controversial: he (at that time) provoked the public to think critically about their rulers. Nedham wrote that Prynne's intention was to rouse the public out of complacency. Nedham's criticism of Prynne's effect over "the weaker sort of men" rejects that such men deserve to participate in political affairs. By encouraging men to "create unto themselves out of what they read," on the other hand, Prynne's work is potentially disastrous, since it prizes the individual's ability to think. In his criticism of Prynne, then, Nedham offers a description of just the kind of power that could be roused from the public, figured precisely as a power of the imagination.

Prynne's enemies waged their battle on a level of reading and interpretation. They sought to counteract his power by interpreting his pamphlets to the opposite effect, hoping to inoculate potential recruits against his writings. In the anti-Prynne pamphlet *The Fallacies of Mr. William Prynne*, for example, a scholar performed the action of interpreting Prynne's text for the benefit of his less well educated friend. The gullible reader, his friend, is described as a simple, unlearned man—"You know my education hath been sufficient neither in the Schools of Divinity, nor law; wherefore I cannot render you any Scholar-like account"—a reader typical of the "Downright Dick," or rustic clown, who was featured in many popular writings of the time. He relies utterly upon betters for guidance: "my conscience hath sufficient information from other learned, judicious, and godly men," and he credits these authorities with wisdom sufficient for him to depend on, swearing, "although I go on other men's legs, and see with other men's eyes, yet the one are so strong, and the other so clear, that I neither fall nor err" (*FP*, 1).

The author plays into the myth that simple folk were passive recipients of political ideas disseminated from above, as Royalists were repeatedly accusing. This myth, expounded by elites, formed the basis for their attack on popular literature, though it also was propagated by some Puritans, who feared that "the people" were too easily deceived. The simpleton in this case admits Prynne was even more influential over his opinions than preachers had been: "Though the people yield credence to their Preachers, yet . . . Mr. Prynne is believed most [of] any of them . . . many judicious persons (so supposed by themselves, and some others too) submit their judgment to Mr. Prynne's books, without any further disquisition"; further, "he [Prynne] is the very Oracle of our times" (*FP*, 1). The simple reader "believes" Prynne, becoming slavish in submission to him: "yielding" and "submitting." In the pamphlet to which this simpleton clings, *The Sovereign Power of Parliaments* (1643), Prynne claimed to have "given such full answers to them, as shall, I trust, in the general, abundantly clear the Parliament's authority, innocency, integrity, against all their clamorous malignant calumnies, convince their judgments, satisfy their consciences, and put them to everlasting silence."[12] And when the uneducated reader asserts his loyalty to Prynne, he echoes verbatim Prynne's own text, exemplifying that people like him are swallowing Prynne's words whole: "He hath given such full answers to all the objections of moment, which the King, or any opposites to the Parliament have made as shall abundantly clear all clamorous malignant calumnies, convince their judgments, satisfy their consciences, and put them to an everlasting silence" (1). By his exact quotation of Prynne's words, the ignorant reader proves he is but a parrot, a passive receptacle for ideas. Prynne's teaching, received wholeheartedly and word for word by this doltish reader and by the "many zealous persons [who] build their Conscience upon the confidence of this most learned and religious Gentleman" (1), is a Royalist's nightmare.

The trick of the pamphlet is to set up a situation where the readers are led to reject Prynne's authority by viewing the inept actions of this ignorant reader. The gullible reader is set on the right course by a more critical observer, one who promises to give Prynne's "tenets their due examination" (2). This writer, in the voice of the more experienced friend, provides a model for all readers to follow: "I will presume to peruse some passages in his Pamphlets; if they convince your Judgment and Conscience, in God's holy name submit your assent" (2). Though this capable reader promises to be an impartial judge of Prynne's work, it is clear that he already has an opinion to impart, an opinion signaled by the pamphlet's point of origin: Oxford, the royalist headquarters. The respondent gives his conclusion away openly: "I conjecture I shall make it appear of his own Books, that as he professeth himself no Papist, so we shall decrie him to be no Pope, that he does not determine è Cathedra, dictate unerring conclusions. So that people of Religion and Reason are not obliged to fix their belief upon his Truths newly discovered" (2). Further, Prynne is reimagined as being as dangerous to English citizens as is the pope. In the rest of the pamphlet, this better reader presents a revision of Prynne's work, showing how Prynne has grossly misread his sources, locating paradoxes in Prynne's argument. He finally condemns the antiking stance in Prynne's writing. In the guise of an impartial and wise friend, the author of this pamphlet aims to convince readers to reject Prynne, adopting an authoritarian stance toward readers, conceiving of them as blank slates upon which to write. The logic, however, dicates that whoever has the last say shall conquer, and this explains in some part the endless back-and-forth attacks of these pamphleteers. Each writer sought to *undo* the evil of his predecessor by retraining readers.

Through subtle manipulations of the reader's attention, writers hoped to convince the readers of new positions and to rescue them from wrong ones. They also incorporated enemy texts right into their arguments. William Walwyn ensnared his readers in *A Helpe to the right understanding of a Discourse Concerning Independency Lately published by William Prynne* (1645) by precisely imitating the typography of Prynne's *Independency Examined* (1644). Walwyn thus appealed to supporters of Prynne who might take it for a work of their master's. Walwyn, however, aimed to win back support for Independents like John Goodwin, who objected to Prynne's opposition to toleration for sectarians.[13] By the reference to Prynne in the title, and by the sense of the title itself, a casual reader might expect this pamphlet to support Prynne.[14] The pro-Prynne signs are not wholly misleading, moreover, since the pamphlet opens with praise for Prynne. The pamphleteer debates Prynne's reputation, telling a story of his merits, though quickly moving on to acknowledge that there are some who do not praise him. The purportedly pro-Prynne narrator soon turns into a skeptic: "in a great example of late it is too sadly proved that he [who] did the greatest service, may live to do the greatest mischief." This previous supporter of Prynne comes to doubt him, "even men who held [Prynne] in great repute for integrity, begin to doubt his ends." By the seventh page the mood has changed, as rhetorical questions directed at the reader replace the narration, and these concern the chief issue in the tale just narrated—liberty of conscience. The writer asks, "who can live where he hath not the freedom of his mind, and exercise his conscience?" The writer complains about the present condition of tyranny over individual conscience, claiming: "So Mr. Prynne would have it continued."[15] Despite his refutation of Prynne's arguments, the writer is sympathetic to Prynne, seeming to offering him gentle correction. By this tactic, the writer hopes to draw readers from among Prynne's supporters.

Readers wait until page 8 for the "I," the voice of judgment, of the work: "And where Mr. Prynne may suppose all liberty of this kind, would tend to the increasing of erroneous opinions, and disturbances to the State; I believe he is mistaken; for let any man's experience witness whether freedom of discourse be not the readiest way both to give and receive satisfaction in all things." The tone in the course of the pamphlet has changed from even-handed narrative to an outright attack, a method whereby the reader is slowly, but inevitably, caught unawares in an anti-Prynne argument. At the end, the writer lets loose a stream of invective, addressing readers directly: "if you weigh [Prynne's reasons] you will find them very light, and little better compacted than mere dreams, or such fumes as men use to have betwixt sleeping and waking." It is by now clear which end is up. The author reveals in the final lines of the tract that he is motivated by the desire to save this reader from the evil effects of Prynne's writing: "I end with his own words, more justly applied *fiat justitia*; better it is that he undergo this my plain dealing, than that either the readers of his books should be seduced, or so many innocent well-affected persons be so grossly abused by him."[16] The appeal to "plaine dealing" is an approach claimed by many sides in such arguments. The writer's claim over readers is to write in their interest, for their benefit, and out of love for them. This pamphlet retrieves those who had followed a leader by appealing to an image of an audience in need of correction and assistance. By not declaring its true political allegiance until the end, the pamphlet addressed readers who were undecided, unaware its exact leanings, and thereby more susceptible, perhaps, to its persuasion.

Many writers in the civil war period used fictional devices to secure their readers' allegiances. Readers, by sympathizing and identifying with the central character, were supposed to imitate his actions. This mechanism of identification which leads to specific action is a rhetorical device used by many forms of propaganda,[17] and it is one that Susan Suleiman has called an "authoritarian fiction." In such a fiction, the role of the reader is "to 'repeat' the protagonist's evolution toward the 'right' doctrine." During the course of the reading experience, "the reader is presumed to undergo an ideological evolution." Writing about ideological novels in France in the 1930s, Suleiman describes the structures of activism in their rhetoric, where authors set up a role for the reader by the structure of the narrative in which the reader is "not indifferent. . . . One can even imagine the transformation of the reader into a 'real' . . . helper. . . . The reader might continue in his own life the struggle in the novel." These novels effect this result by a strategy she calls "persuasion by cooptation," where the reader, identifying with the hero, finds himself "necessarily—on the right side." In *A Helpe to the right understanding of a Discourse Concerning Independency Lately published by William Prynne*, Walwyn worked upon his readers by engaging them in the activity of reading and reconsidering their favored author, Prynne. Like authoritarian novels that aim for a "single meaning," this pamphlet and other like it sought to convince their readers by a process of engagement that looks like sympathetic identification rather than overt polemic.[18]

Jacques Ellul writes that the aim of propaganda is to make the public act, and because it is so action-oriented, propaganda "does not tolerate discussion; by its very nature it excludes contradiction and discussion. . . . It must produce quasi-unanimity, and the opposing faction must become negligible."[19] Propaganda depends on a one-sided discourse, to which the propagandees assent. Adolf Hitler understood that propaganda could ill afford to entertain true dialogue, explaining in *Mein Kampf*: "Propaganda's task is, for instance, not to evaluate the various rights, but far more to stress exclusively the one that is to be represented by it. It has not to search into truth as far as this is favorable to others, in order to present it then to the masses with doctrinal honesty, but it has rather to serve its own truth uninterruptedly."[20] The principle is not that of debate, but of "uninterrupted" monologue; not "doctrinal honesty," but one-sided promotion. Milton could not have put it better than Hitler when in *Paradise Lost*, he represented the failed debate in hell, in which Satan "prevented all reply" (2.467). Milton's authorial voice rebukes those hellish troops when they have decided upon their plan: "O shame to men! Devil with Devil damn'd / Firm concord holds, men only disagree / Of creatures rational" (2.496–98). Concord, Milton suggests, may not always be the best solution to disagreement; it may, rather, signal satanic manipulation. Yet in the pamphlets of the English Revolution, we see that authors were concerned to involve readers in a discussion, even if it was only a fictional discussion. Propaganda aims to lock its consumers into a single meaning, a single way of looking at the world; as Ellul explains, the propagandist mobilizes the public by effectively narrowing the range of thought permitted, and by giving that public a sense of urgency, showing its members what to do.[21] The authors of the pamphlets of the English Revolution we have been considering here do not achieve this aim simply by bludgeoning their audiences with scare stories (though there was plenty of that); rather, they seemed willing to entertain the reader's objections and interests. Propaganda may be a kind of monologue, to which the public lends a willing ear, as Ellul asserts, yet the authors we have been examining saw that their readers wished to become active participants in political conversations. Therefore, the propaganda of the English Revolution had to take into account the desires of such an audience for debate.

The pamphlets we are considering here use fiction for ideological or political conversion. Through the fiction, the reader would be caught up in the entertainment, while propaganda invites the reader to play a role demanded by the pamphlet, a role that has political significance. John Taylor, a popular royalist pamphleteer in the hire of the king, for instance, wrote the satirical *Crop-Eare Curried* (1644) in order to provoke his audience to take a position against Prynne. In the pamphlet, the ghost of Tom Nashe acts as an inspiring Muse, sent with an "errand" to Taylor and, by extension, to all Royalists: "I conjure thee to take this Railing fellow in hand, look upon his wicked works, view his villainies"—an injunction first to see, and then to act. And act Taylor does. As soon as he awakens from his dream, he begins a storm of motion, reexamining Prynne's books with a newly sharpened eye, spurred by the ghost's offer of protection: "Fear not, go on Boldly, I will leave my genius with thee, which shall inspire thee, and infuse into thee such terrible, Torturing, Tormenting, Termagent flames and flashes as shall Firk, Ferret, and force Prynne and his partners quite out of the little wit that is left them." Taylor's critical abilities, aroused and inspired by the ghost's admonition, find much to oppose, and the rest of the pamphlet—another forty pages—is a close reading and rebuttal of Prynne's work. In it, Taylor finds examples of Prynne's "adulterate precedents," which are found to be "a mess of musty precedents, like the mouldy bread, ragged clothes, and clouted shoes of the Gibeonite when they deceived Joshua." Inspired by his ghoulish muse, the author accuses Prynne of using the precedents of "damnable Treasons, and perditious Treacheries in all the Kingdoms of the World, maliciously and purposely, to defend, maintain, and countenance this odious Rebellion, now on foot in England." Through humor, the congeries of accusations, and the entertaining vehicle, Taylor hopes to win the reader to his side. Entertainment aside, Taylor had designs on his audience.[22]

In the case of John Taylor we have a writer compelled to show readers how to act by reading: the reader must read the enemy argument properly. The dramatic action in the ghost-story prologue urges any reader, here represented by Taylor, to reread Prynne's works. The body of the pamphlet provides the "right" way of doing so, with the correct interpretation provided. This pamphlet promotes activism in two ways: it represents the activism of the character, showing John Taylor driven by the inspiration of the ghost to reevaluate Prynne, and it forces readers to take up that challenge as well, if they should choose to read the next forty pages of the tract. The author of the pamphlet compels his readers to go through the very steps the fictional ghost has urged upon him by the mere activity of their reading the pamphlet from cover to cover. Once informed of the wickedness of the enemy author, the reader comes away knowing not only what is wrong with Prynne's work, but also how to perform similar critical acts in the future. Taylor gives a point-by-point analysis of Prynne's work, and he shows how criticism ought to be conducted by practicing it himself. The pamphlet finishes the ghost story by page 4, turning sober when the author begins to make a close refutation of Prynne's writings. It is clear that he has the texts by Prynne in front of him, since he quotes them directly in his counterargument, urging his own reader to do so as well. In *Crop-Eare Curried,* John Taylor used fiction to compel readers to follow the path of his protagonist, to follow the plot leading inevitably toward the Royalist party. By identifying with the protagonist, the readers would undergo a conversion along with him. The premise underlying this technique is that readers must be led by an an authority, in the manner that the ghost of Nashe led Taylor, and that Taylor will then lead his readers.

We do not know precisely how readers were affected by this barrage of opinions, whether they changed opinions each time they laid hands on a new pamphlet; whether "the whiff of every new pamphlet should stagger them out of their catechism," as Milton joked in his *Areopagitica* (*CPW* 2.537), or whether readers were "fast reading, trying all things, assenting to the force of reason and convincement" (2.554), as he had hoped. But we do know that many writers were troubled by the coexistence of contradictory opinions. While they sought to attract readers to their own cause and to discredit all the others along the way, they were also concerned about the plight of their readers in the hands of their rivals' pamphlets. Gaining a monopoly on truth was no easy task.

By expressing their fears about a duped populace, the writers of the English Revolution were noting that they were living in a world glutted with deceptive stories. The author of the weekly *Mercurius Civicus* (1643) warned readers against enemies' distortion of truth. The newsbook's truthfulness was announced in the title: "Truth Impartially related . . . To prevent misinformation."[23] With "mis-information" circulating, this writer hoped to save readers from its effects. The author of a royalist newsbook, *Mercurius Elencticus,* announced, "I know 'tis the constant desire of the common-people to hear of News! Strange tidings! Be they never so untrue, ever relish with the multitude, provided they suit with their affections . . . to tickle the Ears of the giddy multitude; which are all of them false, and very unbecoming the Pen of any man that pretends the service of the King; because that by this means Truth itself is often blemished and obscured amongs such Lies and Forgeries; and things Real looked upon as futilous [*sic*] and absurd." The author added, "so good a Cause as we have shall (I hope) never stand in need of Lies to support it."[24]

The conflict in the press was especially worrisome to partisans because so many pamphlets were aimed at the populace. Royalists and anti-Royalists alike expressed a particular nervousness about the powerful effect of pamphlets on the populace. As Milton scoffed, the king's portrait in *Eikon Basilike* was "set there to catch fools and silly gazers," and was again alarmed about the power of deceptions over a rude audience; Milton feared that the king's supporters "intend [*Eikon Basilike*] not so much the defence of his former actions, as the promoting of thir own future designes . . . to corrupt and disorder the mindes of weaker men, by new suggestions and narrations" (*CPW* 3.338). Royalists, too, worried about the susceptibility of the common folk to dangerous opinions culled from pamphlets, as the author of the *England's Remembrancer of Londons Integrity* (1647) noted: "a generation of men are sprung up . . . whose employment is to write Pamphlets filled with false relations, to deceive the people, and to lay on fair beautiful colors upon the horrid and deformed faces of sedition, and faction, and to put the Ensign of Innocency and Peace into their hands, whose actions are guileful. . . . O how are simple-hearted Readers abused with feigned stories, and shadows without substances, and all to hold them in suspense."[25] Writers on all sides of the political spectrum represented their task as education of an audience of "simple men." They were concerned about a specific audience of political illiterates, those unaccustomed to being the targets of political appeal.

The pamphlet battles during the English Revolution offered such uninitiated readers nothing less than different versions of the truth. Astrology books, long a medium associated with a popular audience, for example, could offer directly contradictory predictions to readers, predictions that would of course depend upon the political allegiance of the author.[26] The author of *Mercurius Vapulans* (1644) accused his enemy of "making cheating and lying pamphlets, and by the calculating of news for the meridian of Oxford," that is, of falsifying the truth according to the perspective of the royalist stronghold.[27] Parliament's astrologer, William Lilly, vouched that "the Parliament's cause shall not want a Champion in Astrology to confute any thing in point of Art that can be alleged from the greatest Clerks in Oxford."[28] John Booker's *Mercurius Coelicus* (1644), another antiroyalist pamphlet, responded to the royalist almanacs, interpreting the heavens according to a proparliamentary stance, with results precisely opposite to those of the Royalists.[29] One antiroyalist pamphlet scoffed that "for the truth of affairs must not walk abroad there, either naked, or in their own clothing, but must be translated into such a habit, as will be most pleasing and acceptable to the hearers." This author makes clear that truth was a matter of political orientation, and thus subject to interpretation. The campaign of misinformation required special ways of interpretation that would "undress" the apparant truth.[30] The defeat of the king's forces in their first battle with the New Model Army at Naseby in June 1645 was to prove the Royalists' predictions utterly wrong. What the whiplashed readers of this popular genre thought at this point, nobody knows.

Language itself was a political battleground, as authors accused their enemies of distorting words to suit their ends. "Hard words, jealousies and fears, / Set folks together by the ears": so runs the prologue to Butler's *Hudibras*, an epic that reduces the very matter of the civil war to insults. Booker, for example, represented the clash of opinions as a clash of terminologies, and urged that a correct dictionary was needed. "Victory" for Wharton's royalist almanac was interpreted as "treachery" in Booker's *Mercurius Coelicus*. Booker explained, "I have gotten these base words by reading."[31] An ally of Wharton's was quick to respond to this pamphlet, avowing that Booker himself had stuffed his "perfidious pamphlets with Ambiguous phrases, thereby to beget new Feares and Jealousies amongst the people." This Royalist was troubled that Booker's language might mislead the people.[32] The antiroyalist author of *Mercurius Vapulans* (1644) also focused on the question of interpretation of language, charging royalist authors with "translating" the truth: "Your party are very sufficient *Railers*, even *Naturalized* into detraction and lying." The Royalists made contradictory uses of language, as the author of *Mercurius Vapulans* asserted: "our grave and religious assembly of Divines, thou callest, *A schismatical Assembly of Taylors, Millers, Cobblers and Weavers, etc.* (so they sew up the rent which you Prelates and their adherents have made in the Church)."[33] This author would have his audience "undeceived" by decoding the enemies' language.

PROPAGANDA AND PERSPECTIVE: CORRECTING VISIONS

With all this factional wrangling, writers were aware of the ways that their words could organize political perspectives. The civil war writers made a system of symbolic oppositions a part of their logic: anti-Royalists railed against *Aulicus* and defended *Britanicus*. Not only were the symbols chosen according to the dictates of propaganda, but even the truth itself was made to serve the warring sides. Parliament voted to pay for favorable books to be dispersed; pamphlets describing war atrocities, for instance, helped to create images of a ruthless enemy. Prince Rupert earned his reputation as the "Prince Robber" in part because of the parliamentary pamphlets that narrated the brutality of his military actions. *Marleborough's Miseries* for example, appeared in 1642 after the sacking of Marlborough by the royalist army as a "most exact and true relation of the Beseiging, Plundering, Pillaging, Burning." The subtitle of the pamphlet, *England turned Ireland, by The Lord Digby and Daniel O'Neale*, accuses the royalist commanders of the most inhumane actions, not only of burning the town, but of torturing prisoners as well. The town's loss was estimated at fifty thousand pounds. A pamphlet like this could have a wide appeal; the Parliamentarian propaganda piece *The White King*, for example, was claimed to have sold eighteen hundred copies in three days in 1644. Well into the Cromwellian Protectorate, printed works helped further political and military causes, as did the broadside ballad "A Dreadful Relation, of the Cruel, Bloody, and Most Inhumane Massacre and Butchery, committed on the Poor Protestants," published in 1656. This ballad sang "with bleeding heart and mournful tear" of the atrocities committed against Cromwell's forces by the French and Irish. The header woodcut showed violent pictures, and the ballad related the news of "a bloody crew of wicked men" who "did fall upon these Christians good, / Who never did them any harm."[34] The ballad tells of the tortures these good Christians underwent at the hands of their enemy. Cromwell needed such stories to rouse support for his campaign in Ireland. It was surely a stretching of the facts of that campaign to allow that the Irish were fighting the English without provocation. As Goebbels remarked in a different era, "we do not talk to say something, but to obtain a certain effect."[35] Writing during the civil war strove for effect. Propaganda such as these horror stories provided a vivid picture of what was happening to readers who were too far away to verify it for themselves, and that picture was so horrifying, it was to rouse in readers a sense of urgency and danger. This propaganda, by offering the Irish as utterly without humanity, made it permissible to hate them and to love their conquerers, Cromwell's men.

English politicians during the civil war period offered many versions of the truth, and these versions were often mutually contradictory. This did not mean, however, that each side had equal validity. Consideration of both sides of a matter did not mean the reader was encouraged to choose freely; rather, the author staged the debate so that the reader would be supplied with adequate means for conviction, as one author explained, "for full satisfaction to all Neutralists."[36] Learning how to defend one's own position against an enemy was an important lesson, since the civil wars offered a variety of positions to which participants could subscribe. As we have seen, the structure of debate could work to encourage these undecided readers, the "neutralists," to choose sides. The inclusion of two contrary opinions in a pamphlet could serve as an invitation for readers undecided about their political position to consider reading it in the first place, and then to make a political decision.

But debates could go only so far to put readers in the middle of the action. Many pamphlet writers did not doubt for a minute that theirs was the *right* interpretation; however, they did recognize that theirs was not the *only* possible interpretation. Readers were to learn how to pierce through rhetoric so as to expose the enemy's true position. At Putney, John Merriman's call that "this Oedipus riddle [be] un-opened, and this Gordian knot untied, and the enemies of the same unmasked" was such a lesson.[37] "Un-opening," "untying," and "unmasking" are hermeneutic activities, those which require solving a mystery and which depend on interpretation. The assumption that some truth resides inside (unopened, tied-up), or underneath (masked by) the apparent surface of things is based upon a spatial metaphor that sees it as necessary, and possible, to get to that inner truth. Many pamphleteers of the civil war period shared the assumptions that proper interpretation would reveal a truth, and they offered a kind of training to their readers in "unopening" the rhetoric of the enemy.

By showing a way of rereading to their audience, pamphleteers strove to attract the support of those whose allegiances were still up for grabs. In *Britannicus His Pill to Cure Malignancy* (1644), for example, the author demands that readers take a new perspective on matters. The title page offers a "laying open" and a "discovery" of plots against Protestants, aimed at a readership of those who "will not see the danger that their Religion and Liberties now lie in." The pamphlet promises to present "the whole Progress of the Adversary's long, and continued Plots, briefly laid open, and discovered . . . Whereby the archest malignant will be either convinced, or condemned, and the weakest of the well-affected sufficiently strengthened and encouraged with all vigour to proceed with the Parliament in the defence of Religion and Liberty." The author provides reasons to convince a diverse audience, one that includes the enemy, the undecided, and the committed. The point is not only to persuade the enemy, but also to strengthen those in one's own camp, who are the "weakest of the well-affected." The title's reference to *Mercurius Britannicus* is a sign of this pamphleteer's support for Parliament, and the author offers a medical antidote to the disease of "malignancy" by drawing a picture of the abuses of the king and queen against Parliament and the people of England. The author of this pamphlet is aware that a challenge to the audience's perspective is necessary to incite his own supporters to action, and not just to convert his opponents.

Writers sought to steer their readers to the right interpretation—theirs—and they illustrated the possibilities for mistaken interpretation by several different metaphors. One common figure denoting the resolution of a clash in perspectives is found in the cliché "religion is a cloak for knavery," repeated so often during this period by Royalists. This figure of clothing and nakedness expresses a firm belief that truth, "knavery," lies hidden under layers, "a cloak" which must be flung off. The antiroyalist author of *Mercurius Vapulans* (1644) also used this metaphor: "For the truth of affairs must not walk abroad there, either naked, or in their own clothing, but must be translated into such a habit, as will be most pleasing and acceptable to the hearers." Special ways of interpretation were needed to expose the royalist falsehoods, and the author of *Vapulans* wrote in order to "unbutton [Wharton] . . . to his Principles, and strip his libellous soul stark Naked, and lash him through the streets of London back again to Oxford."[38] By use of this metaphor, the writer pointed to a situation rife with competing interpretations, suggesting that, finally, his was only one truth, like that of naked skin.

The English revolutionary pamphleteers often used the metaphor of seeing to represent the process of political interpretation. Commenting on the multiplicity of opinions offered by the press, writers used visual metaphors—figures of blindness and sight, telescopes, spectacles, and other visual equipment—to register their concern that an audience make sense of the battle of views. By using a language of "seeing properly," writers expressed their intense desire to control the interpretations of readers. By their use of optical metaphors, the authors of the controversial literature of the English Revolution attempted to instruct readers how to read, encouraging their audiences to view any political text with critical eyes. These writers conceived of revolutionary readers as those who could root out truth from among conflicting interpretations, who could make political choices based on a critical practice of reading.

By using metaphors pertaining to sight, writers explicitly recognized the presence of rival interpretations. Their use of this metaphor touches upon several important epistemological issues. First, opinions appear as evident truths: "true sight" as equivalent to "true knowledge" becomes the goal of the reader, and of course, true knowledge is what the writer believes he has. And second, the "truth" of the matter is to be attained through a perceptual process: vision. Not only accusing their enemies of falsehood, the pamphlet writers who used metaphors of true sight spurred their readers to act to correct "faulty vision." The modern relativistic idea that "every image embodies a way of seeing" that is equally valid would be unheard of for the engaged writers of the English Revolution, however. Some ways of seeing, they would argue, were right and others were wrong, and it was most important to see the right way.

The boldest instance was the king. Was the king a traitor? This question alone was the issue in countless pamphlets, and the polemicists working to persuade an audience to fight against Charles held that though there were many images to choose from, there must be a right way of seeing him. The debate over the "right" image of the king was central to *The Converted Cavaliers Confession*, which referred to changes in opinion as a matter of seeing properly, "opening eyes," "discovering," and "seeing." This pamphlet, published in 1644, presented the secrets of a "Cavalier" who recanted. This is a familiar form of propaganda to us, the "confession" narrative. In the title, the author represented a process of political enlightenment that echoed Parliament's 1642 declaration of war, but in personal terms: "*The Converted Cavaliers' Confession of Their Design When first we drew the King away from his Parliament. As also (now our eyes are in some measure opened) that we see there was a deeper Plot and Design in hand, at that time by the Papists; who made use of us, to accomplish their own Design, which then lay hid from us, but now discovereth it selfe: With our Resolution to forsake the Papists.*" The Cavalier explained that the source of this new discovery was a book: as "Mr. Prynne in his late book at large setteth forth," highlighting the place of reading, a process, in acquiring knowledge. Now awakened from his dream, the converted Cavalier urges others to see as clearly as he does, "that others that still prosecute the design that we did, may now take notice of the Papists, how they make use of us to our own destruction; and then I hope, you likewise will forsake them." This Cavalier was to be a pattern for others to follow—others who must read, understand, and see differently. "And this is my persuasion, and my Resolution is to adhere to the King's forces no more": the implication of this conclusion is that readers were to follow suit.[39]

It is doubtful this was a "real" confession. The author used the device of a fictional persona of a reformed Royalist who now toes the Presbyterian line, in hopes of reaching other Royalists who might do the same thing. By this literary impersonation, the author could evade possible charges of treason ("after all," one might say in his defense, "it's only a fiction"), but the use of a fictional persona was a signal too of the hermeneutic structures embedded in the practices of ideological conflict. The Cavalier's confession revealed that a special way of reading civil war events was necessary, with Mr. Prynne's book offering the key. By the use of the metaphor of sight, the author invites readers to understand that finding the truth is a process of penetrating through mediations, and that truth is not an immediately apprehensible fact.

Pamphleteers who used the metaphors of sight and seeing represented truth as mediated by acts of reading. The royalist newsbook *Mercurius Elencticus* (1644) performed such a "reading" using the metaphor of true vision. The author of this pamphlet offered an interpretation of Parliament's restrictions on the press in October 1649, typographically presenting his own meaning within brackets beside Parliament's own language in italics. By this presentation, the author was able to give a running commentary on the language of Parliament, to direct the reader to interpret Parliament's words properly:

> *God is pleased to bless our endeavors abroad,* [that you shall know anon] *and by that means to put an awe upon a great number* [the more Cowards they] *that wish us no good. And is pleased also to open mens Eyes by degrees* [to see your Perfidiousness and Treason] *to a discovery of their true Interest* [swallowed up by your State-Cormorants] . . . *some that were taken in their honest and Candid simplicity, by the cunning insinuation of a* [pretended, but a really Bloody] *Parliament, who lay in wait to deceive, have seen through the imposture, and delivered themselves from the Enchantment* [very properly indeed, for there is not much difference betwixt Rebellion and Witchcraft]."[40]

This author turns the parliamentary gesture of "opening mens Eyes by degrees" back against Parliament, explaining that what men will see when their eyes are opened is "to see your Perfidiousness and Treason." This

author suggests that reading the civil war pronouncements required especially keen eyesight, an ability to read between the lines. This pamphleteer
showed the reader just how to do so.

Writers fought over the political allegiances of their readers by acknowl-
edging the mediation of truth through distorting perspectives, and by providing ways for them to overcome such distortions. As in the *Converted Cavaliers Confession,* the new perspective would offer a pattern for choosing a
side. The language of perception is used to arm readers against being taken
in, against being deceived, by others. Renaissance ideas about visual perspective underlie the recurrent metaphors of sight and deception in these
civil war pamphlets. We recall the application of systematic linear perspective, which arrived in fifteenth-century Italy with Alberti. The "science" of
perspective was a mechanical one, with rules about ratios and vanishing
points providing geometrical certainty in the pictorial representation of
space. Renaissance men and women were fascinated with games of illusion
and about multiple perspectives, such as anamorphic puzzles, as in the
elongated skull across the lower portion of Holbein's *Ambassadors* (1533).
There was of course a connection between visual "wit" and literary wit—for
example, in the metaphysical images of John Donne or George Herbert—
as a favorite Renaissance provenance. This visual wit always depended upon
fixed perspectives between which to shift; that is how the anamorphic skull,
for example, may be "read" at all.[41] Once the "key" to the visual puzzle is
known, the strange shape "looks like" a skull, and with the right point of
view, the picture snaps into place. Visual ambiguities rely on the beholder's
knowledge of the conventions of seeing, like the anamorphic skull, which
may be read as a strange, elongated mark in the foreground of a painting
and which may also be read as a skull—depending from which vantage
point it is viewed. The games played with perspective serve only to show
how much perspective itself began to be seen as a convention, subject to
manipulation and distortion.[42]

Once true perspective became easy to distort, by a shift in the physical
position of the beholder, by the optical lens, and by the free press, writers
found an image for the problem of the multiplicity of opinions. The Renaissance discovery of visual perspective and the seventeenth-century refine-
ment of scientific instruments like the telescope and optical lens gave authors figures for representing manipulated views. The seventeenth-century
political writers who used these figures asserted that once the mediating
perspective was removed—either by an optical lens or through cleansing of
the eyes by a potion—a correct and true account would result. In their use
of the mechanical devices, authors admitted that there were more ways
than one to see the world. The rhetoric of the English Revolution, which
constituted its audience as subjects who were equipped with reading skills,
able both to make political decisions and to decide among possibly conflicting interpretations or "deceptions," also constituted an audience ripe for

the workings of propaganda. By their frequent use of the metaphors of sight and the images associated with seeing, the authors of these pamphlets signaled that propaganda needed to be decoded.

OPTICAL ILLUSIONS

The authors of the pamphlets written during the English Revolution did not surrender their claims to true perspective by engaging in games of multiple perspectives, however. The contrary was the case. They wished to highlight the mediated quality of civil war writing only to assert that once the mediations were recognized, readers would accept their truth as the only one, and would be realeased from the vicelike grip of their enemies' rhetoric. In *Eikonoklastes*, a pamphlet about destroying images, Milton replaces the king's image of a martyr with one of Charles as tyrant.[43] Once the king is pictured as a tyrant, it becomes legitimate to topple his regime. This is a shift in perception that also effects a political change.[44] Milton does not simply substitute one image for the other, however; he induces his audience to reinterpret the king's self-representations by a process of reading. Nevertheless, by his very engagement of the doubling effects of ironic language, Milton did not want to threaten the stability of his position by admitting a plurality of readings. In his desire to replace one image with another, Milton did not express skepticism about the possibility of reaching a true perspective. Interpreting political events became troped as problems of proper "sight" not in order to make room for more interpretations, but rather to show readers that distortion was taking place.

By using visual metaphors to represent the process of viewing political events, writers forced readers to think of political opinions as if they were physical, material truths, truths of nature. The royalist author of *Cuckoo's Nest at Westminster* (1648) makes use of this trope: "Therefore the People may now see (without spectacles) how grossly they have been deceived, and juggled out of their Lives and Estates," clearing away the deceptive writing of the parliamentary press. Likewise, *The Eye Cleared; or, A Preservative for the Sight* (1644) pictures a beaker filled with a potion, a "vial of preservative water for clearing eyes" on its title page, a medication that works to undo the damage of other pamphlets. The author recants "in honest English" of past mistakes: "now our eyes are open we cannot but confess that we have abus'd the King, abus'd the State and abus'd our selves all this while."[45] Armed with new sight, the author admits he has has succumbed to misprisions in the past: "How we have been cozened, how blinded, how enchanted? When we consider how unreasonably our reasons have miscarried, we cannot but doubt that there's more Art than honesty at Oxford." Here the the king and the Malignants are exposed for what they are by the metaphor of cleared vision.

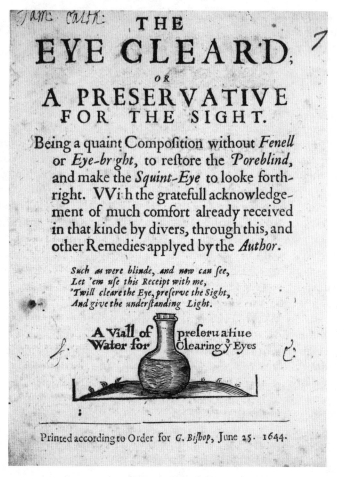

5. Title page to *The Eye Cleared* (1644).

Further, the optical metaphors and the mechanical aids to sight in many pamphlets—spectacles, telescopes, magnifying glasses—give the necessary equipment to readers to be able to see the defective mediations of their enemies. The pamphleteers' interest in the problems of mediation was an obsession, as revealed in the quantity of pamphlet titles using this figure: *A Prospective Glass, Wherein the Child in understanding is enabled to see what the wicked Counsellors did* (1644); *A Paire of Crystal Spectacles . . . Counsels of the Army* (1648); *A New Pair of Spectacles of the Old Fashion* (1649); *A New Invention; or, A paire of Cristall Spectacles* (1644): all these put the matter of proper interpretation and mediation squarely on the title page. Several of these pamphlets fill their title pages with a woodcut illustration of a pair of spectacles.[46]

The author of *A New Invention* explains the value of this visual aid for the reader: "they have such a special virtue in them, that he that makes right

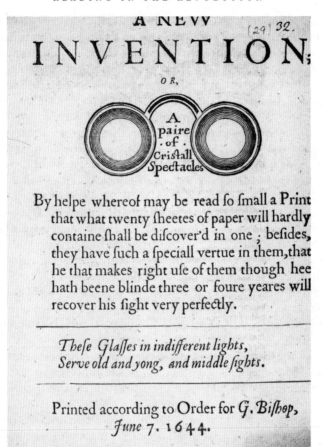

A NEVV

(29) 32.

INVENTION;

O R,

A paire ·of· Cristall Spectacles

By helpe whereof may be read fo fmall a Print that what twenty fheetes of paper will hardly containe fhall be difcover'd in one ; befides, they have fuch a fpeciall vertue in them,that he that makes right ufe of them though hee hath beene blinde three or foure yeares will recover his fight very perfectly.

Thefe Glaffes in indifferent lights,
Serve old and yong, and middle fights.

Printed according to Order for *G. Bifhop,*
June 7. 1644.

6. Title page to *A New Invention* (1644).

use of them though he hath been blind three or four years will recover his sight very perfectly."[47] The spectacles in *A New Invention* signal that a clearer "point of view" will be expressed than before—twenty times clearer, if we take the title-page promise seriously. The "three or four years" of blindness in *A New Invention* refers to the "blindness" since the outbreak of conflict up to the moment of the pamphlet's publication in spring 1644. The moment was a crucial one for Parliament's suriving its own factional disputes after the deaths of a group of ideological moderates, including Pym, Hampden, and Brooke.

Yet this pamphlet, like many others that use this trope, does not make its position clear right away. Rather, readers must pierce a false image of the king. By detecting the author's irony, they choose a political position, and thus the pamphlet works to train readers by indirect literary means rather than by persuasion through explicit political argument. By involving the reader in a game of correcting a false impression, the author of the pamphlet encourages a process of reading by which a reader becomes capable of resisting propagandistic assault. As an example of this process, *A New Invention* opens with a flattering portrait of the king, yet increasingly calls into question that picture over the course of its pages. The author suggests that the papists and Irish, traditional enemies of Protestant England, have been tamed by Charles, asking readers, "Dost thou not see the very Papists themselves that were wont to make nothing of stabbing and poisoning Princes, now become so pious and zealous that none are forwarder to take their King's part?" (A2). Despite the strong anti-Irish sentiment found at the end of the pamphlet, the Irish are shown at the beginning to be politically servile to this king: "that we in our rage pleased to call Rebels lately because they killed a few Roundheads there, come over as fast as they can possibly to protect the King here against the fury of Traitorous Schismaticks: Shall these exceed us in loyalty?" (A2) But when this author recommends, "let us join with those honest Irish, faithful Papists, and other loyal followers of his Majesty, and so make an end of these unnatural wars an unnatural way" (2), a tinge of irony can be detected.

With increasing venom, the author implies that the king of England himself had succumbed to Irish influence. The author is here concerned with Charles's armistice with the Irish following the Scottish rebellion in 1644; in this view, such an accord is a sellout to the Catholics. When the author offers a picture of an England reconciled to its Catholic inhabitants and neighbors, the pamphlet's true political position becomes clear: "That the Pope may domineer, his Majesty rejoice, and all his cut-throat Counsellors be as free from fear as they are from honesty; then will there be a brave new world for them that shall live in it, then there will be no Sects nor Schisms but all of one Religion. . . . This will be a Reformation indeed worth talking of, a Peace to the purpose, no more fears, no more jealousies, no more plots, no more Petitions then" (3). This peaceable kingdom is any English Protestant's nightmare, and the echo of Shakespeare's *Tempest* ("O brave new world") signals to readers that this is yet a fantasy. That such a union would bring about a pleasant peace is only a fiction, one that the king and his supporters would like the people of England to believe.

In this dark fantasy of a papist utopia, the author outlines the benefits to Protestants of the political arrangement, where "The Protestant Religion is to be maintained, and that it is the care and endeavor of the King's party to do it must and (no doubt) will be made apparent" (3). The speaker then brings out examples dating from the late 1620s that could hardly convince readers of Charles's purported protection of Protestant interests. Consider, he asks, the bungled attempt by the duke of Buckingham's commission at La Rochelle to relieve the Huguenots, where supplies were short, officers absent, and even instructions delayed. Or Charles's attempt to relive Elizabeth's victory over Spain, the failed mission at Cadiz of 1625; "we lost a lot of men there, but the honour we got is not to be spoke of" (3). These examples are hardly comforting, and they are followed by a list of others, all of which call the earlier pro-Irish position into question: "To what end was that Army readied against the Scots, Soldiers billeted in most parts of this Kingdom, an Army of eight thousand in Ireland in readiness, and the Protestants there disarmed . . . but only to maintain the Protestant Religion?" (6). The pamphlet writer has the luxury of never condemning Charles outright (in 1644, after all, direct accusation against the king was still dangerous).

On the face of it, this is a royalist pamphlet, with the king represented as a true defender of the Protestant religion. But the careful reader, one practicing "right use" of the spectacles, concludes that this story is completely false. The pamphlet is laced with irony, so that readers "see" a true image of the king and "recover . . . sight very perfectly," as the title page had promised. All the contradictions between statements and reality—"the Pope was turned Protestant" (3), for example—reveal the words on the page as lies. The "crystal spectacles" lead the reader of this pamphlet to dispose of uncertainty about the king's real motives. The mechanical device signals to readers that they must employ special reading skills in order to grasp a true political picture.

Their pamphlets made the truth about Charles into an issue of the activity of *perceiving* him. The pamphleteers offered mechanical means of "Undeception" of some of the political rhetoric that was flying about during the early years of the civil wars. They worked to make readers "see" that rhetoric does not always equal reality, that when the king says he is fighting for the improvement of the Protestant Reformation, he may not be entirely truthful. Responding to the dangers of propaganda to ensnare unwitting readers, writers used the figures of optical instruments to encourage readers to understand that what they were seeing might be merely an illusion created by a false interpretation or mediation.

The technique of forcing readers to make political distinctions is found in *The Second Part of the Spectacles,* which appeared around nine days after the previous spectacles pamphlet. The pamphlet offered an illustration on the title page: a monocle, with the image of a tear-filled eye in the center, offering "this Multiplying Glass," a magnifying glass, "in pity to those poor-blind Brutes." The author revises the viewer's perspective of the prior spectacles pamphlet, *A New Invention,* explaining the irony in the previous pamphlet. This time, the speaker ventriloquizes a Royalist, repeatedly boasting of his "true Protestantism"—a phrase used both by the king and by his enemies as justification for their actions. To call oneself a "true Protestant" would make a very specific claim at this time, when the Reformation of the Protestant church was the aim of the Presbyterians, who called themselves "true Protestants." It was the Presbyterian belief that Charles and his cohort were not acting as "true Protestants," and Presbyterians made it their mission to bring England back to the "true Protestant" faith.

But this fictional character also identifies himself as a "Malignant," using the term of abuse coined by the Parliamentarians for their royalist enemies,

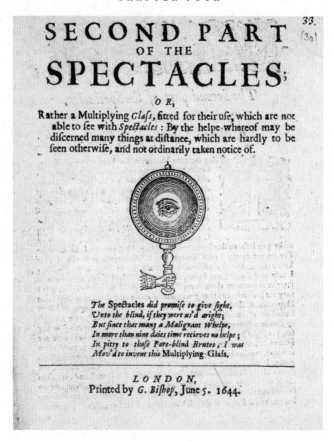

33.
(30)

SECOND PART
OF THE
SPECTACLES;

OR,

Rather a Multiplying *Glafs*, fitted for their ufe, which are not able to fee with *Spectacles* : By the helpe whereof may be difcerned many things at diftance, which are hardly to be feen otherwife, and not ordinarily taken notice of.

The Spectacles *did promife to give fight,*
Unto the blind, if they were us'd aright;
But fince that many a Malignant Whelpe,
In more than nine daies time recieves no helpe ;
In pitty to thofe Fore-blind Brutes ; I was
Mov'd to invent this Multiplying *Glafs.*

LONDON,
Printed by *G. Bifhop*, June 5. 1644.

7. Title page to *The Second Part of the Spectacles* (1644).

and the speaker thus immediately identifes himself with the *opposite* political allegiance. For someone to be identified as a "true Protestant" and then to claim one is a Malignant, as the speaker here does, presents a paradox that would immediately be recognized by readers of the day. The answer to this paradox is that this presentation is meant to be read in a special way. The "Malignant" but nonetheless "true Protestant" speaker in *The Second Part of the Spectacles* goes on to give "an account of my faith," and here we begin to resolve the paradox. If the reader perceives the conscious manipulation of key words, this text may be read as utterly ironic. "To be a *true Protestant*," the author explains, "it is very necessary first, that a man should be so far a Papist, as to maintain an implicit faith, and blind obedience to the Church," invoking the image of "blindness" to talk about allegiance to Rome. This "blind obedience" is understood to negate the rhetoric of freedom of real "true Protestants," whose very identities are pinned on independence from Rome. The author continues, "Nor will I believe, notwithstanding all the evidences, that they or His Majesties or Her Majesty, or her

Priests, Friars and Jesuits, ever intended anything but the maintaining of the *true Protestant Religion*." The author is self-incriminating, and also incriminates Charles, since to admit that the king and queen have a coterie of papist characters—priests, friars, Jesuits—hanging about is to expose the royal household as Catholic. The next five pages discuss the Spanish match and the Scottish war, and conclude that these seem incongruous with a true upholder of the Protestant faith.[48]

The "*true Protestant*"—and now the words ring hollow—provides evidences to prove that the king is in no way disloyal to the Protestant cause, yet these evidences cannot but accuse him—letters between Charles and the pope are said to show the king's friendliness to Catholics, and the marriage match between the king's son and the infanta of Spain are mentioned to prove his unswerving loyalty to the Protestant religion; yet the mere *fact* of such a correspondence would slur the king as pro-Catholic, as would negotiations with archenemy Spain, as an interpreting reader would recognize. The meaning of this pamphlet is triggered by the key words "true Protestant Religion," and these words are shown to be open to two competing interpretations. The text is finally to be understood as a savage antiroyalist polemic. The pamphlet shows a "way of seeing" through the language of enemy Royalists, and exposes the "Malignants" as hypocrites. *The Spectacles*, then, provides two perspectives, the one narrated in the pamphlet that is the phony Malignant's version of the story, where the king is defended as a "true Protestant," and the other side revealed through irony. The capable reader would see that the ironic perspective won.

In their mechanical actions of "undeception," the writers of the pamphlets made use of irony. Irony presents language by which we understand "something which is the opposite of what is actually said," according to Quintilian.[49] Irony was a key method writers used to oppose their enemy's propaganda during the English Revolution. It requires that readers recognize the simultaneous presence of two alternative accounts, between which the correct one must be discerned. In *A Rhetoric of Irony*, Wayne Booth calls "stable irony" the case where "the central meaning of the words is fixed and univocal, regardless of how many peripheral and even contradictory significances different readers might add," and the English revolutionary use of the trope of vision is such an instance.[50] This kind of irony allows readers to work to construct meaning, but the authors of the revolutionary pamphlets reined in the possible "contradictory significances" different readers might add. The civil war writers expressed anxieties precisely because of the existence of various possibilities for misinterpretation of their words, and those who made use of these tropes of vision sought to control their readers' responses by providing other possible readings, of which only one could be seen as true.

Attic drama gives a formula for irony, by which we can see irony as the master trope for literature in a world rife with propagandistic writing: "In the comedic form, a contest (*agon*) takes place between two types of characters, the *alazon* or Imposter and the *eiron*. The Imposter enters the scene full of pretension, but is finally routed by the Ironical Man, who proves not to be the fool he originally seemed to be."[51] This drama of "unmasking" is analogous to the "undeception" performed by Booker's pamphlet, where Booker "stripped" his royalist enemy naked. Through this kind of unmasking, authors aimed to control their readers' interpretation of other texts.

EIKONOKLASTES AND RIGHT READING

This drama of unmasking is also the story of Milton's *Eikonoklastes*, his response to *Eikon Basilike*, the "king's book." Milton was ordered by the Council of State to respond to *Eikon Basilike*, which, published on the day of the king's execution, was an immediate publicity success, appearing in forty English editions in its first year alone.[52] Milton's reply, published in October 1649, took the king's book on its own terms, examining it chapter by chapter. In *Eikonoklastes*, Milton shot at the king's "idolatrous" rhetoric with the artillery of rational argument.[53] He consistently aimed to show that while *Eikon Basilike* patently defended the king's actions before God, it was really a crafty defense before the citizens of England. Milton registered that his enemy's motive was to achieve "that what he could not compass by Warr . . . by his Meditations" (*CPW* 3.342), arguing that those still loyal to Charles "intend it not so much the defence of his former actions, as the promoting of thir own future designes, making thereby the Book thir own rather than the Kings, as the benefit now must be thir own more then his, now the third time to corrupt and disorder the mindes of weaker men, by new suggestions and narrations" (3.338). Like those pamphleteers concerned about the fate of the gullible reader, Milton was worried that the king's book would corrupt "weaker men" because it disarmed readers by rhetorical tricks, and would thus strengthen the royalist cause.

Milton did not just replace the king's image of a martyr in *Eikon Basilike* with one of a tyrant in *Eikonoklastes*, but he also offered readers a way to perform such readings in the future, that "they that will, may now see at length how much they were deceiv'd in him, and were ever like to be hereafter" (3.364); that readers "may find the grace and good guidance to bethink themselves, and recover" (3.601). While *Eikonoklastes* was a circumstantial and topical tract, by these words Milton expresses his worry about the effect of such propaganda for the future; and his own writing urgently essays to teach his own readers how to "read aright" any such piece of propaganda. Milton, throughout his writing career, sought to provide readers not only with images, but also with strategies for reading and ways of seeing. He relied upon readers who wielded reason "sufficient both to judge aright and to examine each matter," as he put it in *Areopagitica* (*CPW* 2.511), to make their way through the quagmire of rhetoric. These properly reading subjects would be able to resist propaganda by relying upon inner judgment to evaluate the statements before them. Milton sought to instruct readers politically in his *Eikonoklastes* by offering a completely different interpretation of an earlier text, and by urging readers to follow his alternative in its methods and in its conclusions. Milton guided his reader through the king's book, chapter by chapter, and performed a textual exegesis for that reader. Milton had become a literary critic in the service of politics.

In *Eikonoklastes*, Milton reinterpreted the king's penitent stance, rewriting the meanings of Charles at prayer. The "king's book," *Eikon Basilike*, had relied heavily on the king's prayers in his drama of self-justification, and the image of the penitent monarch at his prayers was one of the most powerful in the book, adorning the frontispiece with a holy show. Compiled and probably written by the cleric John Gauden, *Eikon Basilike* presented a defense of Charles, included a narration of the events from the meeting of the Long Parliament in 1641 until the king's imprisonment, and was supplemented by the king's own personal reminiscences and feelings. With the brilliance of a master propagandist, Gauden had presented Charles's prayers at the end of each chapter, which called upon God to bear witness to the rightness of his actions. In fact, the prayers became the most popular portions of the book itself, surviving in printed royalist collections well into the eighteenth century in translations, versifications, and musical settings.[54] *Eikon Basilike* was received by its contemporary readers less as a work of polemical persuasion than as a remembrance for a martyr.[55]

Aside from the prayers' appeal as popular songs, they provided an airtight piece of propaganda for the king: How could anyone quarrel with his prayers, the utterances of the king's own conscience? The testimony of Charles's conscience was a powerful tool because conscience was thought to be an irrefutable source of authority, unassailable because it derived power from a source outside politics, from God. The king insisted again and again on the primacy of his conscience in justifying his actions: "I know no resolutions more worthy a Christian King than to prefer his own conscience before his Kingdom's."[56] For Milton, the image of the king was not only dangerous as an instance of theatricality, but because that image was a specific representation: the king at prayer. Prayer held special meaning for a Protestant; it was the direct and, above all, the *sincere* communication between humans and God, and it represented the voice of conscience. In *Eikonoklastes*, Milton exchanged the religious meanings of conscience for political ones as he sought to catch the conscience of the king, hoping to expose the "facil conscience [which] could dissemble satisfaction when it pleas'd" (*CPW* 3.371–72). The king's invocation of conscience as the bedrock of political action in *Eikon Basilike* exposes a conceptual difficulty for Milton, who agrees that conscience is a fundamental guide of human conduct, but who refuses to exempt the king from his responsibilities to his people on the grounds of such a guide.

In *Eikon Basilike*, Charles repeatedly appealed to the testimony of his prayers as a defense, using the expression of his inward conscience to lend authority to the image of his piety, martyrdom, and Christian worthiness. The king's self-fashioning as a Christian martyr relied upon the traditional Protestant sense of conscience as an infallible moral judge to be obeyed regardless of human censure. The king insisted on the propriety of his actions on these unimpeachable grounds: "I may, without vanity, turn the reproach of my sufferings, as to the world's censure, into the honour of a kind of martyrdom, as to the testimony of my own conscience" (163). By fashioning himself as a martyr, the king presents a self-authorizing exemption from the ordinary strictures of civil behavior.[57] A martyr answers to a higher law, and the king goes so far as to justify his opposition to the Parliament's requests on the grounds that they would "wound that inward quiet of my conscience, which ought to be, is, and ever shall be, by God's grace, dearer to me than my Kingdoms" (53). Like the conventional martyr, Charles owes his allegiance to God, not to the humans who have judged him: "Thou, O Lord, art my witness in heaven and in my heart if I have purposed any violence or oppression against the innocent or if there were any such wickedness in my thoughts" (13). Repeatedly stressing his inward piety over his outward circumstances, the king concludes, "I am confident the justice of my cause and clearness of my conscience before God and toward my people will carry me as much above [my enemies] in God's decision as their successes have lifted them above me in the vulgar opinion" (178).

Given that the language of conscience was so often used during the English Revolution as justification for opposition to the king, it is surprising is that the king himself employs this defense. Milton and many others had preached resistance to an "unjust" king like Charles on grounds of conscience, and as we saw in chapter 1, conscience was an important ground on which radicals staked their claims for a potent public.[58] Rebelling against unjust kingship in the *Tenure of Kings and Magistrates*, Milton argued that "God put it into mans heart to find out that way at first for common peace and preservation, approving the exercise therof" (*CPW* 3.209), and he applied the theory that citizens could judge rulers by the workings of an inner natural law, the law of conscience. Milton himself had subscribed to such a view of conscience in his poetry and prose, and would present figures who exemplified conscientious resistance (Abdiel and Enoch are two) in *Paradise Lost*. Because conscience made humans answerable to God alone, it could not be refuted on ordinary civil grounds, as Milton was well aware, and it could provide a defense of unprecedented actions like a tyrannicide (*Tenure of Kings and Magistrates*, *CPW* 3.237).

Conscience was Milton's "umpire" in *Paradise Lost*, which hears cases, and was also termed God's "Secretary" (*Reason of Church Government*, *CPW* 1.822). A "secretary" is one who is entrusted with private or secret matters in addition to being the name for one whose office it is to write for another. Conscience is a secretary in that it is entrusted with the commands of God, and it is also a secretary in the sense that it takes down God's dictation on the heart of the individual. Conscience as a secretary is "written," and the metaphor Milton uses in an echo of Calvin is "engrave," a form of writing that is lasting, as on stone. In opposing those prelates who would force conscience, Michael in *Paradise Lost* describes to Adam that forcing conscience violates that inner writing:

> . . . from that pretense,
> Spiritual Laws by carnal power shall force
> On every conscience; Laws which none shall find
> Left to them inroll'd, or what the Spirit within
> Shall on the heart engrave.
>
> (12.520–24)

Like the words on the tablets of stone of the Ten Commandments, the words of conscience are written by God.

The Puritan sense of conscience was commonly translated into an image of a physical guide, as Milton does in his sonnet "To Mr. Cyriack Skinner upon His Blindness," where he uses an image of the conscience that follows Calvin's usage. Even though the poet is now blind,

> . . . Yet I argue not
> Against heav'n's hand or will, nor bate a jot
> Of heart or hope; but still bear up and steer
> Right onward. What supports me, dost thou ask?
> The conscience, Friend. . .
>
> (*CP* 170, lines 6–10)

Conscience is that inner faculty which liberates the poet from the need for external sight. He is "content though blind" (line 14), and "yet" he harbors hopes about the future. The short, sharp words (bate, jot, heart, hope, bear, steer) are pricks and prods which portray that journey as uneven, even a stumbling one, as if the way is strewn with sharp stones. Conscience provides a steady help through these. Conscience is a kind of internal navigational device, both in land as it is in the "blindness" sonnet, and at sea, as it is in the most memorable of Milton's lines on conscience, where it is the "umpire Conscience" that leads humans to "safe arrive" (*Paradise Lost* 3.195–97).

In Milton's early poem, "On the New Forcers of Conscience under the Long Parliament," the poet sought to protect the spiritual freedom of conscience from encroachments by the civil realm. Milton railed against "the new forcers of conscience" in 1646, against those who seemed to encroach upon the freedoms of individual conscience to decide how to practice religion. Milton asked the civil authorities,

> Dare ye for this adjure the Civil Sword
> To force our Consciences that Christ set free
>
> (*CP* 144, lines 5–6)

The poem makes a clear distinction between the "Civil Sword" and that which "Christ set free," two spheres of action that Milton's two separate lines of poetry tried to keep apart.

For the king to use this defense is thus an alliance with the more radical reformers of his day. In writing his answer to *Eikon Basilike* in 1649, Milton is put in the position of having to explain why conscience may not always authorize actions, since the king relied so heavily on conscience to justify his actions. The king's invocations of conscience were deeply troubling to Milton, who was fighting for freedom of conscience but who saw in the king's words a terrible hypocrisy. In seeking a way to eliminate the king's conscience from the public realm, Milton's main strategy was to to cloud the testimony of the king's conscience by proving that the king was an utter hypocrite, and he did this by rereading the tract and by explaining that the king's plagiarism was a flagrant example of his hypocrisy. Milton used the example of the stolen prayers, both from Sidney's *Arcadia* and from David's psalms to discredit the king's account, proving by literary means that the king's book was a plagiary, a forgery, not a true prayer. The biblical heist was more opprobrious than the literary one for Milton, because of the connection between prayer and conscience in Puritan theology, as outlined above. To Milton, as to the reforming godly of the civil war period, prayer was an especially inflammatory cause, not only as a religious cause, but also as a political one. The first actions of dissent against the king had responded to his imposition of the prayer book by prerogative in Scotland in 1637. At stake was Charles's desire for a uniform church, to be dictated by set forms of worship, what Milton and others would call the forcing of conscience. The Laudian interest in linguistic regularity in set prayers, along with all the other signs of ritual, seemed to reformers to smack of idolatry. In Puritan minds, institutionalized forms of worship were evil, since they interrupted the conversation between an individual's conscience and God. These reformers echoed Jesus' attack on the Pharisaic hypocrisy in the New Testament.

Charles' prayers required rereading, Milton asserts. Not only were the stolen prayers signs of the king's general usurpation of his people's right, of his false dramatic role as a penitent martyr, and of his odious prayer book reforms, but most importantly, they were signs of the dangerous gap between Charles's words and his heart's intentions: "Had he borrow'd *Davids* heart, it had bin much the holier theft" (547). Especially in prayer, there ought to be a correlation between the inner condition of the soul and the outward use of forms, but Milton claimed that one's inner condition is unreadable. The king had no right to the words spoken by others because of this gap between inner thoughts and outward manifestations of those thoughts. Only God can know to whom the property, literary and otherwise, rightly belongs: "It is not hard for any man, who hath a Bible in his hands, to borrow good words and holy sayings in abundance; but to make them his own, is a work of grace onely from above" (553).[59] Inner spirit

must accord with external presentation: "But transported with the vain os-
tentation of imitating *Davids* language, not his life, observe how he brings
a curse upon himself and his Fathers house (God so disposing it) by his
usurp'd and ill imitated prayer" (555). Thus Milton's own readers will learn
proper habits of reading in knowing what may be read—acts—and what
may not—intentions.

The theft of Jesus' words was an ultimate act of hypocrisy because,
through his deeds, Charles had proven himself most unlike Jesus: "eev'n his
prayer is so ambitious of Prerogative, that it dares ask away the Prerogative
of Christ himself" (502). It is interesting to note that Milton used the familiar language of Parliament in its attacks on Charles's abuse of prerogative.
The king's literary borrowing was the same as his political acts of usurpation, tyrannical because it depended upon the king's will alone. Milton's
attack on the plagiarism is analogous to the parliamentary interpretation
that the king has stolen authority that was originally in the people. Just as
the king has stolen from his people, "in whom the power yet remains fundamentally, and cannot be tak'n from them, without a violation of thir natural birthright" (*Tenure, CPW* 3.202), he has stolen their literary works, having none of his own to provide for his own sufferings. Milton opposed the
king's use of the prayers of others because they were inauthentic, and as
stolen words, they were proof that the Charles's piety was an artful construction. As Milton saw it, the king was proving nothing in using Jesus' last
words on the cross, since "it is an easy matter to say over what our Saviour
said"; instead, Milton demanded that Charles be judged by his actions,
"how he lov'd the People, other Arguments then affected sayings must de-
monstrat" (*Eikonoklastes, CPW* 3.447). Though the king has spoken the same
words as Jesus, his inner worth was in no way the same.

Further, in politics, prayers alone do not count. Milton writes: "But
Kings, above all other men, have in thir hands not to pray onely but to doe.
To make that prayer effectual, he should have govern'd as well as pray'd. To
pray and not to govern is For a Monk and not a King" (3.531). Milton works
himself into the position of denying the king any rule by his personal conscience at all, drawing the reader's attention to the disparity between the
king's words and his actions, and claiming that by those actions alone may
Charles be judged: "As for the truth and sinceritie which he praies may be
alwaies found in those his Declarations to the people, the contrariety of his
own actions will bear eternal witness how little carefull or sollicitous he was,
what he promis'd, or what he utterd there" (3.469). Words should not substitute for facts: since actions occur in the public realm, they alone can be
subject to public evaluation. The danger of judging the king by his words
alone is that the words cannot be trusted: "meer words we are too well
acquainted with," Milton remarks with a sneer (3.497). The King's words
alone are as dangerous as kingly prerogative, authority without checks.

Milton distrusts the king's claims of conscience in the public realm at all:
"To wipe off jealousies and scandals, the best way, had bin by clear Actions,

or till Actions be clear'd, by evident reasons" (3.497). The king especially is not entitled to follow the callings of his private conscience because the king is not a private man. In Milton's *Treatise of Civil Power,* and also in the two poems on conscience, Milton separated the realms of civil and ecclesiastical jurisdiction, allowing each human to preserve a private inner space for conscience, as Luther had done before him. But Milton presses this distinction: Kings do not enjoy the same privacy of conscience as private citizens do. A king in *Eikonoklastes* is a wholly public figure; his conscience is not admitted to resolve political situations. Milton proposes a model for political justification that is based upon "evident reasons," not upon inner faith, where the readership of English citizens, rather than God, must act as judges of the king's actions. Milton denies that conscience may stand as an authority for a public man like the king by asserting his account of the political responsibilities of the magistrate: "This we may take for certain, that he was never sworn to his own particular conscience and reason, but to our condition as a free people" (3.519). The king's loyalty is to public, not to his private morality. As Milton writes in *Tenure of Kings and Magistrates,* "to say Kings are accountable to none but God, is the overturning of all Law and Government" (2.204). The king's conscience then is not utterly free, but accountable, as was kingly prerogative, to his subjects.

Rather than to accept the private—and unreadable except by God—calling of the king's conscience, Milton sought to place *Eikon Basilike* firmly in the public realm so that it could be refuted. Since the king was "making new appeale to Truth and to the World," Milton would offer a counterappeal to the king in an "op'n and monumental Court of his own erecting" (3.340–41). That court would be the court of public opinion rather than the private court of Charles's conscience. Because of his assertion that the real audience for *Eikon Basilike* is the English citizenry, Milton rejects the king's claims that God is his authority and judge of his actions. Milton substitutes the English nation as judge, insisting the the king's actions must be evaluated in the public realm.

SIGHT, INSIGHT, AND POLITICAL VISION

Just as Milton did in response to *Eikon Basilike,* many authors of pamphlets sought to educate their readers in ways of reading and conducted that education before the eyes of the world, in the press, in public. They thought about conflicting points of view in perceptual terms. By use of the figures of mechanical optical devices, writers signaled that readers had to practice special reading skills. "True Protestant" was a term that might be employed for opposite purposes. However, one thorny issue remained: how could writers be sure that their perspective was any more secure than the one they had displaced?

In *Paradise Lost*, Milton finds a solution by having Adam's faulty vision relieved through divine means. In book 11, Michael applies a potion to correct Adam's sight:

> . . . to nobler sights
> Michael from Adam's eyes the Film remov'd
> Which that false Fruit that promis'd clearer sight
> Had bred; then purg'd with Euphrasy and Rue
> The visual Nerve, for he had much to see;
> And from the Well of Life three drops instill'd.
> So deep the power of these Ingredients pierc'd
> Ev'n to the inmost seat of mental sight
>
> (11. 411–18)

Michael's "preservative for sight," as the civil war pamphlets would call it, gives Adam the perspective needed to view human history with clarity of true vision. Michael rids Adam of the distorting perspective that had been "promised" as "clearer" by the "false Fruit."[60] The language of this passage cannot but recall in our minds the rhetoric of the civil war pamphlets, which also offered restoration for faulty vision: *Eye-Salve for the City of London* (1648); *Eye-Salve for the English Armie* (1660); and *Eye Salve for England* (1667). Michael's educative mission to Adam and Eve provides a way for them to see, and books 11 and 12 of *Paradise Lost* chronicle that education in perception, guided by divine impulse. At other moments in *Paradise Lost*, readers hear echoes of that civil war trope of correcting eyesight. Milton converts it, however, into a spiritual condition, as when Adam exclaims to Michael, "I was far deceived; for now I see" (11.783); "now I see" is repeated in 12.286; and in a redemptive moment, Adam reports, "Now first I find / Mine eyes true op'ning, and my heart much eas'd" (12.273–74). Of course, greater than the scope of the poet, yet straining to be contained within his language, is the ultimate panoptical perspective, that of God, who "beholding from his prospect high, / Wherein past, present, future he beholds" (3.76–77). This is like the position of the king at the center of the English Renaissance masque's audience; the king sat in the only position where true perspective would be possible.[61] In the case of the civil war pamphlets, however, readers themselves would have to assume this primary seat of view. In Milton's lexicon, sight is often a metaphor for spiritual enlightenment; humans strive for such a total perspective.

Yet lack of sight also has its value. Milton takes his own blindness to be a spiritual advantage in his *Second Defense of the English People*, answering his supposed enemy, Alexander More: "As to my blindness, I would rather have mine, if it be necessary, than . . . yours. Your blindness, deeply implanted in the inmost faculties, obscures the mind, so that you may see nothing whole or real. Mine, which you make a reproach, merely deprives things of color and superficial appearance. . . . there is hope that in this way I may approach more closely the mercy and protection of the Father Almighty. . . So in this darkness, may I be clothed in light" (*CPW* 4.589–90). We might contrast More's blindness, "deeply implanted in the inmost faculties," to Adam's cleared "inmost seat of mental sight." In his *Second Defense*, Milton presents some kinds of blindness as offering a sign of "divine favor," a benefit: "Nor do these shadows around us seem to have been created so much by the dullness of our eyes as by the shade of angels' wings. And divine favor not infrequently is wont to lighten these shadows again, once made, by an inner and far more enduring light" (4.589–90). This "inner light" language echoes the language of conscience, which we have seen Milton so roundly reject in the king's book. Yet in the case of his personal blindness, or that of Adam, inner vision is obtained through personal, not public, means. There is a difference between the two realms, the public and the private, in the way conscience may act.

Is this blindness also a political advantage, as Milton suggests in these remarks in *Second Defense*? That is, will the stripping of all mediations (including sight) lead to political truths? In *Eikonoklastes*, Milton supports the political value of "blindness," as evidenced in his scorn for the visual tricks of the frontispiece of the king's book. But Milton's *Paradise Lost* does not argue this line. In the last books of *Paradise Lost*, Adam does see truly; the problem for Milton is those readers who, lacking a divine interpreter, may not. Without direct divine intervention—and such interventions do not happen frequently—sight may be a dangerously misleading. For Milton, few had the special qualifications to be blind.

There are many examples of the difficulty in seeing properly in *Paradise Lost*, and indeed, Satan exemplifies the dangerous power of deception.[62] As my final example, I take one optical metaphor in *Paradise Lost*, by which Milton himself plays visual tricks on his reader in presenting Satan early on as an epic hero, and that is Satan's shield:

> . . . his ponderous shield
> Etherial temper, massy, large and round,
> Behind him cast; the broad circumference
> Hung on his shoulders like the Moon, whose Orb
> Through Optic Glass the *Tuscan* Artist views
> At Ev'ning from the top of *Fesole*,
> Or in *Valdarno*, to descry new Lands,
> Rivers or Mountains in her spotty Globe.
>
> (1.284–91)

This passage relies on the double outlook of mock-epic that both asserts and takes away comparison with the shields of Homer's Achilles and Spenser's Radigund; it has also been read as an instance of the Miltonic sublime.[63] But there is another tool of perspective at work here, namely, the telescope, and by using this figure, Milton seems to respond to the civil war trope. Satan's shield looks "massy, large and round" like the moon, yet only when seen through the magnifying lens of a telescope. The line break in the poetry leads readers to expect an epic comparison between the shield's brightness and the moon's, but readers' hopes are dashed by the next line, which explains the optical illusion: "Hung on his shoulders like the Moon, whose Orb / Through Optic Glass the *Tuscan* Artist views." We know as well as Milton how small the moon looks in the sky without optical aid. Satan's shield may appear a huge, massy, and intolerably bright thing—Galileo's telescope in 1610 showed objects thirty times nearer and one thousand times larger—but only from a perverted perspective. Thus, Satan's false heroism is revealed by an act of visual perception, and his power is deflated once readers see that the image is mediated by a telescope. Just as the civil war pamphleteers had used the figure, Milton exposes illusion of a specifically political kind through the simile. Like those authors, Milton provides the reader with the view of the behind-the-scenes of epic machinery: since we see the telescope magnifying Satan's shield to its epic proportions, Satan's heroism is diminished.

In *Paradise Lost*, however, Galileo's telescope does not necessarily lead to truth. As we follow the figure throughout the poem, we find a metaphoric structure based on the use of the telescope references.[64] It has been argued that because the new optics revealed imperfections in heavenly bodies, the new science could be allied to the work of "skeptical political analysis."[65] Indeed, it is not clear from Milton's other use of telescope references that the perspective derived from the optical instrument is any truer than other perspectives, despite Milton's positive image of Galileo. Milton may share some of the skepticism of Thomas Hobbes, who asserted that philosophy was the truest form of knowledge, by contrasting it to science: "by opticks I can multiply at will."[66] In optics, Hobbes suggests, distortion and multiple perspectives could actually prevent the acquisition of true knowledge.

That the telescope would not necessarily lead to a truer perspective is an opinion of at least one other civil war writer. In the royalist pamphlet *The Great Assizes Holden in Parnassus* (1645), the author accuses the parliamentary newsbook:

> Old Galileo's glasses to have used,
> Which represented objects to his eye,
> Beyond their measure, and just symmetry,
> Whereby the faults of many did appear,
> More and far greater, than indeed they were.[67]

In this allusion to Galileo's telescope, the author criticizes the interpretations of the parliamentary propagandist, who saw more than was actually there. The mechanical visual aids did not lead to a truer picture, but rather to a tainted one. If we follow the telescope image in *Paradise Regained*, moreover, Milton's position is closer to this writer than to those who sought a single truth by means of optical aids. In *Paradise Regained*, Satan employs an optical lens in order to display the kingdoms of the world, to tempt the Son in book 4: "By what strange Parallax or optic skill / Of vision multiplied through air, or glass / Of Telescope" (40–42). Further on, Satan uses an instrument to give an impossible perspective: "Many a fair Edifice besides, more like / Houses of Gods (so well I have dispos'd / My Airy Microscope) thou mayst behold / Outside and inside both . . ." (55–58). In both allusions, the lens does reveal more to see than the naked eye can behold. But it is not a truer vision. Rather, the Son must reject these perspectives.

In Milton's view, then, the telescope can only be a figure representing manipulation of sight. In the case of Satan's shield, the true perspective is reached by the reader who is capable of recognizing irony, who is able to distinguish the right reading from a distorted perspective. Satan himself appears like an epic hero only through a mechanical act of distortion, for which the act of proper reading will itself be a cure. Common to Milton's representation of Satan's shield and to the pamphleteers who made use of the optical metaphors is an invitation to readers that they read differently—that they read with the knowledge that what they are seeing *is* a perspective, a mediated representation, and not necessarily the truth. The English Revolution was asking readers to become hermeneuts, reading between the lines. Leo Strauss's essay "Persecution and the Art of Writing" outlined the strategy by which writers "write between the lines," a technique the ancients developed to evade detection for heterodox views. Yet Strauss's formulation goes beyond the conditions of censorship; he suggests that "writing between the lines" is a condition of all serious writing that attempts to exclude the many from its precious teaching; a writer's exoteric and his esoteric meanings are not intended for the same audience. Only qualified readers will attend to the esoteric meanings, that "philosophic teaching concerning the most important subject, which is indicated only between the lines."[68] Annabel Patterson has offered a contrary understanding of the effects of persecution on writing, preferring instead of Strauss's sense of a privileged few readers a tradition of "intellectual and political liberalism of an egalitarian bent," and its service in a "more open society than Straussianism aims to promote." Patterson's understanding of "writing between the lines" thus differs fundamentally from what she calls Strauss's cynical belief that texts "should *never* be made public except to a chosen group of acolytes."[69] In our study here, however, we find that many civil war writers would have agreed with Strauss that political truths, and political action, should be restricted to the few who were qualified to inhabit their roles as leaders. Writing between the lines could embrace *either* the author's search for a wide public *or* for a narrow few; and the writers of the English Revolution differed in attitudes toward elliptical writing because of their contrastive views about the capability of the public. I have found that persecuted writing does not signify one type of audience or another just because it is persecuted writing; rather, authors' use of obliqueness depended upon their assumptions about their audiences.

ALLEGORY AND PERSPECTIVE

If writers saw that competing representations of truth were circulating in the pamphlets, they also saw the political uses of ambiguity as well. Under the conditions of censorship, writers had to take care not to be too explicit about their allegiances, but covert writing could help to get a message across in a hostile climate. Interpreting such oblique literature, however, did require special skills of readers. Though we return to *Paradise Lost* and to its political meanings in the next chapter, we glimpse it here to illustrate the uses of ambiguity in this climate of conflicting interpretations. Milton used an astrological image loaded with topical political meanings in his poem: precisely which political meaning he intends, however, he leaves unclear. Multiple perspectives offered by ambiguous language did not always lead to clearer sight.

Allegedly a censor—L'Estrange, perhaps—objected to the following passage in which Milton presents Satan:

> . . . As when the Sun new ris'n
> Looks through the Horizontal misty Air
> Shorn of his Beams, or from behind the Moon
> In dim Eclipse disastrous twilight sheds
> On half the Nations, and with fear of change
> Perplexes Monarchs.
>
> (1.594–599)

The someone who blinked at the poem—or at least those who spread the legend about that someone—saw potential political danger in this image of an eclipse.[70] This would not have been an idle objection. Since the monarchy in England had long assumed the iconography of the sun, the image of an eclipse could be read as a sign of monarchy's temporary abatement; this might be seen as a treasonous image. In popular belief, eclipses were thought quite literally to portend evil for monarchs, and Milton's use of this laden image has led at least one modern scholar of the poem to sniff out Milton's hidden rebellious message.[71] Milton's contemporary readers, too, were becoming practiced in interpreting such political allegories, since political meanings were never far from the surface of the many astrological predictions and images used in this period. As one prescient author remarked, "But as Astronomers who converse with bodies above, do frame and invent certain imaginary circles and lines to verify their conclusions, and make reason good; So in the Regions of state it often falls out that Politicians do oftentimes raise imaginary fears, doubts, and ombrages to make their proceedings more plausible."[72]

The political meanings of any given figure were rarely unequivocal however, and the image of the eclipse was worked by both sides during the civil war period for different purposes. In his allegorical play, *The Distracted State, A Tragedy* (1651), the royalist John Tatham (fl. 1632–64), a dramatist and city poet who succeeded John Taylor and Thomas Heywood as laureate to the lord mayor of London's show, presented the character Mazarus, a "Machiavell" who seized power from his brother Evander. When a lord opposed Mazarus's rule, he talked of the "Eclipse" of Evander's "right,"and the play's chorus also expressed a worry that the national church would follow Mazarus: "Let not this sudden change / Possess the [the church] with a fear of her Eclipse."[73] Read from a royalist vantage point, the image shows the moon or another planet covering the sun's position like a political usurper, just as Mazarus/Cromwell had taken over the position of the true king, Evander/Charles, in the first instance and the church in the second. In a similar manner, the devils in the royalist pamphlet *A Trance; or, News from Hell* (1649) represent members of Parliament who boast : "we have *eclips'd* the glory of the English Nation, we have made them by all people far and near that ever had knowledge of them, to be pitied by some, to be derided by others, to be scorned of all, and to become the very tail of all Nations" (italics mine).[74] The eclipse metaphor condemns opponents of King Charles. But on the parliamentary side, the image of an eclipse was used with a different key to the allegory. In *The Great Eclipse of the Sun; or, Charles his Wain* (1644), for example, the pro-Parliament author sets out his cosmic analogy thus: "The Common-wealth may most fitly be compared to the Glory of the Heavens. The King is the *Sun*, the Parliament are the bright *Stars*; Malignant Counsellours to the King, are the evil aspected *Planets*, such as *Bristol, Cottington*, Lord Keeper *Littleton, Digby, Jermyn*, and others; whereby the King hath been Eclipsed." As in the previous example, the sun is the king. The eclipsing body, however, is different: "the King was eclipsed by the [papist] Queen, and she persuaded him that Darkness was Light."[75] In this instance of proparliamentary allegory, the bodies that shield the sun (king) are both the stars (his "Malignant Counsellours") and his queen.

How were readers to distinguish between these contrary uses of the same image? Milton compounds the problem by presenting the eclipse several times in *Paradise Lost*, with different meanings, as if to challenge his readers to give up on a conclusion at all. In *Paradise Lost* Milton could be seen to blacken the image of Charles II simply by comparing both him *and* Satan to the sun; both are like "the Sun new ris'n" (1.594). But later Milton questions this political allegory by putting it in Satan's mouth: "Another now hath to himself ingross't / All power, and us eclipst under the name / Of King anointed" (5.775–77). At the moment Satan rallies the troops in his counterfeit speech to his army, he sees himself as the eclipsed sun. Even though his point of view renders the reference patently spurious, the allegory corresponds to heavenly hierarchy, unlike in the image in book 1, where there was no exact key: the interposing body here is Christ, whom God preferred to Lucifer in heaven. Yet the language of "ingrossing" ties Satan's complaint in with that of the radicals of the English Revolution, and by using this language, this author suggests that the "King anointed" may not just be the approved Christ, but also the engrosser Charles. Thus at the same time, the second presentation of the image is clearer and less clear than the first; it is clearer in terms of its religious allegory, but it is less clear in its political meanings, and finally not trustworthy because the origin of the comparison is satanic. The censor may have understood the various meanings of these passages, and judged them to be damaging political attacks against an earthly king's authority.

Conflicts in perspective thus might not lead readers down a clear path toward truth. Though authors of the pamphlets used the optical metaphors in order to clear the field for their own truth, Milton in *Paradise Lost*, though not in *Eikonoklastes*, took a more skeptical route: readers themselves would likely stumble if they attempted to resolve the poetical ambiguity. The metaphors of true sight that were scattered throughout civil war literature were a marker of writers' awareness of the problems of reading and interpreting propaganda, of the problem of engaging an audience for political action. As polemicists of the civil war period struggled to replace the "erroneous" perspectives of their enemies with their own "true" ones, like Cromwell's "undeceptions," which attempted to cancel further "undeceptions," Milton's *Eikonoklastes* also attempted to recover the "true" portrait of Charles, despite using metaphors that could undermine that very effort. Milton used the figure of the telescope in *Paradise Lost* to call for readers to realize that the danger for political rhetoric was that there would always be another "deception" to "undeceive." Perhaps the readers of *Paradise Lost* would not come to political truths as a result of their reading, but they would become warier of mediated language, perhaps better able to defend themselves from the imprisonment of a single view.

Paradise Lost may serve to trip up the reader with its ambiguous eclipses and mediated visions; nevertheless, Milton's references to topical, political images reveal his interest, shared by the civil war pamphleteers, that readers be instructed in how to read and deflect propaganda. Milton's education of readers in *Paradise Lost* may be thought of as a response to the hermeneutic problems posed by propaganda, as we shall see later. If the poem is read through the pattern offered in *Eikonoklastes*, where Milton chose to present his education in perception as a lesson in reading, this specifically sets aside a divine resolution to the problem of finding political truths. Milton, of course, did not reject divine guidance in *Paradise Lost*, yet he does follow the implicit logic of the "spectacles" pamphlets to its skeptical conclusions, offering methods, and not results, for the achievement of true sight. Milton pursued an option other than placing God as the source of all true perspective, that is, placing readers at the center of a new practice of polemical discourse.

In the next chapter, *Paradise Lost* will be seen as a reflection on these rhetorical conditions of the English Revolution. As many critics have shown, Milton's *Paradise Lost* pursues a task of educating its readers. When we compare this literary task to the kind of hermeneutic training writers imposed on the readers of propaganda we have examined here, we find that Milton, completing *Paradise Lost* after the failure of the Commonwealth and Protectorate, pursued a task of responding to the rhetorical practices that had misled so many during the English Revolution. Milton, like the other writers who engaged in the propaganda wars of the English Revolution, wished to constitute subjects who were equipped with reading skills to meet the challenge posed by propaganda. These writers conceived of political subjects as those who could root out truth among conflicting interpretations, who could make political choices based on a critical practice of reading.

Milton and the Fit Reader

PARADISE LOST *AND THE PARLIAMENT OF HELL*

> But now the Mystic Tale, that pleas'd of Yore,
>
> Can charm an understanding Age no more;
>
> The long-spun Allegories fulsom grow,
>
> While the dull Moral lyes too plain below.

Joseph Addison, *An Account of the Greatest English Poets* (1694)

THE ANONYMOUS ROYALIST AUTHOR of *We have fish'd and caught a Frog; or, The History of Several new Fishermen* (1649) indirectly condemned Cromwell's printing orders and urged a restoration of the rightful king after the execution of Charles: "although every lie be an untruth, yet every seeming untruth is not a lie," this author admitted, revealing a surprising candor about his use of the mode of fiction. The explanation continues: "There are in History and Poetry many allegories, tropes, types, figures, comparisons, similitudes and fables; which though they seem to be false, yet (if they be rightly interpreted) they carry in their Morals truth, sense, and reason."[1] Partisan poetic practice seemed to revel in allegory during the Interregnum, as authors protected themselves from persecution by casting their political ideas in fiction. Because of the increasing effectiveness of Cromwell's censors, many writers willingly threw veils over their true meanings in order to escape detection for politically dangerous views. Before 1644, all newsbooks were subjected to the gaze of a clerk of the Stationers' Company; in 1644, the job fell to a clerk assistant to the House of Commons; in 1647, when the army threatened mutiny, Parliament and its committees renewed their censorship efforts, passing a new ordinance in 1647. With the execution of the king, Parliament took even stricter control over the press in the Treason Act of 14 May 1649, specifying that writing against the government or the army was to be considered treason. The act was to be enforced by the military; authors were liable to execution. During the Protectorate, the Council of State rather than the Stationers' Company acted as the chief regulatory body of the press, and in 1655, Cromwell himself ordered the most effective measures yet: no other journal but Marchamont Nedham's *Mercurius Britannicus* was licensed to appear.[2] As Annabel

Patterson has argued in her brilliant *Censorship and Interpretation,* allegory had been a means for writers to evade censorship since the Tudors. During the Interregnum, those supporting Parliament made less frequent use of allegory, perhaps on the ideological grounds of iconoclasm, but also because they did not have to cower under the same kinds of press restrictions.

I see the aesthetic principle of a limited readership underlying much revolutionary allegorical practice, not solely because of censorship, however. There is another reason for the ubiquity of this literary royalist mode, irrespective of censorship conditions. Allegories require that readers do something when they read, and only properly equipped readers can do what is required.[3] In using allegory as a political mode, partisan writers required distinctions to be made by their audiences. Their readers had to, in some sense, come to share the particular vision of the author, who divided the audience into those who read and understood and those who did not—either because they lacked the reading skills or because they disputed the raw premise. In this chapter, we shall see how in using allegory, partisan writers embodied certain assumptions about a coterie readership, as had the anonymous author in *We have Fish'd,* who insisted that his work is to be "rightly interpreted." In his book *The Veil of Allegory,* Michael Murrin traces this theme of a select audience in Renaissance allegorical theories of Harington, Boccaccio, Spenser, and others. As Murrin sees it, the allegorist is like "the hierophant of the mysteries [who] habitually classified people into the categories of the sacred and the profane, the initiate and the uninitiate, those who knew the secrets of salvation and those who do not."[4] In the charged political context of the English Revolution, such categories took on the particular colors of the respective parties, and thus it is not surprising that Royalists should devote themselves to a marked set of royalist tropes: the martyr king, Babel, women on top. Northrop Frye in his *Anatomy of Criticism* shows disdain for allegory precisely because of the kind of authorial control it exerts over readers (as Samuel Johnson had before him): a "continuous allegory prescribes the direction of [the reader's] commentary, and so restricts its freedom."[5] Allegory, consequently, serves political propaganda well. During the English Revolution, writers sought to effect political persuasion, to consolidate support from a select audience, and thus to limit the "freedom" of their readers to come to any conclusion. Maureen Quilligan adds to Frye's conclusion that "what the reader loses in freedom, he makes up in significance," insisting that readers themselves become part of the process of understanding the allegory.[6] In a way, the readers of allegories become unwitting participants in political discussion as they flesh out the author's vision.

Allegory, as I see it, becomes the hinge on which rest the issues of interpretation, polemical practice, and audiences we have been dealing with in the previous chapters. In the Interregnum, while Royalists wore the bridle of censorship, allegory seemed to be the only way for these writers, now underground, to express opinions.[7] But Royalists persisted in using their allegories even after the Restoration, when presumably there was no incentive for writing indirectly. This curious persistence leads me to seek for what else Royalists found advantageous in allegory. In a highly divided political climate, writers could use allegory to exclude readers, not solely because of censorship, but because they wished to distinguish the members of their audience from a general reading public, and they distinguished their audience by appeals to recognizable literary habits. The fit reader of allegory in this political context was to become a partisan reader, one who became bonded to a writer through shared, recognizable political opinions, and also by the shared hermeneutic customs.

John Bunyan's *Pilgrim's Progress* may now be trotted out as an important counterexample to this royalist practice of allegory, since *Pilgrim's Progress* is no royalist work, though it is most clearly an allegory. There could be Puritan allegories that relied, rather than on the royalist Neoplatonic representational scheme, instead upon Christian providentialist, apocalyptic, or millenarian schemes.[8] At the time it was published in 1678, moreover, it was underground literature, and Bunyan may have chosen his mode for this secondary reason. But there is a difference between Bunyan's aim and that of the Royalists with respect to their audiences. Bunyan aimed to educate his everyman Christian in proper habits of reading, and his own readers, of course, would practice these by reading Bunyan's own allegory. *Pilgrim's Progress* is its own hornbook, inviting any soul to become qualified; Bunyan supplies marginal notes, repetition, and a plain style to insure that all do. Bunyan, through allegory, appealed to an audience of dissenting souls, writing in code that would be understood by them. The book, however, begs for a wide audience to become part of that distinct group; its message is restricted only by interpretive means, not by social, economic, or political allegiances.

Royalist allegory, like divine right theory in politics, was based on a vision of hierarchy in which there was not only proper order in the political realm, but also in the representational realm, a scheme described by Angus Fletcher as constitutive of allegory in general as a fixed, essential relation between metaphysical truth and earthly representations.[9] Thus, when they compared Charles to the sun, for instance, Royalists asserted a cosmically significant order.[10] One of the Royalists' favorite fictions was the "Parliament of hell," in which parliamentary figures were lampooned as devils meeting in the underworld. This particular allegory was a means by which royalist writers could evade censorship; by holding fictional figures responsible for political ills, authors were relieved from the full responsibility for their opinions or actions. As the American comedian Flip Wilson, in his transvestite character "Geraldine," used to snap, "The Devil made me buy this dress!" In the climate of the Interregnum, this Parliament of hell genre was not only a favored mode for Royalists to evade censors and still to write opposition literature, however; substantively, the genre also presented a cosmic justification for their political position. By representing the struggle between Charles and Parliament as a contest between God and the Devil, Royalists assimilated earthly political events into a cosmic scheme. These writers relied upon their readers' commitment to this cosmically ordered view to sustain other analogies, such as could be found in the social order, the family, gender hierarchy, and in the church. With the Parliament of hell genre, which we shall be examining here, Royalists placed human events in a cosmic scheme, providing a reading of contemporary events through supernatural characters. This allegory also required that its readers agree that the natural order was equated to political order; both could then be equated to representational order. John Cleveland, as we saw in a chapter 2, made such a demand upon his audience.

Is is mere coincidence that Milton writes a Parliament of hell scene into his first books of *Paradise Lost?* Milton dallies with forms of allegorical representation that became conventional during the English Revolution in representing Satan in *Paradise Lost*, especially in the first two books. Milton's task, to "assert Eternal Providence / And justify the ways of God to men" (1.25–26), would seem to echo the royalist belief that contemporary events might represent a cosmic narrative of order. When we place Milton's *Paradise Lost* in contact with the royalist Parliament of hell tradition, we find many specific allegorical resonances. Milton's crossing with the genre has bizarre political consequences: Milton's Satan in *Paradise Lost* most closely resembles the Royalists' post-Restoration view of Cromwell.[11]

In considering Satan as an allegorical figure—and the Parliament of hell pamphlets demand that we do so—I may seem to run against the current of Milton scholarship, which has just about given up on the "Satan controversy," which entranced readers of *Paradise Lost* for the centuries from Dryden on down. Several earlier generations of critics had waged war on the Blakean topic, *whether Mr. Milton was of the Devil's party without knowing it*, a debate that was finally drawn to a silent close by Stanley Fish, who turned critical attention away from Milton's coded messages and toward the reader's making of meaning. After Fish's masterful analysis, somehow Milton's purported sympathy with the Devil seemed to be a mere projection of readers' fallible wills, a psychological crutch, or a heuristic tool; we—the readers—were made to feel ashamed for our naïve affection for the father of lies. Our mea culpas rang round the library: "In *Paradise Lost*, the reader is repeatedly forced to acknowledge the unworthiness of values and ideals he had previously admired."[12]

Yet the Satan-hero as a politician has returned as an object of inquiry in Milton studies with the return of historicist approaches. Though without explicitly positing Satan as Milton's champion, or presenting an allegorical reading of Satan as a revolutionary radical, scholars have seen Milton fighting for liberty and against tyranny in general with the figure of Satan. With their current interest in history, some critics have brought back a kind of authorial intention as a fit object of study in their look into Milton's political commitments, and Satan consequently has been aligned to Charles I, representative of the "false heroic image" that must crumble before the strength of Christian liberty and right reason, freely and properly applied.[13] If Satan is to be read allegorically at all nowadays, goes this line of thinking, then he must be seen as a representation of a general type, and not specifically as a stand-in for King Charles (or for Milton).[14]

The move in modern Milton scholarship has been to resist reading Satan as an allegory, whether for Milton or for Charles—or for any other figure, for that matter. Merritt Y. Hughes seized the bull by the horns in his important essay, "Satan and the 'Myth' of the Tyrant," where he argued that "Milton's Satan is 'the false image' of the true orator Milton wanted to become," and thus is not reduciable to any particular figure in history. Hughes saw the "attribution of any topical political intention to Milton's epic plan" as involving "irreconcilable hypotheses" about the nature of Milton's political commitments, especially given Milton's other writings.[15] Even Stella Purce Revard, who in *The War in Heaven: "Paradise Lost" and the Tradition of Satan's Rebellion* assessed "how the seventeenth-century political scene might have affected Milton's presentation of Satan's conspiracy in books Five and Six of *Paradise Lost*," nevertheless shrank from seeing precise topical references in his image of the fallen angel. Revard argued that that "while theological, political, and social traditions exerted considerable influence on *Paradise Lost*"—the 1605 Gunpowder Plot is one instance—nevertheless, "the literary tradition exerted still more," that literary tradition being one of representing Satan as a figure for general evil.[16] Stevie Davies would "utterly reject any attempt to allegorize the poem," and roundly pressed for silence on the whole question of Satan's roman-à-clef identity: "Any suggestion of a one-to-one ratio between Milton's creation of the king of Hell and the bygone king of England is not only fruitlessly reductive but ridiculous."[17]

If we take into account the literature of the English Revolution, and especially the political genre of the Parliament of hell, we might subsequently reconsider Milton's approach toward this material, however. During the English revolutionary period, we find that allegories of Satan were used to express a variety of political positions, aside from the common designation of Satan as a general principle of evil, held responsible for all the social ills of the day: Satan was, variously, the Catholic church, the sects, Parliament, Cromwell, or an assortment of other historical figures. In all these roles, writers adapted the medieval notion of Satan either as God's rebel or as the Antichrist.[18]

Milton's political intent may be impossible to pin down by reading the image of Satan allegorically, yet by examining the tradition from which Milton drew, we might set Milton's poem into the literary culture of his own day, a literary culture that was intensely interested in political analysis. In my view, this setting includes the literature of the street, where Milton's quasi-allegorical representation of Satan in *Paradise Lost* would have resonated with contemporary polemical uses of the character of Satan and other quasi-allegories. The result, I think, enriches our understanding of

Milton's poetry as engaged with contemporary polemic, both in theme and in style. I shall argue that, in wielding a recognizably royalist trope in his epic, Milton commented on the current uses of allegory in political expression. The relation between literary representation, allegory, and polemical—or political—intent is at the heart of Milton's task; and secondary accounts that attempt to disentangle these, or to purge Milton's *Paradise Lost* of its contemporary political resonances are, in my opinion, guilty of suppressing one of the poem's essential meanings, that is, of training fit readers within this context.

THE GENRE OF THE PARLIAMENT OF HELL

The 1647 pamphlet *The Devil in his Dumps* is exemplary of the Parliament of hell genre since it sets out its story so succinctly. The pamphlet takes up the issue of toleration for the sects, a debate that came to a head with the army's consolidation of a political program and the Agitators' mutiny in the army in 1647. At the beginning of the summer of 1647, the lawyer and general Henry Ireton had assembled army regiments and had drafted the *Solemn Engagement of the Army*, outlining a political program, which, among other things, fixed the duration of Parliaments, pressed for religious toleration, and opposed arbitrary rule. These demands were presented to the king on 2 August as the *Heads of Proposals*. The Presbyterians in Parliament opposed the Army radicals' demands, specifically on the issue of toleration for the sects. The Presbyterian author sees the demands for toleration as a consequence of Satan's work. The author of *The Devil in his Dumps* opposes toleration, tracing the origin of sectarianism to a meeting of underworld characters:

> Know, that about the beginning of this present *Summer* the Prince of darkness, called a general Assembly of all the infernal *spirits*, who with winged host attended his summons, and being met and the grand *Diabolo* mounted on a throne of *sulphur*, accompanied with his Cabinet Council the *seven deadly sins*, he began a very passionate complaint of the great decay and imminent ruin of his Kingdom, if some speedy course were not taken to prevent it, for which he had called them together requiring their devilish advice. He recounted unto them, how they were altogether cast out of heaven by the Almighty Power, for which common wrong although their confederate malice did oblige them all to seek revenge, yet himself had done it by a most subtile insinuation, withdrawing the *first man* that ever was from's obedience to his *Maker*.

The author explains the current political and religious crisis as Satan's plan to avenge his ejection from heaven, and gives the Devil a political backdrop. The "general Assembly" of devils is called a "Cabinet Council," for example; the Devil sits on a throne as he meets or holds a council of infernal spirits; oral arguments are made; the temptation of Adam is recalled;

and there is a warning to readers that the Devil is yet at work. Further, there is a contrast and comparison between the Devil's kingdom and England, as Pluto brags that though the glory of his empire was ended by Luther, it gains strength in England nevertheless: "At that very instant hatcht another brood of Crocodiles"—Anabaptists and other sectaries, the author notes in the margin—"who by their fained tears, counterfeit humility and shews of holiness, inticed thousands to run after them, and by new lights . . . of their own giddy heads, lead them about such vagaries, that they brought 'em at last to a grosser darkness than that they escaped." According to the author, those advocating toleration specifically do the work of the Devil in weakening the English Protestant church, thus making England easy prey to the tyranny of popery: "We are warned hereby . . . what black ends their fair *pretences so suriously drive at*, that are so zealous for *toleration. . . . Rub your eyes, be wise, and see in time whom you trust.*"[19] In *The Devil in His Dumps*, we observe the essential features of the Parliament of hell genre: there is a topical political aim, as the conventional story of the Devil is applied to a current historical situation. Here we have an instance of what Northrop Frye would call "simple" allegory, where there is an easy one-to-one correspondence between the signifier and thing signified; the grand Diabolo, perhaps, is Ireton. The devils "stand for" the sectaries.[20]

We find a similar scene in the first two books of Milton's poem. Satan, "Hell's dread Emperor with pomp Supreme" (2.510), sits "High on a Throne of Royal State" (2.1), presiding over a "great consult" (1.798) in an "infernal Court" (1.792) of his fallen underlings. He considers "once more / With rallied Arms to try what may be yet / Regain'd in Heav'n" (1.268–70), speaking with "high words, that bore / Semblance of worth, not substance, gently rais'd / Thir fainting courage, and dispell'd thir fears" (1.528–30), persistent in his prideful pursuit, revenge, a "Vain War with Heav'n" (2.9). Even from the start of *Paradise Lost*, then, Milton seems to embrace this conventional representation of Satan as the cause of all "our woe," as he asks, "Who first seduc'd them to that foul revolt? / Th'infernal Serpent; hee it was" (1.33–34), and the poet reels off a political narrative in form very like the one found in the Parliament of hell representation:

> . . . what time his Pride
> Had cast him out from Heav'n, with all his Host
> Of Rebel Angels, by whose aid aspiring
> To set himself in Glory above his Peers,
> He trusted to have equall'd the most High
> If he oppos'd; and with ambitious aim
> Against the Throne and Monarchy of God
> Rais'd impious War in Heav'n and Battle proud
> With vain attempt.
>
> (1.36–44)

In this passage, Milton expresses cosmic events through explicitly political language: God's rule is represented as a "monarchy," as Milton seems to press the royalist equation between monarchy and divine right. This equation was severed by radicals in the English Revolution, however. Strangely enough, in his first books of *Paradise Lost*, Milton's representation of the "devilish Counsel" (2.379) resembles the worldview of the antitolerationist pamphlet *The Devil in his Dumps*.

Although it would be premature or fallacious at this point to set *Paradise Lost* alongside of *The Devil in his Dumps* and to construct a precise link between these two texts, the Devil's appearance in the first two books of *Paradise Lost* now can be seen to resonate with possible topical meanings. Before I explore whether such precise links may be drawn, there is the history of this genre of the Parliament of hell during the English Revolution to consider, a history that will complicate our understanding of Milton's representation of Satan. For during the English Revolution, the image of Satan was, regardless of the party using it, one central way writers could understand and represent current political and historical events.

There was a worldview implied by these stories of the Devil acting in England. As Keith Thomas has colorfully documented in his exhaustive study of the beliefs in witchcraft and magic in Renaissance English culture, *Religion and the Decline of Magic*, the Devil was a "literal reality for most devout Englishmen," well into the seventeenth century in England. Such a belief coexisted with more orthodox church doctrine, and indeed, Thomas argues, complemented it. The Devil's evil, for example, was opposed to the Christian God's good. Sectaries were quite literally thought to be "possessed" by the Devil, and the prevalence of exorcisms of such "possessions" is evidence of this belief.[21] The images of the Devil literally at work within England's shores, as were found in a pamphlet like *The Devil in his Dumps*, then, were not far from the common views of ordinary English citizens.

Still, we should explain the popularity of these images not solely in terms of this set of beliefs. The Devil imagery could also be used rhetorically to mask possibly dangerous political positions. In the early years of the civil war period, the parliamentary side, along with the Royalists, had represented the Devil as the source of schism. By blaming the Devil—often a stand-in for the pope—those who opposed the king could find a secure metaphor through which to express their potentially treasonous opinions. Thus the allegory of the Devil in hell was one response to a political climate where it was as yet unacceptable to express criticism of the king or his favorites outright. Relying upon the safety and conventionality of this image, the pro-Parliament author of a 1644 pamphlet, *The Devills White Boyes*, for example, explained that in England, it was not papists themselves but "Malignants [who] are the Devil's Agents still." Railing against ecclesiastical innovations, the author suggested that the king was being led astray by devilish, Catholic, "Malignant," counselors: "this Religion would serve the Malignants, who are half Epicures, half Papists, and half Atheist, and a medly of mad wickedness, they and the Devil have been in Counsell a great while, to devise a plot how to destroy all the honest Religious Protestants in *England*." This author makes use of the traditional English link between the Devil and Catholicism as he connects the current court to popish subversion, including evidence of the Gunpowder Plot, and the Irish uprising. At the end of the pamphlet, the author issues a warning about future evils to be wrought by these devils' men: "what a number of black malignants are there now in this Land, being a kind of smooth-faced Machiavellian Devils, some with flattering bellows blowing the coals of dissention between the King and Parliament; then there be horned malignant Devils that will roar, swear, domineer. . . . but these Malignants are not Dormant Devils, but active and stirring to do mischief."[22] All England is festering with their evil effects, specifically, political unrest and dissension.

In a clearly propagandistic act, however, alluding to a Popish plot, this pro-Parliament author names one of the "devils": "the Earl of *Strafford*, he sits in Counsell every day about it with *Pluto, Ashteroth,* and the other Infernall Counsellors." England, quite literally, has become hell. As the Devil's henchmen, Strafford and others corrupt the king; they are at once "Machiavellian" and satanic figures, sowing discord and disorder wherever they go:

> like those pictures which have a double aspect, one like a man, the other like a Devil, when they are to do mischief by flattering the King, or making the country people rise in the Kings behalf, then they put on smooth faces, and tell them of the Kings power and Prerogative, and that the Parliament is no Parliament, and therefore they may fight against it, that the King is wronged, when indeed no body wrongs him but his malignant Counsellors, that they fight for the Protestant Religion, that is for Popery, and to defend the Laws, that is the Law of tyrannical slavery, which the King would impose upon his subjects.

The author applies conventional motifs of devilishness—the "smooth face," flattery, the love of inversion—all to the current scene, where "Parliament is no Parliament," and where there is surreptitious popery. Though the author notes that he is fashioning a literary "conceit," still his direct explanation of his allegory is surprising, as it sets his accusation against Strafford, the king's former counselor, in full view.[23]

The Parliament of hell was not a stable genre between the years 1640 and 1660, however. Over the course of the English revolutionary period, the images of Satan went through an evolution. In the early 1640s, Satan represented an assortment of evil figures and was held responsible for the sects; Satan in 1648–49 (around the time of the king's execution) stood for Parliament itself; and Satan after the Restoration was identified with Oliver Cromwell or John Bradshaw, the chief justice of the court that had tried and condemned Charles I. The genre of the Parliament of hell itself was thus the product of cultural change, both in literary and in political terms. In political terms, we see the genre used more exclusively by Royalists than by anti-Royalists over the course of the period. In literary terms, the writers grew bolder and bolder in naming their targets of satire outright, making fewer and fewer demands on readers to interpret, and also denoting the decreasing risks of writing political allegory. Before turning to *Paradise Lost*, then, we shall examine these various angles.

In some pamphlets in the revolutionary period particular figures were imagined as devils, not because they had led the king astray, as they were seen to have done in the 1640s, but simply because they were creating serious political unrest. For example, in *Mercurius Poeticus* (1648), the author promises to "Turn Treasons darker inside out / Unto the view of All," accusing parliamentary leaders John Pym and Viscount Saye and Sele—outspoken critics of the king—of being lured by Alecto and Megara, "snake-haired sisters," and "inspired with hellish ire / Against their Sovereign and the Church conspire."[24] These authors wished their readers to perform the task of filling in the gaps in their analogies, to continue the process of seeing the Devil at work by viewing the actions of living politicians according to their scheme. Thus, the authors ask the readers to read a cosmic allegory as a key to current politics. Allegory then is a means to provoke such political interpretations of current history.

Used both by those opposing and those supporting Parliament, the image of Satan as the fomenter of political intrigue and rebellion accords with medieval and Renaissance accounts of Satan as the prototypical traitor. Milton condemned political treachery in general by drawing upon this tradition as he portrayed Satan.[25] The evidence from the pamphlet literature suggests, however, that this is only part of the story. Satan was not just a general political type but was also a representation of specific historical beings, as we saw above, for example, in the case of Strafford, Pym, and the Viscount, where the devils quite literally *were* the political opposition. In these cases, the representation of Satan was deployed specifically in order to delegitimize and quite literally, to "demonize" particular political or religious figures, and to prompt readers to fill in the blanks. There were frequent casual references—"The depth of their Designe, was hatch'd in hell" and "Shall such Imposters be Obeyed, when / They Act like Devils, and cease for to be Men?"—and full-blown representations of Parliaments in hell in their pamphlet dramas.[26] Through these tropes, writers found the figure of Satan, and allegory in general, useful to promote their causes within this climate of political conflict, training their readers to interpret in this frame.

Whether they used it as a ploy to shore up support among an underground readership or were expressing a literal belief in the Devil, by the years 1648–49, Royalists had taken over the exclusive rights to the genre in their attacks on the parliamentary leaders and on Parliament itself. By then, political events had unraveled to lead those loyal to the king to question whether the world had indeed been turned upside down, and in their pamphlets of this period, they seem to believe the Devil was actually at work in England. Charles was in custody, awaiting a trial for treason by a political body that considered its own sovereignty superior to the king's; the royal family had been spirited away to the Continent; all lords had been removed from Parliament; preachers, including women, from unheard-of sects, had emerged from unknown quarters of the land. Defeated royalist soldiers rambled over the countryside, beaten down by two successive civil wars; an archbishop and a highly placed earl, the kings' right-hand men, had suffered deposition and execution, according to the will of the people. As the king purportedly penned his meditations in the Tower that was to be his final home, the chaos outside the prison walls seemed almost inexplicable except by appeal to some cosmic interference, the Devil's work.

Bewildered Royalists explained recent events by reference to Satan's hold. Especially as the king's cause appeared more and more in danger, they represented Parliament with devil imagery. In these representations, they held Satan responsible for the general condition of anarchy, but also, more specifically, saw Parliament itself as driven by satanic forces. Especially as options for the king seemed to narrow to nil, Royalists found no other explanation for his fall but that the Devil's hand was in it. For example, a 1648 royalist pamphlet taunts Parliament for being "a combined medley of Traitors and Rebels, and far different from the Nature of a Parliament (by reason of their Luciferian Pride, to be flung down to hell) and to be deserted by Loyal Subjects, as disjointed, severed and mangled in its members [was] . . . incapable of any just Act, but wading in blood"[27] According to this view, Parliament was an anti-Parliament, as Satan was the Antichrist, in a topsy-turvy universe.

In 1648–49, there appeared a number of royalist pamphlets representing Satan as in Parliament. These exemplify a literal belief in the Devil, as writers offered readers a way of understanding contemporary history as a Manichaean struggle between good and evil. On the eve of the king's trial, one Royalist wrote a poem on his magazine's title page:

> The Rebels rage like mad, their greedy minds
> Remain unsatisfied; like blustering winds
> They roar for Blood; and with unwearied toil,
> Pursue Destruction, Murder, Rapine, Spoil.
> They've entered into Covenant with Hell;
> Rebels beyond the line of parallel;
> Who trampling on Allegiance, do defy
> The Powers of earth, and scorn the Deity.

The pamphlet continues with a narration of the themes of cosmic chaos of this poem, denouncing the members of Parliament who "have lately with much Machiavelical [*sic*] policy, drawn up a form of Government, or rather a Chaos of disorder; the pattern whereof was certainly fetched from Hell, and the matter was contrived by the Devil, the Parliament and armies' grand Agent; for both matter, substance, and method, savor of his style."[28]

God and the Devil have been translated into Charles and Parliament. The idea of a Faustian "covenant with hell" of course derives from the medieval tradition where Satan made a contract for human souls. But "covenant" also echoed the political language of Puritan theology. Many royalist pamphleteers played up this analogy between Puritan "covenanting" and the Devil's contract, as in the pamphlet *The Devill and the Parliament* (1648), where Satan insists that Parliament live up to the terms of its contract, saying, I "needs must have thy soul that is my own, by contract, and 'twas for that that all this while I aided thee." Satan's contract, however, turns the world upside down by reversal of proper social hierarchy, as in this pamphleteer's 1648 portrayal of the Devil singing a prideful tune: "Now topsy turvy, ring the knell, / Come Parliament with me to hell. / There thee and I will ever dwell; / Thus Rebells, must I pay you well." Speaking to Parliament, this Devil explains that "he that threw me down from Heaven for conspiring against him, permitted me to be the Patron, and Protector of your Rebellion" (1–2), boasting, "to thee have I given all my power, taught thee to lie, dissemble, & to cheat a Nation of their Birthright; to know Law, have I persuaded the deluded vulgar, to hearken to thy poisonous Rhetorick and to believe thou meanest to Reform, and building on that weak foundation, to bring their Plate, Coin, and all theair treasure, and throw it at thy feet; have I infus'd contentious spirits into them, which stirred them up to Faction, and Rebellion," explaining "that is my own, by contract." The Devil has contracted Parliament to oppose the king.[29]

In viewing the world as a contest between God and the Devil, royalist writers justified conservative social hierarchy. As in the passage immediately above, the class issue comes up over and over in these royalist attacks on Parliament, and it seems to be part of the genre's thrust to reinstate social order. By these conventional attacks on the lower orders, writers also shored up support for their political positions among their elite readers. In *Mercurius Melancholicus* (1649) the author slurs the "Sanctified Council of Mechanicks at White-hall," members of an illegitimate Parliament, which has "voted the King to be Deposed." This royalist author fulminates: "what Diabolical Rascals they have cried up; but let them Vote themselves to the Devil, their Master."[30] Another example where the allegory of Satan was used to express an attitude toward the lower orders is *A Trance; or, News from Hell* (1649), whose speaker imagines himself visiting hell, where he witnesses the devil Megara boasting of her accomplishments: "To effect which our practice hath been to bring the *beggerliest* and *toughest* people upon the *richest* and *softest*," overturning the distinctions of rank. "In sum," Megara reports to Lucifer, her lord, "We have reduced that Kingdom to a new conformity with this of your Majesties', to a sweet Chaos of all confusion, we have brought thy sway solely into the common peoples' hands; And never did the common people more truly act the part, and discover the genius of a common people more lively, whose nature is still thirsting after novelties and Utopian reformations, though they fool themselves thereby into a baser kind of slavery."[31] Chaos here is quite literally seen in the overturning of proper social hierarchy; Satan's victory is the defeat of the aristocracy by the vulgar. By evoking these fears of the common folk, writers appealed to an elite audience.

The Parliament of hell genre explained that disarray in the social fabric was the result of the political disorder. The genre also called attention to the disorderly political conduct of Parliament itself. One pamphlet burlesques the Jacobean cry "no Bishop, no King" with the new slogan "no Devill, no Parliament, is a sure *maxime.*"[32] The royalist newspaper *Mercurius Elencticus* (May 1649) saw the Devil's love of inversion in Parliament's actions: "An Act (forsooth) was this day read and debated of, whereby they intend to make falsehood be called truth, Rebellion Loyalty, the Devil a Saint: Treason it must be for me or any man, to affirm their present Government to be Tyrannical, Usurped, or Unlawfull: Or that the Commons are not the Supreme authority of the Nation: Or for any one to endeavor the alteration of that Government."[33] These words mock the 1650 Engagement Oath, in which Parliament required all adult males to swear loyalty to the new Commonwealth. Westminster, wrote one author, "has become such a Den of Devils . . . there is not such a subtle deceiver in the world, as an Angel of light: a Devil in the shape of a Saint (especially at Westminster) hath done more mischief, than all the honest men there can ever do good."[34]

Contemporary parliamentary practice also came under fire, as royalist writers drew upon class fears to delegitimize more "democratic" involvement in government. In the pamphlet *The Parliaments Petition to the Divell* (1648), for example, the author mocks parliamentary petitioning, a practice that surged during the tenure of the Long Parliament, where everyone—including the "ten thousand citizens of London," women, and apprentices—seemed to offer advice to Parliament. In this pamphlet, Parliament petitions the Devil himself. By implication, the petitioners of Parliament, too, seek the Devil's favor. This Parliament swears "that we (to serve you) have laid aside all service of God, all Loyalty towards our King, and all Christian love and charity towards men, we have robbed God of as much of his glory as we possibly could." The means they have used are sects, traitors, ignorance, the press—"the bellows of Sedition"—laws, the breaking of all trusts, and the demolition of the king. "Concerning the King," Parliament claims, "we have played our parts sufficiently with him, we have handled him to some tune, we have coursed him like a Partridge over the Mountains, we have robbed and divested him of all Royal dignities, and deprived him of all Regal Revenues and Possessions, insomuch, as we have not left him a house of his own to put his head in, except a jail." In repayment for its service of "more than 7 years," Parliament asks the Devil to "speedily bestir yourself," to act in its defense, reminding him of their contract: "though God made us men, yet you were ungraciously pleased to make us Rebels and Traitors, in which point we are your creatures." Parliament also begs the Devil to continue in his work, to extend "your best assistance either by force or by fraud, power or policy, to free us from the inevitable dangers which threaten our destruction; it is feared greatly by us, that God and the King will get the upper hand over us. . . . destroy not therefore the works of your own hands." Parliament is figured as a tool of the Devil, the members of Parliament wholly loyal to their leader's commands.[35]

By mocking the language of Parliament, royalist writers urged their readers to view Parliament's actions with skepticism. In *A Declaration of Great Lucifer, Prince of the Air, and of Devils, and of all the damned crew in Hell* (1648), the Devil responds to the petition, praising his "obedient servants," in Parliament for what they have done "to the advance of our Kingdom, and have countenanced treason, and rebellion, applauded Rebels, rewarded murders, fomented untruths, falsified Oaths, broken Covenants, robbed the people, and used that most excellent art of equivocating; for these Acts . . . we accept, affect, applaud, and approve . . . for what have we not power to command the whole earth? Yea we have, and it will obey." Lucifer praises specifically the "sundry Acts, Orders and Ordinances, by you commanded, and by the people in general performed to the great advance of our Kingdom." This language, which contains echoes of the language of the parliamentary thanksgiving prayers to God, confirms that those in Parliament are merely the Devil's lackeys. The Devil reassures his minions: "we are the great paymaster in the world, and if we set you on work be sure we will pay you your wages"; he congratulates his earthly workers: "we do approve of all and every act by you done, or shall do in this kind, for its done to the advancement of our Kingdom, and we are joyful to hear that we have such faithful and diligent servants, that are so willing to perform our will."[36] Lucifer praises Parliament, the "you" here—though this is a tacit address to the pamphlet's readers as well—for a job well done.

Not simply indicting a general topsy-turvy climate, the author of *A Declaration of Great Lucifer* attacks Parliament for its deeds, including, among other things, taxes, which the author accuses Parliament of worshipping as idols: "whether Parliament's Idols, Goldsmiths Hall Idols, or Excise Idols." This Parliament also is accused of condoning as lawful political conduct for its members to "satisfy our lusts"; to "live without order"; and to "back-bite, slander, revile, and betray any one, be they friend or foe." The author of the pamphlet continues with his ironic scheme by having Lucifer swear an oath of loyalty to his earthly servants: with the "approbation of our infernall privy Counsel," Lucifer swears that "I with the rest of my devilish Counsellours, will maintain, defend, preserve, and put in practice, set forward, and help these and the like designs."[37] The reader will notice the similarity between this Devil's oath and the coronation oath to be sworn by England's ruler— by implication, then, the Devil is indeed ruling in England instead of Charles. It seems that the new political conditions—where the "common people" have a say in government, with a newly powerful Parliament and new governmental structures, committees, taxes, and public appeals—are all the effects of the Devil's involvement in English politics.

Proof of the Devil's activity was thus witnessed in the contemporary political scene. Publicity in the press especially was seen as the Devil's work, as writers adapted the traditional image of Satan as the "father of lies" to meet the current conditions of polemical writing: "Will these Sainted reprobates never leave their lying?" asks one royalist newswriter, in *Mercurius Fidelicus* (1648). The answer of course, is, "No, they are it seems resolved to continue their correspondency with the Father of their faction, Laurence Lucifer, author of their Rebellion, who for his pride was thrown down to hell, and they for their presumptuous insolence I fear, will never go to Heaven." Was this "Laurence" the figure for Henry Lawrence (1600–1664), lord president of the council under Cromwell? According to this writer, "Saints" are like Devils on account of their deceptive writing, and furthermore, the common people would be especially vulnerable to these satanic manipulations: "When they ["Sainted reprobates"] have invented what they think may make the Kings party odious, then they immediately send it abroad, and afterwards cause it to be intercepted and read at the house of mischief, and then ordered . . . forthwith to be printed, this is one of the Westminster Devils' chief projects, and they find it takes much with the weaker sort of people, but for those who have any ingenuity or common sense, being to smell out their Knavery, and will not be gulled by their fopperies any longer."[38] In this royalist account, the "Saints" imitate the Devil's delight in inverting the truth, with the help of the press. Likewise, in *A Trance; or, News from Hell* (1649), which we examined above, the Devil's servant boasts that "The most advantageous instruments we have used to bring all this [turmoil] about, have been the *Pulpit* and the *Press*; by these we diffus'd those surmises and suppositious fears formerly spoken of, to intoxicate the brains of the people."[39] A royalist sermon entitled *The Devilish Conspiracy*, appearing very soon after the regicide, inveighed against the "*Hypocrites, a Generation of Vipers, Sons of Belial, Children* (indeed) *of the Devil*," charging that "Devils, Beasts, and such Jews as these degenerate in this from all mankind, and therefore are not alone content to murder *Ch.* their King, but that they will crucify him again when he is dead; and that not only in his Disciples and Servants, but in his never-dying name, which (like Flies) they endeavor to corrupt, and to blast."[40] The press is a kind of weapon, capable of hellish murder. In these examples, Parliament was likened to the Devil specifically in spreading "lies" in the press. What is surprising is the consistency of intention and the flexibility of technique of this royalist effort, the attempt to put the traditional image of the Devil to contemporary use, "upgrading" the Devil's falsifying media to include the modern technology of the printing press.

Especially after the execution of the king, this genre of the Parliament in hell came to full flower. It was one central way Royalists expressed their view of historical events. One royalist newpaper condemned the act instituting a Commonwealth in terms of a cosmic struggle between heaven and hell:

> Black as Hell it self: Lo! There it stands,
> The Workmanship of the Imperious Hands.
> Look down, (O Heav'n) & view their ugly Acts.
> Vouchsafe to open all the Cataracts
> Of thy just Wrath. . .[41]

In choosing the language of heaven and hell to condemn his enemies, the writer pleads to God to render judgment. The events he is witnessing seem truly acts in sacred time, and he allies his perspective with that of God: both view history truly, and that view of history is a providential struggle betwen forces of good and evil.

After the regicide, not only was Parliament in general represented as the satanic in the way it had overturned natural order, but specific members continued to be lampooned as devils. In *The Famous Tragedie of King Charles I* (1649), a tract that appeared soon after the regicide, we have a drama that opens with Oliver Cromwell speaking to Hugh Peters, the fiery Independent preacher: "My fine facetious Devil," Cromwell addresses his cohort, "who wear'st the Livery of the Stygian God, as the white Emblem of thy innocence: Hast thou prepar'd a pithy formal speech against the essence and the power of Kings?" Cromwell urges his "fine facetious Devil" friend to spread lies among the populace: "That when tomorrow all my Myrmidons do meet on Onslow heath, like the Greek Exorcist, renowned Calthas, . . . by thy insinuating persuasive art, their hearts may move, like Reeds." Cromwell knows his mate has a special talent for such persuasion: "I know that nectar hangs upon thy lips, and that the most absurd Syllogism, or ear-deceiving paradox, maintained by thee, shall seem oraculous, more dangerous to question than the Sacred Writ."[42] We have here, of course, an appropriation of the trope of the Devil as expert liar and falsifier. With this pamphlet, however, we see a precise allegory between members of the Commonwealth regime and the devils, a special case of the genre discussed above.

The Famous Tragedie of King Charles I is emblematic because it presents not only the hellish deeds but the men who were behind them, in no uncertain terms, as Cromwell is represented as Satan himself.[43] Likewise, in *Bradshaw's Ghost* (1659), the figure of John Bradshaw is named outright as satanic. Bradshaw meets King Charles in the afterworld, and explains that he is doomed to wander ceaselessly in a kind of purgatory, punished for his sin of chairing the regicide commission. It turns out that Pluto, king of hell, has denied Bradshaw entrance into his world, for fear he will usurp his throne. "For in hell I find no company," Bradshaw laments, "the fact that I did was so unparalleled, that it is with me as the *Preacher* said once it was with the *Jesuites*, there was a *little Hell* prepared for them on purpose, lest they should breed *confusion* among all the rest: so I find there is not only a *little Hell*, but *peculiar torments*, for such heaven-daring *regicides*, for *Pluto* himself is afraid to be condemned and *unthroned*, if I might be admitted at large in a Hell."[44] The author played on deeply held beliefs that recent events in history could be understood as taking place on a cosmic plane of action. This story, and others like it, helped to fuel the animosity toward Cromwell, Bradshaw, and other opponents of Charles I, part of a campaign of vilification that burst like the fireworks that greeted the king's return in 1660.

"To the Knowing Reader": Royalist Practice of Allegory

For royalist pamphleteers in the Interregnum, allegories were means through which the truth of historical events could be expressed and rendered apprehensible to informed readers. The royalist James Howell explained in the preface to his prose allegory, *Dodona's Grove, the second part* (1650), that his "knowing reader" was to be "impartiall, discreet, and no *blockhead*."[45] Howell, born in 1594, was an international businessman and a member of Ben Jonson's literary circle. He had previously published the first part of *Dodona's Grove* (1640) as an allegory covering the political events between 1603 and 1640. The work narrated the political troubles of the Jacobean reign through a conceit of a forest of trees, ruled by an oak, in which various other trees, from hemlock and yew to thistle, play a role. Siding with Charles in the civil war, Howell was imprisoned often, purportedly for debt, between 1643 and 1651. When he emerged, it was into a career of political pamphleteering; however, like Nedham, Howell sought patronage from Cromwell during the Rump, only to appeal to Charles II after the Restoration. He was granted employment as historiographer royal in his final years, dying in 1666. In *Dodona's Grove, the second part*, Howell, at this point in his career yet a Royalist, continued his arborial allegory, with the oak as "the Tree-paramount of this *Forest*, and that not altogether improperly, for this Iland bears the best vegetable of that kind upon the Earth. . . . besides the *oak* above all other *vegetalls* deserves to have the precedency, for his strength, his durance and vigor, and those varieties of productions which nature hath assign'd to that Tree above all others" (5).

Though the vehicle might seem to us to be reductively crude, still Howell insisted that his meaning in 1650 would be understood by only a few. He explains his reason for shrouding his true meaning as both economy of length and something like decorum: "Let not that unpassionate, and well weighted Reader . . . that while he runs over this historical parley of *Trees*, he must not expect in so narrow a compass the whole thread of an exact story drawn out at full length, for that would fill up huge volumes, and this *arboricall* discourse aims only at the *pith* of things, yet without omission of any important passage; No, he will find this *twist* of matter to be like a ball of cotton thread which may peradventure be drawn out hereafter to a larger work when the times are more proper" (7). The times will be "more proper," presumably, when clear royalist writing will not be prosecuted by the state, "When the King enjoys his owne again," as the ballad refrain would have it. Howell thus signals to an audience of readers who were persecuted but in secret alliance with one another.

In his remarks to this "Knowing Reader," Howell also expresses concern about a vulgar audience: "though [this method] may render the matter more difficult at first, yet, it will enhance the value thereof, and endear it more to the fancy of the knowing Reader afterwards by way of Recompence. . . . Those notions which at first sight stand obvious to every capacity, are as . . . plain and common ware, but that knowledge which requires a second or third indagation [*sic*], and puts the peruser to his quaeres and researches, to scratch his head, or bite his lips peradventure, that knowledge, I say, will prove far more pleasant and precious at last." The hiddenness of meaning makes the work more valuable, in a hermeneutic economy analogous to that of the market: "We find that the best commodities are kept in boxes under locks, when the coarsest of wares lies prostitute upon the stall, and exposed to every common view, and dirty fingers" (8–9). The "knowing reader," then, needs to read twice, having the leisure and the wit to understand.

Royalists, in expressing these ideas about a fit readership, and in their underlying worldview of a struggle between cosmic good and evil, give us an explanation of how the genre of the Parliament of hell survived in the Restoration, even after there was no motive of censorship to prohibit much royalist expression. Even after the Restoration, however, writers attempted to make sense of the previous period and to justify the return of the king by construing the Interregnum leaders as agents of the Devil. They held on to and amplified a preexisting genre, spelling out often what was only hinted at before. The pamphlet we saw above in 1649 called *The Famous Tragedie* appeared under a new title in 1660, for example, renamed so as to mark its meaning explicitly: *Cromwell's Conspiracy. A Tragicomedy, Relating to our latter Times. Beginning at the Death of King Charles the First, And ending with the happy Restauration of KING CHARLES the Second* (1660). Its author now professed himself a "Person of Quality."[46] The depiction of Cromwell and Peters, a "fine facetious Devil," now bears a politically orthodox meaning, as the king's cause is vindicated and the allegory proven prophetic. With the coming of the Restoration, Cromwell and his cohorts could be freely represented in the now-victorious royalist press as satanic; and they were, not just in offhand remarks or epithets—though there were plenty of these—but in elaborate and extended dramatic episodes that mapped Cromwell, or some other parliamentary figure's life and deeds, onto those of the Devil. The gates were opened for a flood of vicious writing to appear that had been building up since the beginning of hostilities between king and Parliament. It was clear who was on top now.

These post-Restoration writers, newly liberated from suppression, smug and giddy with power, condemned the politicians of the Interregnum in the same literary manner as before. Though they were free from the bonds of censorship, they still used the Parliament of hell genre over and over to ramify their victory. The popularity of the genre seems to be based upon their royalist worldview, confirmed in hindsight, of a cosmic struggle where God was on the side of the king. When promonarchists continued the royalist tradition by fashioning Cromwell and the regicides as devils, they made a one-to-one relation between their allegorical literary representations and this cosmic view of history. The collection of royalist poetry called *The Rump; or, An Exact Collection of the Choycest poems and songs relating to the late times* (London, 1662) contains poems mocking the Interregnum's political figures; among these are several that play out the story of Cromwell or Bradshaw as the devil.[47] In the *Rump* song with the prolix title, "The Rump Ululant; or, Penitence per force. Being the Recantation of the Old Rusty-roguy-rebellious-rampant, and now ruinous rotten-roasted RUMP," we hear the rebels apologize: "Hell was our Text, though Heav'n were our Gloze / And Will our Reason, / Religion we made free of *Hocus* trade, / And voted Loyalty Treason."[48] Colonel Baker makes fun of Cromwell's nose, long a target for royalist sharp satire. The nose, along with the rest of him, newly unearthed in proceedings that exhumed Cromwell's body and laid it before all to see, presents an explanation for the civil unrest of the preceding twenty years in his poem:

> Wherein is set down, the Acts of all those
> In Pluto's Black Court, that guarded Noll's Nose,
> As Harrison, Hewson, and Cook that curst Pigg,
> With Cobbet, Vaine, Scot and Nurse Haslerig.
> And next those Black Chaplains that preach'd up Nolls Nose,
> Goodwin, Milton, and Peters i'th close.
> Hells Counsel's agreed, and now do dispose
> Of Nedham to write for Lucifer's Nose,
> He being a Vagrant that always did live ill,
> Is thought a fit Member to write for the Devil.

The squib is titled *The Blazing Star; or, Nolls Nose Newly Revived, and taken out of his TOMB*. Here, "Hell's Counsel" includes parliamentary actors, preachers, pamphleteers—even John Milton. We see the conjunction of false counselors, a hellish cabal, and deceptive writing—all jumbled together and condemned as satanic. In the poem's final lines, Baker comes out with his summary judgment: "The land of Darkness this we may call, / When the Devils Nose did govern all."[49] During the Interregnum, then, England had become a "land of Darkness," hell itself. Now that the Interregnum Parliament, the Rump, has been dissolved, the author of *The Downfall of Cerberus* (1660) supposes, "'tis like thou'lt be / In *Pluto's* Parliament a *Mercury,* / From whence perhaps thy friends may look to hear / From thee, what news, and the nocturnals there."[50] What was a "diurnal," a daily newspaper, before will be a "nocturnal," a nightly newspaper, more fitting the eternal darkness in hell. All the figures associated with the Commonwealth and Protectorate, from the politicians to the pamphleteers, are to be banished from England to find a home in hell. Thus Royalists after the Restoration could be vindicated; the cosmic scheme was now delivering divine retribution.

In naming their enemies outright and equating them to devils, those supporting the Restoration fashioned a perspective through which to view all history. In the 1660 broadside *Lucifer's Lifeguard: Containing a Schedule, List, Scroll, or Catalogue,* for example, the author offers a list that plays nonsense against sense, in a pile of names that includes not only devils, but all manner of evil men, drawn from history, again asserting a worldview based on timeless hierarchies:

1. *John Pontius Pilate* Ravilac Belial *Bradshaw,*
2. Nimrod Herod *Oliver* Aceldama *Cromwell,*
3. *Henry Caiphas* son of Perdition *Ireton,*
4. Fawkes Catiline Boutefeu L. Grub *Gray,*
5 *Oliver* Mountebank Achitophel *John* no St.
6. Sir Machiavel *Bulstrode* Amphibion *Whitlock,*
7. Judas *Henry* Iscariot *Vane* Father and Son,[51]

By relating Bradshaw's sins to Pilate's, the writer insists that there is a correlation between the one who brought down Charles I and the one who brought down Christ, here expressed through the list's metonymic relations between the names. Cromwell is also compared to Nimrod, an example of archtyranny, and also to Achitophel, a type of treacherous political underling. By these lines, the author compresses all treasons into one name. By these analogies, which conflate classical, biblical, historical, and literary sources, the author reduces the sins of particular current historical figures into an alembic of every cosmic and historical sinner. This scheme, though not properly an allegory, represents a kind of cosmic thinking that underlay the genre of the Parliament of hell in the Restoration, where writers made sense of history by appealing to universal tropes of good and evil.

In Restoration mythopoetics, writers explained historical events of the previous twenty years as the result of an essential struggle between good and evil, God and Satan, which was translated into a struggle between King Charles and Cromwell. Dryden's poem, "Astrea Redux," subtitled "A Poem on the Happy Restoration and Return of His Sacred Majesty Charles the Second" (1660), sums up this thinking: "(What King, what Crown from Treasons reach is free, / If *Jove* and *Heaven* can violated be?)"[52] In these analogies between English political events and cosmic history, royalist writers encouraged readers to view the drama of history in this frame. The Restoration Royalists insisted that cosmic order buttressed political order, and their view was seemingly vindicated by the restoration of monarchy in 1660. The pro-Restoration press was as merciless toward the reputations of the Interregnum Parliament-men as had been the leaders who ordered the exhumation and mutilation of the bodies of the regicides. In the single-page broadside entitled *The Arraignment of the Devil, for Stealing away President Bradshaw* (1660), the author justifies the exhumation by reminding readers that Bradshaw had "rais'd by spell / Last Parliament from Hell."[53] As Bradshaw put Charles on trial, now Bradshaw must be tried. The verdict, of course, is guilty: "Satan, y'are guilty found / by your Peers, by your Peers, / And must die above ground." The sentence is read: "You must die out of hand, / *Satanas, Satanas,* / This our Decree shall stand, / without control." The author here calls Bradshaw "Satan" and Satan "Bradshaw" interchangeably.

In their imaginative response to the Restoration, Royalists evoked the cosmic myth as a way to read history, not just the history of the past twenty years, but to read present and future history as well. The broadside *News from Hell* (1660) relates hell's reaction to the Restoration in political, not moral, terms. The story is told by "one of Pluto's band," come from hell to bring the "doleful news" of England's restored monarchy:

> A great man lately to us came
>   And tidings thither brought
> That treason 'gainst great *Pluto's* State
>   The *English* Nation wrought.
> That very word of Treason did
>   *Beelzebub* so affright,
> That of all courage for a while
>   He was bereaved quite.

The Restoration itself is deemed treason against Satan. Satan responds:

> What? *England* my sweet darling dear
>   Against me Treason-plot!
> *England* so late by us regain'd?
>   Tush I believe it not.

He recites the list of his successes in England over "these sixteen years"— 1644 to 1660—including the "successful labours" of his "trusty sprites," Pride, Mammon, Lust, and others, and he asks, "Shall all this labour, care and pains / (My *England* to regain) / Which I, and all my Spirits have tane, / Prove fruitless and in vane,"—punning here on the parliamentary names "Pride" and "Vane." The Devil continues:

> Will *England* now from me revolt,
>   And plot against my State?

> Without whose help and council they
>   Themselves will ruinate.
> 'Tis true, they broke their Oaths and Vows
>   Which they to heaven made,
> But yet with me to break their League
>   I am sure they are afraid.

Satan recovers his optimism, and charges his messenger to "Make haste now to return again" to England:

> I'll muster Legions of my Spirits,
>   And with them council take,
> How 'mong the sottish Elves I may
>   Greatest confusion make.[54]

The author's representation that the Devil has been ruling in England for sixteen years by "pride, Mammon, lust, envy, and lies" is an indictment of the Interregnum leaders. Parliament's rule was the Devil's rule, and the language of contemporary political intrigue is applied to this supernatural scheme. By these examples we see that the Parliament of hell motif was a literary trope that carried specific political meanings, especially in the royalist press during the English revolutionary period. The story promoted a worldview of a fixed order and prompted a group of fit readers to identify themselves in it. When members of Parliament were repeatedly referred to as devils, both during the Interregnum period and especially after the Restoration, this was an expression of a cosmic order that had been upset, and an appeal to readers to retaliate.

The royalist practice of allegorical writing also reflected the polemical context of propaganda; it held up a worldview as well, one that translated into a hermeneutic practice. Royalist writers invoked an elite audience of believers—a hearty band of those who understood, and who were to remain committed to their cause through their shared practices of reading. On the epistemological level, further, these writers insisted that there was some essential correspondence between the signifier and the thing signified, and that that correspondence was immediate, as in the case of John Cleveland, who drew an analogy between anarchy in language and anarchy in politics, and who fastened on correct definition and proper grammar as a means to express his commitment to a stable system of royally authorized meaning. Though the signifiers in the royalist allegories we have been looking at in this chapter were not always the same one (either a tree *or* a planet could represent King Charles, for example), the allegories insisted upon unalterable connections between signs and the things they signified. It is the scheme described in Angus Fletcher's theory of allegory, where there is a fixed, essential relation between metaphysical truth and representations.[55]

In their wildly inventive, and witty, uses of the genre of the Parliament of hell in the Restoration, the Royalists read the last age as a cosmic struggle between good and evil, with good finally reigning supreme with the return of the king. Charles II triumphed over the Devil, Bradshaw or Cromwell. Determining whether these writers actually believed in the Devil or merely used the Devil as a safe way to express their concerns is beyond the scope of the treatment here. Yet their ascribing motives to supernatural beings is in keeping with the literary conventions of epic poetry, where the gods—or a supernatural figure like the Devil—are held responsible for human actions. The Devil imagery set up English political events as taking place on a cosmic plane. Thus Milton's *Paradise Lost* would have been entirely in keeping with revolutionary representations of current events as divinely motivated. How the losing side—Milton's—made sense of the same period would be another matter altogether, and this other perspective gives rise to a distinct attitude toward allegory, and toward the requirements such allegories made upon their audiences. We find this other attitude in Milton.

PARADISE LOST AND THE PARLIAMENT OF HELL

Paradise Lost is no squib nor a polemical barb in some pamphlet war; it is, rather, an extraordinary epic poem, encompassing far more than simply a topical political intention. Marvell summed it up best by listing the ingredients of *Paradise Lost* as an almost unimaginable heap: "*Messiah* Crown'd, God's Reconcil'd Decree, / Heav'n, Hell, Earth, Chaos, All."[56] In that frail "All" hangs the entire tale. However, in its mission to justify the ways of God to men, and also to find a "fit audience . . . though few," Milton's poem is consistent with the ethical concerns voiced in his prose. Soon after his Interregnum books were indexed, Milton's great poem appeared, with the approval of the licenser Thomas Tomkins, and was duly entered into the Stationers' Registers in 1667. Milton did not put his name on the title page of several of these 1667 editions, only his J.M., and he may have found some anonymity in that; he also sold the rights to the publishers so that any risks of scandal would involve the publisher rather than the author; he did name himself, however, on the title page of the 1674 edition.[57] Was Milton one of those adaptable loyalists, like Marchamont Nedham, or even Dryden, who was to be forgiven for the sins of his Interregnum politics?[58]

Did Milton purge his magnificent poem of all political intention? It appears not, especially since in the first two books of his epic, Milton repeated certain words and situations that were constantly appearing in pamphlets of The Parliament of hell genre. In *Paradise Lost*, the Devil is the "author" of "woe"; devils appear as fallen angels or saints; they embark on a mission to retrieve former glory through deceit: "our own loss how repair, / How overcome this dire Calamity" (1.188–89); they take their revenge in the form of political seduction: "Seduce them to our Party"; they contrive to make "that thir God / May prove thir foe. . . . This would surpass / Common revenge"

(2.367–71); they use persuasion and false rhetoric as their tools, with Belial using "words cloth'd in reason's garb" (2.226) and Beelzebub speaking as the Devil's mouthpiece; they appeal to the multitude, "the popular vote" (2.313); the hellish crowd is "the hasty multitude" (1.730) or a "captive multitude" (2.323), over which skilled orators exert power. The poem even seems to share the very words of *Bradshaw's Ghost* (1660), for example, a pamphlet in which Bradshaw insists, "To drive black *Pluto's* Coach I'd rather dain, / Than to be Wagoner to *Charles'* wain," just as Satan in *Paradise Lost* refuses, "To bow and sue for grace / With suppliant knee, and deify his power" (1.111), insisting, "Better to reign in Hell, than serve in Heaven" (1.263). In *Bradshaw's Ghost*, Bradshaw boasted, "for where / So e're I am, Hell properly is there," just as Mephistopheles in Marlowe's *Doctor Faustus* remarked, "but where we are is hell. / And where hell is, There must we ever be" (2.1.122–23).[59] In these lines, we also hear Satan in *Paradise Lost* who has "The Hell within him, for within him Hell / He brings, and round about Him" (4.20–21). In the case of *Bradshaw's Ghost*, there is a precise analogy to current English history, as the "hell" described in that pamphlet is the chaos that resulted from the Interregnum period. In Milton's case, any analogy between the demons of *Paradise Lost* and the Interregnum political figures is imprecise, yet the language is similar.[60] The Miltonic representations of hell build force within the context of the other like references to particular political figures in the pamphlet literature of the English Revolution. To me, these similarities suggest that the author's involvement with this genre may be quite deep indeed.

There are several possible explanations for this resemblance. Though Milton does not allegorize particular figures in the manner conventional to Parliament of hell pamphlets, nevertheless, by drawing upon the same tropes, Milton might still raise fears about current popish or radical plots, and thus signal his continuing commitment to the Protestant cause. In picturing Satan in his *Paradise Lost*, Milton loads him with images from antipopery propaganda. And it is true, Milton remained a fierce enemy of all popery throughout his life. It would have been important for Milton, an advocate of religious toleration, to oppose Catholicism with virulence, especially in the Restoration, where defenders of religious toleration were accused of also defending Catholicism. However, Satan more closely resembles the parliamentary figures lampooned in the Parliament of hell genre of the Interregnum than he does the conventional papist.

Milton's use of this royalist convention could lead us to draw a surprising conclusion, that *Paradise Lost* expressed not only a general anti-Catholic sentiment, but specifically voiced an anti-Cromwellian, and even a royalist, message. Given the pervasiveness of the Parliament of hell conventions in the revolutionary period, we might infer that Milton's own readers would compare his Satan to the Royalists' accounts of the rebels during the English Revolution. There is much to compare. In *Paradise Lost*, Satan begins his second war campaign with a rally to his troops, using republican rhetoric (5.772–907) which recalled that of the Interregnum leaders: "what if better counsels might erect / Our minds and teach us to cast off this Yoke?" (5.785–86). Abdiel's response, that Satan "hast'n to appease / Th'incensed Father, and th'incensed Son, / While Pardon may be found in time besought" (5.846–48), is perhaps that of the post-Restoration parliamentarian, who hoped for mercy and an "act of oblivion" to be dispensed by the returning king. Could Milton have welcomed the second Charles, like Marvell, who in disavowing the "Good Old Cause," reported, "I think the Cause was too good to have been fought for"?[61] Milton has been associated with Royalism before; this evidence of his condemnation of the revolution could be used to deliver a fatal blow to the recent Marxist-inspired image of Milton as a left-leaning radical even to the end of his days. If Milton adopted the royalist genre, then perhaps we ought to reconsider Milton's political allegiances in the Restoration.

Yet Milton just never gave in and supported Charles II. Just a little more than a month before the king returned, Milton brought out a second and enlarged edition of his *Readie and Easie Way*; "What I have spoken," he revealed in its introduction, "is the language of the good old cause."[62] Though he might have come to disapprove of the Interregnum government's means, he never wavered in his commitment to the fundamental principles of "spiritual or civil libertie," as he described them in *The Readie and Easie Way*. His opposition to arbitrary power as a kind of self-enslavement keeps popping up in the poem, and so at many times his beliefs conflicted with the Restoration Royalists' scheme.

Or could Milton have presented this episode to throw Royalists off his scent? By evoking the royalist tradition in the first pages of his book, Milton could be steering potentially hostile readers toward a judgment that he had indeed changed his mind about the Interregnum, while covertly remaining loyal to the Good Old Cause. Any reader who picked up *Paradise Lost* in 1667 looking for political intent could have seen those fallen angels in hell in the first books as the convention dictated: as a condemnation of Cromwell and his crew. By opening with this recognizable genre, perhaps Milton evaded the Restoration censors. In his account of *Paradise Lost*, Christopher Hill suggests that vigilant readers will penetrate beyond the "deliberate mystification" of his poetry to get at Milton's true meaning, as, for example, in Milton's epithet "sons of Belial," which Hill argues "everyone would understand" to refer to Cavalier and new-Cavalier "bullies."[63] Yet if all we need is a "key," as Hill recommends, if Milton encodes his poem with things "everyone would understand," then we might imagine the censor's job to be quite easy. If this were the case, we would have no *Paradise Lost* in the seventeenth century.

Paradise Lost, of course, is a censored text, but not in the way that Hill sees it. *Paradise Lost* is not merely a stump for Milton's revolutionary political ideas, now unpopular in current political climate, ideas that under specific circumstances could not be voiced overtly. The very circumstances of Milton's work—the restoration of monarchy, the new literary milieu, the tempering of religious enthusiasm—are all integral to Milton's poem. We cannot merely remove such aspects in order to find the "real" meaning of the poem—for these constitute the meaning of the poem. I see *Paradise Lost* as a work that expresses anxieties about the status of indirect, allegorical, and censored writing, conditions specific to the Restoration literary milieu but ones that, as Milton sadly came to realize, were inherent in public writing.

I argue here that in *Paradise Lost,* Milton not only thwarted the expectations that might be raised by the Parliament of hell trope; he also rejected a simple ratio of literary representation to history and cleared the way for his revolutionary reader to perform interpretive acts in the future. Milton evoked this genre in order to convey his loyalty to the spirit of the revolution, though not to its agents. Milton shared with the Royalists a degree of contempt for actors on the Interregnum political stage. But he did not go so far as to condemn the revolution. With his representation of the devils in hell, Milton showed that a single set of signs could bear numerous interpretations; that political allegory—and allegory in general—required special skills in reading; and that, finally, the failure of the English Revolution was not a matter of God's decree, but of human weakness. Consequently, I focus on Milton's search for a "fit audience" in light of the demands of the mode of allegory on its readership. In *Paradise Lost,* Milton summons readers to become more keenly aware of their susceptibility to political deception. Milton aimed to promote readerly skills as a means for English citizens to regain the individual freedoms that had slipped through the revolutionary leaders' fingers.

Milton and the Parliament of Hell: Political Intention in *Paradise Lost*

Mixing bejeweled imagery of Oriental splendor with the mundane tropes of republican rhetoric, Milton creates an entirely original Satan in his first two books of his poem. But Milton begins *Paradise Lost* with a conventional Parliament of hell scene, as Satan greets his host and convenes his stygian council. Just as the Devil, who, represented in numerous pamphlets in the Restoration, plotted to regain England from his hellish headquarters, Milton's devils in *Paradise Lost* vowed to "reascend" and "repossess thir native seat" (1.633–4; 2.75–76). Moloch's plan of "open War" (2.51) mirrors the parliamentary strength, its New Model Army. Satan's throne, "of Royal State, which far / Outshone the wealth of *Ormus* or of *Ind*, / Or where the gorgeous East with richest hand / Show'rs on her Kings *Barbaric* Pearl and Gold" in *Paradise Lost* (2.1–4) resembles that of the illegitimate parliamentary leaders in the royalist pamphlet *Mercurius Elencticus* (1649): "They have murdered the King; Banished or Imprisoned his Consort, Children, seized upon his Palace, set his Crown on their heads; wear his Apparel, and Furniture; and then they cry out—see in what splendor we sit."[64] Much like Hugh Peters in *The Famous Tragedie of King Charles I* (1649), whom the dramatic character Cromwell praises for his "insinuating persuasive art," Milton's Belial touts a "persuasive accent," making "the worse appear / the better reason, to perplex and dash / Maturest Counsels" (2.118, 113–15).[65]

Worst of all, Satan in *Paradise Lost* has become a tyrant. In hell, the obedient fallen angels "towards him they bend / With awful reverence prone; and as a God / Extol him equal to the highest in Heav'n" (2.477–79). Fawning and idolatrous, these minions have surrendered their liberty to their diabolical master. In the royalist Parliament of hell genre also, the devil's sway over his underlings was envisioned as a tyranny. In *A Trance; or, News from Hell* (1649), one underling gleefully reports to Lucifer her lord: "We have reduced that Kingdom to a new conformity with this of your Majesties'."[66] This royalist picture matches Milton's estimation of Satan's power over his fleet: "Devil with Devil damn'd / Firm concord holds" (2.496–97). Full obedience to Satan is also presented in *The Parliaments Petition to the Divell* (1648), in which Parliament swears "that we (to serve you) have laid aside all service of God, all Loyalty towards our King, and all Christian love and charity towards men, we have robbed God of as much of his glory as we possibly could"; later, Parliament grants, "we are your creatures," wholly merging with their creator and owner, Satan.[67]

In *Paradise Lost*, Satan's tyranny consists partly in not allowing free debate. For the debate in hell is not really a free exchange of ideas; Satan wrote a script in which Beelzebub would propose his plan, and then Satan himself "prevented all reply" (2.467). This is not a true dialogue, such as that in which truth and "Falsehood grapple; who ever knew Truth put to the worse, in a free and open encounter" (*Areopagitica, CPW* 2.561). Rather, Satan coerced his audience by his sole voice's power: "But they / Dreaded not more th'adventure than his voice / Forbidding; and at once with him they rose" (2.473–75). The debate in hell is one example of falsified public speech, a context in which Truth may not "open herself faster" (*Areopagitica, CPW* 2.521).

Yet the Royalists found the Devil's reign politically unsatisfactory only in that it placed the wrong man on top. According to the royalist renditions of the Parliament of hell, once God reinstated Charles II in his proper spot at the top of the pyramid, all Satan's evil effects would be reinverted. In the Restoration Parliament of hell genre, this is so. In *The Trial of Traytors; or, The Rump in the Round* (1660), for example, the Rump Parliament is represented as a coven of Devil's minions who futilely attempt to stop "time's wheel" from revolving, to stop the Restoration of monarchy. Too late. The figures in the illustration—half beast, sporting heads of animals like goats, cats, and foxes and cloven hoofs—all wear the dress of Puritans, stand upright, and are labeled with the names of Parliament-men and other Interregnum figures, including Judge Cook (ram), Hugh Peters (buck), Arthur Haselrig (fox), and Henry Vane (wolf). The "Rump's Scout," parodying the name of the parliamentary newsbook, is represented as the Devil himself, with his wings, curled tail, horns, and staff prodding his men on. The author of the piece reveals that,

> These Traitors all who had the World at will,
> Have now their *Scout* continues with them still;
> He pokes them forward with a Fork of steel,
> Urging Sir *Arthur* [Haselrig] for to stop the Wheel
> A while, but stay Time's Wheel is turned round,
> All's for the KING, but traitors in the Pound.[68]

In this Restoration Royalist's opinion, the return of the king was God's way of reasserting control over satanic forces; there was something inevitable, and surely providential, about the proper reinstating of cosmic hierarchy.

Yet in Milton's eyes, the hierarchy itself was part of the problem; in thinking that earthly politics mirrored celestial politics, Royalists were making a mistake. As Joan Bennett has persuasively argued, Satan's logic of analogy between his own realm and God's—and, by implication, the earthly arena and the divine—is completely flawed.[69] But a further argument against Satan's rule is that his hierarchy did not allow for the exercise of free reason. In spite of Satan's rhetoric of "mutual league," the outcome of Satan's regime was conformity. For Milton, forcing conformity is sin: "How goodly, and how to be wished, were such an obedient unanimity as this, what a fine conformity would it starch us all into!" (*Areopagitica*, *CPW* 2.545), Milton writes of censorship. Conformity not only bridled the human spirit, but it went against conscience, a view Milton expresses in his poem "On the New Forcers of Conscience under the Long Parliament," where he railed against the tyranny of the Presbyterians:

> Dare ye for this adjure the Civil Sword
> To force our Consciences that Christ set free,
> And ride us with a classic Hierarchy . . . ?

Those newly in power may be tyrants just like those whom they have evicted, as Milton asserts as he ends his poem: "*New Presbyter* is but *Old Priest* writ Large."[70] In *Paradise Lost*, tyranny in hell and on earth may be the same. Milton disavows the kind of tyranny Satan imposes—not because it is Satan's—but because it is tyranny. Milton raises the question of legitimate or coerced persuasion as a kind of satanic tyranny in his example of Abdiel, who refused to adhere to Satan's program. In fact, the kind of tyranny Satan projects is like any other kind of tyranny, including that of Charles I and even that of the parliamentary leaders.

In finding Interregnum leaders were satanic, Milton puts himself in the same camp as the Royalists. Royalists had also blamed individual figures for ambition: meeting in hell in the pamphlet *Bradshaw's Ghost* (1659), Charles asks John Bradshaw, What is the good old cause? "As for the thing called the *Good Old Cause*," Bradshaw answers, "it is no other than the *Quarrel* at first begun with *you*, and now newnamed, nicknamed, or indeed rather *rebaptised*, but it was not long reverenced either for its *age*, or *goodness*, but like an old Almanack laid aside as useless, and this was it that broke my heart, the air of a *Common-wealth*, with the profit arising thereby, might have lengthened my life, but to see *Mars* triumphant, and yet *ourselves* cashiered, would it not even vex a *Saint?*"[71] But Milton's resemblance to the royalist critique of the Interregnum leaders stops there. For Milton, the Interregnum leaders exerted tyranny over free conscience, and that was their sin. Even as early as the *Second Defense*, Milton expressed apprehensions about the ambitions of the leaders of the new government. When he praised Cromwell for refusing the crown, he also warned him that to have taken it would make it seem "as if, when you had subjugated some tribe of idolators with the help of the true God, you were to worship the gods you had conquered"; Milton also cheered Fairfax for having overcome "ambition . . . and the thirst for glory which conquers all the most eminent men" (*CPW* 4.672). But Milton's worst fears did come true; the leaders of the revolution did prefer their own ambitions to the country's interest. Milton, it has been argued, began to lose faith in the English rulers as early as February 1649.

We are treading on the dangerous terrain of analyzing *Paradise Lost* for topical political intention. Of course, *Paradise Lost* is no political pamphlet. But in his masterpiece of poetry, Milton expresses ethical concerns that arise out of his political moment, though they are not restricted to it. In a different manner, but not perhaps with a different intent, Milton also voices ethical aims in his prose writings; as we have seen in *Areopagitica*, Milton works to promote a reasoning, virtuous subject. In his *History of Britain*, Milton explicitly states his sour views about Parliament, and it is to these we shall turn in exploring the meanings of Milton's "Parliament of Hell" scenes in *Paradise Lost*. Because of its thorny publication history, it is not clear whether the views Milton expresses in the *History of Britain* are those of 1649, a warning to the Interregnum Parliament leaders, or of 1660, as an intervention in Restoration politics. The *History* itself was published in 1670, yet the section in which Milton comments directly on his political milieu, the *Character of the Long Parliament*, also called the "Digression," was not released until well after his death, withheld from print until 1681, and at that late date it was made to serve Tory political interests in the Exclusion crisis.[72] Only in 1932 did the full text of Milton's Digression appear. It is not clear why the Digression was omitted from publication in 1670, whether it was Milton's decision or that of L'Estrange, the censor. Perhaps Milton struck the passage because it was terribly dark. Masson thinks the excision was Milton's decision, since the passage had become "irrelevant."[73] But the Digression is relevant to us, for in it, Milton gives not only his opinions about the Long Parliament—even if he withdrew them later—but also, and most importantly here, an image of a revolutionary reader.

Vociferously in the Digression, Milton voices dissatisfaction with Parliament. In his complaints, he sounds like the satirical Royalists who used the

Parliament of hell genre to demolish the Parliamentarians during the Interregnum. Milton refers to the committeemen as "Children of the Devil" (*History, CPW* 5.449). He reviles them and the Presbyterian divines for having "set up a spirtual [*sic*] tyrannie by a secular power to the advancing of thir owne authorit[ie]" (447). Rather than reforming the Commonwealth, the end for which they were raised to power, they acted "unfaithfully, unjustly, unmercifully, and where not corruptly, stupidly" (449). What is more, the people blindly followed them. "Thus they who but of late were extolld as great deliverers, and had a people wholy at thir devotion," Milton wails, "by so discharging thir trust as wee see, did not onely weak'n and unfitt themselves to be dispencers of what libertie they pretented [*sic*], but unfitted also the people, now growne worse & more disordinate, to receave or to digest any libertie at all" (449). Like the Royalists who mocked the giddy multitude, the people were rendered "unfit" for liberty by their traitorous leaders in Milton's view: "For libertie hath a sharp and double edge fitt onelie to be handl'd by just and virtuous men, to bad and dissolute it become[s] a mischief unweildie in thir own hands" (449). In like manner, Milton had chided the people of England for swallowing the king's book whole: "that people that should seek a King . . . would shew themselves to be by nature slaves, and arrant beasts; not fitt for that liberty which they cri'd out and bellow'd for, but fitter to be led back again into thir old servitude, like a sort of clamouring & fighting brutes, broke loos from thir copyholds, that know not how to use or possess the liberty which they fought for" (*Eikonoklastes, CPW* 3.581). Milton concurs, then, with the royalist author of *A Trance; or, News from Hell* (1649): "And never did the common people more truly act the part, and discover the genius of a common people more lively, whose nature is still thirsting after novelties and Utopian reformations, though they fool themselves thereby into a baser kind of slavery."[74]

Milton may agree with the Royalists in finding that the behavior of the common people in the Interregnum was wholly despicable, but he comes to a different conclusion about what is to be done in consequence. The royalist solution was to reinstate the king and restore the lower sorts to their lower places. In his *History of Britain*, however, Milton may have reviled his beloved English and their leaders, but he would not wish them to be placed under a leader's thumb. Rather, Milton thought that the common people must be prepared for freedom in the future better than they were in 1649. What was needed was a "fitter" people, able to withstand corrupt leaders. A fitter people would be hard to find in Britain, whose citizens succeeded at the arts of war rather than at those of peace: "For Britain (to speake a truth not oft spok'n) as it is a land fruitful enough of men stout and couragious in warr, so is it naturallie not over fertil of men able to govern justlie & prudently in peace; trusting onelie on thir Mother-witt, as most doo, & consider not that civilitie, prudence, love of the public more then of money or vaine honour are to this soile in a manner outlandish; grow not here but in minds well implanted with solid & elaborate breeding" (*CPW* 5.451). Milton urges that leaders, like farmers and husbandmen, implant "solid & elaborate breeding" in the people in the future. Writing poetry was a like task, as he remarked in the prologue to the second book of his *Reason of Church Government*: the aim of poetry was "to inbreed and cherish in a great people the seeds of virtue and public civility" (*CPW* 1.816).

The antidote to the miserable state of unfitness of the English people lay in their pursuit of that "strenuous liberty" Milton alludes to in *Areopagitica*, a liberty that is to be obtained through proper education, and their reading. He remarks in the Digression that virtue may be culled from the past by reading stories: "for stories teach us that libertie out of season in a corrupt and degenerate age brought Rome it self into further slaverie" (*CPW* 5.449). In his *History*, Milton believes that the public and its leaders could withstand these temptations if they knew more history. Milton urges his public to become educated in "civilitie, prudence," and "love of the public." For the English do not know history, "bred up, as few of them were, in the knowledge of Antient and illustrious deeds" (451). Because of their lack of this kind of training, like their forbears, the Britons, "what in the eyes of man cou[ld] be expected but what befel those antient inhabita[nts] whome they so much resembl'd, confusion in the end" (451).

In writing the *History of Britain*, Milton wants to make sure that, should another opportunity present itself, the people of England will not be so ill-equipped to meet it. His own writing will help to prevent that unfortunate outcome, for the failure of the Long Parliament was its "ill husbanding of those faire opportunities" (*CPW* 5.443). The story of the fate of the Britons after the demise of Roman rule offers an enlightening analogy: "Considering especially that the late civil broils had cast us into a condition not much unlike to what the *Britans* then were in, when the imperial jurisdiction departing hence left them to the sway of thir own Councils" (129). Milton knows he makes an unappealing comparison, but it is one that offers lessons in England's current weaknesses. Milton writes in his opening paragraph to the third book:

> Which times by comparing seriously with these later, and that confused Anarchy with this intereign, we may be able from two such remarkable turns of State, producing like events among us, to raise a knowledg of our selves both great and weighty, by judging hence what kind of men the *Britans* generally are in matters of so high enterprise, how by nature, industry, or custom fitted to attempt or undergoe matters of so main consequence: for if it be a high point of wisdom in every private man, much more is it in a Nation to know it self; rather than puft up with vulgar flatteries and encomiums, for want of self knowledge, to enterprise rashly and come off miserably in great undertakings. (129–30)

In this extremely rich and promising paragraph, Milton urges self-knowledge on the part of the entire nation as a first step in political liberty. Milton's political vision is premised on a personal vision of the individual self-scrutinizing soul, "a high point of wisdom in every private man," which is to be the model for an entire nation. If individuals are prideful, "puft up with vulgar flatteries and encomiums, for want of self knowledge," so much more are they a danger to the people over whom they are stewards. Milton presented another case of failed self-knowledge that led to a divine punishment in his account of David's taking the census in *Christian Doctrine.* There, Milton recollects language very like that of the passage from the *History of Britain*: "as a result of his power King David's spirit was so haughty and puffed up" (*CPW* 6.333). The lesson in *Christian Doctrine* of this failure in self-knowledge was that David suffered punishment for his sins, but also that "God always produces something good and just out of these" (333). In his *History of Britain,* Milton hopes to help English citizens gain knowledge from their sins, offering a remedy to his troubled times of renewal and giving the entire English people a task to complete. When Milton draws a connection between the nation and an individual reader of texts, he recommends that reading itself is a means to a political end, of which self-knowledge is to be the base. Thus Milton asks his readers to pay especially close attention to history, which "may deserve attention more than common, and repay it with like benefit to them who can judiciously read" (*CPW* 5.129). By appealing to those who can "judiciously read," Milton understands his political analogy to include an ethical mission, one in which he presses for citizens of his nation to become readers, educating themselves in spiritual matters and history. Such ethical training may resolve the question of responsibility for the failure of the English Revolution.

The royalist allegory of the Parliament of hell put the responsibility for the Restoration squarely in God's hands. Milton, on the other hand, blamed humans. By casting such blame, Milton finds that God's justice allows for free will: "So we must conclude that God made no absolute decrees about anything which he left in the power of men, for men have freedom of action" (*Christian Doctrine, CPW* 6.155). By encouraging humans to learn how to read as a first step toward ethical and political improvement, Milton vouches for the exercise of the will. By this logic, just as Adam and Eve's Fall in *Paradise Lost* was not proof that God foreordained it, the English Revolution was not divinely fated to fail. Rather, its current leaders, like their prototypes, Adam and Eve, freely fell by making bad political choices, by reading history badly or not at all.

Since humans, and not God, had failed England, what remained then was for humans to make themselves capable of succeeding in the future when another opportunity for liberation reared up. In the mean time, Milton believed, preparation was needed, to make "the people fittest to choose and the chosen fittest to govern" (*CPW* 4.615), through an education in "moulding the minds of men to virtue (whence arises true and internal liberty), in governing the state effectively, and preserving it for the longest possible space of time" (615).[75] These goals, while patently republican in their political vision of an "immortal commonwealth," as Harrington would put it, also are ethical, as Milton expresses a continued optimism about human capacity for change and growth. Harrington, by contrast, never gave the people a chance, sneering in 1656,

> A people, when they are reduced unto misery and despair, become their own politicians, as certain beasts when they are sick become their own physicians and are carried by a natural instinct unto the desire of such herbs as are their proper cure; but the people, for the greater part, are beneath the beasts in the use of them. Thus the people of Rome, though in their misery they had recourse, by instinct as it were, unto the two main fundamentals of a commonwealth, participation of magistracy and the agrarian, did but taste and spit at them, not (which is necessary in physic) drink down the potion and in that their healths. . . . But if you do not take the due dose of your medicines (as there be slight tastes which a man may have of philosophy that incline unto atheism), it may chance to be a poison; there being a like taste of the politics that inclines to confusion, as appears in the institution of the Roman tribunes, by which magistracy, and no more, the people were so far from attaining unto peace that they, in getting but so much, got but heads for eternal feud.

Milton, in opposing this shabby portait of the people, believes that individuals may be made fit to govern themselves effectively; he believes they may be made so by acquiring habits of reading. It is true that Milton had pictured the mob as "a herd confus'd / A miscellaneous rabble, who extol / Things vulgar, & well weigh'd scarce worth the praise" (*Paradise Regained* 3.49–51). But their leaders had been even worse. The people may be yet molded: "to guide Nations in the way of Truth / By saving Doctrine, and from error lead / To know" (*Paradise Regained* 2.473–75). Over the passage of time, Michael explains in *Paradise Lost*, humans will be brought "Up to a better Cov'nant, disciplin'd / From shadowie Types to Truth, from Flesh to Spirit" (12.302–3), finally able to convert their "works of Law to works of Faith" (12.306). Satan will not be destroyed until the Second Coming, but his ability to affect men will diminish before that time: "nor so is overcome / Satan, . . . but his works / In thee and in thy Seed" (12.390–95).[76]

Thus in the first two books of *Paradise Lost*, Milton agreed with the royalist judgment on the leaders of the English Revolution; the leaders had become "thyself not free, but to thyself enthralled," as Abdiel had taunted Satan (6.181). But Milton disagreed with the Royalists about who was responsible for that fact. While the Royalists blamed Satan and praised God for his victory in 1660, Milton blamed the individual men who had failed so miserably in their pursuit of liberty. In *Paradise Lost*, Milton corrected the current notion that Providence had designed the Restoration from the start.[77] As he wrote on Providence in *Christian Doctrine*, "even in sin, then, we see God's providence at work, not only in permitting it or withdrawing its grace, but often in inciting sinners to commit sin, hardening their hearts and blinding them" (*CPW* 6.331). Evil does not come from God, "but he directs a will which is already evil" (332; Guns don't kill people; people kill people). Milton's example showing God's leaving the human will free to sin is David's evil action of taking the census. In that case, Milton explains, God "was the instigator of the deed itself, but David alone was responsible for all the wickedness and pride which it involved" (333). The lesson in *Christian Doctrine* of this failure in self-knowledge was that David suffered punishment for his sins. The general lesson is this: "God always produces something good and just out of these and creates, as it were, light out of darkness" (333).[78] How would humans in Milton's own time attain the understanding of the light that comes out of darkness, the good that comes out of evil, when their own leaders, from David on down, had failed to understand this?

"Darkness Visible": Milton and the Reader of Allegory

They would do so by reading. "Light out of darkness"; "From shadowie Types to Truth": Milton writes of the spiritual education of humans as if writing about reading allegory. Milton presents these inscrutable images to portray his process of educating readers to become virtuous, to become revolutionary readers. Learning how to read is no easy project, and Milton scatters hard-to-read passages all over his text as a means to test his own readers' strenuousness, and to prepare them for the more difficult task of reading history. Over and over in representing hell in *Paradise Lost*, for example, Milton presents scenes that challenge his readers to work, not only in the mirroring of the Parliament of hell genre, but also in those passages in which we find the motif of darkness visible, a literal paradox. When Satan is compared to the eclipse (1.595–600), he is "Dark'n'd so, yet shone" (1.600). Before Satan leaves the strange, indistinct geography of hell, he must pass through Chaos, but before that, he must exit the gates that are guarded by two figures who present the clearest instance of allegory in the poem; but its very clarity throws all the other semiallegories in dark relief.

Sin is a figure identified with the eclipse. Her hellhounds, repeatedly returning into the kennel of her womb, follow her as they follow "the Night-Hag, when call'd / In secret, riding through the Air she comes / Lur'd with the smell of infant blood, to dance / With *Lapland* Witches, while the laboring Moon / Eclipses at thir charms" (2.662–66). The eclipse metaphor, as we saw in the last chapter, appeared frequently as a royalist political allegory. It is significant that the eclipse image frequently served in a circuit of meanings during the English Revolution, specifically to do with the activity of interpreting political rhetoric. The author of *Mercurius Bellicus*, for example, used the eclipse metaphor to protest printing conditions: "Nothing but *Lyes* may bee now *Printed*: Truth hath received a *totall Eclipse*: else sure, the last *Lyurnall* had never had so strict a charge, to *conceale* the *Coppy* of the *Kings* last *Letter*. . . . they will Print nothing that shall tend to the least *distur-*

bance of their own *Peace,* or *quiet.*"[79] Truth, like the sun, is masked by Parliament's avid press corps, the diurnals, which this author derisively nicknames "Lyurnalls." If truth was often equated with King Charles, it was also likened as often to the sun in the civil war pamphlets. The Royalist Sir George Wharton, in his *Mercurio-Coelico-Mastix* (1644), opposed his accuser John Booker's almanac: "your opacious, dark, and unweildy stars at Westminster, who reject to be enlightened with the lively and wholesome rays of the Sun (I mean our Gracious King Charles)."[80] In a similar spirit, *The Downfall of Cerberus* (1660) cheered the return of monarchy and the demise of the Interregnum press. The three-headed "Cerberus" was explicitly taunted as the triumvirate of parliamentary mercuries, *Britannicus, Pragmaticus,* and *Politicus*: "'tis like thou'lt be / In *Pluto's* Parliament a *Mercury,* / From whence perhaps thy friends may look to hear / From thee, what news, and the nocturnals there."[81] Rather than a "diurnal," these writers will produce business of the night, of darkness, "nocturnals."

Yet, as Joan S. Bennett has shown in her excellent analysis *Reviving Liberty,* Milton makes ample use of the image of an eclipse, or of the shadowed sun, fashioning a metaphoric structure in *Paradise Lost* to play against a very familiar royalist image. Though Bennett's account stops at the Restoration, the recurrence of this allegory even after 1660 takes on a significance like that of the Parliament of hell, vindicating the royalist perspective of a cosmic, natural hierarchy. Restoration Royalists used this eclipse image in their panegyrics to the returning monarch to justify a divine right theory of monarchy, as a theory that was not just a theory, but a natural reality. Among other poems greeting Charles II to the throne of England were Cowley's "Ode on the Blessed Restoration," Dryden's "Astrea Redux," Davenant's "Upon His Sacred Majesties Most Happy Return," and Waller's "To the King, Upon His Majesties Happy Return": all use the image to refer to Charles's recovery of his throne. Thomas Higgins, in "A Panegyrick to the King" (1660), writes: "As the sun, though he breake out but late, / Darkness dispells, and drives all Clouds away. / A gloomy Morn turn to a glorious day."[82]

Milton's contribution, the antipanegyric to Satan, virtually echoes this Restoration royalist figure, both before and after his success (2.486–95).[83] But Milton uses the eclipse image to turn it on its head. After Satan's victory, we have:

> At last as from a Cloud his fulgent head
> And shape Star-bright appear'd, or brighter, clad
> With what permissive glory since his fall
> Was left to him, or false glitter: All amaz'd
> At that so sudden blaze . . .

> (10.449–53)

According to Bennett, Milton uses the sun imagery to mark instances of false rulers (Satan in *Paradise Lost* and Charles I in *Eikonoklastes*) who fail to shine with the light given them, in contrast to the true ruler who keeps a proper balance of power and maintains God's law and spirit, and thus shines as a vehicle of those qualities. In his use of this image throughout the poem, then, Milton undermines the doctrine of the divine right of kings.[84] Yet in the passage above, Milton makes clear that the shadows that fall upon Satan's head come from the true light of God, who has dispensed "permissive glory." The passive mood, "with what permissive glory since his fall / Was left to him," makes clear that Satan shines from no light of his own, but purely from reflected light, which the reader views glancing off his fallen form. Milton forces the reader to coincide with his point of view: who, after all, finds Satan's glory "permissive" or "left," but Milton? By calling into question the purity of the image of Satan as the returning ruler in eclipse, by parodying the Restoration panegyric, Milton asks readers to call into question the whole scheme of representation.

As we saw in chapter 4, the eclipse was one sign of the problems of reading allegorically. Milton used the allegory of Charles or Satan as the sun not merely to evoke and to reject pervasive royalist imagery, but also to mark the difficulties of proper interpretation within an allegorical scheme of representation. In *Paradise Lost*, even for monarchs, the eclipse is something that "Perplexes"; the word *perplex* itself follows a chain of association denoting acts of failed or incomplete interpretation. For Milton, *perplexity* is a mark of interpretive challenge to make readers fit, as the first step to enlightenment. We recall Belial, who can make "the worse appear / The better reason, to *perplex* and dash / Maturest Counsels" (2.113–15, italics mine). Milton's own readers must push beyond Belial's words to discover their inner worthlessness. One of Milton's first readers, Andrew Marvell, also used the term *perplex* to denote the beginning of his readerly task. Marvell linked his poem to Milton's when he revealed the difficulty of the task of reading. As Marvell grew "less severe" in his reading, he grasped the success of Milton's "Project." Marvell describes his own readerly conduct rather in the same manner as does the royalist James Howell, writing that his "Knowing Reader" should read more than once to obtain the valuable truth hidden inside his text; in response to *Paradise Lost*, Marvell was first "misdoubting his Intent," but "growing less severe" as he read. When Marvell started to "fear" that project's success, he admitted,

> Yet as I read, soon growing less severe,
> I lik'd his Project, the success did fear;
> Through that wide Field how he his way should find
> O'er which lame Faith leads Understanding blind;
> Lest he perplex'd the things he would explain,
> And what was easy he should render vain.[85]

Marvell applauds Milton for not making things too difficult. Marvell's use of the word *perplex* in his dedicatory poem might then reflect his understanding of the process of reading as a rocky path toward understanding. Significantly, the word *perplex* features in the passage on which the censor allegedly choked. Marvell's term *perplex* directly links his own response and the passage in Milton's *Paradise Lost* that supposedly ran into trouble with the censor, and Marvell may be said to exonerate Milton from a dangerous kind of perplexity.

In Milton's poem too, "perplex" is both a physical and a mental condition, one involving the difficulties of finding one's way in a confusing field of signs. As a physical condition, it is associated with a difficult journey: Satan's tour of earth is "pensive and slow," because the thick "undergrowth / Of shrubs and tangling bushes had perplext / All path of Man or Beast that pass'd that way" (4.175–77). *Perplexed*, Satan finds his way obstructed by the rich foliage in Eden. Journeying in *Paradise Lost* is not something those in Eden generally want to do; the only human journey—the expulsion of Adam and Eve—is an unwanted one. However, of all the creatures in Eden, only Satan actually wants to *go* somewhere. For the beasts and the humans, this undergrowth is not an impediment, but "fram'd"—as are all things made by God—"to man's delightful use" (4.691–92). Satan's "wand'ring quest" (2.830) through Chaos and beyond, "alone, and without guide, half lost" (2.975), signifies not only his moral condition, but also his interpretive fallen state.

In the poem, *perplexity* in general is a satanic mode, both as a physical and a mental act, similar to Spenserian error but also to Milton's own concept of failed virtue.[86] After Satan's announcement to his hellish assembly, for instance, the angels bide time until their leader's return, "wand'ring, each his several way / Pursues, as inclination or sad choice / Leads him perplext, where he may likeliest find / Truce to his restless thoughts" (2.522–26). The fallen angels hope to ease the psychological torment of "restless thoughts" by physical wandering; we find them later "in wand'ring mazes lost" (2.561), mazes that are not material, do not resemble the Renaissance genre of romance and errantry, but that are intellectual, "vain wisdom all, and false Philosophie" (2.565). Their perplexity consists in the devils' failings in—or in their being prevented from—apprehending the simple truth of God's eminence. This satanic perplexity contrasts to Adam and Eve's manner, both before and after the Fall. The angels have free will in hell, but the direction of their wandering is a "sad choice"; it contrasts with the better choice of Adam, who, responding to Raphael's lesson, becomes "clear'd of doubt." Having been "freed from intricacies" by his lesson before the Fall, Adam is "taught to live / The easiest way, nor with perplexing thoughts / To interrupt the sweet of Life" (8.179, 182–84). The angels, in contrast, choose the physical directions that get them morally lost, erroneously searching for inner peace by exterior voyage.

After the Fall, Adam too loses this "easiest way" to the "sweet of Life." In the final book of *Paradise Lost*, however, Adam's condition may resemble in many ways that of the fallen angels in book 2, except that he rises above perplexity:

> now first I find
> Mine eyes true op'ning, and my heart much eas'd,
> Erstwhile perplext with thoughts what would become
> Of mee and all Mankind; but now I see
> His day, in whom all Nations shall be blest,
>
> (12.273–77)

The lessons of Adam in book 8 are different for the fallen man in book 12; that experienced man lives with perplexities he must himself solve.[87] In the passage from book 12, Adam relates a narrative, a before-and-after story. Yet unlike Satan's before-and-after, Adam recognizes the changes within himself.

Perplexity thus stands as a starting point for Milton's revolutionary reader. Michael Wilding has suggested that the Fall of the humans may be seen as a fall into a world of politics, that, "when both have eaten the apple, their plight is described in political terms. As a result of the fall they have become political beings. Political—Satanic—language enters," and thus, "part of the knowledge achieved by eating the fruit of the tree, then, is a political knowledge."[88] Wilding makes a mistake in equating political language with Satan or the Fall, however, by implying that there is another, preferable, kind of language. My point here is that Milton insists that humans have no access to this language, even if it existed. This is as much to say that books are inherently bad, an argument Milton opposed in *Areopagitica* when he wrote, "wholesome meats to a vitiated stomack differ little or nothing from unwholesome, and best books to a naughty mind are not unappliable to occasions of evill" (*CPW* 2.512). The effects of books—evil or good—depend on the reader's state to begin with. The lesson there was, "to the pure all things are pure" (512). In the case of postlapsarian language, there can be no inherently "satanic" language either: Milton appears to agree with Hobbes that language does not form a natural connection to the signified. Fallen, political language is the only language to be had, Milton seems to say, and Adam and Eve had better get used to it. It is neither inherently "satanic" nor "angelic"; as the last two books of *Paradise Lost* show, Adam has as much difficulty conversing with the Angel as he might have with the Devil.

After the Fall, though, reading takes on a new role, because there is another kind of representation to deal with. There is first of all history, which offers the human pair new perspectives and occasions upon which to test their ability to discern truth. Understanding history and politics after the Fall are equivocal tasks, because there are multiple ways of seeing and of speaking. But these tasks are vital to Milton's intention voiced in his *History*: history teaches humans the lessons they so often fail to learn in life. Adam has to learn to interpret the equivocal signs so that he sees properly. His heart may be repentant after the Fall, but his eyes are yet clouded. In the final books of *Paradise Lost*, Adam undergoes a training in hermeneutics under the tutelage of Michael. David Loewenstein has eloquently mapped Adam's education in *Milton and the Drama of History*, in which Adam learns that history will be "an essentially tragic process full of confusion and violence"; further, this is a vision Adam can perceive only by resisting false appearances. Loewenstein focuses on the content of this history, its dark, almost deterministic patchwork of repeated failures and its ambiguous relation to typological, progressive history. But after the Fall, there is something aside from the simple lessons of history; there is the fact of mediation for humans to cope with. Adam's current clear sight is the result of a vision of history that has been properly mediated, in this case, by Michael's narrative.[89]

After the Fall, however, Adam and Eve are separated from God, and their understandings are shaded by that distance.[90] The heavens recede to a great height; the human pair must be removed from their birthplace. In the process is Adam's learning how to read, a process that, it has been argued, is the subject of the epic.[91] Reading is explicitly and inherently a mediated process. After the Fall, Adam no longer stands in a direct relation with God. He fears the disunion, and it prompts his first query to Michael:

> This most afflicts me, that departing hence,
> As from his face I shall be hid, depriv'd
> His blessed count'nance; here I could frequent,
> With worship, place by place where he voutsaf'd
> Presence Divine
>
> (11.315–19)

Michael explains that though it appears there is a gap between Adam and the divine, God will be with him. When he reassures Adam, however, his language is vague: "Yet doubt not but in Valley and in Plain / God is as here, and will be found alike / Present" (11.349–50): the "is as here" presents a muddle: is God or is God not here? Michael insists that God may be felt by marks of his presence, though he may no longer be perceived directly:

> . . . and of his presence many a sign
> Still following thee, still compassing thee round
> With goodness and paternal Love, his Face
> Express, and of his steps the track Divine.
>
> (11.351–54)

Adam will have to learn how to read those signs. We hear an echo of Milton's abject state, "In darkness, and with dangers compast round, / And solitude" (7.27–28).

Even before his history lesson, however, Adam has already felt abject on his own, and this condition requires some kind of practical response: reading. In his first deed of repentance, Adam feels the presence of God, but this presence is only surmised, and it involves interpretation: "Methought I saw him placable and mild, / Bending his ear; persuasion in me grew / That I was heard with favor" (11.151–53). Adam's solution is based upon conjecture; "Methought" is an opinion, a "persuasion," not an unmediated fact. His first fallen act thus involves interpretating his station relative to God, which is now a state of abjectness. Unlike Satan, however, he fully accepts it. Adam's second interpretive action follows immediately on the first, and it involves reading the world around him. There is something new, animals hunting one another, in a glorious dance of airy predator and prey; and there is the figure of the eclipse:

> Nature first gave Signs, imprest
> On Bird, Beast, Air, Air suddenly eclips'd
> After short blush of Morn; nigh in her sight
> The Bird of *Jove*, stoopt from his aery tow'r,
> Two Birds of grayest plume before him drove:
>
> (11.182–86)

Viewing nature's new way, Adam interprets, only gropingly:

> O *Eve*, some furder change awaits us nigh,
> Which Heav'n by these mute signs in Nature shows
> Forerunners of his purpose, or to warn
> Us haply too secure of our discharge
> From penalty . . .
>
> (11.193–97)

His second lesson in reading is reading death. Though he does not know what these signs are, he knows they are bad. He is sure that they mean something. After the Fall, there are immediate changes in his perceptual powers: "doubt / And carnal fear that day dimm'd *Adam's* eye" (11.211–12).

But Adam also inhabits an unfamiliar world, and needs knowledge for new purposes. In his new world, he must do more than sing praises to God or chat with Eve. For Adam, there is now the knowledge of politics, of society, and of sin to contend with. This knowledge, further, is mediated through Michael's historical representations. Such clear sight, however, is not so readily available to the rest of humanity. Adam, presumably, will go out of Eden equipped with the ability to apply his lessons. How will Milton's own readers be so well supplied?

In *Paradise Lost*, Milton takes on Michael's mission, performing for his reader the intermediary acts that will justify the ways of God to men. Just as Adam's knowledge is received through the intercession of Michael, the reader's knowledge is received through Milton. But first, those readers must be made fit. How are they to be made so? Michael supplies the answer. Attending for the grace of the Lord's Second Coming, Adam in the meantime must be "disciplin'd / From shadowy Types to Truth, from Flesh to Spirit, / From imposition of strict Laws, to free / Acceptance of large Grace" (12.302–5).[92] Until that time, there is an earthly rent in the representational order. In his lesson in reading, Adam has begun to learn how to work through this disjunction, but it will take many more steps along the way. The problem is one and the same as the angel's "lik'ning spiritual to corporeal forms, / As may express them best" (5.573–74): that of understanding how meaning might from "corporeal to incorporeal turn" (5.413). It is the task of reading allegory. To return to the image of the eclipse, then, and to its "perplexity," we find Milton making an early signal by this image in the first book of *Paradise Lost*, that representational imagery, whether it is the holy image of the divine or the polemical use of allegory, is to be treated with suspicion.

The first book is spattered with epic similes and classical allusions, and critics have associated these with Milton's rejection of the classical epic. But these similes also perform a task of separating the reader from immediate experience of the events transpiring in hell. These call for the readers to make interpretations, to be prompted to apply readerly skills and power. Milton sometimes gives a poor guide for the reader's understanding, offering only qualification upon qualification through these difficult similes. When Satan alights on dry land, for example, Milton does not present a clear picture: "if it were Land that ever burn'd / With solid, as the Lake with liquid fire / And such appear'd in hue; as when the force / of subterranean wind transports a hill" (1.228–31). We can know this landscape only by comparison, but it is by comparison to things we have never seen.[93] It appears that Milton, and not just the sociable angel, must liken "spiritual to corporeal forms, / As may express them best" (5.573–74) in his representation of Satan in hell.

Similitude and conditionality both are forms of negation. And negation is the prime means by which Milton expresses the features of hell. Satan walks with "uneasy steps / Over the burning Marl, not like those steps / On Heaven's Azure" (1.295–97). Satan's hell is most unlike Lucifer's heaven, but only through a negative analogy can one know hell. When Satan's legions come awake, "Nor did they not perceive the evil plight / In which they were, or the fierce pains not feel" (1.335–36). Negative upon negative: Milton's language asserts that they did perceive their plight and feel their pain—or did they?

Simile offers another form of negation, because it asserts what exists in the form of what does not. Readers see the hellish figures summoned by Satan only indistinctly:

> As when the potent Rod
> Of *Amram's* Son in *Egypt's* evil day
> Wav'd round the Coast, up call'd a pitchy cloud
> Of *locusts*, warping on the Eastern Wind,
> That o'er the Realm of impious *Pharaoh* hung
> Like Night, and darken'd all the Land of *Nile*
> So numberless were those bad Angels seen.

> (1.338–44)

Satan wields his wand like Moses, now lord of the flies. Readers must make their way through this terrain by groping. Satan's crew hearkens to its leader as from the mists of sleep (1.332–34), much like the reader of these scenes who sees only as through a glass, darkly. The crowd throngs "numberless" (1.780), like "Faery Elves, / Whose midnight Revels, by a Forest side / Or Fountain some belated Peasant sees, / Or dreams he sees, while over-head the Moon / Sits Arbitress" (1.781–85). The reader's position is marked as that of the "belated Peasant"—perhaps the rustic shepherd of pastoral, perhaps Spenser's Colin Clout—but also as the poet, the ever-belated Milton. The way to understand hell is tenebrous indeed: does that peasant "see," or merely "dreams he sees"? With the hellish throng turning a stygian day into night by masking the sun, we have an image of "darkness visible," very much like that of the sun in eclipse.

Milton refused to allegorize in his representation of Satan and in the account of the war of the angels in *Paradise Lost*, and Michael Murrin has suggested that "this choice signals the end" of a literary tradition of allegory in epic. Milton's biblical poetics and his preference for typology were partly responsible for his choice, Murrin argues, but the poet's "iconoclastic theology" was what finally determined his literary mode. "Linguistically," Murrin writes, "iconoclasm cut Milton off from the traditional language of analogy. . . . The tradition of neither biblical nor secular allegory was available to Milton. He was a literalist in his scriptural interpretation."[94] The only instance of allegory—the brief Sin and Death scene—is strictly satanic, continues Murrin; allegory is itself rendered a satanic mode.[95] Though others have disputed Murrin's claims, explaining that with *Paradise Lost* we have not the end of a particular allegorical tradition, but rather an epistemological complication of it, it is generally agreed however, that, whether in the Spenserian high mode or in Bunyan's "mechanick Puritan mode," allegory as a literary kind died out in the seventeenth century. Stephen Fallon attributes this to a "decline in the status of universals."[96] I suggest that there is another factor to take into account: the crisis in hermeneutics that was the result of the writing of the English Revolution. *Paradise Lost* engages with contemporary allegorical representations of Satan in hell as a response to this crisis, and as a rejection of the royalist interpretation of cosmic hierarchy.

What Happens at Night: Making Darkness Visible

What does Milton do to offset the political investment in allegory? He interprets perversely, like Abdiel in his opposition to Satan. God rewards Abdiel: "To stand approv'd in sight of God, though Worlds / Judg'd thee perverse" (6.35–36), and Milton offers the example of Abdiel as a mark that individuals may take actions against the forces of tyranny by performing seemingly perverse acts, which, when properly interpreted, are glorious. Abdiel's actions may be judged "perverse" by the world (6.29–37), but they are the virtuous ones. Reading allegories may also be reading perversely. Until the Second Coming, all reading is somewhat perverse. Until that day, "so shall the World go on, / To good men malignant, to bad men benign" (12.537–38). Since humans, and not God, had failed the revolution, humans needed better preparation before they could reform the world, and part of their preparation was in learning how to read.

In *Paradise Lost*, Milton uses the motif of darkness as a figure for this condition of hermeneutic struggle, inverting the common sense in which darkness connotes a spiritual condition of abjection from God. Like Abdiel's perversity, blindness itself can be a virtue, as we saw in chapter 4. The sun in *Paradise Lost* is not always preferable to the moon. Indeed, much happens under cover of darkness, starting with the creation of Milton's poem. As we know, Milton's muse assaults him at night. Urania, "who deigns / Her nightly visitation unimplor'd, / And dictates to me slumb'ring" (9.21–23; see also 7.29) is the patroness of astronomy and queen of the night. But the muse is also "Light" itself, whom Milton claims "Nightly I visit" (3.32). Thus when Milton invokes "The meaning, not the Name" of his muse (7.5), he presents a linguistic obfuscation, a mimetic paradox, light in the midst of darkness.

Adam and Eve, even before the Fall, have to explain the presence of darkness in their world as a necessary absence of light. In book 4, before Adam and Eve first consummate their marriage and share in God's creation, they have a little discussion about what happens at night. In this conversation, Adam reveals that he knows something about the universe, well before his celestial instruction. Eve asks, "But wherefore all night long shine these, for whom / This glorious sight, when sleep hath shut all eyes?" (4.657–58); to which Adam answers:

> Those have thir course to finish, round the Earth,
> By morrow Ev'ning, and from Land to Land
> In order, though to Nations yet unborn,
> Minist'ring light prepar'd, they set and rise;
>
> (4.661–64)

The stars first express a cosmic order, a cycle of nature in which the whole earth is held. But further, they express a spiritual order as well:

> Lest total darkness should by Night regain
> Her old possession, and extinguish life
> In Nature and all things, which these soft fires
> Not only enlighten, but with kindly heat
> Of various influence foment and warm,
> Temper or nourish, or in part shed down
> Thir stellar virtue on all kinds that grow
> On Earth, made hereby apter to receive
> Perfection from the Sun's more potent Ray.
>
> (4.665–73)

The stars keep night at bay, but they also prepare the human world for the light of the sun. Adam suggests that the sun is too powerful at times, and needs its way muted before the sensitive apprehension of humans. Adam stresses the limitations of human perception, knowing the frailty of human abilities: those on earth, too, need to be made "apter to receive" the sun's light. What happens at night, when the moon holds sway, is a planning, a "fomenting" and "nourishing."

Adam's account matches Milton's explanation of his own writing process, as Milton, too, uses nighttime to advantage. Adam continues, in one of the loveliest passages in the poem:

> These then, though not unbeheld in deep of night,
> Shine not in vain, nor think, though men were none,
> That Heav'n would want spectators, God want praise;
> Millions of spiritual Creatures walk the Earth
> Unseen, both when we wake, and when we sleep:
> All these with ceaseless praise his works behold
> Both day and night: how often from the steep
> Of echoing Hill or Thicket have we heard
> Celestial voices to the midnight air,
> Sole, or responsive each to other's note
> Singing thir great Creator: oft in bands
> While they keep watch, or nightly rounding walk,
> With Heav'nly touch of instrumental sounds
> In full harmonic number join'd, thir songs
> Divide the night, and lift our thoughts to Heaven.
>
> (4.674–88)

The stars have work to do. They "shine not in vain," and at night give the light by which the "millions of spiritual Creatures" may praise God. The stars illuminate the world for those who "keep watch," the faithful many who sing unheard songs. Milton echoes the Puritan language of preacher Francis Woodcock, who explained his mission as God's "people's Watchmen, and his own Remembrancers," an allusion to Isaiah's watchmen on the walls of Jerusalem.[97] Adam's unfallen description of what happens at night sounds like a benign version of Milton's description of his own condition. Rather than sweet succor, though, Milton finds the stars give him only intermittent comfort:

> fall'n on evil days,
> On evil days though fall'n, and evil tongues;
> In darkness, and with dangers compast round,
> And solitude . . .
>
> (7.25–28)

Like those unseen millions of "Spiritual Creatures," singing while Adam sleeps, "Sole, or responsive each to other's note" (4.81), Milton is not alone, but is joined by his muse. His nightly visions encourage him to "shine on" in his writing, "as the wakeful Bird / Sings darkling, and in shadiest Covert his / Tunes her nocturnal Note" (3.38–40). With the failure of the English Revolution, with "*Bacchus* and his Revellers" (7.33) carousing until dawn, in *Paradise Lost* Milton urges his fellow countrymen not to give up faith in their cause; he seeks a fit audience, "though few" (7.31), to prepare and keep watch in the meantime.

With this concept of stellar virtue, Milton expresses his own spiritual hopes, and he also explains his literary impulses. In the nighttime of the earthly kingdom launched in the Restoration, these faithful few, keeping watch, await the true light of day, the true Kingdom of God. For Milton, the task ahead was to keep up the faith, either "Sole, or responsive each to other's note." In my reading, Milton never gave up on the people of England, and these passages in Eden explain the value of night, offering us a method for understanding how Milton thought the faithful ought to spend their time in the meanwhile. The period of darkness affords time to nourish "all kinds that grow" to become "apter to receive / Perfection from the Sun's more potent Ray," a time of heuristic growth. What follows this passage is the first lovemaking in Eden, an episode that seals the bond between husband and wife, and through which Milton links humanity to the order of God's Creation. Creation thus follows darkness, just as Milton's poem emerges after nightfall.

While they wait for a better future, however, there is night, the cover of darkness, in which both Satan and the poet take wing. Under that cover, however, the distinctions between good and evil are veiled. When Beelzebub speaks, for instance, the crowd is fixed, "still as Night / Or Summer's Noon-tide air" (2.308–9): either apogee will do.[98] Back in hell, Mammon fails to see the difference between the condition of true light and the light they might re-create in hell:

> This deep world
> Of darkness do we dread? How oft amidst
> Thick clouds and dark doth Heav'n's all-ruling Sire
> Choose to reside, his Glory unobscur'd,
> And with the Majesty of darkness round
> Covers his Throne; from whence deep thunders roar
> Must'ring thir rage, and Heav'n resembles Hell?
> As he our darkness, cannot we his Light
> Imitate when we please?
>
> (2.262–70)

When Mammon claims the devils can make a heaven out of hell, he reads the figure of the sun behind the clouds as a token of the commensurability of the two realms. But in this reading, he expresses a flawed theory of imitation: he believes since hell bears a physical resemblance to heaven at times, as when clouds cover the sun, hell may thus become a heaven to its inhabitants. Erroneously thinking that the qualities of light and darkness are reversible, Mammon interprets the figure of the sun and clouds as encouragement that those in darkness may yet recover light. But Milton and his readers know that this can never be. The state of hell is evil in its imitation of God's true state in heaven. In thinking the fallen angels can "imitate" God, they are reading incorrectly, incorrectly transcribing the text of heaven in another text, the text of hell. Milton offers his own text as an authentic rewriting of heaven's text, though one that is aware of its status as thoroughly mediated.

Milton suggests there is a discrepancy between interpretations made in hell or on earth and those made in heaven. True intepretation comes from without, as God's word is rewritten in a man's heart. Abdiel in his "testimony of Truth" (6.33) rebukes Satan for his reading of matters, first on doctrinal grounds, and then on experiential ones: "by experience taught we know how good, / And of our good, and of our dignity / How provident he is" (5.826–28). Abdiel is commended by God, for withstanding the hellish ridicule; "though Worlds / judg'd thee perverse" (6.35–36), in God's perspective he is on the right path. Authentic signification is difficult to distinguish in the lower realms, and may indeed appear "perverse." Milton thus resists the satanic practice of allegory, in which there is a one-to-one relation between the political order, the cosmic order, and the representational order. In so doing, Milton resists the Royalists' appeal to an audience to read history along the fixed lines of those correspondences. Milton acknowledges the mediation required to understand the figures of history.[99] *Paradise Lost* is principally concerned with proper interpretation, given the human condition of contingency, both in spiritual and in political terms.

Milton's repeated strategy of provoking allegorical interpretations while refusing to supply unequivocal "keys" to the allegory is meant as a lesson, a challenge, and more importantly, as a warning to his revolutionary readers. He presses the stress points of a popular contemporary political allegory, and baffles readers' expectations of a clear meaning. Doing so, Milton, in two books of *Paradise Lost,* sets before the reader a subtext of the multiple political possibilities of literary genres, and the rest of the poem leads readers down a path toward spiritual enlightenment that involves learning how to read. Milton used what Annabel Patterson has called "the concept of functional, intentional ambiguity,"[100] not to encode a particular meaning, as if the fit reader could find the "key" to unlock Milton's cabinet. Rather, Milton exposes the dangers of such allegories for the unwary reader. This is not to say that Milton "gave up" on his public, or even on history, in playing indeterminately upon this allegory, or that he retreated into an unpolitical "Paradise within." The lessons of *Paradise Lost,* on the contrary, are activist and engaged. Milton urged his readers to become a fit audience, revolutionary readers, and they were to do this by reading between the lines, by becoming adept at detecting and resisting propaganda: not because rhetoric and propaganda were inherently evil or satanic; nor because a plain style was better (in fact, there was no such thing as a plain style, except in Eden and in heaven: the one irrevocably in the past, and the other presently always mediated through fallen language). Members of Milton's fit audience sit and wait in the darkness, but they read by the candlelight in the meantime.

IN THIS STUDY of Milton's ideas about his public in his revolutionary prose and major poems, I have chosen to compare Milton's sense of his audience with that of his fellow writers: the pamphleteers, poets, and polemicists of the English Revolution. This comparison brings to light a common impulse in the writing of the period: the desire to shape a new kind of public. That public was imagined as active, rational, and deserving of a place in political decision making. Writers, including Milton, addressed their works to such a public, demanding that their audiences read and respond to contemporary issues; they also presented models for public debate by fighting pen-battles in print. Theirs was an imaginative contribution to the English Revolution, and I have underscored the rhetorical dimension of the writers' efforts to instill in their readers certain qualities. I express a strong claim for the power of rhetoric; indeed, that their rhetorical imagining of a new kind of public both responded to and brought into existence a reflective political subject.

In considering the question of reading subjects to be significant, I may seem to propose a deconstructionist reading of Milton's great poem, where I find that the meaning of *Paradise Lost* is inevitably about the "problem" of meaning. Rather, because of his need to make sense of recent history, and the rhetorical conditions of the Restoration public sphere in which he lived the final years of his life, I find that in *Paradise Lost*, Milton makes interpretation a chief concern. In his prose writings, notably *Eikonoklastes* and the *History of Britain*, Milton found that interpretation was a chief deficiency of England's political leaders, and he thought that the solution was for the English people to acquire reading skills. In *Paradise Lost*, Milton challenged his readers by using a conventional political allegory, forcing his readers to press beyond such facile representations. In the Restoration, this blind author wrote literature to help his people to learn how to bear up better in the future should another occasion for spiritual transformation present itself. But Milton aimed not simply to pass on his revolutionary or theological ideas in code, but also to stress training in fit reading as a political lesson. In his aim to transform his own readers into a "fit audience," Milton made the "revolutionary" content of the poem not an overt political statement, but the very process of training readers.

Over his writing career, Milton repeatedly sustained an interest in shaping his own readers. In opposing certain forms of censorship, he pointed explicitly to the powers of the public when he asked, "consider what Nation it is whereof ye are, and whereof ye are the governours: a Nation not slow and dull, but of a quick, ingenious, and piercing spirit, acute to invent, subtle and sinewy to discourse" (*Areopagitica*, *CPW* 2.551). Creating a positive image for the public and appealing to the English people as "quick and ingenious," supplied with reason "sufficient to judge aright" (2.511), Milton encouraged that public to continue its rapid production and reading of pamphlets. In the pamphlets of the English Revolution, many other writers exhorted their readers in a similar manner, urging them to make decisions and to join in the action.

That new kind of public enjoyed a mixed reception, both in Milton's great poems and in the writings of Milton's contemporaries, who feared that the public would be taken in by propaganda. Writers and readers, after all, were coming to terms with the new phenomenon of widespread propaganda from all points along the political spectrum. From Cleveland's biting attacks on the mob whom he deemed unable to resist propaganda, to Milton's persistent urging that the public make themselves fit to see through it, authors were confronting the free press as a press also free for distortions and manipulations. Rather than dismissing the public as an audience for politics, Milton aimed to create revolutionary readers, those who would be able to read and understand the coercive nature of many printed opinions. The revolutionary reader would be well armed to see through the manipulations of future politicians.

In his aim to construct a revolutionary reader, Milton chose as his final political mode a commitment not only to a specific cause, but to a process. In insisting that we pay attention to Milton's figuration of his audience as a significant contribution to the history of political thought, I urge Milton scholars to understand Milton as a writer who made a series of engagements and interventions with contrary—and often contradictory—political positions concerning his audience, specifically in the context of the English Revolution. This series does not necessarily add up to a sum total nor is it a story of Milton's growth toward some final achievement, whether that growth represents triumph over time, or disillusionment because of it. Rather, I have sought how Milton's political allegiances were expressed in response to particular political events, not to a singular "cataclysmic" event like the Restoration. Thus in my own work, I leave aside the monolithic Milton, who is either a "good" Milton (who furthered the cause of liberty) or a "bad" Milton (who was elitist and repressive); or a Milton who fits into a teleological narrative of the "rise" of capitalism or the "rise of the bourgeois subject." These models, though simplistic, are regularly adopted by my undergraduates in Milton class, and the students are indeed responding to something that *is* a drive toward the unified self in Milton, perhaps what Harold Bloom finds in a "strong poet." In light of my work, however, it will be important to see Milton's rhetorical opportunism, that is, the political choices he made at different times during the course of a terrifyingly turbulent period. To say that the Milton here is rhetorically opportunistic is not to condemn him for political insincerity; rather, perhaps it is to understand his flexibility and political strength (in a Machiavellian sense). This might mean that we set aside a quest for a coherent Miltonic biography in order to pay attention specifically to the incoherences in Milton's thought. These are not to be seen as failures of intellect, but rather as natural consequences of a man who constantly struggled to reconcile his ideals with historical realities, who was no idle theorist about politics, but an engaged man of action. Those incoherences might be the starting point for our renewed debate about literature and politics in the mid-seventeenth century, and for a renewed attention to the neglected literary output of the Interregnum period.

In the book, I have considered how the "low" polemical practices of the midcentury, especially its figuration of the public, intersected with Milton's "high" conceptions, and I argued that those "low" practices bear on an interpretation of Milton's great poems. But they also bear on the history of political thought. My work contributes to the ways we think about the relations between authors and audiences, and by fastening on rhetoric as a way to understand these ways, my conclusions bear not only on literary study, but also offer a neglected chapter in the history of political thought. I find that the rhetorical modes that writers used to address their readers depended on fundamental understandings of the moral capacity of individuals for acquiring knowledge. We see this in the discussion over state-sponsored censorship in 1644, when Milton argued that in states bound by censorship, "the privilege of the people [is] nullified" (*Areopagitica, CPW* 2.541). Censorship would deny that people have the capability to make decisions for themselves. In censored states, people "are not thought fit to be turned loose" to read what they will. Milton opposes this conception of human capabilities with a model of an active, able reader, graced by God with "the gift of reason to be his own chooser" (514). In their explicit appeals to a public, as well as in their rhetoric of a revolutionary reader, pamphlet writers helped to cultivate an ideology of an active and cohesive public that had a role to play in political affairs.

In sum, the literature of the English Revolution gave an image for a political subject. The writers' rhetoric of an active public contrasted with the idea that politics belonged behind closed doors. Writers acted upon the assumption that texts and readers belonged wholly in the public sphere, and this idea would change the way the political arena operated after the revolution. The press was not entirely free during the revolutionary years, yet there arose a fiction and a fantasy of free dialogue and debate, a fiction I have sketched in my study. Through the circulation of books, pamphlets, ballads, sermons, and broadsides, citizens became used to the practice of public debate. This was a fiction and a practice that did not disappear with the restoration of monarchy, moreover. By the eighteenth century, the press was accepted, if only warily, as a battleground for varying literary and political opinions.

In the book, I also offer a counterexample to the revisionists' complaint about the lack of a coherent ideology or even an ideological consequence of the purported English Revolution. I have emphasized that the rhetorical practices themselves constitute a form of ideology. My claim that the writers of the midseventeenth century brought into existence a concept of the revolutionary reader bears on our understanding of the rise of the "modern political subject." I recommend that political historians imagine that entity in light of revolutionary rhetoric, not solely as a repository of rights, but as a reader: as a sum of polemical and rhetorical processes, not as a product.

In our own age, where political symbolism and rhetoric seem to have taken over politics, this book is a meditation on the power of symbolism to shape thought itself. My study is an implicit argument for taking political rhetoric, symbolism, tropes, and images—and the propaganda that sprouts from these—very seriously. Though in late-twentieth-century America, our hair might curl at the notion that political rhetoric verges on propaganda, my study shows that the two share many things. My study, in fact, calls for a more thorough understanding of the differences and similarities between rhetoric and propaganda. In my understanding, and in the evidence I have given here, both political rhetoric and propaganda are two faces of the same coin. I have conceived of rhetoric (regardless of local conditions of "censorship") as *always* ambiguous and obscure. I showed how the civil war writers made use of this fact by writing literature that played on that obscurity. The problem for the revolutionary readers was to learn to distinguish between rhetoric that allowed room for choice and dissent and rhetoric that did not. The difficulty for the actors involved was to develop means to distinguish between these dangerously compatible uses of language.

Milton and the Revolutionary Reader also calls into question the assumptions underlying our current understanding of censorship. If audiences are thought to be passive recipients of ideas, then censorship is acceptable, since otherwise the audience would have no protection from pernicious writers. If audiences are thought to possess powers to make decisions, then censorship is an affront to their reasoning capacities. Writers during the civil war period were addressing readers that were increasingly figured as rational, judging publics. Yet that made audiences all the more susceptible to the dangers of rhetorical manipulation. My study should make us ask, What are the political needs of interested parties in particular moments that make censorship attractive (the "political" causes)? and Who are the bodies "protected" by censorship (the "theory of the audience")? But I also shift attention to the question, What is implied about the ability of the people to withstand danger under conditions of censorship or propaganda? What do leaders imply when they claim it their right to protect others? We know the effects of censorship as historical events: fines, punishments, martyrdoms, and book burnings; so, too, do we know the workings of propaganda: political or judicial machinery and its effects. But what assumptions do those who create these rhetorical forms make about their readers? When we press for forms of censorship or when we go in for publicity campaigns and sound bites for political candidates in our own country, what suspicions do we harbor about the abilities of the American people to make judgments based upon their own sound, individual, and independent authorities?

Though the people fighting for change in the seventeenth century failed in their political aims, they did leave a legacy. The revolution may have been in name a colossal failure: the fundamental structures of society were not altered; both king and Anglican church were restored; hierarchies within social structure hardened—even a commonly used name for the period, the Interregnum, is a sign of the failure, positing what happened during the English Revolution as an aberration from English monarchical tradition—nevertheless, even so, after the civil war period, the press was ever used as a means of address to a widened electorate, as an organ of party politics, and it provided a new livelihood for a cadre of writers like Dryden, Defoe, Swift, Steele, and Addision, now professional pundits. The establishment of the free press after 1695 was an extension of gains made by the public appeals of the English Revolution, and an acknowledgment of the press's place in political and intellectual life, despite the possibilities of propaganda. An interest in political debate in the press is one outcome of the English Revolution, and it is our inheritance from the seventeenth-century war of words. The idea of the revolutionary reader in the English Revolution thus heralds a dramatic and enduring turn in Western political culture. In our own age, where censorship threatens to reduce the scope of public expression, we should take care to understand the hard battles fought to accept public expression in the first place, nor should we forget that a free press is also a press free for propaganda. We should also take care not to degrade our own portraits of our democratic political subjects.

• N O T E S •

INTRODUCTION

1. *Catalogue of the Thomason Tracts in the British Museum, 1640–1661* (London, 1908), xxi. This collection is not complete for the period, but gives some idea of the volume. For printing history during the English revolutionary period, see Frederick S. Siebert, *Freedom of the Press in England, 1476–1776* (Urbana: University of Illinois Press, 1952), 166–76; Cyprian Blagden, "The 'Company' of Printers," *Studies in Bibliography* 13 (1960): 3–15; J. Frank, *The Beginnings of the English Newspaper, 1620–1660* (Cambridge: Harvard University Press, 1961); Cyprian Blagden, "The Stationers' Company in the Civil War Period," *The Library*, 5th ser., 13, no. 1 (1958): 1–17.

2. There has been a flurry of interest recently in linking the high literature of the seventeenth century to the rich pamphlet lore of the English Revolution. Collections of essays such as R. C. Richardson and G. M. Ridden, eds., *Freedom and the English Revolution: Essays in History and Literature* (Manchester: Manchester University Press, 1986); and Thomas Healy and Jonathan Sawday, eds., *Literature and the English Civil War* (Cambridge: Cambridge University Press, 1990), attempt to bring to the literary texts the full political meanings that have been missed by literary scholars. Recent studies such as Thomas Corns, *Uncloistered Virtue: English Political Literature, 1640–1660* (Oxford: Clarendon Press, 1992) and Nigel Smith, *Perfection Proclaimed: Language and Literature in English Radical Religion, 1640–1660* (Oxford: Oxford University Press, 1989) have aimed to bridge the high and the low literature of the period. Elizabeth Skerpan, *The Rhetoric of Politics in the English Revolution* (Columbia: University of Missouri Press, 1992) examines the traditions of university rhetoric used by politicians during the English Revolution, and her study complements my literary approach.

3. C. Hill, "Parliament and People in Seventeenth-Century England," *Past and Present* 92 (1981): 100–124, argues that the motions of parliaments during pre–civil war years did reflect real change, a voice of the middling sort seeking representation, though J. H. Hexter, "Power Struggle, Parliament, and Liberty in Early Stuart England," *Journal of Modern History* 50 (1978): 1–50, disagrees. Derek Hirst, *The Representative of the People? Voters and Voting under the Early Stuarts* (Cambridge: Cambridge University Press, 1975), 192; Mark Kishlansky, *Parliamentary Selection: Social and Political Choice in Early Modern England* (New York: Columbia University Press, 1986), 226. One of the chief disputes in historiography of the seventeenth century is whether such principles as the authority of the House of Commons led to the revolution or whether the civil war was a kind of road accident in history, without long-term structural or ideological causes. David Underdown, *Revel, Riot and Rebellion* (Oxford: Oxford University Press, 1987): "Englishmen of the middling sort were becoming more involved in national politics in the early seventeenth century than ever before" (123), e.g., ship money: "the divisions which led to the civil war were sharpened by the intrusion of the popular element into national politics" (132).

4. Conrad Russell, *Parliaments and English Politics, 1621–1629* (Oxford: Oxford University Press, 1979), 1. The preferred revisionist term however is *rebellion*. Chris-

topher Hill, vigilant antirevisionist, defends the term *revolution* in "The Word 'Revolution,'" in *A Nation of Change and Novelty: Radical Politics, Religion and Literature in Seventeenth-Century England* (New York: Routledge, 1990), 82–101. The extreme revisionist position, not uniformly embraced by revisionists, is put forward by J.C.D. Clark, *Revolution and Rebellion: State and Society in England in the Seventeenth and Eighteenth Centuries* (Cambridge: Cambridge University Press, 1986), which considers the period from the curious vantage point of its eighteenth-century outcome.

5. G. R. Elton, "A High Road to Civil War?" *Studies in Tudor and Stuart Politics and Government* (Cambridge: Cambridge University Press, 1974), 164–82; Conrad Russell, "Parliamentary History in Perspective, 1603–1629," *History* 61 (1976): 1–17, 21. The first crop of revisionist historians has included, in addition to Elton, Kevin Sharpe, *Faction and Parliament* (Oxford: Clarendon Press, 1978); Mark Kishlansky, "The Emergence of Adversary Politics in the Long Parliament," *Journal of Modern History* 49 (1977): 617–40; also, his "Consensus Politics and the Structure of Debate at Putney," *Journal of British Studies* 20, no. 2 (1981): 50–69; and John S. Morrill, *The Revolt of the Provinces: Conservatives and Radicals in the English Civil War, 1603–1650* (Allen and Unwin, London: 1976); and his "Religious Context of the English Civil War," *Transactions of the Royal Historical Society*, 5th ser., 33 (1983): 155–78. All these have focused on local politics and parliamentary history. Their interpretations have been countered recently by Thomas Cogswell, "Coping with Revisionism in Early Stuart History," *Journal of Modern History* 62 (1990): 538–51; and Johann P. Sommerville, *Politics and Ideology in England, 1603–1640* (London: Longman, 1986). See also Derek Hirst, fighting back against the revisionists in "Revisionism Revised: The Place of Principle," *Past and Present* 92 (1981): 79–99. For the best and most readable overview of recent historiography of this period as well as an analysis of the "functional crisis," see Lawrence Stone, *The Causes of the English Revolution, 1529–1642* (New York: Harper and Row, 1972).

6. Judith Shklar, "James Harrington," in Lawrence Stone, ed., *Social Change and Revolution in England, 1540–1640* (London: Longmans, 1965), 108, seeks to place the intellectuals of the English Revolution at quite a distance from the actual political arena.

7. My notion of an "ideology" or "political ideas" is much narrower than a neo-Marxist conception of ideology, where "ideology is a system (with its own logic and rigour) of representation (images, myths, ideas or concepts, depending on the case) endowed with a historical existence and role within a given society," according to Louis Althusser, *For Marx*, trans. Ben Brewster (New York: Pantheon, 1969), 231; my application of political analysis is more precisely located in the workings of high politics than that of a literary critic such as Terry Eagleton, who examines literary texts from the vantage point of the power processes that sustain social orders.

8. Quentin Skinner, "Motives, Intentions and the Interpretation of Texts" and "Meaning and Understanding in the History of Ideas," both essays in James Tully, ed., *Meaning and Context: Quentin Skinner and His Critics* (Princeton: Princeton University Press, 1988), 77–78, 64. By encouraging the interpreter to understand the text's conventionality, Skinner also encourages the literary critic to enter the archive. Stanley E. Fish, "Literature in the Reader: Affective Stylistics," in *Is There a Text in This Class?* (Cambridge: Harvard University Press, 1980), 65. See also William J. Bouwsma, "Intellectual History in the 1980s: From the History of Ideas to the History of Meaning," *Journal of Interdisciplinary History* 12, no. 2 (1981): 279–91.

9. C. B. Macpherson, *The Political Theory of Possessive Individualism: Hobbes to Locke* (Oxford: Clarendon Press, 1962), 1; Lawrence Stone, "The Results of the English

Revolutions of the Seventeenth Century," in J.G.A. Pocock, ed., *Three British Revolutions* (Princeton: Princeton University Press, 1980), 61; Also see the classic essay by Wallace Notestein, "The Winning of the Initiative by the House of Commons," *British Academy Proceedings* 2 (1924–25): 125–75, which makes the "new individualism" (170) responsible for the empowerment of the Commons; B. Bailyn, *The Ideological Origins of the American Revolution* (Cambridge: Harvard University Press, 1967).

10. Thomas Hobbes, *Leviathan*, ed. C. B. Macpherson (Harmondsworth, Middlesex: Penguin, 1968), 81.

11. As argues Terry Eagleton, *Ideology: An Introduction* (New York: Verso, 1991), 1–24, drawing upon Althusser, *For Marx;* and see Michael J. Shapiro, ed., *Language and Politics* (New York: New York University Press, 1984) for considerations of these Marxist and *marxisant* ideas. My point of departure is that any ideology is mediated through language, as Michael Ryan suggests: "Form is . . . a bridge concept between rationalism and materialism, between the realm of thought, in as much as it can only exist in the form of representations, and materiality, in as much as it can only exist in certain forms of being." *Politics and Culture: Working Hypotheses for a Post-Revolutionary Society* (Baltimore: Johns Hopkins University Press, 1989), 6. For a non-linguistic analysis of ideology in media, see David E. Proctor, *Enacting Political Culture* (New York: Praeger, 1991).

12. Sheldon S. Wolin, *Politics and Vision: Continuity and Innovation in Western Political Thought* (Boston: Little, Brown and Company, 1960), 17–19. His *Hobbes and the Epic Tradition of Political Theory* (Los Angeles: William Andrews Clark Memorial Library, 1970) exemplifies the principle that political writing is a kind of literature. I am also influenced by Ernst Cassirer, *The Myth of the State* (New Haven: Yale University Press, 1946). My work here does not extend into such epistemological concerns. For a more thorough, and controversial, treatment, see Sabina Lovibond, who in *Realism and Imagination in Ethics* (Minneapolis: University of Minnesota Press, 1983) applies Wittgenstein's language theory to politics, and breaks down the distinction between prescriptive and descriptive statements, denying the epistemological opposition between facts and values.

13. Barbara Lewalski, "Milton: Political Beliefs and Polemical Methods," *PMLA* 74 (1959): 191–202, emphasizes the occasional aspects of Milton's political writings, yet stresses his continuities of thought.

14. Jürgen Habermas, *The Structural Transformation of the Public Sphere: An Inquiry into a Category of Bourgeois Society*, trans. T. Burger (Cambridge: MIT Press, 1989), 25–26, 27, 42–43, 88–93.

15. Keith Baker, "Politics and Public Opinion under the Old Regime: Some Reflections," in Jack R. Censer and Jeremy D. Popkin, eds., *Press and Politics in Pre-Revolutionary France* (Berkeley: University of California Press, 1987), 204–46; and Mona Ozouf, "'Public Opinion' at the End of the Old Regime," *Journal of Modern History* 60, suppl. (1988): S1-S21.

16. Thomas Browne, "To the Reader," *Religio Medici*, in *Sir Thomas Browne: The Major Works*, ed. C. A. Patrides (Harmondsworth, Middlesex: Penguin, 1977), 59.

17. *Mercurius Aulicus*, no. 84 (4–10 August 1644); [John Birkenhead], *News from Smith the Oxford Jailor* (1645).

18. On the relationship between literacy and social status, see Lawrence Stone, "The Educational Revolution in England, 1560–1640," *Past and Present* 28 (1965): 41–80; David Cressy, *Literacy and the Social Order* (Cambridge: Cambridge University Press, 1980); Margaret Spufford, "First Steps in Literacy," *Social History* 4 (1979): 407–35.

19. On Nashe, see Sandra Clark, *The Elizabethan Pamphleteers: Popular Moralistic Pamphlets, 1580–1640* (Rutherford, N.J.: Fairleigh Dickinson University Press, 1983), 141–42; Margaret Spufford, *Small Books and Pleasant Histories: Popular Fiction and Its Readership in Seventeenth-Century England* (Cambridge: Cambridge University Press, 1985), 51.

20. George Wharton, *Mercurio-Coelico-Mastix* (1644), 2.

21. For an excellent overview of the radical and popular traditions between Elizabethan and Stuart writing, see Christopher Hill, "From Marprelate to the Levellers," in *Writing and Revolution in Seventeenth-Century England* (Amherst: University of Massachusetts Press, 1985), 75–95; E. Arber, *The Martin Marprelate Controversy* (London: Archibald Constable and Co., 1879); William Pierce, *A Historical Introduction to the Marprelate Tracts* (London: Archibald Constable and Co., 1908); William Pierce, ed., *The Marprelate Tracts* (London: James Clarke and Co., 1911).

22. On this press, see H. R. Plomer, "Secret Printing during the Civil War," *The Library*, n.s., 5 (1904): 374–403, esp. 382–85.

23. John S. Coolidge, "Martin Marprelate, Marvell, and *Decorum Personae* as a Satirical Theme," *PMLA* 74 (1959): 526–32: "the memory of old Martin remained a Puritan possession" (529).

24. Nigel Smith, "Richard Overton's Marpriest Tracts: Toward a History of Leveller Style," in Thomas N. Corns, ed., *The Literature of Controversy*, (Totowa, N.J.: Frank Cass, 1987). On the connection between seventeenth-century literature and the Protestant reforming tradition, see David Norbrook, *Poetry and Politics in the English Renaissance* (London: Routledge and Kegan Paul, 1984), who, in chap. 2, links radical humanism and radical Protestantism; also, Barbara Kiefer Lewalski, *Protestant Poetics and the Seventeenth-Century Religious Lyric* (Princeton: Princeton University Press, 1979), who argues "Biblical poetics is itself the most important component of an emerging Protestant aesthetics" (8).

25. John Taylor, *Crop-Eare Curried* (1644), 3, t.p.

26. Richard Brathwaite, *Whimzies; or, A New Cast of Characters* (1634), 19.

27. Cyprian Blagden, *The Stationers' Company: A History, 1497–1959* (Stanford, Calif.: Stanford University Press, 1960), 188; Spufford, *Small Books*, 100.

28. Spufford, *Small Books*, 93; Hyder E. Rollins, "The Black Letter Broadside Ballad," *PMLA* 34 (1919): 258–339. On the spread of popular literature, see B. Capp, "Popular Literature," in B. Reay, ed., *Popular Culture in Seventeenth-Century England* (New York: St. Martin's Press, 1985), 198–243; Louis B. Wright, *Middle-Class Culture in Elizabethan England* (Chapel Hill: University of North Carolina Press, 1935); H. S. Bennett, *English Books and Their Readers, 1558–1603* (Cambridge: Cambridge University Press, 1965); T. Laqueur, "Cultural Origins of Popular Literacy in England, 1500–1850," *Oxford Review of Education* 2, no. 3 (1976): 55–75; C. J. Sommerville, "On the Distribution of Religious and Occult Literature in Seventeenth-Century England," *The Library*, 5th ser., 29 (1974): 221–25.

29. Samuel Hartlib, *A Description of the Famous Kingdom of Macaria*, quoted in Siebert, *Freedom of the Press*, 192. On penny merriments, see Spufford, *Small Books*, chap. 3.

30. Edith Klotz, "A Subject Analysis of English Imprints for Every Tenth Year from 1480 to 1640," *Huntington Library Quarterly* 1, no. 4 (1938): 417–19; D. F. McKenzie, "The London Book Trade in the Later Seventeenth Century," Sandars Lectures, Cambridge University, 1976, chap. 2.

31. *The King's Cabinet Opened* (1645), A3v; Derek Hirst, *Authority and Conflict: En-*

gland, 1603–1658 (Cambridge: Harvard University Press, 1986), 257; E. Symmons, *A Vindication of King Charles . . . from those Aspersions cast upon Him* (1648), A1.

32. Stanley Fish, *Surprised by Sin: The Reader in "Paradise Lost"* (Berkeley: University of California Press, 1971), sees the poem as a means to make readers fit, but those readers perform their acts solo; my interest is in the collective audience Milton imagines, the "to men" to whom he addresses his poem.

33. Andrew Marvell, "On *Paradise Lost*," in Merritt Y. Hughes, ed. *John Milton: Complete Poems and Major Prose* (Indianapolis: Bobbs-Merrill, 1957), 209.

34. C. S. Lewis, *A Preface to "Paradise Lost"* (Oxford: Oxford University Press, 1979), 135; J. Carey and A. Fowler disagree with this stylistic elitism, in *The Poems of John Milton* (London: Longmans, 1968); Milton, in designating his "fit audience, though few" of *Paradise Lost*, was "not necessarily implying esoteric intention" (277). For Mary Ann Radzinowicz, "The Politics of *Paradise Lost*," in Kevin Sharpe and Steven N. Zwicker, eds., *Politics of Discourse: The Literature and History of Seventeenth-Century England* (Los Angeles: University of California Press, 1987), 204–29, Milton's audience is to be made "fit" to receive his epic teaching, though she does not deal with her implication that the audience is not *yet* fit. See also Hugh Trevor-Roper, "The Elitist Politics of Milton," *Times Literary Supplement*, 1 June 1973. The debate about Milton's elitism has also been seen in the theological context of Calvinist ideals of "the elect." See John Guillory, "The Father's House: *Samson Agonistes* in Its Historical Moment," in Mary Nyquist and Margaret Ferguson, eds. *Re-Membering Milton: Essays in the Texts and Traditions* (New York: Methuen, 1987), 157.

35. Marvell, "On *Paradise Lost*"; Annabel Patterson, "'Forc'd Fingers': Milton's Early Poems and Ideological Constraint," in Claude J. Summers and Ted-Larry Pebworth, eds., *"The Muses Commonweale": Poetry and Politics in the Seventeenth Century* (Columbia: University of Missouri Press, 1988), 9–22.

36. Roberta F. Brinkley, ed., *Coleridge in the Seventeenth Century* (Durham, NC: Duke University Press, 1955), 473.

37. Christopher Hill, *Milton and the English Revolution* (New York: Viking, 1977), 459, 464; Michael Fixler finds an "aristocratic and theocratic" Milton, in *Milton and the Kingdoms of God* (Evanston, Ill.: Northwestern University Press, 1964), 169.

38. For a Marxist analysis of Milton's class bias, see David Aers and Gunther Kress, "Historical Process, Individual and Communities in Milton's Early Prose," in Francis Barker, Jay Bernstein, John Coombes, Peter Hulme, Jennifer Stone, Jon Stratton, eds., *1642: Literature and Power in the Seventeenth Century* (Essex: University of Essex, 1981), 296; "elitist radical": Patterson, "'Forc'd Fingers,'" 22; "ideological failure": Thomas N. Corns, "Milton's Quest for Respectability," *Modern Language Review* 77, no. 4 (October 1982): 769–79.

39. See James Turner, "The Politics of Engagement," in David Loewenstein and James G. Turner, eds., *Politics, Poetics, and Hermeneutics in Milton's Prose* (Cambridge: Cambridge University Press, 1990), 257–75; Joan S. Bennett, *Reviving Liberty: Radical Christian Humanism in Milton's Great Poems* (Cambridge: Harvard University Press, 1989), 210 n. 46; Don M. Wolfe, *Milton in the English Revolution* (New York: Humanities Press, 1963), 240–46; and Hugh Trevor-Roper, "Milton in Politics," in *Catholics, Anglicans and Puritans: Seventeenth Century Essays* (Chicago: University of Chicago Press, 1988), 231–82.

40. J.G.A. Pocock, *The Machiavellian Moment: Florentine Poltiical Thought and the Atlantic Republican Tradition* (Princeton: Princeton University Press, 1975), 369–80; J.G.A. Pocock, *The Ancient Constitution and the Feudal Law* (Cambridge: Cambridge

University Press, 1957), 21, 44–49; Edmund Morgan, *Inventing the People: The Rise of Popular Sovereignty in England and America* (New York: Norton, 1988), chap. 3; see William Haller, *Tracts on Liberty in the Puritan Revolution*, 3 vols. (New York: Columbia University Press, 1934), 1.24, on this doctrine in the civil war period.

41. The humanist practice of reading for examples of virtue is explained brilliantly in John Wallace, "'Examples Are Best Precepts': Readers and Meanings in Seventeenth-Century Poetry," *Critical Inquiry* 1, no. 2 (December 1974): 273–90.

42. Blair Worden, "Providence and Politics in Cromwellian England," *Past and Present* 109 (November 1985): 55–99, 90 n. 165.

43. Lewalski, *Protestant Poetics*, 131.

44. David Loewenstein, in *Milton and the Drama of History: Historical Vision, Iconoclasm and the Literary Imagination* (Cambridge: Cambridge University Press, 1990), calls the history involved in this "millennial vision" a "cosmic Drama in which God and men perform their competing spectacles" (11), brilliantly studying the ways in which Milton was troubled by the different possiblities of "literary configuration" (124) of that history.

45. Steven N. Zwicker, *Dryden's Political Poetry: The Typology of King and Nation* (Providence, R.I.: Brown University Press, 1972), 22.

46. Victoria Kahn, *Rhetoric, Prudence and Skepticism in the Renaissance* (Ithaca: Cornell University Press, 1985), 11, 182.

47. Not strictly the kind of activist discussed in Annabel Patterson, "The Civic Hero in Milton's Prose," *Milton Studies* 8 (1975): 71–102, where the prose is seen to articulate a concept of "civic fortitude," a Ciceronian ideal of the public hero, but rather a "radical saint." See Perry Miller, *The New England Mind: The Seventeenth Century* (Cambridge: Harvard University Press, 1954); William M. Lamont, *Godly Rule. Politics and Religion, 1603–1660* (London: Macmillan, 1969).

48. Anthony Fletcher revives providentialism for understanding the political theory of the seventeenth century in, "Oliver Cromwell and the Godly Nation," in John Morrill, ed., *Oliver Cromwell and the English Revolution* (New York: Longman, 1990), 209–33, but overstresses the spiritual component, at the expense of the constitutional side; Worden, "Providence and Politics," 55–99, sees providentialism as conservative politically; and Keith Thomas, in *Religion and the Decline of Magic* (New York: Scribner's, 1971), 104–12, as conservative socially. For contrast, Christopher Hill, "'Till the Conversion of the Jews,'" in Richard H. Popkin, ed., *Millenarianism and Messianism in English Literature and Thought, 1650–1800* (New York: E. J. Brill, 1988), 12–36, argues for the the radical nature of millennialist, typological thought.

49. Arthur E. Barker, *Milton and the Puritan Dilemma, 1641–1660* (Toronto: University of Toronto Press, 1976), 201.

50. Boyd Berry, *Process of Speech: Puritan Religious Writing and "Paradise Lost"* (Baltimore: Johns Hopkins University Press, 1976), 127, 129; see also Norman Cohn, *Pursuit of the Millennium*, rev. ed. (New York: Temple Smith, 1970), 179–94; Earl Miner, ed., *Literary Uses of Religious Typology from the Late Middle Ages to the Present* (Princeton: Princeton University Press, 1977).

51. Keith W. Stavely, *The Politics of Milton's Prose Style* (New Haven: Yale University Press, 1975), 112; likewise, Wilbur E. Gilman argued that in *Areopagitica*, Milton relied to heavily on the "pathetic proof," that is, the emotional appeal to the beliefs and prejudices of his audience, rather than on logical argument. *Milton's Rhetoric: Studies in His Defense of Liberty* (Columbia: University of Missouri Press, 1939), 170; Wolin, *Politics and Vision*, 17.

52. Fixler, *Milton and the Kingdoms of God*, 97.

53. Harold Fisch, *Jerusalem and Albion: The Hebraic Theme in Seventeenth-Century Literature* (New York: Schochen, 1964); Steven N. Zwicker talks about the clash between these two systems of imagery in the literature of the English Restoration, though not in Milton, in his "England, Israel and the Triumph of Roman Virtue," in Richard H. Popkin, ed., *Millenarianism and Messianism in English Literature and Thought, 1650–1800* (New York: E. J. Brill, 1988), 37–64.

54. My notion of a "language" here derives from J.G.A. Pocock's essays, "Languages and Their Implications," in his *Politics, Language and Time: Essays in Political Thought and History* (New York: Atheneum, 1971), 3–41; and "The Concept of a Language and the *métier d'historien*: Some Considerations of Practice," in Anthony Pagden, ed., *The Languages of Political Theory in Early Modern Europe* (New York: Cambridge University Press, 1987), 19–38; and also Quentin Skinner, "Language and Social Change," in Tully, *Meaning and Context*, 119–32.

55. Ernest Sirluck, "That Grand Whig Milton," *Modern Philology* 52 (August 1954): 63–67. Thomas Corns has written persuasively that this image of Milton reflects the moment in which it was written: "the initiators of the *Complete Prose*, unsurprisingly, approach Milton within a problematic wholly congruent with then prevailing American approaches to late Renaissance culture. It is a humane and decent tradition, which foregrounds notions of intellectual continuity and of the importance of the individual in political crises, but it belongs to its age. The writing of Milton and his contemporaries is unconsciously appropriated by midtwentieth century liberalism." "The *Complete Prose Works of John Milton* in Retrospect (review article)," *Prose Studies* 7, no. 2 (September 1984): 185.

56. Mary Ann Radzinowicz, *Toward "Samson Agonistes": The Growth of Milton's Mind* (Princeton: Princeton University Press, 1978), 146; and her essay, "'To make the people fittest to chuse': How Milton Personified His Program for Poetry," *CEA Critic* 48, no. 8 (1986): 3–23. On Milton's secularism and consistency, see Robert Thomas Fallon, "Milton in the Anarchy, 1659–1660: A Question of Consistency," *Studies in English Literature* 21, no. 1 (Winter 1981): 126.

57. Zera Fink, *The Classical Republicans: An Essay in the Recovery of a Pattern of Thought in Seventeenth-Century England* (1945; reprint, Evanston, Ill.: Northwestern University Press, 1962); also Perez Zagorin, *A History of Political Thought in the English Revolution* (London: Routledge and Kegan Paul, 1954), 111. Judith Shklar's, "Ideology Hunting: The Case of James Harrington," *American Political Science Review* 53 (1959): 662–92, has raised doubts for revisionists about the role of intellectuals in the political history of the English Revolution.

58. In his introduction to the *Prima Defensio*, for example, Don M. Wolfe takes up the question of Milton's conception of the people as a "central weakness of Milton's intellectual position" (*CPW* 4.113). Wolfe "saves" Milton, however, by pointing out the ways in which Milton revised his position through qualifications in later works. Ernest Sirluck also uses a biographical account to explain the contradictions in Milton's political views. Such a turn to biography has its own problems, and it has fostered a whole cottage industry in the dating of Milton's later works; we have yet to see what the reconsideration of the dating of *Christian Doctrine* might do to this argument, for example.

59. The recent collection of essays edited by Margaret W. Ferguson and Mary Nyquist, *Re-Membering Milton: Essays on the Texts and Traditions* (London: Methuen, 1987), sought to apply the findings of poststructuralist and feminist thought, opposing the impulse to surrender to Milton's own masterful self-fashioning as a national

poet. See also Paul Stevens, "Discontinuities in Milton's Early Public Self-Representation," *Huntington Library Quarterly* 51, no. 4 (Autumn 1988): 261–80, who also opposes such a notion of a coherent authoritative biography.

60. Laura Lunger Knoppers, "Rewriting the Protestant Ethic: Discipline and Love in *Paradise Lost*," *English Literary History* 58, no. 3 (1991): 545–60. Another application of Weber is found in Andrew Milner, *John Milton and the English Revolution* (Totowa, N.J.: Barnes and Noble, 1981).

61. Many of these critics are responding to Christopher Hill's account in *Milton and the English Revolution* (New York: Viking, 1977), which overturned the view of Milton the Christian humanist and placed Milton in the context of the radicals of the English Revolution. See Aers and Kress, "Historical Process," 283–300; Trevor-Roper, "Milton in Politics," 231–82; Fredric Jameson, "Religion and Ideology," in Barker et al., *1642: Literature and Power*, 315–36. However, John Illo, in "The Misreading of Milton," in Leo Baxandall, ed., *Radical Perspectives in the Arts* (Harmondsworth, Middlesex: Penguin, 1972), 178–94, criticized the "liberal" view of Milton by emphasizing the limited nature of Milton's notion of freedom *Areopagitica*.

62. Thomas Corns, "Milton's Quest for Respectability," *Modern Language Review* 77, no. 4 (October 1982) 776; Nathaniel H. Henry also saw Milton distinguishing himself from the radical sectarians in "Who Meant License When They Cried Liberty?" *Modern Language Notes* 66, no. 8 (December 1951): 509–13, a reading of sonnets 11 and 12, judged to have been written not against the Presbyterian Westminster Assembly but against radical sectarians; Milton was trying to distance himself from these radicals. Milner, *John Milton*, too pits the "bourgeois" Milton against the "petit-bourgeois" Levellers (199); Aers and Kress, "Historical Process," 295.

63. Lawrence Stone, "The Bourgeois Revolution of Seventeenth-Century England Revisited," *Past and Present* 109 (1985): 45–54. See also G. E. Aylmer, "Gentlemen Levellers?" in Charles Webster, ed., *The Intellectual Revolution of the Seventeenth Century*, Past and Present Series (London: Routledge and Kegan Paul, 1974), 101–8; G. E. Aylmer, "Office-Holding as a Factor of English History, 1625–1642," *History* 44 (1959): 228–40; J.C.D. Clark, *Revolution and Rebellion: State and Society in England in the Seventeenth and Eighteenth Centuries* (Cambridge: Cambridge Unviersity Press, 1986), 185. See also, for the anticlass argument, R. Howell, Jr., "The Structure of Urban Politics in the English Civil War," *Albion* 11 (1979): 111–27.

64. Barker, *Milton and the Puritan Dilemma*, 184.

65. W. M. Lamont, "Puritanism as History and Historiography," *Past and Present* 44 (1969): 133–46.

66. G. R. Elton, *Policy and Police: The Enforcement of the Reformation in the Age of Thomas Cromwell* (Cambridge: Cambridge University Press, 1972); C.S.L. Davies, *Peace, Print, and Protestantism, 1450–1558* (London: Hart Davis, MacGibbon, 1976).

67. Klotz, "A Subject Analysis"; Sommerville, "On the Distribution of Religious and Occult Literature," 221–25, defines best-sellers as books that go over twenty editions; between 1600 and 1711, fourteen books of popular religious literature went over this mark; only a few nonreligious works went over ten editions. It is clear from evidence of book ownership that of all books, the Bible was the most commonly owned, with other religious literature rating next highest on the list.

68. David Cressy, *Literacy and the Social Order* (Cambridge: Cambridge University Press, 1980), 177, 189; Keith Wrightson and D. Levine, *Poverty and Piety in an English Village: Terling, 1525–1700* (New York: Academic Press, 1979), 144; I have also learned from A. G. Dickens, *The English Reformation* (New York: Schocken, 1964),

137; L. Stone, "The Reformation," in *The Past and the Present* (London: Routledge and Kegan Paul, 1981); B. Reay, "Popular Religion," in *Popular Culture in Seventeenth-Century England* (New York: St. Martin's Press, 1985), 91–129.

69. John King, *English Reformation Literature: The Tudor Origins of the Protestant Tradition* (Princeton: Princeton University Press, 1982), chap. 2, examines the Reformation book trade and its propaganda.

70. Leo Braudy, *The Frenzy of Renown: Fame and Its History* (New York: Oxford University Press, 1986); Garth S. Jowett and Victoria O'Donnell, *Propaganda and Persuasion* (New York: Sage, 1986), chap. 2. The word's first appearance in the *Oxford English Dictionary* bore its religious heritage, and the definition referred to proselytizing missionary religious activity of the 1840s. Some of the most fruitful work of historians of early modern propaganda takes a semiotic perspective, and Lynn Hunt, *Politics, Culture and Class in the French Revolution* (Berkeley: University of California Press, 1984) on the French Revolution, and Robert Scribner *For the Sake of Simple Folk: Popular Propaganda for the German Reformation* (Cambridge: Cambridge University Press, 1981) on the German Reformation are two outstanding examples of this semiotic approach. Some other excellent earlier studies are James Alan Downie, *Robert Harley and the Press: Propaganda and Public Opinion in the Age of Swift and Defoe* (Cambridge: Cambridge University Press, 1979); and Tim Harris, *London Crowds in the Reign of Charles II: Propaganda and Politics from the Restoration until the Exclusion Crisis* (Cambridge: Cambridge University Press, 1987), though these do not explore the meanings of the concept of propaganda used by the historical figures they describe.

71. In *Literature and Propaganda* (New York: Methuen, 1983), A. P. Foulkes focused almost exclusively on exposing capitalist myths in works of modern fiction. This is the only work by a literary critic I have come across so far devoted to the specific question of the relationship between literature and propaganda, and it draws heavily on the still-reigning model put forward in Jacques Ellul's *Propaganda: The Formation of Men's Attitudes*, trans. Konrad Kellen and Jean Lerner (New York: Vintage, 1973).

72. Terence Qualter, "Propaganda: What It Is," in *Opinion Control in the Democracies* (New York: St. Martin's Press, 1985), chap. 6, gives an excellent sketch of the history of propaganda studies in the twentieth century. Harold Dwight Lasswell focuses on the use of symbols in *Propaganda Techniques in the World War* (1938; reprint, New York: Garland, 1972). Definitions of propaganda are found in Harold Lasswell, "The Theory of Political Propaganda," *American Political Science Review* 21 (1927): 631; Harold Lasswell, *Allied Propaganda and the Collapse of the German Empire in 1918* (Stanford, Calif.: Stanford University Press, 1938), v; Gladys Thum and Marcella Thum, *The Persuaders: Propaganda in War and Peace* (New York: Atheneum, 1972), 12.

73. For starters, no mass public, or even the idea of public opinion, existed until the French Revolution, according to Paul A. Palmer, "The Concept of Public Opinion in Political Theory," in *Essays in History and Political Theory in Honor of Charles Howard McIlwain* (Cambridge: Harvard University Press, 1936), 231. See Keith Baker, "Politics and Public Opinion under the Old Regime: Some Reflections," in Jack R. Censer and Jeremy D. Popkin, eds., *Press and Politics in Pre-Revolutionary France* (Berkeley: University of California Press, 1987), 204–46. In England, the "multitude" was an idea feared by elites, but was not a coherent force that could be called "public opinion." See Christopher Hill, "The Many-Headed Monster," in *Change and Continuity in Seventeenth-Century England* (Cambridge: Harvard University Press,

1975), 181–204; Annabel Patterson, "The Very Name of the Game: Theories of Order and Disorder," in Thomas Healy and Jonathan Sawday, eds., *Literature and the English Civil War* (Cambridge: Cambridge University Press, 1990), 21–37; and Eamon Duffy, "The Godly and the Multitude in Stuart England," *Seventeenth Century* 1, no. 1 (January 1986): 31–55.

74. Habermas, *The Structural Transformation*, 58–59.

CHAPTER ONE
REVOLUTION IN PRINT: LILBURNE'S JURY, *AREOPAGITICA*,
AND THE CONSCIENTIOUS PUBLIC

1. Eric Cochrane, Charles M. Gray and Mark Kishlansky, eds., *Early Modern Europe: Crisis of Authority* (Chicago: University of Chicago Press, 1987), 393–94; H. L. Stephens ed., *State Trials*, 4 vols. (London: Duckworth, 1899), 1:371–89.

2. J. A. Sharpe, "Last Dying Speeches: Religion, Ideology and Public Execution in Seventeenth-Century England," *Past and Present* 107 (1985): 160, 144–67.

3. J. Fidoe, *Parliament Justified* (27 February 1649), 15.

4. M. Simmonds, *The Execution of the Late King Justified, and the Parliament and the Army therein, Vindicated* (26 February 1649, 25); J. Goodwin, *HYBRISTIKAI* (1649); R. Robins, *Reasons to Resolve the unresolved PEOPLE of the legality of the King's Trial and Judgment* (26 February 1649), 8.

5. Christopher Hill, "Parliament and People in Seventeenth-Century England," *Past and Present* 92 (1981): 100–124, versus J. H. Hexter, "Power Struggle, Parliament, and Liberty in Early Stuart England," *Journal of Modern History* 50 (1978): 1–50. See also, Derek Hirst, *The Representative of the People? Voters and Voting under the Early Stuarts* (Cambridge: Cambridge University Press, 1975), 192; Mark Kishlansky, *Parliamentary Selection: Social and Political Choice in Early Modern England* (New York: Columbia University Press, 1986), 226; David Underdown, *Revel, Riot and Rebellion: Popular Politics and Culture in England, 1603–1660* (Oxford: Oxford University Press, 1987), 123–32; Lawrence Stone, "The Results of the English Revolutions," in J.G.A. Pocock, ed., *Three British Revolutions* (Princeton: Princeton University Press, 1980); and Geoffrey Holmes, *The Electorate and the National Will in the First Age of Party* (Lancaster: University of Lancaster Press, 1976), 2.

6. J. P. Kenyon, ed., *The Stuart Constitution, 1603–1688* (Cambridge: Cambridge University Press, 1966), 84.

7. See John M. Wallace, *Destiny His Choice: The Loyalism of Andrew Marvell* (Cambridge: Cambridge University Press, 1968), esp. chap. 1, for a literary and historical attitude toward the constitutional problems.

8. Henry Parker, *Jus Populi* (1644), in Haller, *Tracts on Liberty in the Puritan Revolution*, 3 vols. (New York: Columbia University Press, 1934), 2.179; J. Lilburne, *Englands Birth-Right Justified*, in Haller, *Tracts* 1.99; W. Walwyn, *Englands Lamentable Slaverie*, in Haller, *Tracts* 3.309; William Overton, *Vox Plebis* (1646).

9. *Vox Populi: The people's humble discovery of their loyalty* (1642).

10. "Theophilus Craterus," *A Calm Consolatory Discourse of the Sad Tempestuous Affairs in England* (1647), 5, cited in J.A.W. Gunn, *Politics and the Public Interest in the Seventeenth-Century* (London: Routledge and Kegan Paul, 1969), 4.

11. *King Charls his Tryal* (1649; reprint, Leeds: Scolar Press, 1966), 14, 15.

12. Ibid., 27; *State Trials*, 4:1005; *King Charls his Tryal*, 11.

13. E. Eisenstein, *The Printing Press as an Agent of Change* (Cambridge: Cambridge University Press, 1985), and her seminal article, "The Advent of Printing and the

Problem of the Renaissance," *Past and Present* 45 (1969): 19–89, have engendered much debate over the deterministic path of print; T. Rabb and E. Eisenstein, "Debate: The Advent of Printing and the Problem of the Renaissance. A Comment," *Past and Present* 52 (1971): 135–44. Also, see Anthony T. Grafton, "The Importance of Being Printed," *Journal of Interdisciplinary History* 11, no. 2 (1980): 265–86; also, F. J. Levy, "How Information Spread, 1540–1640," *Journal of British Studies* 21 (1982): 11–34.

14. The issues raised by a burgeoning popular literature are also discussed in Natalie Davis, "Printing and the People," in her *Society and Culture in Early Modern France* (Stanford, Calif.: Stanford University Press, 1975); in Robert Darnton, *The Literary Underground of the Old Regime* (Cambridge: Harvard University Press, 1982): 167–208; and in Margaret Spufford, *Small Books and Pleasant Histories: Popular Fiction and Its Readership in Seventeenth-Century England* (Cambridge: Cambridge University Press, 1985). For the background and tradition of printing and religious reform, see J. King, *English Reformation Literature: The Tudor Origins of the Protestant Tradition* (Princeton: Princeton University Press, 1982), chap. 3.

15. Louis B. Wright, "Propaganda against James I's 'Appeasement' of Spain," *Huntington Library Quarterly* 6 (1942–43): 150.

16. Also, see Christopher Hill, "The Pre-Revolutionary Decades," in *Writing and Revolution in Seventeenth-Century England: The Collected Essays of Christopher Hill*, 3 vols. (Amherst: University of Massachusetts Press), 1:3–31.

17. For a survey of the royalist propaganda machines, see Lois Potter, *Secret Rites and Secret Writing: Royalist Literature, 1641–1660* (Cambridge: Cambridge University Press, 1989), 7–22; P. W. Thomas, *Sir John Berkenhead* (Oxford: Oxford University Press, 1969); and Joyce Lee Malcolm, *Caesar's Due: Loyalty and King Charles, 1642–1646* (London: Royal Historical Society, 1983), chap. 5. On the parliamentary side, see J. Frank, *Cromwell's Press Agent: A Critical Biography of Marchamont Nedham* (Lanham, Md.: University Press of America, 1980).

18. These high figures were the direct result of Reformation ideologies and propaganda practices: Lawrence Stone, "The Educational Revolution in England, 1560–1640," *Past and Present* 28 (1964): 41–80; Keith Wrightson, "Learning and Godliness," in *English Society, 1500–1800* (New Brunswick, N.J.: Rutgers University Press, 1986), chap. 7. On the relationship between literacy and occupational demand, see David Cressy, *Literacy and the Social Order* (Cambridge: Cambridge University Press, 1980), 177, and his critique of the equation between literacy and democracy (189); on schooling of the lower orders and upholding the thesis that reading was a far more socially diffused skill than writing, Margaret Spufford, "First Steps in Literacy," *Social History* 4 (1979), 407–35; on the impact of literacy on custom in popular society, Keith Wrightson and D. Levine, *Poverty and Piety in an English Village: Terling, 1525–1700* (New York: Academic Press, 1979), 144; and T. Laqueur, "Cultural Origins of Popular Literacy in England, 1500–1850," *Oxford Review of Education* 2, no. 3 (1976): 55–75.

19. For the history of parliamentary coverage, see, in addition to Frederick S. Siebert, *Freedom of the Press in England, 1476–1776* (Urbana: University of Illinois Press, 1952), esp. 166–92; William M. Clyde, "Parliament and the Press, 1643–1647," *The Library*, 4th ser., 14 (1934): 399–424; Sheila Lambert, ed., *Printing for Parliament, 1641–1700*, List and Index Society, Special Series, vol. 20 (London, 1984).

20. William Prynne, *Sovereign Power of Parliaments and Kingdoms* (1643), A3. King, *English Reformation Literature*, chap. 2, talks about the forthrightness of publication in Edward VI's reign; that literature was aimed, he argues, to issue propaganda in

defense of religious reform, and it was patronized by prominent lords. While some of the writing of the English Revolution was patronized by aristocrats, much of it, very much, came from the hands of ordinary citizens.

21. Richard Cust, "News and Politics in Early Seventeenth-Century England," *Past and Present* 112 (1986): 60–90; Folke Dahl, "A Short-title Catalogue of English Corantos and Newsbooks, 1620–1642," *The Library*, 4th ser., 19 (1939): 44–98. Carolyn Nelson and Matthew Seccombe, eds., *British Newspapers and Periodicals, 1641–1700* (New York: Modern Language Association of America, 1987) is indispensable for the study of these materials.

22. *To the Right Honourable, the Supreme Authority of this Nation, THE COMMONS OF ENGLAND*, in Don M. Wolfe, *Leveller Manifestoes of the Puritan Revolution* (London: Thomas Nelson, 1944), 327.

23. Arthur E. Barker, *Milton and the Puritan Dilemma, 1641–1660* (Toronto: University of Toronto Press, 1976), 140–44.

24. William Walwyn, *A Helpe to the right understanding of a Discourse concerning Independency* (1644), in Haller, *Tracts* 3.199.

25. William Overton, *A Remonstrance of Many Thousand Citizens*, in Wolfe, *Leveller Manifestoes*, 128, 117.

26. Lilburne, *Englands Birth-Right Justified*, in Haller, *Tracts* 1.269.

27. Ernest Sirluck's introduction to vol. 2 of the *Complete Prose Works* gives an account of contemporary arguments about the press; also see William Haller's "Before *Areopagitica*," *PMLA* 42, no. 4 (1927): 875–900.

28. Lilburne, *Englands Birth-Right Justified*, in Haller, *Tracts* 1.268.

29. For a historical study of anti-Catholicism during this period, see the excellent essay by Peter Lake, "Anti-Popery: The Structure of a Prejudice," in Richard Cust and Ann Hughes, eds., *Conflict in Early Stuart England: Studies in Religion and Politics, 1603–1642* (New York: Longman, 1989), 72–106; and T. N. Corns, W. A. Speck, and J. A. Downie, "Archetypal Mystification: Polemic and Reality in English Political Literature, 1640–1750," *Eighteenth-Century Life* 7 (1982): 1–27.

30. Henry Robinson, *Liberty of Conscience* (1644), in Haller, *Tracts* 3.173.

31. John Lilburne, *A Copie of a Letter to Mr. William Prynne* (1645), in Haller, *Tracts* 3.182–83.

32. Taking or not taking off one's cap was about as clear a message as could be expressed in this tightly coded society. Lilburne was not the first to make use of its dramatic effect; Henry Marten refused to do so, and urged his jury to don their caps "to demonstrate the fact that they were 'the Chief Judges in the Court,' " according to Christopher Hill, *Puritanism and Revolution* (London: Mercury Books, 1962), 77.

33. Lilburne, *A Copie*, in Haller, *Tracts* 3.182.

34. Walwyn, *A Helpe to the Right Understanding*, in Haller, *Tracts* 3.200.

35. Lawrence Palmer, *St. Pauls Politiques* (1644), A2v.

36. King, *English Reformation Literature*, 443–56, examines the continuities between Reformation and seventeenth-century literature as a tradition of religious reform and toleration.

37. On the correlation between printing and the Protestant Reformation, see Eisenstein, *Printing Press*, 366–91; H. S. Bennett, *English Books and Readers, 1475–1557* (Cambridge: Cambridge University Press, 1952); Lawrence Stone, "Literacy and Education in England, 1640–1900," *Past and Present* 42 (1969): 77. Studies of English Puritanism leading up to, and comprehending, the civil war years include: William Hunt, *The Puritan Moment* (Cambridge: Harvard University Press, 1982),

esp. chaps. 4 and 11; Brian Manning, *The English People and the English Revoluion* (London: Heinemann, 1976); Underdown, *Revel, Riot and Rebellion,* chap. 5, 129; see also W. M. Lamont, "Puritanism as History and Historiography," *Past and Present* 44 (1969): 133–45. For the sixteenth-century church conflicts, see Patrick Collinson, *Godly People: Essays on English Protestantism and Puritanism* (London: Hambledon, 1983), 155–89, 335–70; A. G. Dickens, *The English People and the Reformation* (New York: Schocken, 1964).

38. Lilburne, *Come out of her my People* (1639), 25, 30.

39. Godfrey Davies, "English Political Sermons, 1603–1640," *Huntington Library Quarterly* 3 (1979): 1–22, argues that sermons played an important part in "the formation of public opinion," pointing to the "significant attempt by the Crown to control pulpit utterances" (1) as a correlate to censorship in the press: "identical factors were operative in both cases" (7), though Davies does not examine the concept of public opinion. Paul Seaver, *The Puritan Lectureships: The Politics of Religious Dissent, 1560–1662* (Stanford, Calif.: Stanford University Press, 1970), 68–72, discusses the radicalism of Puritanism and the means by which lecturers communicated their radical political ideas to the populace.

40. William Mewe, *The Robbing and Spoiling* (1643), in *Fast Sermons to Parliament . . . Nov . 1640–April 1653,* 34 vols. (London: Cornmarket, 1970–71), 9: 55. In November 1640, the Long Parliament resolved to hold a weekly fast, when sermons would be preached by designated preachers. Facsimiles of the sermons themselves have been recently reprinted as part of the series of English Historical Documents. Other "Fast Sermons" will be cited hereafter as FS. For the background and history of these Fast Sermons, see John F. Wilson, *Pulpit in Parliament: Puritanism during the English Civil Wars, 1640–1648* (Princeton: Princeton University Press, 1969).

41. Eisenstein, *Printing Press,* chap. 2, esp. 88–124.

42. Charles Herle, *Davids Reserve* (1645), FS 14:121, Mewe, *The Robbing,* FS 9:55.

43. For the historical background to the Puritan sermons, see William M. Lamont, *Godly Rule: Politics and Religion, 1603–1660* (London: Macmillan, 1969); W. Hunt studies Puritanism in Essex in *The Puritan Moment* (Cambridge: Harvard University Press, 1983), 87–112; Seaver, *Puritan Lectureships,* 289–94; P. Collinson, *Religion of Protestants* (Oxford: Clarendon Press, 1982), 129–39; C. Hill, *Society and Puritanism in Pre-Revolutionary England* (New York: Schocken Books, 1964), chaps. 2 and 3.

44. Hill, *Society and Puritanism in Pre-Revolutionary England,* 80.

45. E. W. Kirby, "Sermons before the Commons, 1640–1642," *Americal Historical Review* 44 (1939): 528–48; H. R. Trevor-Roper, in "The Fast Sermons to the Long Parliament," *Essays in British History Presented to Sir Keith Feiling* (London: Macmillan, 1964).

46. L. Palmer, *Saint Pauls Politics,* A2v. There was an economic motive behind publication of sermons, since religious literature was the most popular genre of printed material.

47. Herle, *Davids Reserve.*

48. M. Newcomen, *A Sermon Tending to set forth the Right use of Disasters that befall our Armies* (1644), FS 12:274, A3v.

49. Francis Woodcock, *Christ's Warning-Piece* (1644), FS 3:27, A3, A4.

50. On book ownership and book production: Peter Clark, "The Ownership of Books in England, 1560–1640: The Example of Some Kentish Townfolk," in Lawrence Stone, ed., *Schooling and Society* (Baltimore: Johns Hopkins University

242

Press, 1976), 95–114; Edith Klotz, "A Subject Analysis of English Imprints for Every Tenth Year from 1480 to 1640," *Huntington Library Quarterly* 1, no. 4 (1938): 417–19.

51. The role of the publication of the vernacular Bible in early modern European political change is a thorny question. To Dickens, *The English People*, Bible publication and circulation had progressive effects since the content of the Bible itself was subversive (137); for L. Stone, "The Reformation," in *The Past and the Present* (London: Routledge and Kegan Paul, 1981), it was no less than a "revolutionary document" (102), assisting in undermining "the existence of a single road toward truth" (116). Yet, as B. Reay argues in "Popular Religion," in *Popular Culture in Seventeenth-Century England* (New York: St. Martin's Press, 1985), literate Protestantism never succeeded with the popular sort, even though the people were thoroughly doused in biblical phrases they knew by heart; instead, "zealous Protestantism," a version of "folklorized Christianity," was what took with them (107–10). G. R. Elton, *Policy and Police: The Enforcement of the Reformation in the Age of Thomas Cromwell* (Cambridge: Cambridge University Press, 1972) holds that the pulpit was still more important than the printing press in "conveying new notions to the people and in stirring up discontent" (211). For a study of the political and the religious elements aroused during the Reformation, see H. Trevor-Roper, "The Religious Origins of the Enlightenment," in his *Religion, the Reformation and Social Change* (London: Macmillan, 1967), 193–236.

52. Godfrey Davies, "English Political Sermons, 1603–1640," *Huntington Library Quarterly* 3 (1979): 1–22.

53. Palmer, *St. Paul's Politics*, A2.

54. Woodcock, *Christ's Warning-Piece*, A4, A3.

55. J. Gauden, *The Love of Truth and Peace*, FS 1:15, A2.

56. *Mercurius Pragmaticus* (24 April–1 May 1649), cited in Pauline Gregg, *Free-born John* (London, George G. Harrap, 1961), 293; *Mercurius Pragmaticus* (23–30 October 1649), Dd. Gregg's is the best biography of Lilburne.

57. *Truths Victory over Tyrants and Tyranny* (1649), 4. M. Heinemann, *Puritanism and Theatre: Thomas Middleton and Opposition Drama under the Early Stuarts* (Cambridge: Cambridge University Press, 1980), chap. 13, argues pamphleteers took over the literary tradition of opposition theater once the theaters were closed down. She presents evidence that some Leveller writers had been involved with the theater before, and turned to popular pamphleteering after the closings. The pamphlets for which Lilburne was accused of treason were *An Impeachment of High Treason*; *A Salva Libertate*; *The Legall Fundamentall Liberties*; the *Outcry of Apprentices*; and the *Hue and Cry*, all from 1649; all attacking Cromwell, Ireton, and the interim government.

58. Gregg, *Free-born*, 81; *The Just Man in Bonds* (1646); Joan Webber, *The Eloquent "I": Style and Self in Seventeenth-Century Prose* (Madison: University of Wisconsin Press, 1968), 74.

59. In Gregg, *Free-born*, 269. *Mercurius Pragmaticus*, (20 March 1649); *Cal. S. P. Dom., 1649–1650*, 55, 56, 59.

60. A. L. Morton, "The Place of Lilburne, Overton, and Walwyn in the Tradition of English Prose," *Zeitschrift für Anglistik und Amerikanistik* 6 (1958): 7; William Haller, *Liberty and Reformation in the Puritan Revolution* (New York: Columbia University Press, 1955), 262. On Lilburne, see also Hill, *Puritanism and Revolution*; and M. A. Gibb, *John Lilburne the Leveller* (London: Lindsay Drummond, 1947).

61. *Mercurius Elencticus* (7–14 May 1649), in Gregg, *Free-born*, 276.

62. Theodore C. Pease, *The Leveller Movement* (Oxford: Oxford University Press, 1916), 6.

63. William Walwyn, *Just Man in Bonds* (1646).

64. R. Overton, *A Remonstrance of Many thousand Citizens*, in Wolfe, *Leveller Manifestoes*, 117; Webber, *The Eloquent "I,"* chap. 3, quote on p. 58. On Lilburne's "martyrology," see also Thomas N. Corns, *Uncloistered Virtue: English Political Literature, 1640–1660* (Oxford: Clarendon Press, 1992), 136–46.

65. Corns, *Uncloistered Virtue*, 146.

66. *Mercurius Pragmaticus. For King Charls II*, no. 27 (23–30 October 1649), Dd1.

67. John Crouch, *Man in the moon, Discovering a World of Knavery under the Sun*, no. 1 (16 April 1649), 8.

68. *Man in the Moon*, no. 2 (16–23 April 1649), 11.

69. T. B. Howell, *Cobbett's Complete Collection of State Trials*, 33 vols. (London: R. Bagshaw, 1809–26), 4:1274.

70. Ibid., 1273. Defendants in treason trials had no right to legal counsel and had to defend themselves unaided, according to D. Veall, *The Popular Movement for Law Reform, 1640–1660* (Oxford: Clarendon Press, 1970), 18.

71. Lilburne, *A Copie*, 2.

72. *State Trials* 4:1286.

73. *State Trials* 4:1379, 1380. Milton makes use of this figure of a cipher in his *Eikonoklastes* to refer to the bishops, in "that foolish and self-undoing Declaration of twelve Cypher Bishops," (3.394). On the myth of the Norman Yoke, see J.G.A. Pocock, *The Ancient Constitution and the Feudal Law* (Cambridge: Cambridge University Press, 1957).

74. Henry Parker, *A Letter of Due Censure, and redarguation* [sic] *to Lieut. Col. John Lilburne* (1650), 21, 22, 39.

75. *State Trials* 4:1314; Parker, *A Letter*, 9–10, 10, 23–24.

76. Parker, *A Letter*, 24, 39. See Annabel Patterson, "The Name of the Game," *South Atlantic Quarterly* 86, no. 4 (1987): 519–43, for discussion of a continuous tradition of reactions against the labels of Warbeck and Tyler.

77. *State Trials* 4:1361, 1305.

78. For a fuller account of the legal traditions and complexities of these arguments, see T. A. Green, *Verdict according to Conscience: Perspectives on the English Criminal Trial Jury, 1200–1800* (Chicago: University of Chicago Press, 1985), chap. 5, from whom I have drawn in this discussion of jury finding law and fact.

79. *State Trials* 4:1379. In fact, Lilburne's is a complete misreading of Coke, since at the end of the cited passage, Coke had made emphatically clear that "judges, not juries are to respond to questions of law; juries, not judges, are to rule on questions of fact." His misinterpretation drove Judge Keble sadly to exclaim, "I thought you had understood the law better than I see you do" (*State Trials* 4:1381); Green, *Verdict*, 175. See also Christopher Hill, "Sir Edward Coke: Mythmaker," in *Intellectual Origins of the English Revolution* (Oxford: Clarendon Press, 1982), 225–65.

80. For history of seventeenth-century legal reform, see B. Shapiro, "Law Reform in Seventeenth-Century England," *American Journal of Legal History* 19 (1975): 288–97; E. W. Ives, "Social Change and the Law," in E. W. Ives, ed., *The English Revolution, 1600–1660* (London: Edwin Arnold, 1968): 115–30; J. S. Cockburn, "Twelve Silly Men? The Trial at Assizes," in J. S. Cockburn and Thomas A. Green, eds., *Twelve*

Good Men and True: The Criminal Trial Jury in England, 1200–1800 (Princeton: Princeton University Press, 1988), 158–81.

81. John Jones, *Jurors Judges of Law and Fact* (1650), 58.

82. *State Trials* 4:1379, 1386, 1385.

83. Sheldon Wolin, *Politics and Vision: Continuity and Innovation in Western Political Thought* (Boston: Little, Brown, 1960), 187, discusses the notion of conscience in political theory. Two fascinating treatments that have creatively misread the Calvinist conscience are Friedrich Nietzsche, "'Guilt,' 'Bad Conscience,' and the Like," in *On the Genealogy of Morals*, trans. Walter Kaufmann and R. J. Hollingdale (New York: Vintage, 1989), 57–96; and Max Weber, who stresses the connections betweeen Calvinism and radical individualism, in *The Protestant Ethic and the Spirit of Capitalism*, trans. Talcott Parsons (London: Unwin Hyman, 1930), 108–25.

84. John Calvin, *Institutes of Christian Religion*, trans. Ford Lewis Battles, ed. John T. McNeill, 2 vols. (Philadelphia: Westminster Press, 1960), 1: 848.

85. *State Trials* 4:1393, 1389.

86. Calvin, *Institutes* 1:1181.

87. Ibid., 1:848, 1:1182, 1:367, 1:849; Cf. Milton, *Reason of Church Government* (1.822), where conscience is God's "Secretary."

88. W. Cargill Thompson, *The Political Thought of Martin Luther* (Totowa, N.J.: Barnes and Noble, 1984); Bernhard Lohsee, "Conscience and Authority in Luther," in Heiko A. Oberman, ed., *Luther and the Dawn of the Modern Era* (Leiden: E. J. Brill, 1974), 158–83.

89. Calvin, *Institutes* 1:1184, 848. Though Luther's position did change on the right to resist unjust authority, especially after 1530, personal conscience was not the authority for resistance but was rather a conception of public versus private duties of the magistrate. See W. Cargill Thompson, "Luther and the Right of Resistance to the Emperor," *Studies in Church History* 12 (1975): 159–202; and his *Political Thought of Martin Luther*, 99–111; also Wolin, *Politics and Vision*, 161ff.

90. Michael Walzer, *Revolution of the Saints: A Study in the Origins of Radical Politics* (Cambridge: Harvard University Press, 1965), 58–59, 64; Quentin Skinner, *The Foundations of Modern Political Thought*, 2 vols. (Cambridge: Cambridge University Press, 1978), 2: 233.

91. On the casuistical tradition, see Camille Wells Slights, *The Casuistical Tradition in Shakespeare, Donne, Herbert, and Milton* (Princeton: Princeton University Press, 1981), which addresses the issue of conscience, but as a kind of practical divinity, an exercise in intellection or moral arithmetic, not of political action.

92. William Ames, *Conscience with the Power and Cases Thereof* (1643), 2.

93. Christopher Hill, *The World Turned Upside Down* (Harmondsworth, Middlesex: Penguin, 1972) discusses these radicals. James Tully, "Governing Conduct," in Edmund Leites, ed., *Conscience and Casuistry in Early Modern Europe* (Cambridge: Cambridge University Press, 1988), 12–71, traces the movement in political thinking away from the radical claims of conscience to the rational theories of assent of Locke that replaced them in the eighteenth century.

94. J. P. Kenyon, *The Stuart Constitution, 1603–1688* (Cambridge: Cambridge University Press, 1966), 309.

95. William Ames, *Conscience with the Power and Cases Thereof* (1643), 5. See also William Jordan, *The Development of Religious Toleration in England*, 4 vols. (Cambridge: Harvard University Press, 1932–40), 2: 212.

96. Blair Worden, "Toleration and the Cromwellian Protectorate," in W. J. Sheils,

ed., *Persecution and Toleration*, vol. 21 of Studies in Church History (London: Basil Blackwell, 1984), 199–233; and Wallace, *Destiny his Choice*, chap. 1, for a survey of the Engagement controversy.

97. The oath was designed to create a bond between the Rump and the Presbyterians by isolating the Royalists, who, it was thought, surely would not agree to it. The outcome of the controversy was contrary to expectations, however. The Royalists who refused could not support the enemy regime, and the Presbyterians refused to do so on the ground that their prior oath of allegiance (the Solemn League and Covenant) still bound them to the king. Many Royalists, however, willingly swore the oath (disingenuously). See Derek Hirst, *Authority and Conflict: England, 1603–1658* (Cambridge: Harvard University Press, 1986), 298; D. Wooton, *Divine Right and Democracy* (Harmondsworth, Middlesex: Penguin, 1986), 68; and Blair Worden, *The Rump Parliament, 1648–1653* (Cambridge: Cambridge University Press, 1974), 228–31.

98. John Dury, *Considerations Concerning the Present Engagement* (7 February 1650), 15; *A Disengaged Survey* (4 December 1649), 9, A2. Essential tools in research in the pamphlet literature are John M. Wallace, "The Engagement Controversy, 1649–1652: An Annotated List of Pamphlets," *Bulletin of the New York Public Library* 68, no. 6 (1964), 384–405; and Quentin Skinner, "The Ideological Context of Hobbes's Political Thought," *Historical Journal* 9, no. 3 (1966): 286–317, which provides another useful survey.

99. Robert Sanderson, *A Resolution of Conscience* (1 December 1649), 5–6. It is a temptation for historians to doubt the sincerity of the appeal to liberty of conscience made by those who were to be persecuted for their religious views, as does Jordan, in *The Development of Religious Toleration in England* 2: 212, yet the appeal to conscience was based on a general philosophical reasoning that did not give way after the Royalists came back to power with the Restoration. See also John Tulloch, *Rational Theology and Christian Philosophy in England in the Seventeenth Century*, 2 vols. (London: Blackwood and Sons, 1874), esp. 1:155–66. My thanks to Richard Kroll for providing references.

100. Calvin, *Institutes*, 1:1184; John Aucher, *Arguments and Reasons to prove the Inconvenience and Unlawfulness of Taking the New Engagement* (14 February 1650), 3, 8.

101. *State Trials* 4:1367, 1394, 1373.

102. Ibid., 1384, 1388. The place of conscience in finding verdict in the criminal justice system of seventeenth-century England was paramount, as detailed in Green, *Verdict*, 167. On jury composition, see Cynthia B. Herrup, *The Common Peace: Participation in the Criminal Law in Seventeenth-Century England* (New York: Cambridge University Press, 1987); on jury independence, Cockburn, "Twelve Silly Men."

103. John Crouch, *Man in the moon, Discovering a World of Knavery under the Sun* (April 1649–June 1650), 221–22; *Truths Victory over Tyrants and Tyranny* (1649), t.p., 6.; Jones, *Jurors Judges*, 58–59.

104. *Mercurius Elencticus* 26 (22–29 October 1649), 203.

105. *Jury-man's Judgment upon the Case of Lieut. Col. John Lilburne* (22 June 1653), 12. In tandem with his own publicity efforts were several pamphlets arguing for or against him: *A Word to the Jury in the behalfe of John Lilburne* (11 August 1653); *More Light to Mr John Lilburne's Jury* (6 August 1653).

106. *Jury-man's Judgment*, title page, 12–13.

107. *State Trials*, 5:446, 450.

108. Compare to Annabel Patterson, "The Civic Hero in Milton's Prose," *Milton Studies* 8 (1975): 71–102. See also, on the rhetorical form of *Areopagitica*, G. K. Hunter, "The Structure of Milton's *Areopagitica*," *English Studies* 39 (1958): 117–19. Wilbur E. Gilman, *Milton's Rhetoric* (Columbia: University of Missouri Press, 1939) shows it strictly conforms to the laws of the oration as set forth by Cicero.

109. Francis Barker, *The Tremulous Private Body: Essays on Subjection* (New York: Methuen, 1984), 41–52; and Christopher Kendrick, *Milton: A Study in Ideology and Form* (London: Methuen, 1986), 35–51, offer a different (Marxist) interest in Milton's distinction between private and public.

110. Jacques Ellul, *Propaganda: The Formation of Men's Attitudes*, trans. Konrad Kellen and Jean Lerner (New York: Vintage, 1973), 31.

111. Yet this is no simple voluntary decision, since it is indeed a fulfillment of God's mission. See Christopher Kendrick's sensitive discussion of the problems of predestination and choice in *Paradise Lost* in *Milton: A Study in Ideology*, chap. 4.

112. This is not a reader, poised after Milton's poetic urgings, ready to act, but not provided with ways to do so, thus ever "disappointed" by inaction, as in Stanley Fish, "The Temptation to Action in Milton's Poetry," *English Literary History* 48, no. 3 (1981): 516–31.

113. An interesting discussion of the role of slogans is Ellul, *Propaganda*, 199.

114. Thomas N. Corns, "The Freedom of Reader-Response: Milton's *Of Reformation* and Lilburne's *Christian Mans Triall*," in R. C. Richardson and G. M. Ridden, eds., *Freedom and the English Revolution: Essays in History and Literature* (Manchester: Manchester University Pres, 1986), 95.

115. William Walwyn, *A Pearle in a Dounghill* (1646).

116. William Walwyn, *A Whisper in the Eare of Mr Thomas Edwards* (1646), 6.

117. Laurence Clarkson, *Lost Sheep Found* (1660), 25.

118. A. Coppe, *A Fiery Flying Roll* (1649).

119. Clarkson, *Lost Sheep Found*, 5.

120. Hill, *The World Turned Upside Down*, 113, 297.

121. William Walwyn, *The Compassionate Samaritan* (1645), 25–26.

122. The limits of that liberty—Catholic writers were an important exemption—depended not upon "fit" readers but on "fit" writers to serve the ends of Truth and the security of the state. Milton is not an advocate for "tolerated Popery," since it "extirpates all religious and civil supremacies" (*CPW* 2:565). See John Illo, "The Misreading of Milton," in L. Baxandall, ed., *Radical Perspectives in the Arts* (Harmondsworth, Middlesex: Penguin, 1972), 178–94. C. Hill, ever the apologist, makes sense of Milton's exclusionism by explaining that "popery" was seen then "not primarily as a religion . . . but as 'a priestly despotism under the cloak of religion,'" a very real threat to the state that justified silencing, in *Milton and the English Revolution* (New York: Viking, 1977), 155–56; also for attempts at reconciling this early Milton with his later role as state censor under Cromwell, see David Masson, *Life of Milton*, 7 vols. (Cambridge and London: Macmillan, 1859–94), 4:324.

123. In Milton's theory of virtue, readers "try" books, "sufficient to judge aright, and to examine each matter" (*CPW* 2:511). Looking at choice in *Paradise Lost* Virginia R. Mollenkott, "Milton's Technique of Multiple Choice," *Milton Studies* 6 (1974): 101–11, argues this theory of reading as choice is a sign of skepticism; for contrast, Mary Ann Radzinowicz, in "'To Make the People Fittest to Chuse': How Milton Personified his Program for Poetry," *CEA Critic* 48, no. 8 (1986): 3–23, discusses the positive values of choice in education.

124. *King Charles his Tryal*, 15.

CHAPTER TWO
ROYALIST REACTIONS: JOHN CLEVELAND, BABEL,
AND THE DIVINE RIGHT OF LANGUAGE

1. H. L. Stephens, ed., *State Trials* (London, 1899), 4:1379.

2. W. K. Jordan, *The Development of Religious Toleration in England*, 3 vols. (Cambridge: Cambridge University Press, 1938), 3: 112–13.

3. Ibid., 134–38.

4. John Wilkins, *An Essay Towards a Real Character, and a Philosophical Language* (London, 1668), 13.

5. Joseph Waite's commendatory poem to Cave Beck's *Universal Character* (1657), A6r, in Murray Cohen, *Sensible Words: Linguistic Practice in England, 1640–1785* (Baltimore: Johns Hopkins University Press, 1977), 2.

6. My meaning of *opposition* here refers to the many souls, some organized into named parties—"The Levellers," for instance—who opposed the king. Of course this lumping together is historically vague, but for the purposes of my argument about antiopposition responses to the press, it reflects the thinking of those who opposed the opposition and saw them as one rebellious mass.

7. Christopher Hill, "Radical Prose in Seventeenth-Century England: From Marprelate to the Levellers," in his *Writing and Revolution in Seventeenth-Century England* (Amherst: University of Massachusetts Press, 1985), 75–95.

8. I share aims with Pierre Bourdieu's analysis of French cultural tastes in the 1960s, in which Bourdieu tested and confirmed the hypothesis that "good taste" is arrived at through specific social and economic paths, through learning the appropriate codes in which the language of art is encoded. See his *Distinction: A Social Critique of the Judgment of Taste*, trans. Richard Nice (Cambridge: Harvard University Press, 1985), 2, though I lay weaker emphasis on the purely economic explanation for such distinctions than Bourdieu does.

9. Margaret Spufford, *Small Books and Pleasant Histories: Popular Fiction and Its Readership in Seventeenth-Century England* (Cambridge: Cambridge University Press, 1985). Though Spufford's book promises to be most appropriate here, her interest is more with the brute facts of literacy's spread and consumption of cheap printed matter than with the cultural impact of such circumstances on the higher orders of society.

10. On Nashe, see Sandra Clark, *The Elizabethan Pamphleteers: Popular Moralistic Pamphlets, 1580–1640* (Rutherford, N.J.: Fairleigh Dickinson University Press, 1983), 141–42; Spufford, *Small Books*, 51.

11. Edward Arber, ed., *A Transcript of the Registers of the Company of Stationers of London, 1554–1640*, 5 vols. (London, 1876), 3: 677. On the vernacular prose literature, see Raymond A. Anselment, *"Betwixt Jest and Earnest": Marprelate, Milton, Marvell, Swift and the Decorum of Religious Ridicule* (Toronto: University of Toronto Press, 1979); on the evolution of comic prose style, Neil Rhodes, *Elizabethan Grotesque* (London: Routledge, 1980), 21–25.

12. B. Capp, *Astrology and the Popular Press: English Almanacs, 1500–1800* (Ithaca: Cornell University Press, 1979).

13. Jerome Friedman, *The Battle of the Frogs and Fairford's Flies: Miracles and the Pulp Press during the English Revolution* (New York: St. Martin's Press, 1993), 41–79, colorfully illustrates the many types of prophetic and astral analyses of the day, in order to show how ordinary English citizens experienced their world, and summarizes thus: "In the end, Englishmen would be hard-pressed to determine which set of

heavenly activities, prodigies, and apparitions or astrology and prophecies best represented God's assessment of the revolution. In the meantime, the civil wars dragged on and everything was getting worse" (79).

14. John Taylor, *Crop-Eare Curried* (1644); George Wharton, *Mercurio-Caelico-Mastix* (1644).

15. See H. Rusche, "Prophecies and Propaganda," *English Historical Review* 84 (1969): 752–70, for the use of astrology to claim truth for either side of an issue. Booker also wrote the astrology books *Mercurius Coelicus*.

16. "A New Ballad, called a Review of the Rebellion" (1647), British Library 660.f.11 (21).

17. "Win at First, Lose at Last" n.d., Bodleian Library Wood Ballads 401.71/2.

18. "The Courtier's Health," n.d., British Library Roxburghe Ballads 3. 395.

19. Ernest Sirluck, "Shakespeare and Jonson among the Pamphleteers of the First Civil War," *Modern Philology* 53 (1955–56): 88–99.

20. "Tragical History of King Lear and his Three Daughters," British Library Roxburghe Ballads 3. 275.

21. Frederick F. Siebert, *Freedom of the Press in England, 1476–1776* (Urbana: University of Illinois Press, 1952), 174.

22. Harry R. Plomer, "An Analysis of the Civil War Newspaper, *Mercurius Civicus*," *The Library*, n.s., 6 (1905), 184–207, suggests Prynne's hand for *Mercurius Civicus*, 200; See also Folke Dahl, "A Short-Title Catalogue of English Corantos and Newsbooks, 1620–1642," *The Library*, 4th ser., 19 (1939), 44–95.

23. *The Great Assizes Holden in Parnassus by Apollo and his Assessours* (1645).

24. [John Birkenhead], *News from Smith the Oxford Jailor* (1645).

25. *A Brief Representation and Discovery of the notorious falshood and dissimulation contained in a Book styled, The Gospel Way* (4 June 1649), A3.

26. Antonia Fraser, *The Weaker Vessel: Woman's Lot in Seventeenth-Century England* (London: Methuen, 1985), 184.

27. Particia Crawford, "Women's Published Writings, 1600–1700," in Mary Prior, ed., *Women in English Society, 1500–1800* (London: Methuen, 1985), 212–13.

28. Patricia Higgins, "The Reactions of Women, with Special Reference to Women Petitioners," in Brian Manning, ed., *Politics, Religion and the English Civil War* (London: Edwin Arnold, 1973), 179–224; Keith Thomas, "Women and the Civil War Sects," *Past and Present* 13 (1958): 42–62; Phyllis Mack, "Women as Prophets during the Civil War," *Feminist Studies* 8, no. 1 (1992): 19–45.

29. *Mercurius Pragmaticus* (23–30 April 1649), A2; *Mercurius Pragmaticus* (24 April–1 May 1649), Qqq3v.

30. John Lilburne, *Englands Birth-Right Justified* (1645).

31. *Mercurius Pacificus* (1648), 2.

32. Ibid., 7; A.S.P. Woodhouse, *Puritanism and Liberty* (London: J. M. Dent, 1951), 104. We should take care to note that Cromwell's idea about an underlying agreement was part of a political push for his own ends.

33. John Wilkins, *Mercury; or, The Secret and Swift Messenger* (1641), 106.

34. Joseph Waite's commendatory poem to Cave Beck's *Universal Character* (1657), A6r, in Cohen, *Sensible Words*, 2.

35. See Cohen, *Sensible Words*, chap. 1, for a survey of these aims and projects; see also, M. M. Slaughter, *Universal Languages and Scientific Taxonomy in the Seventeenth Century* (Cambridge: Cambridge University Press, 1982); James Knowlton, *Universal Language Schemes in England and France, 1600–1800* (Toronto: University of Toronto

Press, 1975); and Vivian Salmon, *The Study of Language in Seventeenth Century England* (Amsterdam: John Benjamins, 1979).

36. Wilkins, *Essay*, B1, B1–B1v. Though Wilkins did not specify the English Civil War as his immediate impetus, in my "The Politics of Babel in the English Revolution," *Prose Studies* 14, no. 3 (December 1991): 14–44, I account for the preconditions of this universalist discourse about language in the pamphlet literature of the English Revolution.

37. As Byron Nelson argues in "The Ranters and the Limits of Language," *Prose Studies* 14, no. 3 (1991): 60–75. In *Perfection Proclaimed: Language and Literature in English Radical Religion, 1640–1660* (Oxford: Clarendon Press, 1988), Nigel Smith comprehensively explores the writings of radical religion during the period, and elegantly weaves together rhetorical criticism and intellectual and social history, to prove that the radicals pursued new uses of language in order to search for adequate means of inspiration. See also the introduction in Nigel Smith, ed., *A Collection of Ranter Writings from the Seventeenth Century* (London: Junction Books, 1983), 7–38.

38. Christopher Hill, *The World Turned Upside Down* (London: Temple Smith, 1972), 160–83. Besides Hill, those arguing the Ranters existed include Jerome Friedman, *Blasphemy, Immorality, and Anarchy: The Ranters and the English Revolution* (Athens: Ohio University Press, 1987); and A. L. Morton, *The World of the Ranters: Religious Radicalism in the English Revolution* (London: Lawrence and Wishart, 1970). Other historians ask whether the so-called Ranter sect was a fantasy created by conservative antisectarian writers of the civil war period and interpreted by leftist historians of the twentieth century: J. C. Davis, in *Fear, Myth and History: The Ranters and the Historians* (Cambridge: Cambridge University Press, 1986); see also the remarks against Davis by Keith Thomas, "On the Rant," in Geoff Eley and William Hunt, eds., *Reviving the English Revolution* (London: Verso, 1988), 153–60; for an insightful analysis of the Ranters in light of literary New Historicism, see James Holstun, "Ranting at the New Historicism," *English Literary Renaissance* 19, no. 2 (1989): 189–225. Ranter for me is a loose designation, a current political construct that unevenly clusters pamphlets and authors.

39. Laurence Clarkson, *The Lost Sheep Found* (1660) in Smith, *A Collection of Ranter Writings*, 180. See also Friedman, *Blasphemy*, 59–63, 96–109. Thomas N. Corns beautifully situates Ranter thought and its literary practices with the other radicals of the period in *Uncloistered Virtue: English Political Literature, 1640–1660* (Oxford: Clarendon Press, 1992), 174–93.

40. Jacob Bauthumley, *The Light and Dark Sides of God* (1650), in Smith, *A Collection of Ranter Writings*, 242, 244.

41. Friedman, *Blasphemy*, 75, incisively comments on the differences in style but emphasizes the unity of purpose among these men. Clarkson quoted in Smith, *A Collection of Ranter Writings*, 182, 183, 174.

42. Abinezer Coppe, *Second Fiery Flying Roll* (1649), in Smith, *A Collection of Ranter Writings*, 108, 107; and *An Additional and Preambular Hint*, in Smith, *A Collection of Ranter Writings*, 73.

43. Derek Hirst, *Authority and Conflict: England, 1603–1658* (Cambridge: Harvard University Press, 1986), 289. As Holstun puts it, "Ranter rhetoric is radical not simply because it attempts to invert social and ethical hierarchies, but because it attacks the very binary principle determining hierarchy and ethics," in "Ranting at the New Historicism," 220.

44. Davis, *Fear, Myth and History*, 101–2; "An Act against several Atheistical, Blasphemous and Execrable Opinions," in C. H. Firth and R. S. Rait, eds., *Acts and Ordinances of the Interregnum, 1642–1660*, 3 vols. (Holmes Beach, Fla.: W. M. Gaunt, 1972), 2.409–10.

45. Henry Peacham, *The World is Ruled & Governed by Opinion* (1641). Natalie Davis, "Women on Top," *Society and Culture in Early Modern France* (Stanford, Calif.: Stanford University Press, 1975), 24–151, explains how this kind of sexual symbolism is connected with issues of power, order, and hierarchy in early modern Europe.

46. Robert Filmer, *"Patriarcha" and Other Political Works of Sir Robert Filmer*, ed. Peter Laslett (Oxford: Blackwell, 1949), 283. See Hans Aarsleff, *From Locke to Saussure: Essays in the Study of Language and Intellectual History* (Minneapolis: University of Minnesota Press, 1982) for discussion of various "Adamic" theories of linguistic origin, where "the relation between signifier and signified is not arbitrary" (25–26).

47. I have profited from conversation with Jim Holstun about this second meaning of Babel. David Loewenstein writes about the antityrannical rhetoric as a component of Milton's mythmaking in *Milton and the Drama of History: Historical Vision, Iconoclasm and the Literary Imagination* (Cambridge: Cambridge University Press, 1990), and about Babel as it is associated with the tyrant Nimrod (109–11), yet fails to note the royalist perspective that Milton has co-opted for his own purposes.

48. Thomas Blount, *Glossographia* (1656), F2.

49. John Gauden, *Eikon Basilike*, in *Eikon Basilike: The Pourtraiture of His Sacred Majesty in His Solitudes and Sufferings*, ed. Philip Knachel (Ithaca: Cornell University Press and the Folger Library, 1966), 175; John Milton, *Eikonoklastes CPW* III.598.

50. *Sampsons Foxes Agreed to Fire a Kingdom* (1644).

51. J. Doughty, *The King's Cause Rationally, briefly, and plainly debated* (1644), 37.

52. Thomas Browne, "To the Reader," *Religio Medici*, in *Sir Thomas Browne: The Major Works*, ed. C. A. Patrides (Harmondsworth, Middlesex: Penguin, 1977), 59.

53. Thomas Jordan, "The Rebellion," in *Rump: or, An Exact Collection . . . 1639 to Anno 1661*, 2 vols., facs. ed. (1662; reprint, London: Henry Brome and Henry Marsh, 1874), 1: 291–95.

54. *A Description of the Famous Kingdom of Macaria* (1641), quoted in Seibert, *Freedom of the Press* 192. Siebert has attributed this utopia to Gabriel Harvey, but Charles Webster has argued more recently that it is the work of Gabriel Plattes, in *The Intellectual Revolution of the Seventeenth Century* (London: Routledge, 1974), 369–85. I thank Jim Holstun for this reference.

55. *A Remedie Against Dissention*, (1644), 13; Margot Heineman, *Puritanism and Theatre: Thomas Middleton and Opposition Drama under the Early Stuarts* (Cambridge: Cambridge University Press, 1980), 27.

56. Or, the reverse, as Annabel Patterson argues in *Shakespeare and the Popular Voice* (Oxford: Basil Blackwell, 1989).

57. See Eamon Duffy, "The Godly and the Multitude in Stuart England," *Seventeenth Centruy* 1, no. 1 (January 1986): 31–55; Annabel Patterson, "The Very Name of the Game: Theories of Order and Disorder," in Thomas Healy and Jonathan Sawday, eds., *Literature and the English Civil War* (Cambridge: Cambridge University Press, 1990), 21–37; and Christopher Hill, "The Many-Headed Monster," in *Change and Continuity in Seventeenth-Century England* (Cambridge: Harvard University Press, 1975), 181–204.

58. Cleveland's works were successful in the press, tallying twenty-five editions between 1647 and 1700, even though he sought a coterie audience. Concerning early editions of Cleveland's works, see John Morris, *John Cleveland: A Bibliography of*

his Poems (London: Bibliographical Society, 1967), which explains the difficulty in ascertaining the Cleveland canon; B. Morris and E. Worthington, eds., *The Poems of John Cleveland* (Oxford: Oxford University Press, 1967), xvii. See also S. V. Gapp, "Notes on John Cleveland," *PMLA* 46 (1931): 1075–86.

59. John Cleveland, "The Character of a London Diurnal," in Henry Morley, ed., *Character Writings of the Seventeenth Century* (London: George Routledge and Sons, 1891), 308. Hereafter, references to Cleveland's work found in the Morley edition will be abbreviated *CWSC* and cited parenthetically in text.

60. Hilda Smith, *Reason's Disciples: Seventeenth-Century English Feminists* (Urbana: University of Illinois Press, 1982), 3–17; Claire Cross, "'He-goats before the flocks': A Note on the Part Played by Women in the Founding of Some Civil War Churches," *Studies in Church History* 8 (1972): 195–202.

61. Peter Hausted, *Ad Populam* (1644).

62. "O Brave Oliver" was a popular ballad of the period.

63. The connection is more than a topos, since cheap pamphlets often served a second role in the privy.

64. Cleveland was not the first to attack the press in a "character"; Richard Brathwait's popular *Whimzies; or, A New Cast of Characters* (1631) pokes fun at "A Corranto-Coiner," as "a state news-monger: and his own genius is his intelligencer," as Ben Jonson had before him in the masque *A Staple of News* (1631). Yet these did not attack Parliament head-on.

65. Thomas Hobbes, *Leviathan*, ed. C. B. Macpherson (Harmondsworth, Middlesex: Penguin, 1968), 368. Hereafter, all references to *Leviathan* will be abbreviated *L* and page numbers will be cited parenthetically in the text.

66. See Gordon J. Schochet, *Patriarchalism in Political Thought: The Authoritarian Family and Political Speculation and Attitudes Especially in Seventeenth-Century England* (Oxford: Basil Blackwell, 1971). Filmer's *Patriarchia* is the keystone of the theory that made an analogy between families and states.

67. J.G.A. Pocock, *The Ancient Constitution and the Feudal Law* (Cambridge: Cambridge University Press, 1957), 17. See Derek Attridge on etymology as fiction, "Language as History/History as Language: Saussure and the Romance of Etymology," in Derek Attridge, Geoff Bennington, and Robert Young, eds., *Post-structuralism and the Question of History* (New York: Cambridge Unversity Press, 1990), 183–211.

68. Mikhail Bakhtin, *The Dialogic Imagination*, trans. Caryl Emerson and Michael Holquist (Austin: University of Texas Press, 1981), 431, 271.

69. I have found the following useful: Terence Ball, "Hobbes' Linguistic Turn," *Polity* 17 (1985): 739–60; Howard Warrender, *The Political Philosophy of Hobbes: His Theory of Obligation* (Oxford: Clarendon Press, 1957); Isabel C. Hungerland and George R. Vick, "Hobbes's Theory of Signification," *Journal of the History of Philosophy* 11, no. 4 (1973): 459–82. I thank Gordon Schochet for his insatiable zest in discussing Hobbes with me.

70. See Terence Cave, *The Cornucopian Text: Problems of writing in the French Renaissance* (Oxford: Clarendon Press, 1979), on the epistemological meaning of the trope of copiousness.

71. Thomas Hobbes, *De Corpore*, in *The English Works of Thomas Hobbes*, ed. W. Molesworth, 34 vols. (London: John Bohn, 1839), 1:16. References hereafter will be abbreviated *DC* and will be given parenthetically in text.

72. Jürgen Habermas, *The Structural Transformation of the Public Sphere: An Inquiry into a Category of Bourgeois Society*, trans. T. Burger (Cambridge: MIT Press, 1989), 53.

73. Leo Strauss, *The Political Philosophy of Hobbes: Its Basis and Its Genesis*, trans. Elsa

M. Sinclair (Chicago: University of Chicago Press, 1984) argues Hobbes's theory of public opinion is the background of Rousseau's sense of public opinion as *volonté générale.*

74. Thomas Sprat, *The History of the Royal Society,* ed. Jackson I. Cope and Harold Whitmore James (St. Louis, Mo.: Washington University Press, 1958), 113.

75. Stanley Fish, in "The Plain Style Question," in *Self-Consuming Artifacts* (Berkeley: University of California Press, 1972), argues that "the triumph of the plain style, then, is a triumph of epistemology" (381).

CHAPTER THREE
DEBATE AND THE DRAMA OF POLITICS IN THE PUBLIC SPHERE

1. Cromwell quoted in A.S.P. Woodhouse, *Puritanism and Liberty, Being the Army Debates, 1647–1649* (London: J. M. Dent, 1966), 22. All further references to the Putney debates will be to this edition, will be abbreviated *PD*, and will be indicated parenthetically in the text.

2. Gal. 2:11 shows that Paul "withstood [Peter] to his face."

3. "The text is a representation of the spectacle of politics, but the action of politics itself, in its public manifestations, demands to be seen." Christian Jouhaud, *Mazarinades: La fronde des mots* (Paris: Aubier, 1985), 242.

4. This account is taken from Woodhouse, *Puritanism and Liberty,* 14–35. On the difficulties in distinguishing clearly the "parties" in the English Revolution, see W. M. Lamont, "Puritanism as History and Historiography," *Past and Present* 44 (1969): 133–46.

5. G. E. Aylmer, *Rebellion or Revolution? England, 1640–1660* (New York: Oxford University Press, 1986), 86–89; Derek Hirst, *Authority and Conflict: England, 1603–1658* (Cambridge: Harvard University Press, 1986), 277–78; On ideology in the army, see Mark Kishlansky, "Ideology and Politics in the Parliamentary Armies, 1645–1649," in John Morrill, ed., *Reactions to the English Civil War, 1642–1649* (London: Macmillan, 1986), 163–83.

6. David Wooton, *Divine Right and Democracy* (Harmondsworth, Middlesex: Penguin, 1982), 274.

7. Woodhouse, *Puritanism and Liberty,* 80.

8. Mark Kishlansky, "The Emergence of Adversary Politics in the Long Parliament," *Journal of Modern History* 49, no. 4 (1977): 640. Kishlansky argues in "Consensus Politics and the Structure of Debate at Putney," *Journal of British Studies* 20, no. 2 (1981): 50–69, that Putney failed to accomplish anything; my interest is not in how they concluded or on what they settled, but rather with the understanding of how political discussion was to take place.

9. Joel B. Altman, *The Tudor Play of Mind: Rhetorical Inquiry and the Development of Elizabethan Drama* (Berkeley: University of California Press, 1978) works out the Renaissance fascination with arguing *in utramque partem.* On the practices of rhetorical debate: K. J. Wilson, *Incomplete Fictions: The Formation of English Renaissance Dialogue* (Washington, D.C.: Catholic University of America Press, 1985); J. Siegel, *Rhetoric and Philosophy in Renaissance Humanism* (Princeton: Princeton University Press, 1968) on public character of oratory; Eliabeth Skerpan, *The Rhetoric of Politics in the English Revolution, 1642–1660* (Columbia: University of Missouri Press, 1992), 13–31, on the genres of rhetorical argument used in the English Revolution, and a survey of rhetorical principles learned in the schools by English gentlemen; on

rhetoric's service to the state, see Anthony Grafton and Lisa Jardine, *From Humanism to the Humanities: Education and the Liberal Arts in Fifteenth- and Sixteenth-Century Europe* (Cambridge: Harvard University Press, 1986), chap. 7. This oral model of service to the state persisted despite the transition into print: the printing press now acted as a forum for oratorical activity.

10. Louis L. Martz, "Introduction" to *A Dialogue of Comfort against Tribulation*, in *The Complete Works of St. Thomas More*, vol. 12 (New Haven: Yale University Press, 1976), lxvii.

11. Margot Heinemann, *Puritanism and Theatre: Thomas Middleton and Opposition Drama under the Early Stuarts* (Cambridge: Cambridge University Press, 1980); and Lois Potter, "*The Triumph of Peace* and *The Cruel Warr.* Masque and Parody," *Notes and Queries*, n.s., 27 (1980): 345–48.

12. *A Dialogue betwixt a Rattlehead and a Roundhead* (1641), A2v.

13. Margaret A. Doody, *The Daring Muse: Augustan Poetry Reconsidered* (Cambridge: Cambridge University Press, 1985), 44–49, on ventriloquism.

14. *The Soldiers Language; or, A Discourse between two soldiers, showing how the Wars go on* (1644), A1v, A4v.

15. Ibid., B3v, B4v.

16. *Dialogue Betwixt a Courtier and a Scholar* (1644), 8.

17. Ibid., 3.

18. *Against Universal Liberty of Conscience* (1644).

19. Dent, *The Plain Man's Pathway* (1601), A4.

20. Sandra Clark, *The Elizabethan Pamphleteers: Popular Moralistic Pamphlets, 1580–1640* (Rutherford, N.J.: Fairleigh Dickinson University Press, 1983), 258, on didactic uses of this popular form.

21. *The Soldiers Catechism* (1644), 4, 5.

22. *A Late Dialogue, betwixt a Civilian and a Divine* (1644), 26.

23. Ibid., 39.

24. W. Prynne, *The Falsities* (1644), 1, 4.

25. Ibid., 1.

26. Ibid., 5. Prynne's is not only a demand that the reader decide; Prynne is also playing the salesman. He exhorts the readers to buy, or at least to lay hands on, copies of the books that will speak in his own defense. This example also tells us about writing in a print culture, according to E. Eisenstein, since it is only after the dissemination of identical texts that a community—in her case a scholarly one—can share enough materials to have a common ground upon which to argue or to prove things, through checking and rechecking. *The Printing Press as an Agent of Change* (Cambridge: Cambridge University Press, 1979), 111, 142.

27. W. L., *A Medicine for Malignancy* (1644), A3-A3v, 83.

28. *A Dialogue betwixt a Horse of War and a Mill-Horse* (1644). On the habits of religious ridicule, see Raymond A. Anselment, *"Betwixt Jest and Earnest": Marprelate, Milton, Marvell, Swift, and the Decorum of Religious Ridicule* (Toronto: University of Toronto Press, 1979).

29. *A Dialogue, or Rather a Parley between Prince Rupert's Dog . . . and Toby's Dog* (1643), A4v.

30. Ibid., A4v. The beast fable as a model of subversive political writing has been examined by Annabel Patterson, in *Fables of Power: Aesopian Writing and Political History* (Durham, N.C.: Duke University Press, 1991).

31. "The Power of the Sword," in *Rump; or, An Exact Collection . . . 1639 to Anno*

1661, facs. ed., 2 vols. (1662; reprint, London: Henry Brome and Henry Marsh, 1874), 1: 333–35.

32. *A Call to all the Soldiers of the Army by the Free People of England*, in Woodhouse, *Puritanism and Liberty*, 439, 441 (29 October 1647).

33. David Underdown, *Revel, Riot and Rebellion: Popular Politics and Culture in England, 1603–1660* (Oxford: Oxford University Press, 1987), 141–43, discusses these and other contemporary stereotypes.

34. Wilbur Gilman calls this "a technique with cumulative significances." "These are the means by which Milton keeps [readers'] repugnance to Catholicism constantly associated with licensing. It is quite apparent that by frequent repetition of this highly charged appeal to prejudice he hopes to extend intolerance of Catholicism to intolerance of licensing." *Milton's Rhetoric: Studies in his Defense of Liberty* (Columbia: University of Missouri Press, 1939), 170, 30. See also Robin Clifton, "The Popular Fear of Catholics during the English Revolution," in Paul Slack, ed., *Rebellion, Popular Protest and the Social Order in Early Modern England* (Cambridge: Cambridge University Press, 1984), 129–61; but also see Peter Lake's revisionary account, "Anti-Popery: The Structure of a Prejudice," in Richard Cust and Ann Hughes, eds., *Conflict in Early Stuart England: Studies in Religion and Politics, 1603–1642* (New York: Longman, 1989), 72–106.

35. For analysis of these kinds of rhetorics, see Kenneth Burke, "The Rhetoric of Hitler's 'Battle,'" in Michael J. Shapiro, ed., *Language and Politics* (New York: New York University Press, 1984), 68.

36. Jacques Ellul, in *Propaganda: The Formation of Men's Attitudes*, trans. Konrad Kellen and Jean Lerner (New York: Vintage, 1973), 31, writes about the repetition of "certain words, signs, or symbols, even certain persons or facts, provoking unfailing reactions," which constitute propaganda.

37. John Taylor, *No Mercurius Aulicus* (10 July 1644); John Booker, *No Mercurius Aquaticus, but a Cable-Rope Double twisted for John Taylor* (19 July 1644); John Taylor, *John Taylor, being yet unhanged, sends greeting to John Booker that hanged him* (July 1644); John Booker, *A Rope Treble-twisted for John Taylor* (27 September 1644).

38. D. Featley, *Sacra Nemesis* (Oxford, 1644), A2v.

39. *Aulicus his Hue and Cry* (1645).

40. *Recantation of Mercurius Aulicus* (1644), 4.

41. *Mercurius Vapulans* (1644), 3.

42. Hezekiah Woodward, *Inquiries into the Cause of our Miseries* (1644) 11, in *Marginal Prynne*, 9.

43. A point M. Smuts misses, in "The Political Failure of Stuart Cultural Patronage," in Guy Fitch Lytle and Stephen Orgel, eds., *Patronage in the Renaissance* (Princeton: Princeton University Press, 1981). On the organizational structure of propaganda, see Ellul, *Propaganda*, 20.

44. Phoebe Sheavyn, *The Literary Profession in the Elizabethan Age* (Manchester: Manchester University Press, 1979), 9.

45. Parliament's votes: *Journals of the House of Commons*, 2.611; Frederick F. Siebert, *Freedom of the Press in England, 1476–1776* (Urbana: University of Illinois Press, 1952), 205.

46. Booker, *No Mercurius Aquaticus*, 2.

47. John Booker worked for Parliament in 1643–50 as a censor of new almanacs and mathematical books, according to R. L. Greaves and R. Zaller, eds., *Biographical*

Dictionary of British Radicals in the Seventeenth Century, 3 vols. (Sussex: Harvester Press, 1982), 1: 80.

48. Booker, *No Mercurius Aquaticus*, 4.

49. Taylor, *John Taylor, unhanged* (1644), 3, 2–3, 7, 7.

50. Booker, *A Rope Treble-twisted*, 4, 7, 8, 6 (see lines above from *John Taylor, unhanged*).

51. P. W. Thomas, *Sir John Berkenhead, 1617–1679: A Royalist Career in Politics and Polemics* (Oxford: Clarendon, 1969), 52; See also Joyce Lee Malcolm, *Caesar's Due: Loyalism and King Charles, 1642–1646*, Royal Historical Society Studies in History, vol. 38 (London: Royal Historical Society, 1983), 140–45.

52. *The manner of the Election of Philip Herbert . . . For the Knight of the Shire for Barkshire, by almost fourty Free-holders* (1649), 6.

53. *Gradus Simeonis, or, the First Fruits of Philip, Earl of Pembroke . . . [sometimes] Knight of the Garter: and [now] Knight of Berk-shire. Presented In a learned Speech upon the Day of his Ascending down into the Lower House of Commons* "the first year of the LORDS Freedome" (1649), 1–2, 3, 6.

54. *The Earl of Pembrokes Speech to Nol-Cromwell* (1649), 4.

55. Kevin Sharpe, *The Personal Rule of Charles I* (New Haven: Yale University Press, 1992), 631.

56. Kevin Sharpe, *Criticism and Compliment: The Politics of Literature in the England of Charles I* (Cambridge: Cambridge University Press, 1987), 272.

57. Sir John Denham is an exemplary figure for this; see Peter Malekin, *Liberty and Love: English Literature and Society, 1640–1688* (London: Hutchinson, 1981), 19–33.

58. Sharpe, *Criticism and Compliment*, 297–301; On the function of the masque to criticize and to destabilize Stuart policies, see Martin Butler, "Politics and the Masque: *Salmacida Spolia*," in Thomas Healy and Jonathan Sawday, eds., *Literature and the English Civil War* (Cambridge: Cambridge University Press, 1990), 59–74. David Norbrook explores the tradition of criticism in masques even from the Jacobean period in "The Reformation of the Masque," in D. Lindley, ed., *The Court Masque* (Manchester: Manchester University Press, 1984), 94–110, and argues that Puritan sympathies were compatible with masquing because the form served to express criticism of and advice to the king.

59. Kevin Sharpe and Steven N. Zwicker, "Introduction," in *Politics of Discourse: The Literature and History of Seventeenth-Century England* (Los Angeles: University of California Press, 1987), 16.

60. Annabel Patterson, *Censorship and Interpretation: The Conditions of Writing and Reading in Early Modern England* (Madison: University of Wisconsin Press, 1984), 178–84, 200. Yet see David Quint, who, in *Epic and Empire: Politics and Generic Form from Virgil to Milton* (Princeton: Princeton University Press, 1993), argues that romance is the literary form associated with antiauthoritarian, republican thinking (9, 322–24). Arcadian genres, as Graham Parry argues in "A Troubled Arcadia," in Healy and Sawday, *Literature and the English Civil War*, rather than signaling a false idyll, could be a place in which writers warned the king that all was not well in his state (38–55).

61. Robert Baron, *Pocula Castalia* (1650), stanza 83.

62. Potter, *Secret Rites and Secret Writing: Royalist Literature, 1641–1660* (Cambridge: Cambridge University Press, 1989), chap. 3, 97, 107, 107, 113.

63. James VI and I, *Trew Law of Free Monarchies*, in D. Wooton, ed., *Divine Right and Democracy* (Harmondsworth, Middlesex: Penguin, 1986), 99.

64. Sir Robert Filmer, *Patriarcha*, in Johann P. Sommerville, ed., *"Patriarcha" and Other Writings* (Cambridge: Cambridge University Press, 1991), 7.

65. J. P. Sommerville, *Politics and Ideology in England, 1603–1640* (London: Longman, 1986), 30, 27–34. The fullest discussion of patriarchalism is Gordon J. Schochet, *Patriarchalism in Political Thought: The Authoritarian Family and Political Speculation and Attitudes Especially in Seventeenth-Century England* (Oxford: Basil Blackwell, 1975).

66. J.G.A. Pocock analyzes the king's *Answer to the Nineteen Propositions of Both Houses of Parliament* in 1642 in, *The Machiavellian Moment: Florentine Political Thought and the Atlantic Republican Tradition* (Princeton: Princeton University Press, 1975), arguing that Charles's admission of a balance in government was a form of classical republicanism, a departure from earlier Stuart theories of government (362–77).

67. John Gauden, *Eikon Basilike: The Pourtrature of His Sacred Majesty in His Solitudes and Sufferings*, ed. Philip Knachel (Ithaca: Cornell University Press and the Folger Library, 1966), 86, 132.

68. Ibid., 44, 92, 32, 39.

69. Annabel Patterson has discussed the royalist interest in separating private from public discourse through the genre of personal letters in *Censorship and Interpretation* (chap. 5).

70. Jonathan Goldberg, *James I and the Politics of Literature* (Baltimore: Johns Hopkins University Press, 1983); see also Graham Parry, *The Golden Age Restor'd: The Culture of the Stuart Court* (Manchester: Manchester University Press, 1981).

CHAPTER FOUR
READING IN THE REVOLUTION: *EIKONOKLASTES*
AND THE BATTLE OF PERSPECTIVES

1. "Advertisements for the Managing of the Counsels of the Army, Walden, 1647," in A.S.P. Woodhouse, *Puritanism and Liberty, Being the Army Debates, 1647–1649* (London: J. M. Dent, 1966), 398.

2. Jacques Ellul, *Propaganda: The Formation of Men's Attitudes*, trans. Konrad Kellen and Jean Lerner (New York: Vintage Books, 1973), 112, 146.

3. Harry Rusche, "Prophecy and Propaganda, 1641 to 1651," *English Historical Review* 84 (1969): 752; Robert W. Scribner, *For the Sake of Simple Folk: Popular Propaganda for the German Reformation* (Cambridge: Cambridge University Press, 1981), 8.

4. Robin Clifton, "The Popular Fear of Catholics during the English Revolution," in Paul Slack, ed., *Rebellion, Popular Protest and the Social Order in Early Modern England* (Cambridge: Cambridge University Press, 1984), 145. On Foxe, see David Birch, *Early Reformation English Polemics* (Salzburg: Universitat Salzburg, 1983), 109. Antipopery and mass propaganda are explored by Tim Harris, *London Crowds in the Reign of Charles II* (Cambridge: Cambridge University Press, 1987), chap. 5, 96–129.

5. Ellul, *Propaganda*, 207.

6. Thomas Hobbes, *Leviathan*, ed. C. B. Macpherson (Harmondsworth, Middlesex: Penguin, 1968), 379. How shall we compare this image, which so frightens and disturbs Hobbes, with that of Locke describing the process of the mind in *Essay Concerning Human Understanding?*

7. Henry Parker, *The Contra-Replicant* (1643).

8. W. Prynne, *Vox Populi* (1642), 23. See W. Lamont, *Marginal Prynne, 1600–1669* (London: Routledge and Kegan Paul, 1963) for biography.

9. *The Fallacies of Mr. Prynne*, (1644), 23. References hereafter are abbreviated *FP* and cited parenthetically in text.

10. Hezekiah Woodward, *Inquiries into the Cause of our Miseries* (1644), 11; Lamont, *Marginal Prynne*, 8.

11. Marchamont Nedham, *The Lawyer of Lincoln's Inn Reformed* (1647), 1; in Lamont, *Marginal Prynne*, 7.

12. W. Prynne, *The Sovereign Power of Parliaments* (1643), 33.

13. For understanding the confusing taxonomy of political parties, see Blair Worden, Valerie Pearl, David Underdown, and George Yule, "Debate: Presbyterians, Independents, or Puritans," *Past and Present* 47 (1970): 116–46.

14. On Walwyn's authorship of these pamphlets, see William Haller, *Tracts on Liberty in the Puritan Revolution* (New York: Columbia University Press, 1934) vol. 1, app. A, 121–27.

15. Ibid. 3.193, 199, 199.

16. Ibid., 200, 200, 201.

17. Kenneth Burke. "The Rhetoric of Hitler's 'Battle,'" in Michael Shapiro, ed., *Language and Politics* (New York: New York University Press, 1984), 61–80.

18. Susan R. Suleiman, *Authoritarian Fictions: The Ideological Novel as a Literary Genre* (New York: Columbia University Press, 1983), 142–43, 144, 143, 22.

19. Ellul, *Propaganda*, 11.

20. Adolph Hitler, *Mein Kampf* (New York: Reynal and Hitchcock, 1941), 236.

21. Ellul, *Propaganda*, 209.

22. J. Taylor, *Crop-Eare Curried* (1644), 3, 3, 32, 27, 30.

23. *Mercurius Civicus* (25 January–1 February 1643).

24. *Mercurius Elencticus: Communicating the unparallell'd Proceedings*, no. 22 (17–24 September 1649), 169–70.

25. *England's Remembrancer of Londons integrity*, no. 1 (1647), 1, 3.

26. Rusche, "Prophecies and Propaganda," 760; B. Capp, *Astrology and the Popular Press* (Ithaca: Cornell University Press, 1979).

27. *Mercurius Vapulans* (1644), 7.

28. William Lilly, *The Starry Messenger; or, An Interpretation of that Strange Apparition of Three suns seen in London* (1645), n.p.

29. John Booker, *Mercurius Coelicus* (25 January 1644), 2. John Booker's almanacs were selling about fifteen thousand copies a year in the mid-1660s—a staggering figure—according to Rusche, "Prophesies and Propaganda."

30. *Mercurius Vapulans* (1644), 7.

31. Booker, *Mercurius Coelicus*, 2; also see *A Rope for a Parrot* (1644), 2.

32. *Mercurio-Coelico-Mastix* (1644), 2, 13.

33. *Mercurius Vapulans* (1644), 3, 8.

34. "A Dreadful Relation, of the Cruel, Bloody, and Most Inhumane Massacre and Butchery, committed on the Poor Protestants" (1656), British Library Ballad c.20 f. 14.

35. Joseph Goebbels, cited in Ellul, *Propaganda*, x n. 1.

36. *The Converted Cavaliers Confession* (1644).

37. Woodhouse, *Puritanism and Liberty*, 35.

38. *Mercurius Vapulans*, 2.

39. *Converted Cavaliers Confession*, 4, 5, 5.

40. *Mercurius Elencticus: Communicating the unparallell'd Proceedings*, no. 25 (15–22 October 1649).

41. Linear perspective became a "category of thought," according to Ernest B. Gilman, *The Curious Perspective: Literary and Pictorial Wit in the Seventeenth Century* (New Haven: Yale University Press, 1978), 28. The relation between verbal and visual wit is discussed by Murray Roston, *Milton and the Baroque* (London: Macmillan, 1980), esp. 104–14; and Mario Praz, *Mnemosyne: The Parallel between Literature and the Visual Arts* (Princeton: Princeton University Press, 1970), 126.

42. Ernest Gombrich, *Art and Illusion: A Study in the Psychology of Pictorial Representation* (Princeton: Princeton University Press, 1968), 212, 252, 249.

43. So argues David Lowenstein, *Milton and the Drama of History: Historical Vision, Iconoclasm and the Literary Imagination* (Cambridge: Cambridge University Press, 1990), 51–73.

44. Hobbes plays this image game the other way around: "no tyrant was ever so cruel as a popular assembly," in *Behemoth*, ed. Ferdinand Tönnies (Chicago: University of Chicago Press, 1990), 23.

45. *The Eye Cleared; or, A Preservative for the Sight* (1644), 3. Other pamphlets using the figure of a potion for eyes are: *Eye-Salve to anoint the Eyes of the Ministers . . . of London* (1649); *Eye-Salve for the City of London* (1648); *An Eye-Salve for the English Armie* (1660).

46. As do *A Paire of Crystal Spectacles . . . Counsels of the Army* (1648); *A New paire of Spectacles of the Old Fashion . . . Scots Commissioners* (1648); *Mercurius Heliconicus* (1651); *The Blind Man's Meditations* (1660).

47. *A New Invention; or, A paire of Cristall Spectacles* (1644). Hereafter, page references appear parenthetically in text.

48. *The Second Part of the Spectacles* (1644), 3.

49. Quintilian, *Institutio Oratoria*, trans. H. E. Butler (New York: Loeb Classical Library, 1922), 3:401.9, 2, 44.

50. Wayne Booth, *A Rhetoric of Irony* (Chicago: University of Chicago Press, 1974), 91. See also Kenneth Burke, *A Grammar of Motives* (Berkeley: University of California Press, 1969), on the conflict between a single perspective ("relativism") and the awareness of many perspectives ("irony") (512).

51. Sue Curry Jansen, *Censorship: The Knot that Binds Power and Knowledge* (Oxford: Oxford University Press, 1991), 196. This drama of irony is also discussed in Northrop Frye, *Anatomy of Criticism* (New York: Atheneum, 1969), 40–41.

52. On the occasion and background for *Eikonoklastes*, see the introduction by Merritt Hughes, *CPW* 3, chap. 8; and Ernest Sirluck, "*Eikon Basilike, Eikon Alethine* and *Eikonoklastes*," *Modern Language Notes* 69 (1954): 497–502.

53. As Thomas Corns has argued in *Uncloistered Virtue: English Political Literature, 1640–1660* (Oxford: Clarendon Press, 1992), 217–20, Milton's first step is to force the English readers to see that *Eikon Basilike* is a work of political polemic, and not a prayer or a memoir. On Charles's idolatry, see Florence Sandler, "Icon and Iconoclast," in M. Lieb and J. T. Shawcross, eds., *Achievements of the Left Hand: Essays on the Prose of John Milton* (Amherst: University of Massachussetts Press, 1974), 160–84; and Lana Cable, "Milton's Iconoclastic Truth," in David Loewenstein and James Grantham Turner, eds., *Politics, Poetics, and Hermeneutics in Milton's Prose* (Cambridge: Cambridge University Press, 1990), 135–51.

54. *The Divine Penitential Meditations and Vowes of his Late Sacred Majestie at Holmby House, Faithfully Turned into Verse, by E. R., Gentleman* (21 June 1649); later set to music as *Psalterium Carolinum*, by John Wilson (1657).

55. Francis F. Madan, *A New Bibliography of the "Eikon Basilike"* (London: Quaritch, 1950); Christopher Wordsworth, *Documentary Supplement to "Who Wrote Eikon Basilike?"* (London: J. Murray, 1825), 16; a review is provided in Hugh Trevor-Roper, *"Eikon Basilike*: The Problem of the King's Book," *History Today* 1 (1951): 7–12.

56. John Gauden, *Eikon Basilike: The Pourtraiture of His Sacred Majesty in His Solitudes and Sufferings*, ed. Philip Knachel (Ithaca: Cornell University Press and the Folger Library, 1966), 28. All further references appear parenthetically in text. On seventeenth-century theories of prayer, see Cynthia Garrett, "The Rhetoric of Supplication: Prayer Theory in Seventeenth-Century England," *Renaissance Quarterly* 46, no. 2 (1993): 328–57.

57. For the king's self-fashioning as a martyr, see John R. Knott, Jr., "'Suffering for Truths sake': Milton and Martyrdom," in Loewenstein and Turner, *Politics, Poetics, and Hermeneutics*, 53–170.

58. For the development of the justification for resistance based on conscience from Luther and Calvin, see Quentin Skinner, *The Foundations of Modern Political Thought* 2 vols. (Cambridge: Cambridge University Press, 1978), 2: 206–38; see also Michael Walzer's discussion of the Calvinist "sacred duty to resist" in *Revolution of the Saints: A Study in the Origins of Radical Politics* (Cambridge: Harvard University Press, 1965); and his "Puritanism as a Revolutionary Ideology," *History and Theory* 3 (1963): 59–90.

59. On the notion of an author's work as literary property, see Martha Woodmansee, "The Genius and Copyright: Economic and Legal Conditions of the Emergence of the Author," *Eighteenth-Century Studies* 17, no. 4 (1984): 443; and Richard Helgerson, "Milton Reads the King's Book: Print, Performance, and the Making of a Bourgeois Idol," *Criticism* 29, no. 1 (1987): 1–25.

60. We are meant to take Michael's story as true, based on the principle of certainty offered by the doctrine of *Sola Scriptura*. See Earl Miner, "Milton and the Histories," in Kevin Sharpe and Steven N. Zwicker, eds., *Politics of Discourse: The Literature and History of Seventeenth-Century England* (Los Angeles: University of California Press, 1987), 181–203.

61. Stephen Orgel, *The Illusion of Power: Political Theater in the English Renaissance* (Berkeley: University of California Press, 1975), describes the king's focal point in the drama.

62. John M. Steadman, "Satan and the Strategy of Illusion," *Milton's Epic Characters: Image and Idol* (Chapel Hill: University of North Carolina, 1968), chap. 5. See also Steadman's "*Ethos* and *Dianoia*: Character and Rhetoric in *Paradise Lost*," in Ronald David Emma and John T. Shawcross, eds., *Language and Style in Milton* (New York: Frederick Ungar, 1967), 193–202; and Irene Samuel, "Milton on the Province of Rhetoric," *Milton Studies* 10 (1977): 177–93.

63. Critics have discussed the literary significance of Milton's use of this figure. Samuel Johnson saw the allusion to the telescope as Milton's striving for the sublime: "he expands the adventitious image beyond the dimensions which the occasion required . . . he crowds the imagination with the discovery of the telescope, and all the wonders which the telescope discovers." "Milton," in *The Lives of the Most Eminent English Poets*, in Scott Elledge, ed., *Paradise Lost* (New York: Norton, 1975), 526–27. Thomas Greene reads Milton's use of the telescope here as part of his mock-heroic program, an instance of the false sublime, in *The Descent from Heaven: A Study in Epic Continuity* (New Haven: Yale University Press, 1975), 415; Barbara Lewalski also sees the shield as typical of Satan's "declination from higher to lower heroic kinds and models," in *"Paradise Lost" and the Rhetoric of Literary Forms* (Prince-

ton: Princeton University Press, 1979), 55–56; Stanley E. Fish, *Surprised by Sin: The Reader in "Paradise Lost"* (Berkeley: University of California Press, 1971), reads this passage as Milton's aim to "provide for his audience a perspective that is beyond the field of its perception" (25), part of Milton's general assault on the reader's senses.

64. Annabel Patterson, "Imagining New Worlds: Milton, Galileo, and the Good Old Cause," in Katherine Z. Keller and Gerald J. Schiffhorst, eds., *The Witness of Times: Manifestations of Ideology in Seventeenth-Century England* (Pittsburgh: Duquesne University Press, 1993), 238–60.

65. This is perhaps another way in which Milton achieves his "things unat-tempted." Milton's Satan has a shield that is explained by a metaphor not available to prior epic poets. Marjorie Hope Nicolson, "Milton and the Telescope," in *Science and Imagination* (Ithaca: Cornell University Press, 1956), 80–110, explores the im-pact of astronomy on Milton's imagination, and sees Milton's use of many astro-nomical metaphors—the telescope, the abyss, the newly perceived vastness of "inter-stellar space"—in light of Milton's "cosmic" poetic vision.

66. Thomas Hobbes, *Autobiography* (London, 1680), 6.

67. *The Great Assizes Holden in Parnassus* (1645), 34.

68. Leo Strauss's phrase is "reading between the lines," in "Persecution and the Art of Writing," *Persecution and the Art of Writing* (Glencoe, Ill.: Free Press, 1952), 36, 22–37, an essay I have found highly stimulating; though see Annabel Patterson's critique of Strauss in her analysis of the "hermeneutics of censorship" in the new introduction to *Censorship and Interpretation: The Conditions of Writing and Reading in Early Modern England* (Madison: University of Wisconsin Press, 1984), 24–48.

69. Patterson, *Censorship and Interpretation*, 25; and Annabel Patterson, *Reading between the Lines* (Madison: University of Wisconsin Press, 1993), 7; Patterson, *Censor-ship and Interpretation*, 26.

70. William Riley Parker, *Milton: A Biography*, 2 vols., (Oxford: Oxford University Press, 1968) 1:600–601.

71. Christopher Hill, *Milton and the English Revolution*, (New York: Viking, 1977), 405. Milton's sun imagery is treated in Joan S. Bennett, *Reviving Liberty: Radical Christian Humanism in Milton's Great Poems* (Cambridge: Harvard University Press, 1989), 37–38.

72. James Howell, *Dodona's Grove; or, The Vocal Forest, second part* (1650),147–48.

73. John Tatham, *The Distracted State, A Tragedy* (1651), 4, 2.

74. Mercurius Acheronticus [James Howell], *A Trance; or, News from Hell* (1649), 12.

75. *The Great Eclipse of the Sun; or, Charles his Wain* (1644), 2.

CHAPTER FIVE
MILTON AND THE FIT READER: *PARADISE LOST*
AND THE PARLIAMENT OF HELL

1. *We have fish'd and caught a Frog; or, The History of Several New Fishermen* (1649). The epigraph is Joseph Addison, *An Account of the Greatest English Poets* (1694), in R. M. Cummings, ed., *Spenser: The Critical Heritage* (New York, 1971), 224.

2. Frederick S. Siebert, *Freedom of the Press in England, 1476–1776* (Urbana: Uni-versity of Illinois Press, 1952), 209–33. See also Blair Worden, "Literature and Cen-sorship in Early Modern England," in *Too Mighty to Be Free: Censorship and the Press in Britain and the Netherlands* (Zutphen: De Walburg Press, 1988), 45–62.

3. Maureen Quilligan, in *The Language of Allegory: Defining the Genre* (Ithaca: Cornell University Press, 1979), talks about the process of "collusion" between the writer and the reader of an allegory (226).

4. Michael Murrin, *The Veil of Allegory: Some Notes toward a Theory of Allegorical Rhetoric in the English Renaissance* (Chicago: University of Chicago, 1969), 19. He explains that one chief function of allegory is to divide audiences into the knowing and the ignorant, iterating a prophetic model of utterance where there is a distinction in audience between the sacred and the profane (13).

5. Northrop Frye, *Anatomy of Criticism* (Princeton: Princeton University Press, 1957), 90.

6. Quilligan, *The Language of Allegory*, 226.

7. Lois Potter, *Secret Rites and Secret Writing: Royalist Literature, 1641–1660* (Cambridge: Cambridge University Press, 1989), argues this necessary indirection gives a new spin to the idea of "subversive literature," since those who were subverting were the ones who wanted hierarchy reestablished (3, 34).

8. On the Puritan use of utopia, which I see as similar in aims to allegory, see James Holstun, *A Rational Millennium: Puritan Utopias of Seventeenth-Century England and America* (New York: Oxford University Press, 1987), 12; Stanley E. Fish has argued that in *Pilgrim's Progress*, though Bunyan attempts to present an allegory in a "plain style," he nonetheless creates a self-consuming artifact, vainly attempting to make a figural journey into a literal one. *Self-Consuming Artifacts: The Experience of Seventeenth-Century Literature* (Berkeley: University of California Press, 1972), 224–25.

9. Angus Fletcher, *Allegory: The Theory of a Symbolic Mode* (Ithaca: Cornell University Press, 1964), 64–65.

10. As expressed in the neo-Platonism of the Caroline court masque, for example; see Kevin Sharpe, *Criticism and Compliment: The Politics of Literature in the England of Charles I* (Cambridge: Cambridge University Press, 1987), chap. 5. For an indispensable discussion of the connections between neo-Platonism and English royal power, see Stephen Orgel, *The Illusion of Power: Political Theater in the English Renaissance* (Berkeley: University of California Press, 1975); and "Platonic Politics," in Stephen Orgel and Roy Strong, eds., *Inigo Jones: The Theater of the Stuart Court* 2 vols. (Berkeley: University of California Press, 1973), 1: 49–75.

11. J. B. Broadbent, though not addressing this genre, finds that "Satan is the devils' Cromwell," and that Milton might even be satirizing Cromwell in his portait of Satan, in *Some Graver Subject: An Essay on "Paradise Lost"* (New York: Barnes and Noble, 1960), 115.

12. Stanley E. Fish, *Surprised by Sin: The Reader in "Paradise Lost"* (Berkeley: University of California Press, 1971), 12; Joseph Summers had argued similarly earlier, in *The Muse's Method* (Cambridge: Harvard University Press, 1962): "the readers as well as the characters have been involved in the evil and have been forced to recognize and to judge their involvement" (30–31).

13. Joan S. Bennett, *Reviving Liberty: Radical Christian Humanism in Milton's Great Poems* (Cambridge: Harvard University Press, 1989), 44.

14. The sole exception to this tendency against framing Satan in a political allegory is Christopher Kendrick, who gives us a Satan who is still the "symbolic expression or fulfillment of Milton's revolutionary desire." *Milton: A Study in Ideology and Form* (London: Methuen, 1986), 151.

15. Merritt Y. Hughes, "Satan and the 'Myth' of the Tyrant,"in *Ten Perspectives on Milton* (New Haven: Yale University Press, 1965), 188. Hughes banishes imputations

that in the poem, Milton is interested in Satan's political effects: "it is questionable whether Milton was as much concerned as we are today about mob-psychology and its part in the evolution of dictatorships" (187).

16. Stella Purce Revard, in *The War in Heaven: "Paradise Lost" and the Tradition of Satan's Rebellion* (Ithaca: Cornell University Press, 1980), 10, 23, 88, 116.

17. Stevie Davies, *Images of Kingship in "Paradise Lost"* (Columbia: University of Missouri Press, 1983), 11–12.

18. During the 1640s and 1650s, according to the historian Christopher Hill, "Antichrist . . . ceased to be exclusively ecclesiastical power and could be a symbol for any kind of political power—monarchy, the Lord Mayor of London, Parliament, the rule of the gentry, the protectorate of Oliver Cromwell." *Antichrist in Seventeenth-Century England* (London: Verso, 1990), 130–31.

19. *The Devil in his Dumps: or, A sad Complaint of Malignant Spirits* (1647), 2, 3, 8.

20. Northrop Frye, "Allegory," in Alex Preminger, ed., *The Princeton Encyclopedia of Poetry and Poetics*, enl. ed. (Princeton: Princeton University Press, 1974), 12–15; called "topical allusion," by Angus Fletcher, *Allegory*, 26.

21. Keith Thomas, *Religion and the Decline of Magic* (New York: Scribner's, 1978), 472, 267, 486–87.

22. *The Devills White Boyes; or, A mixture of Malicious Malignants, with their much evil, and manifold practices against the Kingdom and Parliament* (1644), 3, 4–5.

23. Ibid., 3, 4.

24. *Mercurius Poeticus* (5–13 May 1648), t.p.

25. Revard, *War in Heaven*, 87. See also Jeffrey Burton Russell, *Lucifer: The Devil in the Middle Ages* (Ithaca: Cornell University Press, 1984).

26. *The Famous Tragedie of King Charles I* (1649), A2; *Mercurius Elencticus*, no. 4 (14–21 May 1649), 27.

27. Mercurius Melancholicus, *The Cuckoo's nest at Westminster* (1648).

28. *Mercurius Melancholicus*, no. 1 (25 December–1 January 1649), 1, 5.

29. *The Devill and the Parliament; or, The Parliament and the Devill: A Contestation between them for the precedencie* (1648), 5–6, 1, 1–2, 5, 6.

30. *Mercurius Melancholicus*, no. 1 (25 December–1 January 1649), 8.

31. Mercurius Acheronticus [James Howell], *A Trance; or, News from Hell* (1649), 6, 9.

32. *The Devill and the Parliament* , 3.

33. *Mercurius Elencticus: Communicating the unparallell'd Proceedings*, no. 2 (1–8 May 1648), 10.

34. *Westminster Projects; or, The Mystery of Iniquity, or Darby-house Discovered*, no. 5 (1648), 1.

35. *The Parliaments Petition to the Divell* (1648), 3, 4, 6, 7, 6–7.

36. *A Declaration of Great Lucifer, Prince of the Air, and of Devils, and of all the damned crew in Hell* (1648), 3–4.

37. Ibid., 6–7, 5.

38. *Mercurius Fidelicus*, no. 1 (17–24 August 1648), 5. Whether this author considered his own pamphlet to be suspected of such devilishness is hinted in the title; by writing a *Mercurius Fidelicus*, a "Faithful Mercury," the author insists upon his innocence. Only the enemy's use of the press is deemed deceptive.

39. *A Trance*, 9.

40. [John Warner, bishop of Rochester], *The Devilish Conspiracy, Hellish Treason, Heathenish Condemnation, and Damnable Murder, Committed, and Executed by the Jewes,*

against the Anointed of the Lord, Christ their King (1649), 21, 40. The sermon was read on 4 February 1649, immediately following the regicide.

41. *Mercurius Elencticus*, no. 6 (28 May–4 June 1649), 45.

42. *The Famous Tragedie of King Charles I* (1649), 1–2.

43. Those defending Parliament or its leaders did not take this sort of attack without fighting back. In *Respublica Anglicana; or, The Historie of the Parliament* (1650), George Wither wrote against those who accused Cromwell of being the Devil: "behold this wretch [Sir Henry Vane, Senior?] dares defile the very name of Saint, as if holiness were a crime. Take heed, O [B]eelzebub, lest he get the lordship of thy hell too, and be preferred to command in chief, as being the more daring Fiend" (28). Wither does see the Devil's hand in the affairs of state, claiming the Scots are "guilty of an Antichristian spirit now, when they arrogate that power to themselves, which none but the Pope (by all Protestants agreed to be the Antichrist, the man of Sin) usurped, except the Devil, whose carriage to our Saviour was not much unlike theirs to their King, both shewing the Kingdoms of the Earth, and the glory of them, and saying, '*all these will we give thee, if thou wilt fall down and worship us*' yet let them take heed" (45). Wither uses the conventional image of the pope as the Devil to castigate the Scots, and he counters a scurrilous attack on Cromwell, accusing his detractor of being "the more daring Fiend," but he does not come up with his own hellish allegory. Parliamentary writers generally did not make use of this trope during the Interregnum.

44. *Bradshaw's Ghost: Being a Dialogue between Said Ghost, and an Apparition of the Late King Charles . . . The third Edition, Corrected and Enlarg'd* (1659), 12.

45. James Howell, *Dodona's Grove; or, The Vocal Forest, second part* (1650), 4. Hereafter, page references appear parenthetically in the text.

46. *Cromwell's Conspiracy. A Tragicomedy, Relating to our latter Times. Beginning at the Death of King Charles the First, And ending with the happy Restauration of KING CHARLES the Second* (1660).

47. "The Arraignment of the Devil for stealing away President Bradshaw," in, *The Rump; or, an Exact Collection of the Choycest poems and songs relating to the late times,* facs. ed., 2 vols. (1662; reprint London, 1874), 2:135–39. This poem also appeared as a single-sheet folio broadside; see note 48.

48. "The Rump Ululant; or, Penitence per force. Being the Recantation of the Old Rusty-roguy-rebellious-rampant, and now ruinous rotten-roasted RUMP," in *Rump*, 2.

49. Colonel Baker, in *The Blazing Star; or, Nolls Nose Newly Revived, and taken out of his TOMB* (1660), t.p., 4.

50. *The Downfall of Cerberus* (1660).

51. *Lucifer's Lifeguard: Containing a Schedule, List, Scroll, or Catalogue, of the first and following Names of the Antichristian, Anabaptistical, Atheistical, Anarchical and Infernal Imps . . .* (1660).

52. John Dryden, "Astrea Redux," in Edward Niles Hooker and H. T. Swedenberg, Jr., eds. *The Works of John Dryden*, 20 vols. (Los Angeles: University of California Press, 1956–89), 1:23, lines 39–40.

53. *The Arraignment of the Devil, for Stealing away President Bradshaw* (1660), 3.

54. *News from Hell; or, The Relation of a Vision* (1660).

55. Fletcher, *Allegory*, 64–65.

56. Andrew Marvell, "On *Paradise Lost*," in Merritt Y. Hughes, ed., *John Milton: Complete Poems and Major Prose* (Indianapolis: Bobbs-Merrill, 1984), 209–10.

57. William Riley Parker, *Milton: A Biography*, 2 vols. (Oxford: Oxford University Press, 1968), I:602.

58. After all, Milton, Marvell, and Dryden, as employees of the Protectorate, all walked in the procession at Oliver Cromwell's funeral in September 1658. Christopher Hill, "Milton and Marvell," in C. A. Patrides, ed., *Approaches to Marvell: The York Tercentenary Lectures* (London: Routledge and Kegan Paul, 1978), 1.

59. *Bradshaw's Ghost* (1660), 1, 2. This is also an echo of Achilles in *Odyssey* 11.460. Christopher Marlowe, *Doctor Faustus*, in Russell A. Fraser and Norman Rabkin, eds., *Drama of the English Renaissance: The Tudor Period* (New York: Macmillan, 1976).

60. Of current scholars, Michael Wilding in *Dragon's Teeth: Literature in the English Revolution* (Oxford: Clarendon Press, 1987), chap. 8, makes the closest concrete connection between the devils in *Paradise Lost* and midcentury political figures, though Wilding argues that Milton was critical of the Interregnum parliament, which, reflecting the tyranny of Satan, exemplified the dangers of democracy.

61. Andrew Marvell, *The Rehearsal Transpros'd*, ed., D.I.B. Smith (Oxford: Clarendon Press, 1971), 135.

62. Austin Woolrych, "Milton and the Good Old Cause," in Ronald G. Shafer, ed., *Ringing the Bell Backward: The Proceedings of the First International Milton Symposium* (Indiana, PA: Indiana University of Pennsylvania Press, 1982), 135.

63. Christopher Hill, *Milton and the English Revolution* (New York: Viking, 1977), 406–9.

64. *Mercurius Elencticus*, no. 6 (28 May–4 June 1649), 42.

65. *The Famous Tragedie of King Charles I* (1649), 1. Barbara K. Lewalski, in *"Paradise Lost" and the Rhetoric*, discusses Milton's treatment of Satan's deliberative rhetoric as a "genre of the damned" (84–97); Michael Wilding urges that we see the first two books in *Paradise Lost* as an example of the dangers of politics, where Milton is warning the reader that beautiful rhetoric can waylay democratic processes. *Dragon's Teeth*, 229.

66. Mercurius Acheronticus [James Howell], *A Trance*, 6.

67. *The Parliaments Petition to the Divell* (1648), 3, 7.

68. *The Trial of Traytors; or, The Rump in the Round* (1660). The same illustration was used in *The Dragon's Forces totally Routed* (1660).

69. Bennett, *Reviving Liberty*, 50.

70. "On the New Forcers of Conscience under the Long Parliament," *CP*, 144.

71. *Bradshaw's Ghost: Being a Dialogue between Said Ghost, and an Apparition of the Late King Charles . . . The third Edition, Corrected and Enlarg'd* (1659), 11.

72. Nicholas von Maltzahn dates the Digression in February 1649, in *Milton's "History of Britain": Republican Historiography in the English Revolution* (Oxford: Clarendon Press, 1991), 31; Hill takes these ominous statements as a sign of Milton's losing hope in 1654, in *Milton and the English Revolution*, 193; Austin Woolrych dates the Digression in 1660, finding that Milton retained optimism until 1659, in "The Date of the Digression in Milton's *History of Britain*," in Richard Ollard and Pamela Tudor-Craig, eds., *For Veronica Wedgwood These: Studies in Seventeenth-Century History* (London: Collins, 1986), 236–41. For the controversy over the dating of the Digression, see von Maltzahn, *Milton's History of Britain*, 22–48.

73. David Masson, *Life of Milton*, 7 vols. (Cambridge and London: Macmillan, 1859–94), 6: 811.

74. *A Trance*, 9.

75. In my argument here I concur with Mary Ann Radzinowicz's superlative account of Milton's late politics in *Toward "Samson Agonistes": The Growth of Milton's Mind* (Princeton: Princeton University Press, 1978), 145–49, though, as I will go on to show, my sense of Milton's educational program involves readers not just learning political truths but acquiring interpretive activities.

76. James Harrington, *Oceana*, in J.G.A. Pocock, ed., *The Political Works of James Harrington* (Cambridge: Cambridge University Press, 1977), 277.

77. Thus I disagree with Don M. Wolfe, who, in *Milton in the Puritan Revolution* (New York: Thomas Nelson and Sons, 1941), 342, found that Milton believed the Restoration was God's punishment to the people of England.

78. On the debate over whether Milton wrote *Christian Doctrine*, see William B. Hunter, who argues that he did not, in "The Provenance of the *Christian Doctrine*," *Studies in English Literature* 32, no. 1 (Winter 1992): 129–42, 163–66; and, arguing that he did, Barbara Lewalski, "Forum: Milton's *Christian Doctrine*," *Studies in English Literature* 32, no. 1 (Winter 1992): 143–54; and John T. Shawcross, "Forum: Milton's *Christian Doctrine*," *Studies in English Literature* 32, no. 1 (Winter 1992): 155–62.

79. *Mercurius Bellicus*, no. 2 (22–29 November 1647), 10.

80. Sir George Wharton, *Mercurio-Coelico-Mastix* (1644), 13.

81. *The Downfall of Cerberus* (1660).

82. Joseph Frank, *Hobbled Pegasus: A Descriptive Bibliography of Minor English Poetry, 1641–1660* (Albuquerque: University of New Mexico Press, 1968), 456.

83. Lois Potter also examines the sun and clouds imagery in such civil war royalist writing, though she does not draw the connection to *Paradise Lost*'s use of this figure. *Secret Rites*, 65–71.

84. Bennett, *Reviving Liberty*, 37–38, 39.

85. Andrew Marvell, "On *Paradise Lost*," in Merritt Y. Hughes, ed., *John Milton: Complete Poems and Major Prose* (Indianapolis: Bobbs-Merrill, 1984), 209–10, lines 11–16.

86. Gordon Teskey, "From Allegory to Dialectic: Imagining Error in Spenser and Milton," *PMLA* 101, no. 1 (1986): 9–23, argues that Miltonic error is represented dialectically, through negation, in contrast to Spenserian error, which is represented diagetically, through narrative (9). In the concept of "perplexity" in *Paradise Lost*, however, I see creatures not only making the wrong choices, but lacking any clear sense of what to choose between: this is more similar to Spenserian error than Teskey's dichotomy would allow.

87. Many critics have seen the lesson in the final books as one in fortitude: George Williamson, in "The Education of Adam," in Arthur E. Barker, ed., *Milton: Modern Essays in Criticism* (New York: Oxford University Press, 1965) stresses the didactic content of the final books, where Adam is given information to keep up his hopes, learning by exemplary teaching, acquiring wisdom and love rather than rational knowledge (284–307); patience is also the lesson in Barbara K. Lewalski, "Structure and Symbolism of Vision in Michael's Prophesy, *Paradise Lost*, Books XI–XII," *Philological Quarterly* 42 (1963): 25–35; Gerald J. Schiffhorst reads patience and optimism in the last two books in "Patience and the Education of Adam in *Paradise Lost*," *South Atlantic Review* 49, no. 4 (1984): 55–63; Lawrence A. Sasek defends the last books by stressing the lesson of "Christian fortitude" (196) in "The Drama of *Paradise Lost*, Books XI and XII," in Waldo F. McNair, ed. *Studies in English Renaissance Literature* (Baton Rouge, LA: Louisiana State University, 1962), 181–96. But

others have detected a discreet revolutionary tone in these books, as, for example, David Loewenstein has done in *Milton and the Drama of History: Historical Vision, Iconoclasm and the Literary Imagination* (Cambridge: Cambridge University Press, 1990). Another option is for readers to "act now": Mary Ann Radzinowicz, "'To Make the People Fittest to Chuse': How Milton Personified His Program for Poetry," *CEA Critic* 48, no. 8 (1986): 3–23; and Wilding, *Dragon's Teeth*, 229.

88. Wilding, *Dragon's Teeth*, 229–30.

89. Arnold Stein, "The Paradise Within and the Paradise Without," *Modern Language Quarterly* 26 (1965): 586–600, sees in the last books Adam taking his "final intellectual step" (598); I would say it is his first intellectual step in the world that resembles Milton's own. I agree instead with Robert L. Enzminger, "Michael's Options and Milton's Poetry," *English Literary Renaissance* 8 (1978): "Accustomed to the purely referential language he has employed in Eden, Adam is not yet equipped to turn to effective use the ambiguities of diction and syntax Milton trusts his readers to appreciate through most of the epic. Adam must come, guided by Michael, to approximate the reader's sophistication" (208), though I disagree that the language in Eden was "purely referential." Rather, the uses of language seem to me to be different in Eden and after the Fall, with the application of the lessons of history. Loewenstein, *Milton and the Drama of History*, 100, 97–120.

90. As Maureen Quilligan has pointed out, Eve was always already in a mediate position, receiving truth only indirectly, even before the Fall. *Milton's Spenser: The Politics of Reading* (Ithaca: Cornell University Press, 1983), 224, 226.

91. Mary Ann Radzinowicz, "'Man as Probationer of Immortality': *Paradise Lost*, XI–XII," in C. A. Patrides, ed., *Approaches to "Paradise Lost"* (Toronto: University of Toronto Press, 1968), 31–51, 37.

92. William G. Madsen, *From Shadowy Types to Truth: Studies in Milton's Symbolism* (New Haven: Yale University Press, 1968); and Regina Schwartz, "From Shadowy Types to Shadowy Types: The Unendings of *Paradise Lost*," *Milton Studies* 24 (1988): 123–39.

93. Stanley Fish's brilliant and indispensable *Surprised by Sin* analyzes these and other impossible metaphors (22–37).

94. Michael Murrin, *The Allegorical Epic: Essays in Its Rise and Decline* (Chicago: University of Chicago Press, 1980), 153, 167, 169.

95. See also Anne Davidson Ferry, *Milton's Epic Voice: The Narrator in "Paradise Lost"* (Cambridge: Cambridge University Press, 1963), 128–40.

96. Stephen M. Fallon, "Milton's Sin and Death: The Ontology of Allegory in *Paradise Lost*," *English Literary Renaissance* 17, no. 3 (1987): 338, 350.

97. Francis Woodcock, *Christ's Warning-Piece* (1644), A3.

98. Albert R. Cirillo, in "Noon-Midnight and the Temporal Structure of *Paradise Lost*," *English Literary History* 29 (1962): 210–33, addresses Milton's use of the structure of the "Platonic Great Year": in the poem, noon and midnight, sunlight and eclipse are not irresolvable opposites; rather, in God's viewpoint, they are resolved in the Crucifixion, "the symbol of the noon of eternal life" (230).

99. Maureen Quilligan has argued that, because of her inherently mediated status, "Eve's intial interpretive situation is closer to the fallen reader's corrected reading than any other perspective in the poem," in *Milton's Spenser*, 242.

100. Annabel Patterson, *Censorship and Interpretation: The Conditions of Writing and Reading in Early Modern England* (Madison: University of Wisconsin Press, 1984), 158.